Every Rock, Every Hill

'Every rock, every hill has its story', Winston Churchill wrote of the North-West Frontier, and here is the full story of these magical lands: from Alexander the Great to the kidnapping of Molly Ellis; from the languages and religions to the women and fighters; from skirmishes, wars and the present-day guerrilla warfare against the Soviets to the life of an Englishwoman there during and since the British Raj.

Against a background of the history and geography of the Frontier area, Victoria Schofield paints a vivid picture of this extraordinary territory, drawing on first-hand material and interviews with people from all walks of life.

Victoria Schofield was educated at the Royal Naval School in Surrey and St Louis, Missouri, before going on to obtain an MA Hons degree in History. She was President of the Oxford Union, and is now a freelance writer and reporter. She is married with one daughter, and divides her time between homes in London and Henley-on-Thames.

'This is a very carefully researched and well-written documentary on the North-West Frontier and the tribes beyond its borders . . .' M. M. Kaye, author of *The Far Pavilions*.

'A work of original research, written with enthusiasm and elegance' *Dublin Sunday Press*

'A new and absorbing history of the North-West Frontier and Afghanistan' *Oxford Mail*

'She [Victoria Schofield] sees the world through the eyes of the tribes, and rightly refuses to impose irrelevant foreign stereotypes upon them' *Standard*

EVERY ROCK, EVERY HILL

A Plain Tale of the North-West Frontier and Afghanistan

VICTORIA SCHOFIELD

Century
London Melbourne Auckland Johannesburg

First published in 1984 by Buchan & Enright Publishers Ltd

© Victoria Schofield 1984

All rights reserved

This edition first published in 1987 by Century, an imprint of
Century Hutchinson Ltd, Brookmount House, 62–65 Chandos Place,
London WC2N 4NW

Century Hutchinson South Africa (Pty) Ltd
PO Box 337, Berglvei, 2012 South Africa

Century Hutchinson Australia Pty Ltd
PO Box 496, 16–22 Church Street, Hawthorn, Victoria 3122, Australia

Century Hutchinson New Zealand Ltd
PO Box 40-086, Glenfield, Auckland 10, New Zealand

ISBN 0 7126 1625 X

Printed in Great Britain by
Richard Clay Ltd, Bungay, Suffolk

Contents

Author's Acknowledgements

I should like to express my thanks to all those who gave me extensive interviews and kind hospitality. Invariably after a day's interview, I was sent home laden with books on a long-term loan for my further reading. Many of the people I spoke to are mentioned by name in the bibliography; others, who also gave me valuable information have requested to remain anonymous. I am grateful to them nonetheless. In particular, however, I should like to thank M. M. Kaye, Major-General Goff Hamilton, CB, CBE, DSO, Major Robin Hodson, MBE, David Page of the BBC Eastern Service, and Gordon Adam of the BBC World Service, all of whom read my manuscript and made many useful comments. I am most grateful to Gerald Sattin, FRPS (London) who allowed me to read his valuable collection of letters relating to the military postal history of India in the nineteenth century. He also let me photograph his collection of lithographs drawn by Vincent Eyre, some of which I have used; my thanks go to Peter Fudakowski for taking the photographs. Many other people offered to lend me photographs; unfortunately I could not make use of them all. However my thanks go to Mrs Wade (Molly Ellis), Mrs Stella Walter, Jill Brown, Major Hodson, Christophe de Ponfilly, Romano Cagnoni, Dr and Mrs Shaw, George Antipas and Andrew Altounyan, whose photographs are used in this book.

I have spent many hours researching in the India Office Library, as well as the School of Oriental and African Studies, the Church Missionary Society, the Royal United Services Institute, the National Army Museum, Chelsea, and the Cambridge Centre for South Asia Studies. I am most grateful for being allowed readership in these libraries, and I am indebted to the India Office Library for permission to quote from their unpublished sources. I would like to thank The National Trust for Places of Historic Interest or Natural Beauty for their permission to quote lines from Rudyard Kipling's Poems, 'The Ballad of East and West', 'The Ballad of the King's Mercy' and 'Arithmetic on the Frontier'. I am also extremely grateful to those people from whose publications I have quoted; my thanks also go to Peter Tickler for his patient editing.

Finally I should like to thank my husband, Stephen Willis, who not only read the manuscript but who was a constant source of encouragement in the writing of this book; also my mother who assisted me with the typing of the manuscript when my deadline was running out.

Introduction

Oh, East is East and West is West, and never the twain shall meet,
Till Earth and Sky stand presently at God's great Judgement Seat;
But there is neither East nor West, Border, nor Breed, nor Birth,
When two strong men stand face to face, though they come from the
ends of the earth!

Rudyard Kipling, 'The Ballad of East and West'

There is a strange magic about the lands of the North-West Frontier which seems to have captured the imagination of all who have travelled there. Part of the attraction lies in the combination of the wild and the beautiful: barren hills which rise to become brilliant white snowy peaks; steep valleys and narrow passes which open out into fertile plains; rivers which can alternate between a trickle and a torrent. It comes almost as a surprise to find such a world unto itself, wedged in between the landmass of the Indian sub-continent and the plains of Central Asia. Yet the North-West Frontier of what is today Pakistan has always been highly prized because of its position along the route to India. At the same time, the people have close links with those in Afghanistan, and so it is impossible to talk of the one and not of the other.

For centuries the peoples on both sides of the border have resisted foreign domination; and the resemblance in their faces gives testimony to their shared history. Nowhere else in the world does the past appear to live so closely alongside the present. Customs and traditions have remained the same; so too has mistrust and suspicion of the outsider. Even so, there are many individual foreigners who have found it possible to become close friends with people whose horizons are a world apart. It may be only for an instant; often it can last a lifetime. I have a particularly vivid personal memory of just such an instant when travelling there during the relatively peaceful and untroubled days before the Russians invaded Afghanistan in 1979. After a dry and dusty drive towards the parched land of Waziristan, one of my companions—a tribesman from Afghanistan—sliced in half a blood-red pomegranate, so swiftly that he could have slit his hand in two in the same moment. Silently, with no language in common, he offered one half to me; and as we consumed it, only the appreciation in our eyes could show that two people of such different cultures and backgrounds were enjoying with the same thirst the goodness of the fruit.

For those who have grown up in the post-colonial era, it may not be easy to imagine the North-West Frontier as an indefinite and at times undefined outpost of the British Empire, and Afghanistan as a potential acquisition. But that was how it was to so many young men and women who lived and worked in British India. Their experience belongs to an age which is gone for ever. With the independence of the sub-continent in 1947, the North-West Frontier Province became part of Pakistan; Afghanistan had already gone its own independent way before it eventually fell within the orbit of Communism. But, in spite of these changes, including the war which has devastated so much of the Afghan countryside and its people, there is still a timeless romance about the whole area. Almost all those who have been there seem to feel a deep sense of belonging; invariably, when they leave, a part of themselves remains behind.

One of the advantages of the nineteenth-century travellers and raconteurs was that they could describe at leisure, in more than one volume if they so wished, their victories and defeats, their joys and sorrows, the climate and the weather. Such a luxury is not permitted to modern writers; and in my research for this book, sifting through diaries and letters, there are clearly many more people I would have liked to mention. But time, space and the fear of inundating the reader with a wealth of names have restrained me. None the less, I have tried to conjure up a picture of the border area as seen through a representative selection of foreigners who have ventured there in the capacity of friend or foe.

I hope that those people who have been to the North-West Frontier and Afghanistan will see in the experiences of others an extension of their own, as well as a vision of the region before and since their time. And for those who have never been to Peshawar, or Khyber or Kabul or Kandahar, perhaps the world revealed here will generate as much curiosity as did the poems of Rudyard Kipling in the minds of schoolboys in days gone-by.

Victoria Schofield

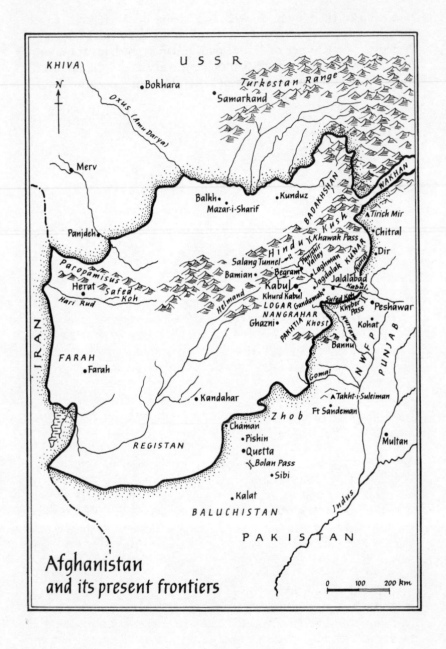

Afghanistan
and its present frontiers

CHAPTER ONE

The Route to India

The East bowed low before the blast,
In patient, deep disdain;
She let the legions thunder past,
And plunged in thought again.

Matthew Arnold, 'Obermann Once More'

Sultan Sikander

The early Europeans knew virtually nothing of India until Alexander the Great. What was known was shrouded in fable and myth, based on the fifth-century BC writings of the Greek historian, Herodotus. India, it was believed, was a place where huge ants dug for gold, and people lived for two hundred years; where men had feet back to front so that they could run fast; and others had one large foot, which, when lying on their backs, they could use as a shade against the fierce sun. And for those, like Alexander, who were curious enough to try and go there, there was the promise of riches untold and of eternal fame.

Alexander was not, however, the first invader to enter India. The tall, fair, straight-nosed Aryans from Central Asia are known to have come through the passes to settle in India around 1500 BC. And the exploits of the Persians—of Cyrus and Darius—form part of the history of the land several hundred years before Alexander came on the scene. In the sixth century BC Darius the Great conquered Kabul and Gandhara (the ancient valley of Peshawar), and annexed the Punjab, incorporating it into the Persian empire.

For a while the north-west frontier of the Indian sub-continent became the eastern frontier of the Persian empire. But then came the son of Philip II of Macedon, Alexander the Great. That we

know so much about him is due above all to Arrian, a Greek
official of the Roman empire who in the second century AD
composed a detailed and reliable account of Alexander's campaigns; this was based first and foremost on the writings of
Ptolemy, the childhood friend of Alexander who accompanied
him to Asia and subsequently founded the Ptolemaic dynasty of
Egypt. Then too there are accounts by Quintus Curtius, Plutarch
and Diodorus, and passing references in many Greek and Roman
writers. All these European accounts were composed long after
Alexander's death. On the Asian side there is no contemporary
reference to the Sultan Sikander, as he was called. In the Indian
tradition he survives only as Skanda, the monster with whom
mothers would threaten their children if they were being
naughty. His armies came to conquer and, almost as though in
revenge, the Indians chose to forget him.

In 331 BC Alexander defeated the Persians decisively at
Gaugamela, and followed up by capturing first Babylon, then
Persepolis. His overall plan was to consolidate his new empire to
the furthest limits of the old Persian one, which would bring him
to present-day Afghanistan, southern Russia and across the
mountains to Pakistan and India. Alexander in fact greatly
underestimated the width of India; and he was unaware of the
Indian ocean, the landmass of Arabia and the Red Sea. For a
time, he even believed that the Indus joined the Nile. His
immediate aim was to capture and execute Bessus who had
incurred his wrath by murdering the defeated Persian king,
Darius Codomannus, and laying claim to the title of King of
Asia. Bessus had fled north across the mountains of the Hindu
Kush to the province of Bactria and the ancient city of Balkh.
Alexander's own feat in crossing the Hindu Kush over the
11,640-foot Khawak pass set an example for future invaders. He
was accompanied by an army of some 30,000 men, but unlike
Hannibal crossing the Alps he was wise enough to leave the
elephants behind, since they would have suffered greatly in the
cold weather; instead they were allowed to wallow in the warm
mud of the elephant park west of Kandahar, known to the
Persians and still in use 1,500 years later.

Journeying in winter, Alexander surprised the local mountain
tribes, but the cost was high: there was a shortage of supplies,
famine spread through the army, and with no firewood his men

had to eat raw horsemeat. When he reached Balkh he found that Bessus had fled across the River Oxus, leaving the people of Bactria to surrender to Alexander. Yet, even when he succeeded finally in capturing Bessus, Alexander proceeded onwards to the most north-eastern part of the ancient Persian empire. He passed Samarkand and reached the river Jaxartes, crushing rebellions in front and behind. He then stayed in the north to build a new city, Alexandria-the-Furthest, on the Jaxartes, and in order to bind the conquered peoples to him, he married a captive princess, Roxane, her name meaning 'little star'. To symbolise their union, they shared a loaf of bread at the banquet—a custom still practised in Turkestan.

In the summer of 327 BC Alexander left Bactria with a strong garrison to defend it and set out on his journey to India. Crossing the Hindu Kush again, part of his army went south-east into the sub-continent and reached the ancient capital of Gandhara, Peucelaotis (modern Charsadda); Alexander himself continued along a route which was 'hilly and rugged' and, according to the geographer Strabo, was to the north. This gave future route-plotters the vital clue that he must have gone through Bajaur and Swat to the north of Peshawar and not through the Khyber as was at one time thought.

Along the way Alexander came across what he believed to be the legendary fortress of Nyasa, which Dionysus, the Greek god of wine, was said to have reached some 6,000 years previously. Wearied by their travels and suffering from the cold, the Greek soldiers lit a fire, inadvertently using cedarwood coffins lying on top of the earth as firewood. The local people, angered at the desecration of their dead, attacked Alexander's troops, but were soon obliged to surrender. Alexander spared them their lives, however, because—according to Arrian—of a discovery which greatly pleased him. To their astonishment, the Greek soldiers found in this far-off place ivy growing in abundance; they also heard the local people talk of Meros, the nearby mountain, which name in Greek means 'thigh'. As ivy was sacred to the Greeks, and Dionysus was said to have been born from the thigh of Zeus, what more could the Greeks ask for as proof that they had indeed found Dionysus's ancient stronghold? The soldiers rested there for a few days, feasting and making garlands out of the laurel and vine.

In 1959 Fosco Maraini, a member of the Rome branch of the
Club Alpino, was travelling to the base camp of Mount Saraghar
when he too stumbled on a place not unlike Nyasa in the
módern-day Bumboret. This is further to the north than Alexander went, the home of the Chitrali Kafirs who, like the people
Alexander came across, bury their dead in coffins lying above the
ground. 'Turning our eyes upon the woodlands of Bumboret, it
was easy enough to recapture the same feeling of passionate
excitement as the Greeks must have experienced on discovering
up here, at the farthest boundaries of their known and imagined
world, on the very threshold of the unknown, a natural enclave
so akin to their native land.' The presence of the vine, he said, 'at
once invested the valley with a mythological atmosphere'.

The route which Alexander was following took him to
Massaga, the 'greatest city in those parts'. The people, the
Assacenians, would not surrender and held out until they saw the
Greek siege engines. According to Curtius, the gates were then
thrown open, and

> . . . the Queen came with a great train of noble ladies who
> poured out libations of wine in golden bowls. The Queen
> herself, having placed her son, a child, at Alexander's knees,
> obtained not only pardon but permission to retain her
> former dignity, for she was styled Queen and some have
> believed that this indulgent treatment was accorded rather
> to the charms of her person than to pity for her misfortune.
> At all events she afterwards gave birth to a son who
> received the name Alexander whoever his father may have
> been.

The legend that Alexander sired a successor to his Asian
empire (and the imperial treasure) was developed by Kipling in
his story 'The Man who Would be King': Alexander was
generally believed to be a god and when his would-be successor
(and supposed descendant) in the nineteenth century desired to
marry a beautiful woman (coincidentally called Roxane) she
feared death—the outcome of union with a god. The people had
long held the superstition that immortal gods did not bleed, but
before the wedding which the 'Man who would be king' insisted
upon, Roxane bit him, drawing blood from his cheek for all to

see. Thus he was deemed not to be Alexander's successor but an impostor and accordingly met an unpleasant end.

Alexander proceeded to subdue the surrounding peoples. In spite of the warlike nature of the local tribes and their obvious desire to defend their liberty, he eventually triumphed over them. Inevitably those who followed his exploits wondered why. Before John Griffiths, who became an expert on that country, went to Afghanistan in 1957, he made a point of travelling in Greece and Yugoslavia—the Macedonia of Alexander's day—to observe the 'sturdy, taciturn, almost phlegmatic peasants' who would have made up Alexander's army in days gone by. Comparing them with the volatile, rather unpredictable tribesmen, he deduced that Alexander's victories were due in large part to temperament; the tribesmen were no match for a well-disciplined, co-ordinated force of men. The personality of Alexander himself also contributed to his success; he was prepared to suffer hardships along with his men; he would help those who fell and he would not drink unless there was enough water for all.

When Alexander's armies attacked the people of Bazira, the Birkot of today, in middle Swat, they fled to a rock called Aornos. Alexander determined to pursue them and sent Ptolemy ahead. But until Sir Aurel Stein discovered it in 1926, no one knew exactly where the rock was. Furnished with the records of Arrian and Curtius, he set out to retrace the steps of Alexander's army. 'It was a day full of eager expectation, but also not free from anxious uncertainty. On the two preceding nights I had carefully read over the descriptions that Arrian and Curtius have left us of Alexander's great exploit at Aornos.' In fact they gave little topographical information other than that Aornos was near the river Indus. It was clear, however, that Alexander would have had problems in laying siege to the rock since, according to Arrian, 'on the summit of the rock there was plenty of pure water, which gushed out from the copious spring. There was timber besides, and as much good arable land as required for its cultivation the labour of a thousand men.'

Robin Lane Fox, one of Alexander's many and best biographers, describes Aornos as being 'a site for mountaineers, but emphatically not for warriors . . . on no side of the rock could his army hope for easy access, and they had to choose between a

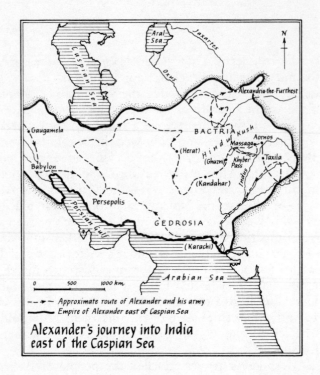

Alexander's journey into India
east of the Caspian Sea

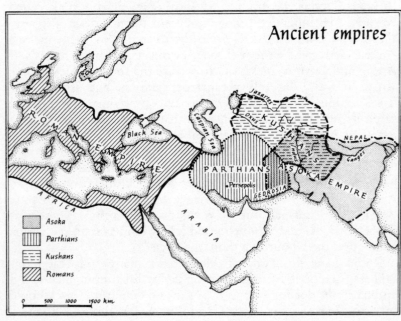

Ancient empires

Asoka
Parthians
Kushans
Romans

ridgeway and a ravine.' On his voyage of exploration Stein and his companions faltered in front of the ravine before realising that it confirmed their own discovery. 'Was this not the deep gap of Aornos which at first baffled the Macedonian attack?' In order to cross the ravine Alexander ordered his men to construct a platform with stakes; he then made the final assault by hauling himself up the rock-face by a rope. After his victory, the customary sacrifices to the gods were offered. So thrilled was Stein with his discovery of Aornos as the modern-day Pir-sar (Holy man's height) that he wrote: 'I had no victory to give thanks for, yet I too felt tempted to offer a libation to Pallas Athene for the fulfilment of a scholar's hope, long cherished and long delayed.'

Alexander's next goal was to cross the Indus and enter India. He crossed at Hind, north of Attock, where a bridge spans the Indus, providing easy access for today's traveller. He was met by King Ambhi of Taxila who had come in a resplendent and solemn procession, with his elephants 'appearing like castles between his troops', to offer his allegiance and incidentally to ask for Alexander's help in defeating his enemy, King Porus. They proceeded to Taxila, a town which flourished at the edge of what was the Persian frontier for hundreds of years.

'Taxila was one of the great metropolises of Asia,' observed Fosco Maraini, who plodded through the ruins in 1959; 'a vast market where Roman glass could be traded for Chinese silk, the furs of the barbarous northern Hyperboreans for jewels from the kingdom of Taprobane, the modern Ceylon [Sri Lanka]. It was also of course, a famous centre of university studies, known for both its philosophical and its medical schools'. But instead of 'chiliarchs and hipparchs, elephants and horsemen wielding the sarissa, the terrible Macedonian pike, all we could see were a few ramshackle petrol-pumps and sordid little shops.'

Alexander left Taxila to go further eastwards, crossing the river Jhelum to defeat Ambhi's old enemy, King Porus. By this time he was using a great many local levies in his army. He had long since relied on native cavalry drawn from Bactria and the countries east of the Persian desert. He then crossed the Chenab and Ravi, but his troops would go no further. 'It was not so much a mutiny as the expression of a deep despair,' surmised Robin Lane Fox. Alexander's men were frightened of the unknown perils ahead and were not prepared either mentally or physically to venture across the Ganges which they believed to be 'sóme four miles wide' and deepest of all the Indian rivers. Exhausted after eight years away from Macedonia, having covered 11,250 miles 'regardless of season or landscape', they wanted to go home, and with inauspicious omens from the gods, Alexander agreed to retreat. While a large part of his army returned by sea via the Indus in a fleet of several hundred ships, Alexander crossed the Gedrosian desert north of what today is Karachi. It was a desperate march, shrinking his army still further in spite of the arrival of reinforcements. He died in Babylon—possibly of poison—soon afterwards in 323 BC.

The successors

After Alexander's death there was anarchy amongst those garrisons of Greeks left behind in his Asian empire. The 'War of the Successors' gave the opportunity for the Mauryas under Chandragupta from the south of India to conquer the north: the prize after which Alexander had yearned. The Greeks under Seleucus were unable to hold on to northern India and Gandhara, and just two decades after his death Alexander's empire had been pushed back well into Afghanistan, ceded to Chandragupta at the cost of 500 elephants. For the first time an invasion from the east countered one from the west.

One story from those times was related to Major John Bowen, a British political officer twenty-three centuries later. It had been handed down by word of mouth 'from generation to generation and is still told when families gather round the fire on winter nights in the hill country of Tirah' began his story teller, Muhammad Zarif Khan. The story which Bowen was the first to record on paper was about a blind man and a king named Chandradev, undoubtedly Chandragupta Maurya.

The story is unusual in that it remained in Islamic folklore, although it originated long before Islam and its moral centred around the preoccupation with caste, more akin to Hindu beliefs. The king, Chandradev, was greatly helped by a blind man who was able to prophesy that a sword the king thought was unbreakable would shatter; and that if he took lean horses into battle instead of fat ones, he would triumph over his enemies, which the king duly did. But the blind man was only rewarded with a small allowance of food each day.

When the king desired to marry a beautiful princess, he again called on the advice of the blind man who counselled that it would be a good match, although he detected that the princess was the daughter of a musician. Later, when the king found out, he angrily asked the blind man why he had allowed him to marry the daughter of a 'low-caste musician'. 'Because you yourself are the son of a tradesman', came the reply; which of itself explained the ungenerous reward: 'Such meanness betokened the narrow outlook of a tradesman rather than the generous character of a king.' The mothers then confessed that they had temporarily forsaken their husbands, the one for a seller of saris, the other for a sitar player. Elsewhere it is recorded that Chandragupta Maurya was illegitimate.

Chandragupta's grandson, Asoka, was esteemed as the greatest of the Maurya kings. Ruling a hundred years after Alexander, he had an empire which stretched from Afghanistan to southern India. As a convert to Buddhism, he did much to spread the religion and was responsible for numerous religious edicts carved on stone pillars, a few of which are discernible to this day.

After his death, the Maurya empire declined; already out of the chaos of the warring Greek generals some semblance of order had emerged. These intruders inevitably mingled with the local inhabitants, creating a dynasty of Graeco-Bactrian kings; their names—Demetrius, Pantaleon, Menander—attesting their origins. 'They took the title of "king" perhaps as much from helplessness as from sinister ambition,' concluded Robin Lane Fox. In the second century BC Menander's kingdom stretched from Kabul to north India, but the Bactrians were unable to resist the incursions of nomads from the fringes of Persia—the Scythians (Sakas), Parthians, and finally the Kushans.

Under its great king Kanishka, who also embraced Buddhism, the Kushan empire was extended to the Ganges valley and its capital established at Peshawar; for the first time, trade flourished between the Roman world of the West and the Orient. But the Kushans were threatened by the Guptas from the south of India and the Sassanians from Persia; by the third century AD the Sassanid empire had reached the Indus.

Fosco Maraini, looking at the coins in the museum at Taxila, could see clearly the generations of rulers who supplanted one another in a continual ebb and flow of conquest. First there were the Greek generals who had been left behind: 'Bareheaded with flowing hair like so many Roman emperors . . . next we inspected the Scythians, Parthians and Kushan coinage: other rulers, different names, but always that veneer of Hellenisation.' Besides being evidence of considerable artistic development, the coins, observed Maraini, also formed a priceless body of historical documentation. 'For decades on end, for entire reigns in fact, they are the only surviving testimony to this period we possess. It is rather as though the world as we know it today had been obliterated in some enormous cataclysm, leaving behind for posterity nothing apart from one miraculously preserved album full of postage stamps.'

The next onslaught was that of the White Huns—a brutal people who came from Central Asia. They crossed the passes to the north-west, conquered Bactria and raided east and west. For a short while the Sassanians in Persia were able to resist them: one of their rulers pretended to buy them off with gold, but then ambushed their army and killed them to a man. In the middle of the fifth century, however, the Huns invaded Gandhara, with the help of a vassal group of tribes, the Gujaras, and destroyed the Gupta empire of the Hindus. But their cruelty led to open rebellion amongst the people, and eventually the Sassanians, helped by the Turks, regained their power in Persia and nominal control up to the Indus.

A Chinese Buddhist monk, Hsüan-Tsang, in the seventh century, noticed the ravages of the Huns as he journeyed to India to learn more about the Buddha. He passed from Afghanistan through the Khyber Pass to Peshawar: 'Towns and villages are almost empty and abandoned and only a few inhabitants are seen in the country', he wrote. 'There are a million Buddhist monasteries which are in ruins and deserted. They are overgrown with weeds and they make only a mournful solitude.' But there were no signs as yet of a new militant religion, whose prophet had just died in Medina in 632. As Hsüan-Tsang returned to China after fifteen years away, laden down with twenty horse-loads of relics, images and manuscripts about Buddha, he was oblivious of this new religion which would sweep through the lands over which he had just travelled, changing its history for always.

There is no God but God
. . . God's Messenger Muhammad is His Prophet

In 870 Yaqub-i-Lais, formerly a coppersmith—*saffar*—from the village of Sijistan in Persia, succeeded in capturing Kabul. He founded the dynasty of the Saffarids and was the first Muslim ruler to bring the power of Islam to the eastern frontier of the old Sassanian empire. Gradually the attraction of Islam spread to the local people; a century later another boost to the number of converts was given by Sabuktagin, the Turkish founder of the Ghaznavid dynasty, which took its name from the city of Ghazni, from where he ruled. He had been a slave to the Turkish rulers of Ghazni but had managed to seize power in 977. He set as his goal the expulsion of the Hindus from the Kabul valley and Gandhara, as the vale of Peshawar was still called.

His son and successor, the Sultan Mahmud of Ghazni, continued his work, carrying the holy war against the Hindus into India. An able ruler, Mahmud managed to consolidate his power over a vast area of northern India, his empire extending from Bokhara in the north to the Persian gulf in the south; from east of the Caspian sea to Peshawar and the Punjab. He also embellished his capital at Ghazni with fine buildings and gardens. After his death in 1030, however, his empire came under attack by the Seljuks from beyond the Oxus, who conquered Persia in 1050, and finally established themselves in Baghdad in 1091. Ghazni was reduced to vassal status within the Seljuk kingdom. The Ghaznavid dynasty was further weakened by the Ghors, their former vassals; and in 1150 Ghazni was sacked by Alauddin Jahnsoz, the 'world burner'; the fire is recorded as having raged for seven days and seven nights and seventy thousand people were said to have been slaughtered.

At the same time the power of Islam was advancing further into India; one of Alauddin's successors, Muhammad Ghori, extended Muslim influence across the Indus, which he crossed in 1178; eventually he took Delhi, which was still the heart of

Hindu power. Henceforward Delhi became a new city, adorned with Muslim mosques built by Hindu craftsmen. When Muhammad Ghori was assassinated in 1206, he was succeeded on the throne by his favourite Turkish slave Qutbuddin Aibeck who began the construction of the Qutb Minar tower outside Delhi. His successors, as slave kings, ruled for the next century in Delhi. Those of Muhammad Ghori's possessions which centred on Ghazni fell to another Turkish mamluk, Ayyaldiz. His name in Turkish means 'the moon and star' which symbols appear in almost every Islamic state to this day.

But the tide of another invasion was already sweeping down from Central Asia. The Mongols from China under Genghis Khan were able to conquer all the lands between the Hindu Kush and the Indus. By 1220 Genghis Khan was on the river Oxus pursuing the remnants of the Turks into Afghanistan. He devastated Balkh, killing its inhabitants. From there he went east to the Indus where he also destroyed Peshawar. Of all the invaders, Genghis is remembered most for the wave of destruction which befell the cities which lay in his path—as John Bowen wrote:

Khan of the Golden Horde, you cannot dupe
The muse of History. She never errs.
I see her comment in the margin reads:
He was an 'atom bomb'—or even worse . . .

In the late thirteenth century the ruler of the eastern Mongol empire, Kublai Khan, received a visit from some Italians. Marco Polo, with his father Niccolo and uncle Maffeo, became famed as the first known Europeans to journey along the famous Silk Road, which linked trade between China and Europe. In so doing they took note of the peoples and lands through which they passed; Balkh was 'still a noble city', in spite of the ravages of the Mongols (or Tartars as they came to be known). Marco Polo described the people as Muhammadans speaking a 'peculiar language', who were excellent archers and much given to the chase. In Badakhshan there were 'fine and valuable gems', such as rubies, as well as azure: "Tis the finest in the world, and is got in a vein like silver.' He also noticed a large sheep, 'whose horns are a good six palms in length'. As he was the first to tell of its existence to the West, it acquired the name *Ovis Poli*—Marco Polo sheep.

Ibn Batuta, an Arab born in Tangier, travelled through northern Afghanistan on his way to India in the fourteenth century. The fame of the Sultan of India, Muhammad bin Tughluq, had spread far and it was known that he was generous to foreign scholars. Originally Ibn Batuta, a student of law, wished to go by sea, but there was no boat at the time and so he travelled overland through Khiva, Bokhara and Samarkand. He found that Balkh was in ruins and deserted. He journeyed in safety as far as the borders of India at the river Indus, but he complained about 'a Persian tribe called Afghans' who harassed him on the road between Kabul and the Indus.

One of Genghis Khan's descendants through his mother was Tamerlane or Timur-i-Lang, Timur the Lame, so-called because of an arrow wound in his foot which made him limp. Tamerlane ruled from Samarkand and crossed the Hindu Kush on several occasions. His greatest expedition was in 1398 to Delhi. At Panipat, north of Delhi, on the plain between the mountains and the desert, he scattered his opponents, before advancing upon Delhi and looting it without mercy. He then returned to Samarkand from where he continued to rule his vast empire.

Gradually Western contact with the strange lands of the east was increasing. One of those who travelled to the court of Tamerlane at Samarkand was the ambassador of Henry III of Castille, Gonzales de Clavijo. He saw the powerful ruler 'upon a raised dais before which there was a fountain that threw up a column of water into the air backwards, and in the basin of the fountain there were floating red apples.' Tamerlane was seated on cushions of embroidered silk, dressed in a cloak of plain silk without any embroidery. On his head was a tall white hat, decorated with a ruby, pearls and other precious stones.

Clavijo also remarked that Timur never gave him his hand to kiss, 'for that is not their custom, no one with them should kiss the hand of any great lord, which to do would here be deemed unseemly.' Timur was seventy years old at the time of Clavijo's visit. Even though he was 'so infirm and old that his eyelids were falling over his eyes', he set out soon afterwards on a voyage of conquest to China, but died on the way.

The Moguls

With the break-up of Tamerlane's empire, which stretched from the Black Sea to Bengal, rival factions laid claim to its various components. One such man was Zahir-ud-din Muhammad Babur—a descendant of both Genghis Khan and Tamerlane. He spent his early years fighting to regain Tamerlane's old capital of Samarkand, but he never succeeded and decided to cut his losses and journey south across the Oxus. At once his fortunes changed. In October 1504 Kabul, a strategically placed city near Begram, one of Alexander's old cities, virtually gave itself to him. 'Without a fight, without an effort, by Almighty God's bounty and mercy I obtained and made subject to me Kabul and Ghazni and their dependent districts,' he wrote in his memoirs.

Babur was well pleased with Kabul as a trading centre: 'Down to Kabul every year come seven, eight or ten thousand horses and up to it from Hindustan come every year caravans of ten, fifteen or twenty thousand heads-of-houses bringing slaves, white cloth, sugar-candy, refined and common sugars and aromatic roots.' He also realised the difficulty an enemy would have in entering his new conquest.

> The country of Kabul is a fastness hard for a foreign foe to make his way into . . . if anyone thinks to cross the Hindu Kush at that time [in winter] over the mountains instead of through a valley bottom, his journey is hard indeed. The time to cross is during the three or four autumn months when the snow is less and the waters are low. Whether on the mountains or in the valley-bottoms Kafir highwaymen are not few.

Soon after he had taken Kabul, Babur, like Alexander, was anxious to set off for India. He crossed the Khyber pass 'in a march or two' and came upon another world. It was the first time he had seen a hot country: 'Other grasses, other trees, other animals, other birds and other manners and customs of clan and horde. We were amazed and truly there was ground for amaze.' They did not cross the Sind water (the Indus), but had heard that there were wealthy tribesmen in an unknown place called Kohat: 'Much cattle and buffalo fell to our men, many Afghans were taken, but I had them all collected and set them free. In the Kohat houses corn was found without limits.'

Babur was fascinated by the customs of the tribesmen: 'We had been told that when Afghans are powerless to resist, they go before their foe with grass between their teeth, this being as much as to say "I am your cow".' On this trip Babur saw the custom in evidence for the first time. But those who were captured as prisoners were beheaded 'and a pillar of their heads was set up in our camp'—the usual practice of the Tartar conquerors. He moved on from Kohat to Hangu and raided the plain of Taq (the modern Thal). His men dismounted on a waterless plain near Bannu. 'The soldiers got water here for themselves, their herds and so on, by digging down from one to one-and-a-half yards, into the dry water course, when the water came.'

Babur's first adventure into Hindustan was not without its discomforts, even for the King himself: 'My own felt tent had to be left from want of baggage beasts. One night at that time it rained so much that water stood knee-deep in my tent; I watched the night out till dawn, uncomfortably sitting on a pile of blankets.'

Two years after this first trip Babur resolved to go back to India; but he had to abandon his project, noting in his memoirs that the Afghans 'multiplied their misdeeds by ten, changing their very merits for faults', accusing Babur of having abandoned Kabul. Even so, he could not forget about India; it was 'always in my heart to possess Hindustan' which he decided to take 'either peacefully or by force'. 'For these reasons, it being imperative to treat these hillmen well, this following order was given: "Do no hurt or harm to the flocks or herds of these people, nor even to their cotton ends and broken needles".' Like others who were to follow him, Babur realised that if he wished to conquer India he would have to have the allegiance of the tribesmen in between, lest they rise up against him while his back was turned.

Babur prayed fervently to be given some sign that he would be successful against his enemies, the Lodis, who were ruling ineffectually at Delhi. The sign he requested was a mango or betel—both fruits of India. When he received a gift of some half-ripened mangoes in honey he saw this as the expected good omen and prepared to move on Hindustan. Yet again the battle was fought at Panipat, and the defeat of Ibrahim Lodi by Babur with his superior artillery meant that as well as being King of Kabul, he was now King of Hindustan. As a result, the centre of power was moved away from Central Asia and Tamerlane's old capital of Samarkand; henceforward, under Babur's successors —who came to be known as the Mogul emperors—Afghanistan and India were ruled from Delhi.

Babur died in 1530, leaving his son Humayun to rule his new empire. The name Humayun was derived from that of the mythical Eastern phoenix, Huma: it was a bird of good omen, and anyone on whom its shadow fell was destined to become a ruler. But Humayun was not of the calibre of either Babur or his own son, Akbar, to whom he relinquished his empire in 1556: at about the same time Charles V left his vast empire in Europe to his son Philip II of Spain.

Akbar dreamed of uniting the people in one 'divine religion'—Din Illahi—in which Muslim, Hindu, Jain, Parsee, Christian and Jew would find themselves united in the worship of One True God. But even though he had the power to do so, he was not anxious to impose such unification by force, on the grounds that truth would and should prevail on its own. Akbar's son, Jehangir, described in his memoirs how his father 'always associated with the learned of every creed and religion . . . and although he was illiterate, so much became clear to him through constant intercourse with the learned and wise in his conversations with them, that no one knew him to be illiterate.'

Over the years the Moguls had lost touch with their Central Asian background, and in 1581 Akbar embarked on a journey through the Khyber to fight his way to Kabul and his grandfather's old capital. He stopped at Attock on the Indus, and began the construction of a huge fort. Its completion five years later was the occasion of another journey west from India. This time Akbar intended to subdue the unruly tribesmen in the hills and plains, at times called Pathans (Pakhtuns), at others Afghans, but he encountered severe opposition from a tribe called Yusufzais, and whatever successes he had were short-lived. The fort, still standing, has walls two miles in circumference.

Neither he nor his successors really managed to rule over the tribes lying to the north-west of their empire. Their control was nominal, and one small tribe, the Khataks, was entrusted by

Akbar with the duty of guarding the imperial route across the Indus at Attock to Peshawar. In return for being allowed to collect the tolls, the Khataks were only too happy to help the Mogul emperor against the Yusufzais, with whom the Khataks also had a feud.

The most famous Khatak was Khushhal Khan; known as the warrior-poet, he set to verse in Pashtu his feelings about the Moguls and the times in which he lived. In some respects Khushhal can be seen as the forerunner of those who fought future foreign domination, whether it was British or Russian. He bemoaned both the lack of discipline and the reluctance of the tribes to work together against a common foe. And today, as the Afghans go to war against the Russians, they sing his epic ballads.

Although as chief of the Khataks, Khushhal admired the Mogul emperors Akbar, Jehangir and Shah Jehan, his admiration turned to hatred when Shah Jehan's son, Aurangzeb took away the Khatak right to guard the imperial route. It may well have been done as part of Aurangzeb's policy of abolishing tolls throughout the empire, but it did not accord with Khushhal's notions of loyalty and honour. What was worse from his point of view, was that the Yusufzais seemed to have found favour, and he himself was imprisoned in 1664 and kept in chains for two years. He used the full power of his poetic invective to inveigh against Aurangzeb.

> No limit is known to Aurang's ill intent;
> His father's curse pursues him to the end,
> False-faced and faithless, fraudulent, forsworn,
> To him truth is lies, and honest men a scorn;
> 'Twixt him and us fair issue is there none.
> If Mogul stand, then broken falls Pakhtun.

Khushhal was eventually freed and allowed to return to his homeland, from where he witnessed the Mogul defeat by the Afridis of the Khyber pass. The Mogul forces had been encouraged to take the route around the Tahtarra mountain near Landi Kotal, but it was a trap and the tribesmen were lying in wait. Khushhal, although not active in the battle, took delight in the victory:

Full five years the tribal sword was flashed,
Keen-edged and bright, since first the battle clashed
Upon Tahtarra, a peak, where at one blow
Twice twenty thousand of the Mughal foe
Perished, wives, sisters, all that they held dear,
Fell captive to the all-conquering Afghan spear.

Having resigned as chief of his tribe, Khushhal spent the rest of his life in open rebellion against the Moguls.

Nearly three hundred years after Khushhal's death, Olaf Caroe, a twentieth-century British political officer, went to visit his grave. He found it in a remote part of the country. 'Why is it here in so lonely a spot?' he asked the custodian. 'The poet desired it,' came the reply, 'for he loved the countryside and flowers, and above all wished that in his resting place he should not be disturbed by the clatter of the hooves of the Mogul cavalry, passing on the King's highway.' It was not Mogul hooves which Khushhal need have feared, however, but Persian. The Moguls never reasserted their power in the northern Punjab or Afghanistan. Their weakness left the way open to further invaders from the west, notably Nadir Shah.

'Afghanistan' emerges

Nadir Quli Beg was of Turkish origin and he set about restoring the power of the Persians, first over the Afghan tribes who for a short time had actually managed to assert themselves in their own lands and advance into Persia. These were the Abdalis of Herat, whose descendants divided into the Saddozais and the Muhammadzais; and the Ghilzais of Kandahar who had temporarily taken power in Isfahan.

Once Nadir Shah, as he styled himself, had conquered Kandahar, there was little in the way to prevent him reaching India. Following in the footsteps of the earlier conquerors, the Persians took Kabul, Peshawar, Lahore and finally Delhi in 1739. The army of the Mogul emperor, Muhammad Shah, was swiftly defeated and Delhi, yet again, was sacked and looted.

Among the booty which Nadir Shah took back from Delhi was a solid gold throne on legs of gold, studded with precious

The early Mogul emperors

Zahir-ud-din Muhammad Babur
1526-1530
|
Humayun
1530-1556 (from 1540-1555 the throne was contested)
|
Akbar
1556-1605
|
Jehangir
1605-1627
|
Shah Jehan
1627-1658
|
Aurangzeb
1658-1707

Throughout the eighteenth and nineteenth centuries there were eight
more emperors. The last of these, Bahadur Shah II, was deposed by
the British after the Indian Mutiny in 1857

The Durrani rulers of Afghanistan

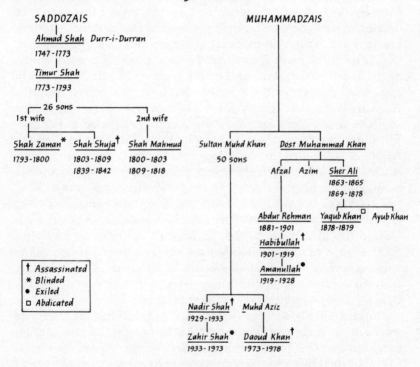

Those who ruled are underlined; only the principle characters are identified

stones and adorned with the outspread tails of two peacocks, also encrusted with jewels. This was the Peacock Throne, symbol of splendour of the Mogul emperors. He also took fabulous jewels, including the 'Mountain of Light', the Koh-i-Noor diamond, first presented to Humayun two centuries previously by a Hindu rajah in return for his protection.

Master of northern India, Nadir went on to extend his empire across the Oxus almost to the limits of the old empires of Darius and Alexander, but he was assassinated in 1747, and, in the confusion that followed, Ahmed Shah Abdali of the Afghan tribe, the Saddozais, took power. He assumed the name Durr-i-Durran, Pearl of Pearls, supposedly after the pearl earring he liked to wear. He also secured the Koh-i-Noor diamond from Nadir's treasure.

To this day the Durrani empire is remembered in Afghan history as the time of their greatest conquests. The power of the Moguls had been greatly weakened, and they were forced to give up all the lands across the Indus as well as the province of Sind. Durrani was also able to consolidate his hold on Afghanistan, which he ruled from Kandahar. He extended his control in the north as far as the Oxus and in the west to Herat. In the south and east he overran the country as far as the Indus. But the Afghans were attacked by the Maharatta confederacy from the south of India. Yet again the issue was to be decided at Panipat. Who would rule northern India? Hindu or Muslim? In 1761 the Afghans succeeded in defeating the Maharattas in a decisive battle. Soon afterwards they also defeated the Sikhs, a warrior people whose holy shrine at Amritsar they had sacked in 1757.

The Afghans could not, however, maintain control of their far-flung conquests from their base in Kandahar. Ahmed Shah Durrani decided to recognise the Moguls as emperors in Delhi. At the same time, he conceded the central Punjab to the Sikhs while retaining Afghanistan, the area to the north as far as Lahore and what came to be considered as the 'frontier areas' of the Punjab, comprising the vale of Peshawar.

Durrani died at the age of fifty in 1773, leaving his favourite son, Timur Shah, to rule the first Afghan empire. Encountering rebellion from his brother in Kandahar, Timur moved the capital to Kabul, making it his custom to retire to the pleasant climate of Peshawar in winter. Although less able than his father, he managed to rule in relative peace for the twenty years up to his death.

The Durrani empire could hardly have been expected to survive the legacy of Timur; out of thirty-six children from numerous wives, twenty-three were sons and there was no named heir. One of the thirty-six, Zaman Shah, succeeded to the throne, but he was ousted by his half-brother Mahmud, who blinded him. But Mahmud remained only three years on the throne when he was overthrown by a full brother of Zaman, Shah Shuja. It was at this time in 1809 that the court of the Afghan ruler, resident at the winter capital in Peshawar, was visited by an Englishman, Mountstuart Elphinstone, who had come to parley with the Afghan ruler on behalf of the British East India Company. He noticed that Shah Shuja was wearing a bracelet studded with a huge diamond, the Koh-i-Noor which Zaman, who had inherited it along with the throne, had secreted in the wall of a fort in the frontier territory. Shah Shuja was deposed soon afterwards by Mahmud, and there was no real outcome to Elphinstone's mission other than his *Account of the Kingdom of Caubul*, which gave many future travellers an interesting insight into the peoples and customs of this strange mountain-land. Mahmud remained uneasily on the throne until he was overthrown a second time. He fled to Herat where he established himself as ruler with his son, Kamran. One province after another broke away from the empire; the most dangerous threat came from the Sikhs, who under Ranjit Singh took both Kashmir and the valley of Peshawar. This last was a loss which the ruler of Afghanistan could not easily forget.

In the 1820s, Charles Masson, a deserter from the army of the East India Company, whose real name was James Lewis, was travelling around the border area. He visited Jalalabad, Kabul, Ghazni and Kandahar, and found that as a foreigner—a *feringhee*—he was the object of much curiosity among the local people. There was none of the animosity which was to greet later travellers. Already, foreigners had a reputation for being doctors; when news of Masson's arrival spread, 'several persons came who were afflicted with disorders or wounds, it being supposed here as elsewhere that a feringhee must necessarily be a *hakim* (doctor) or physician. I could not help regretting that I had no knowledge of medicinal remedies as it would have afforded me the highest satisfaction to have administered to the necessities of these poor people.' Regardless of his ignorance he had to do his best: for wounds, 'generally inflicted by the sword or by stones, I proposed the use of sweeter oils, or in default of which butter, or even honey—strongly urging cleanliness and absolutely forbidding the use of cotton rags which tended to irritate and inflame the sores, and directed leaves to be applied in their stead.' He was pleased to note that he received many thanks for his advice.

While Masson was wandering around the frontier areas of India and Afghanistan clad 'in garments of little worth', other foreigners were enriching themselves in the pay of one or other ruler. An American from Pennsylvania, Josiah Harlan, who had been invalided to India from Burma, went to Afghanistan disguised as a dervish to try and work for the return of Shah Shuja, who had fled to India. Although unsuccessful, he was rewarded with the titles of 'Companion of the Stirrup' and 'The King's Nearest Friend'. He switched allegiance, however, to work for Ranjit Singh. At the time Dost Muhammad Khan of the Muhammadzais, who had made himself ruler of Afghanistan, was intent upon regaining some of the provinces of the Durrani empire. When, in 1835, Dost Muhammad managed to amass an army to recover Peshawar, Harlan was sent by Ranjit Singh to corrupt the Afghan soldiers with money. He did so with such success that, according to his own account, the army 'faded away'.

However, Harlan fell out with Ranjit Singh and turned to Dost Muhammad; again he took most of the credit for the Dost's successful attack against the Sikhs at Jamrud at the entrance to the Khyber pass in 1837. Ranjit Singh and the Sikhs were defeated: his famed general Hari Singh, was slain. Dost Muhammad was poised once more to take Peshawar, but before doing so he turned to a new authority which was asserting itself in northern India—the British, who exercised control over large parts of India through the agencies of the East India Company. In 1803 they had reached Delhi and made the Mogul emperor a virtual prisoner in his palace. In Dost Muhammad's opinion, however, there seemed to be no reason why Britain would not favour his claim on Peshawar and he welcomed the arrival of a new Governor-General in 1835, George Eden Auckland, with great anticipation: 'The field of my hopes, which had before been chilled by the cold blast of wintry times, has by the happy tidings of your Lordship's arrival become the envy of the Garden of Paradise.'

CHAPTER TWO

Frontier Panorama

Every rock, every hill has its story.

Winston Churchill, Despatch to the *Daily Telegraph* 1897

The turbulent history of Central Asia served to turn the land over which the invading armies passed on their way to India into a beaten track. When the land to the east of the former Durrani empire, including the valley of Peshawar, fell out of Afghan hands, first into those of the Sikhs, then into those of the British, it came to be known as the North-West Frontier, rather than the eastern frontier of Afghanistan or, as had once been the case, of Persia. Geographically, the North-West Frontier stretches from the plains of Mekran and the Arabian Sea to the mountains of Kashmir; but in political terms it is the land between the Pamir mountains and the eastern Hindu Kush stretching down to where the Gomal river divides Waziristan from Baluchistan.

Long before any effort was made to draw a boundary, the British East India Company jealously guarded the north-west entry into India from Afghanistan. It was not so much that they feared an invasion, as in the days of old, from hordes of barbarians, sweeping through the passes and across the plains to fight yet another battle of Panipat; but rather, the British saw their opponent as being the invading army of Tsarist Russia which, they believed, could come either from Herat in the west, across the Hindu Kush, or maybe even over the Pamir mountains in the north.

Throughout the years, British explorers, soldiers and administrators became familiar with the territory which still formed a buffer between their interests and the Russians. Each aspect of it was of great importance: the mountains, the rivers, the passes. Whereas the mountains could act as a defensive barrier, the rivers

and passes which intersected them might provide a comparatively easy passage. And for all those who became directly
associated with it, the land came to have an enchantment all of its
own, in spite of the battles which were fought in its barren
mountains and fertile valleys. There have been, of course,
changes on the face of the Frontier: roads and railways were
built; rivers dried up; plains were irrigated, thus increasing their
verdure. But to this day there is a timeless element about the
whole area which captivates the traveller for a lifetime. 'Who is
there, indeed, among those who have experienced it, who will
not testify to the indescribable delight of long days of glorious
toil among the mountains, followed by night beneath the stars
crowned with the golden glory of the dawn?' asked the Earl of
Ronaldshay who served on the Frontier at the turn of the
century. And to successive generations, certain names, places,
towns, bring forth a whole panorama of images which has made
the Frontier's past live, as it were, alongside the present.

The roof of the world

Higher than the Alps piled upon the Pyrenees, the Pamirs form
one of the highest mountain ranges in the world; it is not for
nothing that they are called 'the roof of the world'. This rocky
tableland is at one of the most inaccessible points in the north of
the Indian sub-continent; so it was only geographical ignorance
which made the British fear the Pamirs as one of the most direct
of the invasion routes for the Russians.

One of the great nineteenth-century explorers, Captain Francis
Younghusband, who became famous for his travels throughout
the area, mapped the mountains and passes. On one occasion he
met and talked with his Russian counterpart Captain Gromb-
tchevsky, who was engaged on a similar journey of discovery. In
his report to the British government, Younghusband described
what Britain most feared. According to the Russian, he wrote:

> . . . every officer and man in the Russian army wished to
> march on India, but when they did come it would not be
> with a small army, but with three or four hundred thousand
> men, and on my suggestion that there might be difficulty

about supplies and transport for so large a force, he said that the Russian soldier went wherever he was ordered to go and did not think about such things; he looked upon the General of an Army as his father, who would provide all that was possible and that if at the end of a hard day's march he found neither water to drink nor food to eat, he would still not complain but he would go on cheerfully until he died and when he died there were many more in Russia to take his place.

Gradually, as their knowledge of the land increased, the British came to realise just how inaccessible the Pamirs were and the fear of invasion by that route receded; however, they were always concerned that the Russians would be able to stir up trouble in an area so close to India. After a series of political crises between Britain and Russia in the late nineteenth century, the Pamirs were taken as the point of departure in fixing the northern Frontier between the great empires of the world, joining, it was believed at the time, Russia, China and Britain. It was a fitting tri-junction, as the Report on the Boundary Commission observed in 1897, 'Here amidst a solitary wilderness 20,000 feet above sea level, absolutely inaccessible to man and within the ken of no living creatures except the Pamir eagles, the three great Empires actually meet.'

To the south of the Pamirs lies the two-hundred-mile range of the Hindu Kush mountains, through the several passes of which so many invaders had come. Their Greek name, Paropanisadae, means 'higher than the ceiling of an eagle's flight'. But their other name, Hindu Killer, is a truer expression of their character. Ibn Batuta attributed the name to the agonies of crossing the mountains. 'So many of the slaves, male and female, brought from India, die on the passage of this mountain owing to the severe cold and quantity of snow.' Hsüan-Tsang in the seventh century found that crossing the Hindu Kush was one of the most painful parts of his journey. 'The route is twice as difficult and dangerous as in the region of the deserts and glaciers. What with the frozen clouds and the swirling snow, there is never a moment when one can see clearly.' Alexander's army had suffered crossing the Khawak pass. So too had that of Tamerlane in 1398: his men had to crawl over the glaciers on hands and knees, and

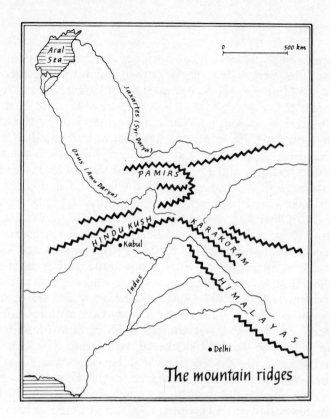

The mountain ridges

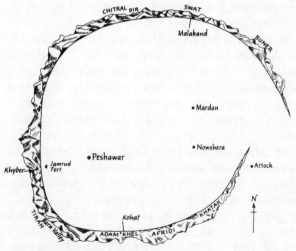

'The coronet of hills'

swing across the ravines on rope bridges attached to large rocks. Even so, the British felt, if Alexander and his successors had crossed the Hindu Kush, so too might the Russians.

Whereas the western Hindu Kush lies in Afghanistan to the north of Kabul, bordering Nuristan (formerly Kafiristan), the eastern mountains lie in Chitral where the highest, the Tirich Mir, stands at 25,263 feet. Further mountain ranges, the Karakorams in Kashmir and Tibet, the Himalayas in Nepal, bind the northern edge of the Indian sub-continent. And in spite of the high altitudes, the British sent agents and explorers like Younghusband to Chitral as well as to the states of Gilgit, Hunza and Kashmir, to keep an eye on the northern frontier, observe the channels of trade and compete with any Russian presence.

It was an exhilarating existence, close to the roof of the world: when Dr Hugh Luard of the Indian Medical Service had to march to Gilgit in the 1890s, all he saw before him was 'a sea of snow peaks as far as the eye could reach on every side, nothing to break the dazzling whiteness but the long drawn line of men and animals, crawling like a black thread over the pass.' Once they had crossed it, 'the descent on the other side was steep and slippery, mules kept sliding; in the pine forest below I saw a mule fall over the edge and down the steep hillside like a cannon-ball, with its legs curled up, till brought to a halt by a tree far below. It was then unloaded, mule and load hauled up, reloaded and continued its journey.'

Whereas, in days of old, men crossed the mountains in order to get to the sub-continent, nowadays they have gone back to climb them and observe the panorama of the snow-capped peaks from the highest altitudes in the world. The hazards of mountaineering in that area, however, meant that in both the nineteenth and twentieth centuries men have climbed and fallen or frozen.

Hugh Carless and Eric Newby considered themselves extremely lucky that worse did not befall them when in 1956 they undertook, in their 'short walk' in the Hindu Kush, to climb the 19,880-foot Mir Samir, overlooking the Panjshir valley. With no experience in mountaineering, other than a few days' rock-climbing in Wales, Eric Newby, a former dress salesman, and Hugh Carless, a diplomat, nearly succeeded in their attempt to reach the top. But they realised that they could not do so and return to their camp before darkness. 'For a moment we were dotty enough to consider going on. It was a terrific temptation: we were only 700 feet below the summit. Then we decided to give up. Both of us were nearly in tears. Sadly we ate our nougat and drank our cold coffee.' Even so, they had been able to admire one of the most magnificent panoramas in the world.

Below us on every side, mountains surged away it seemed for ever; we looked down on glaciers and snow-covered peaks that perhaps no one has ever seen before, except from the air. To the west and north we could see the great axis of the Hindu Kush and its southward curve from the Anjuman pass around the northern marches of Nuristan. Away to the east-north-east was the great snow-covered mountain we had seen from the wall of the east glacier, Tirich Mir, the 25,000-feet giant on the Chitral border, and to the south-west the mountains that separated Nuristan from Panjshir.

The lands of Dir, Swat and Chitral

'The dominant note of Chitral', wrote Sir George Robertson, who was to become only too familiar with the area through tribal warfare in the 1890s, 'is its bigness combined with desolation; vast silent mountains cloaked in eternal snow; wild glacier-born torrents, cruel precipices and pastureless hillsides.' Separated from Dir and Swat by the 11,000-foot Lowarai pass, which provides the most direct but treacherous route of approach from the south, it can also be reached from Gilgit to the east.

Chitral's inaccessibility has added to its allure. There remains in Chitrali folklore the story of a weary traveller who managed to reach Chitral. He sits down to rest by the side of a stream on green velvet grass. Floating in the stream he sees luscious fruits, mulberries, apples, pears, grapes, cherries mingled with ice cubes. He eats his fill and lies down to sleep. When he finally returns to his village he recounts his experience in the local mosque. But the mullah silences him, since he is anxious that the people should not think that the traveller has come back from Paradise.

Both Dir and Swat are bound by the river basins of the Swat and Indus rivers. Swat was the place of sacred pilgrimage for the Buddhists; at one time there were over a thousand monasteries there, and Hsüan-Tsang made a point of going to Swat on his way to India: 'Often the snow flies in whirling storms, mingled with rain and, reflecting the five colours, it looks like flying clouds of flowers.' Khushhal Khan, too, wrote of the beauties of Swat:

In climate it is glorious, lovelier far than Kabul;
Bleak is Kabul, Swat is mild and gentle,
Its air and verdure are like unto Kashmir
Though it spreads not out so finely.

Entrance from the south to Dir and Swat is by the Malakand pass which Winston Churchill, who served with the Malakand Field Force in 1897, described as 'a great cleft in the line of mountains . . . On every side steep and often precipitous hills, covered with boulders and stunted trees, rise in confused irregularity.' But he was not so helpful as some in his portrayal of the beauties of Swat.

I repress with an effort the impulse to describe, or try to describe, the sunrise over the mountains. All the available and suitable words have doubtless been used before by several writers and skipped by many readers. Indeed I am inclined to think that descriptions of this kind, however good, convey nothing to those who have not seen the lovely spectacle and are unnecessary to those who have. Nature will not be admired by proxy.

Hazara

Hazara, once called Urasha, is separated from the Frontier territory by the river Indus which flows down from Swat towards Attock, leaving Hazara on the right. Lieutenant-Colonel Lever, who, when on casual leave in 1945, went to visit the lands of those who had served him so loyally in arms, found Hazara to be a land of incredible beauty:

Low hills, valleys, flat lands, high mountains in the distance, many snow-capped, the hills clothed with pines, firs,
deodars, the flat lands bearing crops, grass and flowers of
varied hues, villages scattered here and there, sparkling
streams and a cloudless sky, brightened the whole scene. It
is true you have desolate regions, barren lands, dry, stony
creeks, sheer crags, bleak mountain sides—all these, to
make one appreciate the more, the beautiful spectacle that is
all around you.

The names of three principal towns bear witness to three
epochs in Hazara's history. The hill station called Nathia Gali,
with its perfect climate, took its name from a local prince Nathia
Khan (*Gali* meaning valley). At an altitude of over 8,000 feet it
became a favoured holiday resort for the British. Abbottabad,
the main town in Hazara, is named after James Abbott who was a
popular nineteenth-century administrator; and Haripur takes its
name from Ranjit Singh's general, Hari Singh, from the time
when the Sikhs ruled the Punjab.

A legend surrounds the name of the lake of Saiful Maluk in the
valley of Kagan at the northern tip of Hazara, near the town of
Naran; a prince of Delhi heard that a fairy queen lived in the
mountains near the great 26,660-foot mountain of Nanga Parbat
('the Naked Mountain') in Chilas State. Inspired by the stories of
her beauty, he went in search of her. After much 'travel of
countries' (*safr maluk*) he arrived at the lake; he was told in a
vision there that he would have to wait for twelve years before he
could see the fairy queen. The time passed, and finally he was
rewarded with the sight of her bathing with her ladies in the lake.
Unobserved, he stole her clothes and only returned them upon
receiving a promise that she would marry him. But the Demon
King of the mountains, who had been pressing his suit upon the
fairy queen without success, chased the lovers along the mountain passes, and gave vent to his wrath by unleashing the waters
of the lake, causing great destruction in the valley. The lovers
escaped and lived happily ever afterwards.

Hazara also includes the barren region around the Black
Mountain. Gerald Curtis, a British political officer in the 1930s,
flew over this 'fierce and difficult country' in 'what would now
be a museum-piece'. He found the mountain itself had:

. . . a somewhat moth-eaten appearance due to the fact that the trees, that perished for one reason or another, lay where they fell. The valleys leading down to the Indus were deep and very dark and it was not always possible to spot the settlements although each had at least one tall, slender tower for defence purposes. The Indus gorge itself was in darkness, but where the sun shone on it the water showed up green, flecked with white foam.

The town of Oghi, lying in the shadow of the Black Mountain, was the starting point for many a British expedition against the tribesmen.

The vale of Peshawar

Upon approaching the town of Peshawar, 'the traveller will find himself in a spreading vale, watered by many streams and surrounded by an unbroken girdle of mountains,' wrote Olaf Caroe. 'The hills that stand around Peshawar not only look like a ring; they are actually set on the map in a circle, almost complete but for one segment to the south-east where the valley-lands slope to the banks of the Indus.'

'The plain with its fat cattle and fatter crops and the green and silver of its fields and rivers stretches away,' wrote Yvonne Gertrude Fitzroy, Lady Reading's Private Secretary in 1921. 'What wonder it has been a debatable land of promise throughout every page of history.'

This was the valley of Peshawar—of Gandhara in the days of old—which invaders regarded as the first prize to plunder on their way to India. With a history that goes back two thousand years, Peshawar, 'the Frontier town', has witnessed the conquering armies of the Greeks, the rule of the Buddhists, and devastation by the Huns. It was rebuilt by the Rajputs from India, to be invaded again from the west by the Ghaznavids under Sultan Mahmud. Moguls, Persians, Afghans, Sikhs, all overran it. Finally in the nineteenth century it was annexed by the British, until the creation of Pakistan in 1947.

Following his visit to the court of Shah Shuja in 1809,

Mountstuart Elphinstone gave a picturesque view of the city at the time of Afghan supremacy.

> The numerous gardens and scattered trees were covered with new foliage which had a freshness and brilliancy never seen in the perpetual summer of India. Many streams ran through the plain. Their banks were fringed with willows and tamarisks. The orchards scattered over the country contained a profusion of plum, peach, apple, pear, quince and pomegranate trees which afforded a greater display of blossom than I ever before witnessed; and uncultivated parts of land were covered with a thick elastic sod, that perhaps never was equalled but in England.

The British found the climate was conducive to growing the flowers to which they were accustomed, like pansies and roses, and it had the added advantage of being able to grow orange trees—successors to those felled by the Sikhs in order to provide fuel for their troops during their ascendancy in Peshawar. Ian Stephens, one time editor of the *Statesman*, believed the roses were the 'pride of the Frontier'. Flowers, he thought, seemed to mean more to the local people than to the Europeans, 'partly because their country is harsh and craggy, partly perhaps because Muslim orthodoxy has banished the human form from painting and architecture, leaving floral designs as substitutes to be graced by tradition.' The local people could be seen 'quaffing the perfume as you would a glass of good wine. "A-ah!" they say in simple delight.'

Sir Herbert Thompson, who came to Peshawar as City Magistrate in the 1920s, explored the city as haphazardly as it had grown up. He found that it had developed as a figure of eight. Originally, it was centred around a piece of rising ground on which the Moguls had built their fort, presiding over the eastern half of the figure of eight. 'From its waist the city swelled out into its second half which was served by the main gate, the Kabul gate, at the end of the great shopping centre, the Qissa Khani (Story-Tellers) Bazaar with its rows of matchbox-sized shops.' In the olden days this was the place where caravans and military adventurers used to meet and where story-tellers would recite ballads and tales of war and love to merchants and soldiers. In the nineteenth century, Herbert Edwardes, one of the early British administrators, called the bazaar the Piccadilly of Central Asia.

Mike Edwards, an American journalist working for the *National Geographic*, travelled to Peshawar fifty years after Thompson. He found that it remained very much two cities in one.

> The cantonment that the British built when Peshawar was their Frontier Headquarters is a gracious tract of wide avenues and flaming bougainvillea. The other part, known as the city, is the heart of hearts, the bazaar, a place of winding alleys and noise and intense aroma, nearly treeless, dense with shops, cyclists, horsedrawn tongas, carts pulled by water buffaloes and put-putting three-wheel taxis.

In the present day it is jam-packed with travellers from Afghanistan, refugees and fighters.

In spite of the girdle of mountains which surrounds the Peshawar valley, there are four natural points of entry through which an enemy might threaten the city. To the north there is the Malakand pass; to the west, the most travelled route of all, lies the Khyber, and, in the south, entry can be made from Kohat. In the east, the traveller must cross the foaming Indus and Kabul rivers which converge in contrasting colours at Attock; here, a bridge built by the British in the late nineteenth century provided road and ultimately rail transport. Before that, a ferry had given less safe but sufficient passage. This was the route leading straight on down to the town of Rawalpindi in the Punjab, which had been guarded so conscientiously by Khushhal and the Khataks.

To the north of Peshawar lies the plain of Mardan: 'A tract of country bounded on the north and west by the mountains of Buner and Swat, and on the east by the river Indus,' said Gerald Curtis. 'A century earlier, when the British took charge of it, it was a poverty-stricken and sparsely inhabited plain with no irrigation except near the Indus where valuable crops of tobacco were watered from wells. British engineers have made use of the Swat river for irrigation.' And once irrigated, the country yielded valuable crops, wheat and barley in winter, maize and sugar cane in summer, which stood 'in squares like pikemen in a seventeeth-century battle scene, and which provided shelter for the outlaw'. Nowadays, around the mud-walled villages there are orchards of peach, apricot, almond and plum, as well as mulberries.

West to Khyber and Tirah

The swiftest way to enter the sub-continent from the west is through the Khyber Pass. Its history has turned it into the most fabled mountain gateway in the world, and to this day it remains a prized passageway to India. Even so, a safe journey still depends on the good will of those who guard it. At Jamrud a huge fort built by the Sikhs lies like a battleship defending the entrance to the Khyber from Peshawar. Midway was the fort of Ali Masjid, named after Hazrat Ali, son-in-law of the Prophet, who, according to legend, had prayed there. However, once the tribesmen had replaced their muskets by rifles, the fort, surrounded by overlooking heights, proved too vulnerable to attack; a new fort was therefore built at Shagai. The third fort, at Landi Kotal, was the 'forward' position of the British Empire along the route to Afghanistan.

Unwelcome entrants have suffered severe losses when trying to pass through the Khyber. When John Griffiths went to Peshawar he could not help but notice the reminders of battles once fought. 'Moving on down the Khyber at dawn to Peshawar, you leave behind the narrow defile speckled with innumerable plaques commemorating the otherwise forgotten deeds of heroism of those who fought to take and hold the pass.' In Colonel Lever's words, 'It twists and turns and winds its way through perhaps the most desolate track of land in the world: sheer mountainside, crag and defile as far as the Afghan border.' And for Mike Edwards it was 'The meanest stretch of country I have ever seen. The pass bristles with reminders of violence: forts, picket posts top every dominating crag, even concrete dragon's teeth, planted to stop German tanks when Britain feared a strike into India during World War II.'

Traditionally the route of the *kafilas* (caravans) taking goods to Peshawar's market, in times of peace the Khyber Pass has, because of its reputation, become one of the biggest tourist attractions. In the time of the British, the advice given to the sightseers in *Murray's Handbook* was quite clear: 'Tribal unrest may lead to the closing of the pass at any time. Visitors must provide themselves with luncheon baskets.' Such advice holds good today.

The Khyber borders the land of Tirah, hostile territory which no foreigner may penetrate. 'They only come fighting—or as prisoners,' said a tribesman to the one person who came in 1923 as a guest, Lillian Starr.

The summer home of the Afridi tribesmen who inhabit Tirah is the Maidan Valley. Twelve miles long and half as wide, it is surrounded by mountains. Captain Shadwell, who was one of those who came fighting into Tirah in 1897, found that it was unlike any valley he had seen before. 'When one talks of a valley, people who have not been in India, especially in the northern part of it, probably picture to themselves a valley such as one sees in England with the meadows gently sloping down to the river, which flows peacefully along in the centre. The valleys among the mountains of Tirah are not, unfortunately, of this nature.' During heavy rainfall the water pours off the spurs on either side in torrents, 'for the soil, which is very scanty on the mountain sides, absorbs very little. This water digs for itself deep water courses or nullahs and, rushing headlong down, tears away the banks till they stand perpendicularly or even jut over in places.'

To Kohat and Kurram

Forty miles to the south of Peshawar lies the town of Kohat. The Kohat pass is the fourth and final exit from the vale of Peshawar. Running through Tirah, the pass is also called the Darrah which means 'valley' and it is famous for the *Darrahwal topak*—the valley-made rifle, manufactured with precision by the local people to shoot their enemies. The road zigzags as it rises steeply to the summit, which is named Handyside Gate after the British Commandant of the Frontier Constabulary, who died in 1926 bravely fighting outlaws on the spot marked by the monument. 'From this position one has an extensive view of the cantonment of Kohat and the countryside around,' observed Colonel Lever. 'Unlike the other passes the scene that meets the eye is pic-turesque, the green of the cultivated fields contrasting with the grey and drab mountain side.' In comparison with mountainous Tirah, the district of Kohat is flat and open.

Skirting the lower edge of Tirah there is a natural route from Kohat district, through the towns of Hangu and Kohat, to the Kurram valley, overlooked by the Samana range of mountains and the Dargai heights in Tirah. The valley, pointing like a finger towards Afghanistan, provides another passage to or from the west. Kurram is beautiful by all accounts, as Peter Mayne, a former RAF officer who came to revisit the Frontier in 1954, discovered: 'Willow trees lined the streams that come tumbling down the hillsides to join the main body of the Kurram river. But the hills are for the most part bare, as if they belonged to a world separate from the watered world of the valley.' The road climbs up-river; suddenly the vegetation stops and the traveller finds himself in 'a wide plain, stone covered'. Beyond is the town of Parachinar and the peaks of the Sufed Koh rising 'like a wall behind the town'.

The Sufed Koh ('White Mountains') are an extension of the long range of the Suleiman mountains which run roughly north-east to south-west from the Khyber through Tirah to Waziristan. The Sufed Koh, which rise to over 15,000 feet, came to form part of the boundary between Afghanistan and British India. In spite of being one of the few places where the frontier followed a geographical line, the head of the Kurram valley remains in Afghanistan.

Bannu's oasis and Dreary Dismal

The town of Bannu is considered to be an oasis in what is otherwise dry and dusty countryside. In the nineteenth century Herbert Edwardes described it as a paradise: 'In Spring it is a veritable emerald and in winter its many-coloured harvest looks as if Ceres had stumbled against the great salt range and spilt half her cornucopia in this favoured vale.' Charles Masson was more specific:

Bunnoo [Bannu], or the plain so-called, is remarkably fertile, producing independently of the several common kinds of grain, sugar, turmeric, ginger and other valuable articles, but in small quantities owing to the disorganised state of society and the want of security. It is undoubtedly capable of yielding any variety of cultivated produce that is met with in the plains of Peshawar, which the inhabitants boast could grow anything. Bunnoo in the distance exhibits a rich and glowing appearance from its verdure.

But for most of the year the area as a whole, comprising the districts of Bannu and Dera Ismail Khan (DIK), lacks water and looks parched because of it. 'Daddy, you have led us to the back side of the desert!' Gerald Curtis's small son exclaimed, quoting from the Bible, as they passed through the sandy wastes of Mianwali bordering Bannu and DIK. It was not without reason that the British used to call Dera Ismail Khan 'Dreary Dismal'.

The mud-walled town of Tank, in the district of DIK but within easy reach of the territory of Waziristan, became an important centre for trade. 'Timber brought down from the hills on camel back was marketed at Tank and other products of the country—wool, hides, potatoes, fruit and nuts—were sold here,' Gerald Curtis found during the time he spent there. The town of DIK, close to the river Indus, provides an interlude from otherwise desolate countryside. 'There was not a blade of grass to be seen,' observed Herbert Thompson, 'but the cattle looked sleek and fat, totally different from the perambulating toast racks of the south'.

The whole area from Peshawar to DIK and down to Dera Ghazi Khan in the Punjab is bounded by the river Indus to the east. The districts of Bannu, Dera Ismail Khan and Dera Ghazi Khan were all known as the Derajat. When the North-West Frontier Province was created, Dera Ghazi Khan reverted to the Punjab. The river Indus formed a natural division between these 'frontier districts' and the Punjab. In winter, when the river was low, the British coming from the Punjab used to cross the Indus near DIK across a bridge of boats, which would run across, 'first a wide island over which a rush and straw causeway was built, and then over the second arm of the Indus to the Frontier side, so making the five-mile crossing of the Indus only a matter of minutes.' The steamer used in summer would take longer, 'And no wonder,' remarked Herbert Thompson. 'It looked like a second-hand acquisition from the Mississippi. When we disembarked on the right bank, I had no doubt where I was—Central Asia.'

Waziristan

'It is a cruel and merciless country, worthy of its sons,' commented Gerald Curtis. Caroe found Waziristan was, in its own way, a fortress like John of Gaunt's England but with ramparts instead of a moat. 'The scale is vast,' said Ian Stephens. 'Everything appears hard and bare. Toothy crags bite the pale sky.'

Several rivers water the hills and valleys of Waziristan, flowing on to join the Indus in the plains. Curtis felt that 'the word "river" conveys too gracious an impression.'

> But to call them torrents would also be misleading. At times they carried a bare trickle wandering amid a wide expanse of sunbaked boulders and sand shingle, or making their way down some dark defile between precipitous cliffs. Suddenly, however, after a cloud burst in the mountains a scanty exiguous stream might become a lethal uncontrollable flood, sweeping all before it.

The Gomal river, dividing Waziristan from Baluchistan, points the way to the Gomal pass. In addition to Khyber and Kurram to the north, this pass could have provided another more southerly route into Afghanistan if the British had been successful in their exploits against the tribesmen. But even though the pass was opened by the British in the 1890s, they never secured complete control, and eventually it was abandoned to be used by the tribesmen and their caravans alone.

No one could be expected to describe Waziristan as beautiful. 'The Afghans will tell you,' said Dr Theodore Pennell, the missionary who spent so much of his life in the area during the late nineteenth and early twentieth century, 'that when God created the world, there were a lot of stones and rocks and other lumber left over, which were all dumped down on this frontier, and this accounts for its unattractive appearance.' Even so, Brigadier John Prendergast, who soldiered on the Frontier in the

1930s, found that there was something about the place which
gave it an appeal all of its own:

> The morning sun picks out the hills and clothes them
> minute by minute with rich, warm colours, as though to
> compensate for their starved aridity. The air is exciting.
> From the tops of the crests down to its little valleys, it varies
> from iced champagne to the heat of a furnace. The sun can
> strike off bare rocks with a blast of heat, which drives the
> accoutred soldier to exhaustion and despair, but rock plants
> are rich in aromatic scent. All this richness to the senses
> makes the Frontier tug harder at the heart strings than all the
> conventionally beautiful places a soldier may see in his
> service.

To Quetta and the Bolan pass

Waziristan, said Arnold Toynbee, who travelled to the Frontier
area in 1960, 'surprises one by the density of the population that
clings to its inhospitable rocks. Vast Baluchistan's emptiness is,
by contrast, just what one would expect in this hard inhospitable
land.'

Situated in northern Baluchistan, the town of Quetta marked
the southernmost point of the 'North-West Frontier' in the
defensive strategy of the British. Originally, Ahmed Shah Durrani regarded virtually the whole territory of Baluchistan as far as
the sea as part of the Afghan empire. But he had given the valley
of Shal, in which Quetta lies, to the local chief, the Khan of
Kalat, who, from this vantage point, was able to control an
important junction into Central Asia.

Like Peshawar, four roads lead to Quetta: to the south-west
lies Persia and beyond, as Toynbee observed, London—5,882
miles away. To the east and south-east are the routes to and from
India, either over the plains of northern Sind or through sixty
miles of the Bolan pass. Toynbee was anxious to see this pass
which had many memories for the British, whose exploits he had
seen portrayed in drawings dating from the nineteenth century.
He found the pass was 'every bit as dramatic as those early
Victorian lithographs had depicted. The perpendicular cliffs, the

winding gorge, the precipitous descent; all the sensational features of the pictures were now being faithfully reproduced in real life.' North-west from Quetta, the road leads directly to Kandahar, from where Durrani ruled his empire, and onwards to Ghazni, Sultan Mahmud's old capital. Then comes Kabul, Babur's first conquest on his way to India.

'The kingdom of Kabul'

'May Kabul be without gold, rather than without snow.' The Pashtu proverb emphasises the great importance of a good snowfall to the Afghan. If there was no snow to melt and thus water the plains, they would produce a meagre yield at harvest time.

Even when severed from the lands to the east which had all been nominally under one authority since the time of Babur, Kabul still retained its importance, sitting on the eastern edge of an irregular circle of roads which linked the main towns of Herat, Kandahar, Ghazni and Mazar-i-Sharif in the north. At the same time there remained several important outlets: the way west from Kabul passed through Jalalabad to Peshawar; the route from Kandahar to Quetta went via Chaman in the south. To the east, Herat led to Persia; and in the north Mazar-i-Sharif and Kunduz pointed towards Russia. In the nineteenth century the routes were dirt tracks; in the twentieth they became all-weather roads.

The 190-mile journey to Kabul from Peshawar takes the traveller through the Khyber pass, following the course of the Kabul river to the north. Between the towns of Torkham on the border and Jalalabad, 'you traverse a characteristic Central Asian scene: a vast stony plateau rimmed by remote mountains, the whole slightly tilted,' observed Ian Stephens. 'The tilt in this case fell to the right, where, pressed against a wall of brown mountain, the Kabul river's distant coils glinted.'

In spite of the long and dusty journey, there are, as Peter Mayne discovered on his travels, compensations, 'such as the sudden emergence of the Hindu Kush sprawled like a snow leopard all over the north'. And on arriving in Kabul, 'the landscape opens out and when this happens you can forget

everything that has gone before and thank God for such loveli-
ness as the climax to such a journey. A high wide plateau, corn,
and the city of Kabul sheltering under its little hills.'

And at least in the present day the traveller can avoid the
treacherous passes which were the scene of the annihilation of the
British army in 1842. Trapped in the Khurd Kabul pass just
outside Kabul on their way to Jalalabad in mid-winter, the
soldiers were an easy target for those on the hills: 'This truly
formidable defile is about five miles from end to end and is shut
in on either hand by a line of lofty hills, between whose
precipitous sides the sun at this season could dart but a
momentary ray,' wrote Vincent Eyre, one of the few survivors.
Today only caravans of camels pass that way.

When Babur was in Kabul, where he lies buried, he took a
special interest in the produce of the country: 'Fruits of hot and
cold climates are to be had in the districts near the town.
Amongst those of cold climate, there are had in the town the
grape, the pomegranate, apricot, apple, quince, pear, peach,
plum,' as well as almonds and walnuts. And he did not agree
with Khushhal Khan who seemed to be the only person who
thought Kabul was bleak: 'It has a very pleasant climate; if the
world has another one so pleasant, it is not known. Even in the
heats one cannot sleep at night without a fur coat.'

In the nineteenth century the British appreciated the horticul-
tural advantages of the city. 'The potatoes thrive well and will be
a very valuable addition to the cuisine,' wrote Lady Sale, at a
time when the Afghan chiefs were rising in rebellion against the
British occupation in Kabul. 'The cauliflowers, artichokes and
turnip radishes are very fine and peculiarly mild in flavour; the
Cabul lettuces are hairy and inferior to those cultivated by us; but
the Cabul cabbages are superior being milder and the red cabbage
from English seeds grows well.'

The city is overlooked by the Bala Hissar fort built by the
Moguls which to this day forms part of Kabul's history. And as
in Peshawar there is a bazaar which, according to Charles
Masson in the 1820s, was 'wonderfully busy and the streets
swarm with people. The display of merchandise is very great, as
well as the necessaries of life, but the exhibition of the fruit shops
might rival competition in any city in the universe.'

Like Peshawar, Kabul was a city divided in two. 'Afghans can live where they please, I suppose: but their foreigners are required to live in barrage-balloons. They must float, gas-filled, in an element in no way their own, with nothing to do but observe, and even their observation is limited by the distance from the earth at which they are moored so securely,' said Peter Mayne of Kabul in the 1950s. 'You feel a prisoner of kindness and perhaps red tape,' observed Ian Stephens, 'cut off from fact, enwrapped in an atmosphere carefully non-Asian.'

Thirty years later under Russian occupation it has become something altogether different and many of the foreigners have left. 'Kabul used to be a gay, gregarious city, with the noise of recorded music and smell of kebab lingering well after midnight. Now it dies soon after the sun is down,' wrote Kudlip Nayar, an Indian journalist who visited Afghanistan in 1980. 'Even otherwise the Afghans have become introverts and quiet.' As in the previous century, Kabul is again occupied by foreign troops, with tribesmen sheltering in the hills trying to descend on the city at night and wreak what havoc they can.

By the end of the nineteenth century, Afghanistan had been invaded twice by British armies. And the 'kingdom of Caubul' so eloquently portrayed by Elphinstone at the beginning of the century had little but sinister memories for those who had been there. British interest in the cities of Afghanistan—Kabul, Kandahar, Jalalabad, Ghazni—arose primarily because of their situation in guarding the north-west frontier of India. Had not the medieval geographers said that Hindustan began at Ghazni? As no boundary was fixed until the close of the century, each town was potentially a forward position in their defensive strategy. And as the Russians were to discover a century later, holding the principal cities meant holding Afghanistan.

The Turkish bath

Benumbing cold and scorching heat combine to make the whole area at times quite unbearable. Arnold Toynbee compared the land over which he travelled between the river Oxus in Afghanistan and the river Jumna in India to 'a Turkish bath on a gigantic scale, with the chilly room at an altitude of 7,000 feet and upwards, opening out of the steam room at 3,000 feet and under.'

Heat is a factor which has caused discomfort (and worse) to many a European.

Jack Lowis, a British political officer in 1935, wrote from Tank to his sister back in the cooler climate of England.

> I have never found the heat so appalling. Only stayed a couple of hours in the office. Four men got heat stroke that day, of which one died in the evening and another nearly died and is still bad. In the middle of the afternoon I thought I was going to blow up myself, but fortunately by that time the water in the bath had cooled to only a little above blood heat and I got into it and then lay under a fan again and things eased slightly.

It was, in fact, a severe heat wave, with a record temperature of 134 degrees Fahrenheit. Tank, said Lowis, was the third hottest place in the world—the first being Tripolitania in North Africa and the second Death Valley in Arizona.

There was also the freezing cold to be reckoned with. In Afghanistan in 1879, camped outside Kabul, Captain Bryce Albert Combe of the Hussars complained: 'It is so awfully cold one simply can't do any writing . . . to say nothing of one's ink being always frozen hard except for a few hours in the middle of the day—over 20° of frost at night and it begins to freeze soon after 5 p.m.' A bottle of medicine which had been mixed in the hospital and sent across to the camp 'was a solid block of ice before it reached us'.

Dr Hugh Luard became very ill with constant diarrhoea all his life due to sleeping out in appalling weather conditions in the 1890s. With no tents the men made a rough hut of stones for the officers with a grass roof to try and afford some protection from torrential rains. But the storm continued:

> . . . with violent wind that threatened to take the roof off; then tremendous thunder roaring round us, lightning and torrents of rain which soon soaked through the roof and ran through like a sieve: I shuffled round in a circle half asleep trying to find a place where my face was protected; roof, mud and water fell everywhere: in the middle of the night [I was] disturbed by fellows walking over me, kicking me,

trying to find a dry place: in the morning the floor was full of puddles in which we were lying.

Colonel Sir Arthur McMahon was more fortunate when touring in the north, in Chitral, in winter time:

> It's awfully cold up in these high altitudes at this time of year and the streams remain frozen all day. It's warmer living in a hut than a tent and so whenever we can find a hut to live in, we do so. They are strongly built houses, but the fire is made in the centre of the floor and the smoke goes or rather ought to go out of a large hole left in the ceiling. The walls and rafters are black with smoke and the cows and sheep generally live inside with the owner's family. The family have vacated the hut I'm in, but the cows and sheep do not approve of the arrangement and keep on trying to come in. The cow has been in twice since I began this letter and a sheep has romped round and upset the washbasin.

Stoic behaviour on the part of the British was the accepted norm in their Asian escapades. It was well known, said Winston Churchill, that the British officers felt the heat more than the Indians, but they could not afford to let the Indians realise this because it would result in a loss of respect.

'Tribal territory' and 'settled areas'

In the end, the disposition of the lands over which the invaders had passed, and which the British spent a hundred years trying to subdue, came to dictate their political future. Whereas those in the plains could be conquered easily and might need protection, those living in the hills could well defend themselves. In addition, because of the severe winters and hot summers, there was continual migration to the plains in winter, to the hills in summer, regardless of who ruled where. At the same time, the poverty of the hill tribes made raiding into the plains an essential part of their daily lives.

The Sikhs, during their supremacy, made no attempt to

control the land of the hill tribes; instead, they preferred to exact taxation from those in the plains and leave the mountainous territory bordering Afghanistan well alone. Ungoverned and lawless, it acted as an additional buffer between India and Afghanistan; it was 'tribal territory,' whereas the plains were 'settled areas'.

When the British took over responsibility of the frontier area, they found it impossible to turn a blind eye to the raids into the settled areas, more especially when their own stores of weapons and ammunition became the objective of a raid. Initially they did not consider that the dividing line as left by the old Sikh administration would remain so clear cut. They hoped eventually that the tribal territory would be incorporated within the overall administration of the British Empire.

But frequent expeditions into tribal territory showed how fiercely the tribes fought to guard their independence. By the next century the line between the settled areas and tribal territory almost amounted to another frontier: 'Settled areas are sort of open level country in which the forces of law and order can fairly easily function,' observed Ambrose Dundas, a British political officer in the inter-war years.

> They are on the whole rich, fertile and tempting. The hills on the other hand are barren and not self-supporting for the hardy population which they breed. Above all they are difficult of access and easy to defend. When we speak of them as hills, it does not mean rolling downs on which tanks or cavalry can operate, but the worst kind of mountain-warfare you can imagine. There are steep precipices, narrow winding valleys, every vantage point commanded by another, and innumerable refuges and routes of escape. It is this country that makes the Frontier problem.

The Durand line

Indirectly, the problem of tribal territory prevented the British from establishing their boundaries between Afghanistan and the British Empire upon what were considered to be the most easily defensible geographical lines. If they could not control the territory in between how could they maintain their lines of communication to their advanced positions?

To defend northern India, the British needed ideally to secure those forward positions in Afghanistan whose occupation had made invasion into India so easy in the past: and for preference the boundary would be fixed along geographical lines. To the north the Kunar river could have provided a point of departure, leading to the Kabul river and down to Kandahar. It was, as the proponents of the 'forward' policy liked to say, a 'scientific frontier', established along more or less natural lines. If this line could not be held, they felt there was very little in between which could act as a barrier, unless the boundary were drawn much further to the east along the line of the Indus, excluding the Frontier districts altogether. But experience had also shown that once reached, the Indus was easy to cross. Alternatively, there was the line adopted by the Sikhs during their occupation; but not only did this leave the mountain tribes free to raid into the open plains, but it also meant relying on them to prevent the passage of the invader.

Finally there was the wavy line in between the forward and backward positions. It was not named after any river or mountain barrier because geography had very little to do with its composition; rather it was named after the man who drew it, Sir Mortimer Durand. Although some have seen the value of a line which separates the tribes which look towards Kabul, Ghazni and Kandahar from those whose focus of attention is Peshawar, Kohat and Quetta, for a long time it was regarded as unsatisfactory.

'It is a vague sort of line, sometimes following watershed, and sometimes not. There is the same mountainous tangle of country on both sides of it, and nowhere is there anything artificial or natural to tell you when you have reached it,' was the disparaging comment of Dundas. Even so, this was the line which came to divide British India and Afghanistan, more by default than for any other reason. In the present day, it is the border which Pakistan adopted when it gained independence in 1947.

In 1893 when Durand went to visit the Amir of Afghanistan, they agreed upon a boundary in territory which neither had fully explored. 'Abdur Rehman,' said Durand afterwards, 'though he knew his frontier country well, knew it from personal visits or hearsay, not from the study of maps; consequently he was at times at fault regarding the position of places. It was no use producing a map, for he would say, "That is no use. It is all wrong. I know, I have been to those places. Your maps are guesswork." '

By their agreement 'tribal territory', as it had been vaguely defined, was cut in two; because of this the border was never a 'frontier' in the accepted sense of the word. It could never be properly sealed, and it made secure those routes of escape which were to plague the British in the first half of the twentieth century, and subsequently the Russians; both were obliged to see fighters come in from one side and flee across the open border to the other. It also sowed the seeds of an embryonic nationalist movement which, on the basis of race and language, would assert its claim to Pashtunistan, the land of the Pashtu-speaking peoples.

The Durand line was only drawn after a great deal of action on the plains of Afghanistan. Throughout the nineteenth century it was by no means certain where the boundary would lie. It was even thought at one time that Britain might absorb the whole of Afghanistan up to the Hindu Kush, leaving Russia to expand as far as the Oxus valley on the other side, but no further. If this had happened, the concept of retaining the buffer would have been abandoned altogether. Alternatively, Britain might have maintained the 'scientific frontier', leaving the buffer kingdom of Afghanistan centred on Kabul. Debate in Parliament raged long and hard as to whether they should retain Kandahar or retire further to the east, to Sibi in Baluchistan, relinquishing even Quetta to the Afghans.

In fact, by the time the British came to agree their border between Afghanistan and British India, they had long since abandoned their 'forward' policy into Afghanistan, which was neither feasible financially nor acceptable morally. They preferred the notion of keeping Afghanistan as a friendly buffer between them and the Russians. The implications of having included over 10,000 square miles of 'tribal territory' were not yet apparent.

That the British ever entered Afghanistan or reached the North-West Frontier could be seen more as another of those accidents of history rather than as any initial grand design.

Certainly when Dost Muhammad, the ruler of Afghanistan, welcomed the new Governor-General to India and encouraged him to consider himself and his country as Auckland's own, he did not think that his Lordship might well do just that.

CHAPTER THREE

Wars Across the Frontier

The welfare of our possessions in the East requires that we should have
on our western frontier an ally who is interested in resisting aggression,
and establishing tranquillity, in the place of chiefs ranging themselves in
subservience to a hostile power and seeking to promote schemes of
conquest and aggrandisement.

Simla Manifesto, 1838

Early moves

British official authority lasted less than one hundred years on the
North-West Frontier: from 1849, when Britain annexed the
Punjab, until 1947, when the whole of the sub-continent was
given its independence. British involvement in India as a whole,
however, goes back to the founding of the East India Company
in 1600. For the next two centuries the East India Company
expanded both its power and possessions. The declining Mogul
empire, the instability of local rulers along with the intrusions of
ambitious chieftains—all exploited at times by the Portuguese
and the French—eventually led the Company to take on military
responsibility for protecting its trade. And as 'John Company'
came increasingly under the control of the British government,
the hopes and fears of the two became indistinguishable. British
policy was enacted through the Governor-General and the
government of India, based in Calcutta.

By the nineteenth century British attention focused on what
was happening to the north-west of India, bringing the Company into contact with an area which was remote from its
assumed trading preserve, that of Central Asia. Far away though
Russia's borders were from the British territories to the east of
the river Sutlej, the British were continually worried about an

invasion. It was with the object of establishing a defensive alliance against the French and Russians, who had signed the Treaty of Tilsit with Napoleon in 1807, that the first British envoy, Mountstuart Elphinstone, was sent two years later to the court of the ruler of Afghanistan, Shah Shuja-ul-Mulk, who was resident at his winter capital in Peshawar. 'As the court of Caubul was known to be haughty and supposed to entertain a mean opinion of the European nations, it was determined that the mission should be in a style of great magnificence,' said Elphinstone.

At the same time another envoy, Charles Metcalfe, went to conclude a treaty with Ranjit Singh and the Sikhs, whose territories in the Punjab could provide a useful barrier between the British and the Russians, in the event of an invasion through the weak and divided kingdom of the Afghans. As the French threat dwindled with the defeat of Napoleon at Waterloo in 1815, that of Russia loomed larger, especially when Russian influence at the court of the Shah of Persia superseded that of Britain. By the Treaty of Turkemenchay in 1828, Russia effectively eliminated Persia as a barrier against her expansion into Turkestan east of the Caspian sea.

As each power strove to make alliance and counter-alliance, they became caught up in a 'game' of diplomacy and intrigue, which was part of a general rivalry between the Russians and the British stretching from south-east Europe and the Crimea to Central Asia. It was of course, as described by Rudyard Kipling, the 'Great Game', an expression which concealed the harsh realities of wars and bloodshed in countries which were both distant and unknown. Russia's own explanation for her advance into Central Asia, as expressed by Prince Gorchakov, Foreign Minister, in 1864, was that it compared with that of Britain's steady engulfment of her unstable neighbours in the previous century:

> The position of Russia in Central Asia is that of all civilised states which are brought into contact with half savage, nomad populations possessing no fixed social organisation; in such cases it always happens that the more civilised state is forced, in the interests of the security of its frontiers and its commercial relations, to exercise a certain ascendancy

over those whom their turbulent and unsettled character makes undesirable neighbours.

Throughout the nineteenth century the whole of British policy was motivated by the fear that if they did not act first, then the Russians would gain the advantage. Britain had no particular desire to possess Afghanistan, but those in power interpreted any Russian advance in the area as a direct threat to India. In so doing, they undertook grandiose ventures which to the onlooker appeared as imperialist and expansionist as the moves of Russia into Central Asia.

Intelligence gathering

The British knew very little about the countries which surrounded their Indian possessions. They relied on accounts, collected in a haphazard way by whoever had travelled in the region, be he soldier, explorer, mapmaker, or even, as in the case of William Moorcroft, horse doctor. Charles Masson's accounts of his adventures secured him a pardon for desertion and a modest pension for life. A young Scotsman, Alexander Burnes, visited Persia and Bokhara in 1832 and his *Travels into Bokhara* gave him early fame and an interview with the King at Brighton.

In order to improve their intelligence, the British evolved a network of agents, stretching from the Black Sea to the Persian Gulf. It was intended to counteract the activities of the Russian spies who were believed to be operating extensively all over the area. The head of the network was Sir John McNeill, a former surgeon in the army of the East India Company, who rose to become Minister in the British Legation in Teheran in the 1820s. Despite the scepticism of others, he took the Russian threat extremely seriously. However, as representatives of a foreign power whose authority was but shadowy to those rulers with whom the British wanted to establish relations, British agents could not always expect a friendly welcome, especially since, as Christians, they were deemed to be 'infidels'.

In December 1838 Lieutenant-Colonel Charles Stoddart was sent by McNeill to visit Nasrullah, the Amir of Bokhara, in order to pre-empt any Russian initiative in the area. Initially Nasrullah was keen to make a treaty with Queen Victoria, whom he described as the 'Example-giver of the Doctrine of Government and Customs', but he became angry when Lord Palmerston did not reply to Stoddart's despatch on the subject of the friendship treaty. Matters were not improved when Captain Arthur Connolly arrived in Bokhara in 1840; whereas Stoddart had converted to Islam under duress, Connolly refused to do so. When the Amir decided they were no longer of use to him, they were imprisoned and eventually executed in 1842.

Dost Muhammad Khan

For the ruler of Afghanistan, who was trying to assert his power once more over the former Durrani empire, the enemy was not Russia but the Sikhs. And in 1837 he had received a British envoy with a certain amount of optimism, anticipating that help against the Sikhs might now be forthcoming. However, the Governor-General, Lord Auckland, did not send a high-level diplomatic mission; instead he despatched the now famous 'Bokhara Burnes'—who had passed through Afghanistan on his previous travels—without entrusting him with the power to negotiate with the Amir. Even the news that Herat, ruled by the son of Mahmud, Shah Kamran, was being besieged by the Persians with Russian assistance, did not change Auckland's instructions to Burnes. Although, in the event of Herat falling to the Persians, Dost Muhammad could have been secured as a useful ally, Burnes was told only to argue and discuss with the Amir and report back to India.

His mission, though, was bound to fail because there was no way the British were going to agree to Dost Muhammad's principal request in return for his own friendship: help against the Sikhs in order to retrieve Peshawar. All Burnes could tell the Amir was that the government of India's main concern was for 'the honour and just wishes of our old and firm ally Ranjit Singh', regardless of the fact that this could be expected to push Dost Muhammad to the side of the Persians and Russians.

As the siege of Herat dragged on through 1838, the British planned a new strategy. Since they felt unable to oblige the Sikhs to surrender Peshawar and considered Dost Muhammad to favour the Russians, they decided that it would suit their interests far better if they could have a ruler in Afghanistan who was well disposed both to the Sikhs and to the British. Such a man was Shah Shuja, the former king who had been in exile in India as a pensioner of the British. He even had a treaty with Ranjit Singh dating from an earlier attempt, in 1833, to retrieve the Afghan throne, whereby he had renounced his claim to the vale of Peshawar.

Assurance even came from Burnes, who had left Kabul in April 1838, that Shuja would be given a 'ready welcome', in spite of Burnes's obvious preference for Dost Muhammad, who he described as 'a man of undoubted ability [who] has at heart high opinions of the British nation.' Burnes, however, also gave the government the information it wanted to hear. 'The British government have only to send Shuja-ul-Mulk with an agent and two of its own regiments as an honorary escort, and an avowal to the Afghans that we have taken up his cause, to ensure his being fixed for ever on his Throne.'

The plan was embodied in the Tripartite Treaty, signed by Lord Auckland, Ranjit Singh and Shah Shuja at Simla in 1838, which stated among other things that Shah Shuja would send Ranjit Singh fifty-five horses in exchange for fifty-five shawls; he also promised to send melons in return for rice; and, most important of all, he confirmed cession to the Sikhs of just about all the lands which came to be the 'North-West Frontier' of British India, including Peshawar.

Originally the Sikhs were to attack Dost Muhammad, but eventually the British took over the responsibility, partly because Ranjit Singh became anxious about using his troops against the Afghans, who had so recently killed his favourite general, Hari Singh, at Jamrud. The British also did not want Shah Shuja to appear in Kabul as the puppet of the Sikhs, which he undoubtedly would have done if Sikhs had been in his entourage. Once the wheels for the operation were set in motion, even the news that the Persians had given up the siege of Herat did not cancel the expedition. The fact that an officer in the Russian Cossacks had been received by Dost Muhammad in Kabul was evidence to the British that he could no longer be trusted as a friend of the British. In October 1838 they issued a manifesto at Simla to the effect that Dost Muhammad, as the enemy of the Sikhs, was also their enemy, and that for their own security they wished to have a stable ally on the throne of Afghanistan.

By determining not to let Dost Muhammad pursue his ambitions into the valley of Peshawar, the British set the scene for the final demarcation of the boundary between Afghanistan and India. Never again would the rulers of Afghanistan be quite so near to making the river Indus their eastern frontier. By backing the Sikhs and Ranjit Singh, by now an old man, the British chose an ally who would be dead before the expedition to Kabul had even set off. Almost unwittingly, they had undertaken one of their most ambitious manoeuvres to date, committing their armies to fight over five hundred miles away from their Indian frontiers.

The First Kabul Tragedy

The History of the War in Afghanistan was written soon afterwards by Sir John William Kaye, from unpublished letters and journals. He compiled two volumes of events in an effort to explain the disaster to the successors of those who died on Afghanistan's plains. 'I have been walking as it were with a torch in my hand over a floor strewn thickly with gunpowder. There is the chance of an explosion at every step.' And ever since Kaye, people have been retelling the story of what came to be known as the First Kabul Tragedy.

The Army of the Indus

Rather than the two regiments as an honorary escort suggested by Alexander Burnes, the British decided to send a vast army from India to seat Shah Shuja on his throne. Kaye described the army which set out from the Punjab in December 1838 as 'a moving city of people': the Bengal regiment of some 9,500 men was to march overland; and the Bombay regiment numbering 5,600 would go by sea from Karachi. In addition there was Shah Shuja's force of 6,000. The greatest numbers, however, were the 38,000 camp followers and 30,000 camels, not to mention the baggage. Officers did not believe in travelling light: sixty camels for the baggage of one brigadier was considered a not unreasonable number at the time; forty servants for a junior officer.

William Macnaghten, Auckland's chief adviser throughout the planning stages, and signatory to the Simla manifesto, was to be the British envoy at the court of Shah Shuja; he was accompanied by Alexander Burnes, who would eventually take over from him. Both Macnaghten and Burnes received knighthoods for services rendered.

Not only did Ranjit Singh manage to avoid supplying the Army of the Indus with any of his own levies; he also diverted its passage out of his territory, causing it to traverse the deserts of Sind and Baluchistan, a distance of some 1,200 miles. A journey which could have taken a few weeks, directly across the Punjab, in fact took several months. Not surprisingly, the army which set out in such high hopes was soon in distress. The march was slowed by the average travelling speed of the camels, which was two miles an hour, and when they finally reached Quetta, on the other side of the Bolan pass, there were virtually no provisions either for the men or the animals.

> Horses already half starved from want of grain and good grass were throughout the day panting in all the agonies of thirst, and in the evening a few drops of water could not be obtained to mix the medicines of the sick . . . All ranks have been taught to understand today how little prized when plentiful, how outrageously demanded when scarce, is that bounteous provision for the wants of God's creatures, water.

For the English soldier the march of the Army of the Indus into the plains of Central Asia was very much a step into the unknown, though hopes of conquest were high. A young lieutenant, Frederick Marriot, was inspired by the grandeur of the venture:

> I suspect this will prove the biggest step that English authority has ever taken at one stride in this quarter of the globe. It is a strike inland to step into the middle at once and afterwards to work outwards. Just look at Caboul on the map. Look at Hehrat. I expect very soon to see Chinese Tartary and Siberia amongst Her Majesty's dominions.

The British considered themselves fortunate in having the services of Mohan Lal, a Kashmiri Indian. Previously he had accompanied Burnes on his travels in Persia and taught him

Persian; then, from being a *munshi* (teacher), he became a spy. As the Army of the Indus entered Afghanistan, Mohan Lal was of great help, not only in collecting information, but in distributing bribes to the local chiefs to encourage them to come over to the side of the British. He was so successful that, when the army reached Kandahar in April 1839, they found that it had been completely evacuated.

At Kandahar, where the two regiments finally met up with each other, they left the heavy guns which they had wearily dragged all the way across the desert and through the Bolan pass. A captain in the Light Infantry, Henry Havelock, believed this to be a mistake because, when they came to the fortress at Ghazni, they had to rely on the ingenuity of an engineer—Lieutenant Henry Durand—to enable them to blow up the only gate of the fortress which had not been walled up. (An informer had let them know which of the gates had merely been barricaded in order to allow supplies to come in.) After Ghazni had fallen, there was little to stop the progress of the army to Kabul, so Dost Muhammad fled across the Hindu Kush mountains.

Shah Shuja—the Luckless Prince, Shah-e-Kam-Naseeb, as he was called by his troops—returned to his kingdom on 6 August 1839, after an absence of thirty years. 'Shah Shuja, dazzling in a coronet, jewelled girdle and bracelet, bestrode his white charger whose equipment gleamed with gold.' Missing from his attire was only the Koh-i-Noor diamond, surrendered some years before to Ranjit Singh. 'But,' said Havelock, 'neither the monarch nor his pageant kindled any enthusiasm with the Cabulees.' As Kaye remarked, 'The inhabitants came to look at the show,' but 'they stared at the European strangers more than at the King who had been brought back to Caubul by the Feringees.' Macnaghten and Burnes rode in splendour; so did Mohan Lal: 'flaunting a majestic turban and looking in his spruceness not at all as though his mission in Afghanistan were to do the dirty work of the British diplomats,' observed Havelock.

In Kabul

Once the ceremonies were over, the British set up garrisons at Ghazni, Jalalabad, Kandahar and Kabul, having despatched the

Bombay division back to India. The original intention was to send most of the army back, but it soon became clear that substantial troops might still be needed either to protect Herat or Shah Shuja or both. A small contingent was sent to Bamian to watch over the passes of the Hindu Kush and over Dost Muhammad. 'For the first and last time in history the British were in actual physical occupation of the great North-Western frontier of their dominions,' noted Sir Kerr Fraser-Tytler, himself British Minister in Afghanistan exactly one hundred years later.

In order to give some semblance of normality to their lives, the officers sent for their wives, children and furniture from India. They introduced their sports, and even constructed a race course. 'They did their best,' said Kaye with a note of caution, 'as they ever do, to accommodate themselves to new localities and their circumstances, and transplanted their habits and, I fear it must be added, their vices with great address to the capital of the Douranee empire.'

Amongst those who came to Kabul was Lady Florentia Sale, a stout woman of fifty-three, accompanied by her twenty-year-old daughter, who in due course married one of the officers, Lieutenant Sturt. Lady Sale's husband, Sir Robert Sale, was kept busy chasing Dost Muhammad, who had succeeded in crossing the Hindu Kush again and causing trouble around Bamian. 'The Afghans are gunpowder and the Dost is a lighted match,' was Macnaghten's assessment. Dost Muhammad preferred to compare himself to a wooden spoon: 'You may throw me hither and thither, but I shall not be hurt.'

The British Army moved in August 1840 from the comparative security of the fort of Bala Hissar to a cantonment on the plain, a move prompted by Shah Shuja, who wanted the fort for his followers. Gradually the soldiers became accustomed to life in this unknown land. One private in the army, James Webb, wrote to his family saying that he longed to be in quarters where there was a church: 'the natives,' he said, 'call us unbelievers.' He was also worried about the post. 'The dakwallahs (I mean postmen) that go from town to town are so often murdered that there is no certainty of them in this country where the army is.' His fervent desire was to hear from his family once a month.

The constant skirmishes with the Afghans taught the soldiers, like Gunner James Black in Jalalabad, something about their new adversaries: 'No sooner had night come on than we was again cauld to stand by ower guns for thay ware to Cowardeley to meet us by Dey. Ower tents are full of shot holes whare they stole [up on] us at night. During this time the firing never ceased we burnt all thare villages not leaving them a place to put thare heads.'

Even Dost Muhammad's surrender and departure into honourable exile in India in September 1840 brought only a temporary lull in the attacks. To the Afghans, the continued presence of the British troops looked very much like an occupation. Much as they might admire the British prowess in skating or their skill at cricket, the British were infidels. The Afghans were also offended by what they felt was the 'traffic' of their women to the cantonment which, said Kaye, was 'open, undisguised and notorious'. The proverb 'Necessity is the mother of invention and the father of the Eurasian' was manifest. Shah Shuja was only too aware of this unpopular feature of the British presence, but he had little influence either with the British or the Afghan chiefs; they resented his entourage of foreigners—feringhees and Kafirs, Hindustanis and Punjabis.

McNeill's intelligence network was still operating out of Teheran. In August 1841 the Political Agent at Kandahar, Henry Rawlinson, reported on the already deteriorating situation:

> The feeling against us is daily on the increase and I apprehend a succession of disturbances in this part of the country till the winter. The moolahs are preaching against us from one end of the country to the other, and we may now be said to hold our position by our military strength. It seems to me that there are but three courses left open to us. We must either evacuate the country and trust to maintain Shah Shuja on the throne by our political influence backed by the location of masses of troops up on the frontier, or we must carry fire and sword through some of the insurgent districts and paralyse the national and religious animosity of the Afghans by a short and sharp course of extreme severity.

The last alternative was to keep military possession of the country 'at one immense sacrifice of blood and treasure; and withhold any prospect of a limit in time to this drain upon our Indian treasure.'

India was indeed 'groaning under the weight' of having to keep the army in Kabul. And the solution adopted of cutting the subsidies to the local chiefs merely increased their problems. The Ghilzais in the east rose in revolt and closed the passes, effectively cutting off communication between Kabul and India. Sale's brigade, which was about to march to India on relief, was ordered to help in clearing the road. He left Kabul in October and had to fight his way to Gandamak, with considerable losses, and injury to himself. Then came the news of further rebellion in Kabul, and the murder of Sir Alexander Burnes.

Burnes, who preferred to live in the city rather than the cantonment, was particularly exposed to attack. But he ignored the warnings of Mohan Lal, even when he was told that several chiefs had sworn on the Koran that they would attack his house. Macnaghten was also oblivious to the real dangers, writing in his reports that everything was the 'couleur de rose' and that the noses of the Afghan chiefs had been brought to the grindstone as late as September. Burnes's murder stunned them all. Apparently he had tried to reason with the mob in his best Persian, but to no avail. He was swiftly hacked to pieces. Mohan Lal managed to escape; he was given protection and continued to carry out his duties 'at the risk of my life . . . if I had feared for my life, there was not a single man to send intelligence to Government at such a crisis, and it is the most wonderful thing that I managed the despatch of letters so regularly and safely, that none of them was ever intercepted by the enemy, while the roads to Jalalabad were watched on every step.'

Soon afterwards, the British launched an attack on the ridge of Beymaru, from where the Afghans had been bombarding the cantonment; their forces, however, were torn apart. Lady Sale described the fighting in her journal: 'I saw the Afghans ride clean through them. The onset was fearful. They looked like a great cluster of bees.'

Swift and effective action could perhaps have stopped the revolt spreading, but unfortunately the general who had arrived in Kabul to take over from General Sir Willoughby Cotton earlier in the year was highly unsuited for the job. General William George Elphinstone, a cousin of Mountstuart, had fought well in the wars against Napoleon but, nearly thirty years later, he was, according to Havelock, 'fit only for the invalid establishment on the day of his arrival in India'. Kaye said that his personal courage was never doubted, but, suffering from severe gout, General Elphinstone had a frame 'almost paralysed by disease and a mind quite clouded by suffering'. In addition, he knew little about 'the political condition of Afghanistan or the feelings of the people; of the language they spoke, or the country they inhabited.'

The second-in-command, Brigadier Shelton, was not much better. He was said to be moody and obstinate, entering into fierce arguments with Elphinstone, and immersing himself in his sleeping bag, pretending to doze off in important meetings.

By early December the situation had worsened still further. Lady Sale managed to get a letter to her husband, Sir Robert, who had reached Jalalabad from Gandamak; she wrote scathingly of both Elphinstone and Shelton. 'It was proposed to go out and attack the enemy who showed themselves as usual, but Shelton would not fight . . . The General is as crippled in mind as body. Shelton seems as bad.' Her letter, sent hidden in the headband of a messenger, added, 'We are all well, tho' anxious.' ·

It was becoming clear that the British Army would have to leave before they were slaughtered in their exposed cantonment. Macnaghten had at last realised the danger, and had opened negotiations with the apparent leader of the Afghan chiefs, who had only recently come on the scene. This was Muhammad Akbar Khan, the son of Dost Muhammad and victor of the battle against the Sikhs at Jamrud in 1837. In her letter to her husband, Lady Sale was already anticipating departure. 'The other women will, I fear, be very helpless with young children; we will load our horses with bags of provisions and walk in the centre of the troops. God bless you; I still look forward to our meeting in better times.'

But the negotiations dragged on, whilst the army was subjected to constant attack, and their supplies diminished. The camels were dying fast and 'the air is most unpleasantly scented at times', wrote Lady Sale. 'The enemy uncommonly quiet, said to be employed in manufacturing powder and shot and hammering such of our shot as they pick up to fit their guns,' she commented on one day. On another she monitored the situation from her roof top: 'I had taken up my post of observation, as usual, on the top of the house, whence I had a fine view of the field of action and where, by keeping behind the chimneys, I escaped the bullets that continually whizzed past me.'

It was an appalling tale of events for Macnaghten to have to recount.

> The whole country, as far as we could learn, had risen in rebellion; our communications on all sides were cut off . . . We have been fighting for forty days against very superior numbers, under most disadvantageous circumstances, with a deplorable loss of valuable lives, and in a day or two we must have perished from hunger, to say nothing of the advanced season of the year and the extreme cold, from the effects of which our native troops were suffering severely.

In spite of everything, he seemed confident that he had obtained the best possible terms. These were total withdrawal of the British troops, a promise of safe conduct, and help with transport and provisions upon payment. Last but not least, Dost Muhammad was to be returned as ruler of Afghanistan. 'We shall part with the Afghans as friends and I feel satisfied that any government which may be established hereafter will always be disposed to cultivate a good understanding with us.' But Macnaghten was deluding himself. His report was later found unfinished in his desk: soon after, Akbar murdered him.

Retreat and defeat

The retreating army set out on 6 January 1842, a total of 4,500: nearly 700 Europeans, 970 Indian cavalrymen and 2,840 Indian foot soldiers; with them were 12,000 camp followers. The unreality which had marked their stay in Kabul was maintained in the retreat. The army was weighed down with baggage, stores, women, children and frightened servants. With a sense of foreboding Lady Sale recorded in her diary a quotation from a book of Thomas Campbell's poems. The book, she said, fell open at 'Hohenlinden' 'and strange to say, one verse actually haunted me day and night':

Few, few shall part where many meet,
The snow shall be their winding sheet;
And every turf beneath their feet
Shall be a soldier's sepulchre.

Vincent Eyre, one of the British officers, likewise felt impending doom. 'Dreary indeed was the scene over which, with drooping spirits and dismal forebodings, we had to bend our unwilling steps. Deep snow covered every inch of mountain and plain with one unspotted sheet of dazzling white, and so intensely bitter was the cold as to penetrate and defy the defences of the warmest clothing.'

The promise of safe conduct was illusory. Akbar could not restrain the Ghilzais, even if he had wanted to. They began plundering and looting the column before it had even left Kabul. After two days it had only managed to advance ten miles. The confusion, said Eyre, was indescribable: 'Suffice it to say that an immense multitude of from 14,000 to 16,000 men, with several hundred cavalry horses and baggage cattle, were closely jammed together in one monstrous, unmanageable, jumbling mass. Night again closed over us, with its attendant train of horrors—starvation, cold, exhaustion, death.'

On the third day they had to go through the five-mile Khurd Kabul pass. 'Down the centre dashed a mountain torrent whose impetuous course the frost in vain attempted to arrest, though it succeeded in lining the edges with thick layers of ice, over which the snow lay, consolidated in slippery masses, affording no very easy footing for our jaded animals,' Eyre recounted.

The slaughter by the Ghilzais from the vantage point of the hills was 'fearful'. 'A universal panic speedily prevailed and thousands, seeking refuge in flight, hurried forward to the front, abandoning baggage, arms, ammunition, women, and children, regardless for the moment of everything but their lives.' Eyre estimated that '3,000 souls perished in the pass'.

Amongst those who died was Lieutenant Sturt, Lady Sale's son-in-law. He would have been hacked to pieces but for 'the generous intrepidity' of Lieutenant Mien, who dragged Sturt through the rest of the pass on a quilt. He did not, however, survive the night. By this time there were only four tents left: one for the general, two for the women and children, and one for the sick. 'Groans of misery and distress assailed the ear from all quarters,' continued Eyre. 'We had ascended to a still colder climate than we had left behind, and were without tents, fuel or food: the snow was the only bed for all, and of many, 'ere morning, it proved the winding sheet.' By the following day Lady Sale estimated that more than half the force was frost-bitten or wounded 'and most of the men can scarcely put a foot to the ground; this is the fourth day that our cattle have had no food and the men are starved with cold and hunger.'

On the fifth day all the women and children were taken as hostages by Akbar; the intention was to provide them with safe conduct to Peshawar. The married officers, most of whom were wounded, went with them. Eyre was among the hostages, and explained the reasons for their departure from the main body of the army: 'The General, hoping that so signal a mark of confidence in Mahomed Akbar's good faith might be attended with beneficial results to the army, and anxious at all events to save the ladies from a prolongation of the hardships they had already endured, readily consented to the arrangement.'

But the plight of the army did not improve: 'Fresh numbers fell at every volley and the gorge was soon choked with the dead and dying.' The hostages, in relative security, found themselves going over the same route as the main column. Lady Sale noted that the road was covered 'with awfully mangled bodies, all naked'. 'The sight was dreadful; the smell of blood sickening; and the corpses lay so thick it was impossible to look from them, as it required care to guide my horse so as not to tread upon the bodies,' adding, with Victorian stoicism, 'but it is unnecessary to dwell on such a distressing and revolting subject.'

As there was no way the wounded could be carried, they had to be left behind. 'However heartrending to all, they were necessarily abandoned, with the painful conviction that they would be massacred in cold blood, defenceless as they were, by the first party of Ghilzyes that arrived.' Those who could struggled on towards the two-mile-long pass of Jagdalak. 'Terrible fire' again poured down. Elphinstone and Shelton had been invited to a parley with Akbar, but they found themselves also his hostages since Akbar would not allow them to return to the column.

At Gandamak the remnants of the army, amounting to only a

few hundred men, tried to open negotiations with the Afghans by waving a piece of white cloth; unfortunately the Afghans thought this meant unconditional surrender, and were angered when the British refused to hand over their weapons. 'The die was now cast, and their fate sealed; for the enemy, taking up their post on an opposite hill, marked off man after man, officer after officer with unerring aim,' wrote Eyre.

Among those stumbling along was Dr William Brydon, who had nearly died at Jagdalak:

> I was pulled off my horse and knocked down by a blow on the head from an Afghan knife which must have killed me had I not had a portion of a Blackwood's magazine in my forage cap. As it was, a piece of bone about the size of a wafer was cut from my skull and I was nearly stunned but managed to rise on my knees and seeing that a second blow was coming I met it with the edge of my sword and I suppose cut off some of my assailant's fingers, as the knife fell to the ground; he bolted one way and I the other—those who had been with me I never saw again.

After Gandamak, Brydon was visibly the only one left. 'I then felt for the pistol I had put in my pocket, but it was gone and I was quite unarmed and on a poor animal I feared could not carry me to Jalalabad, though it was now in sight—suddenly all energy seemed to forsake me, I became nervous and frightened at shadows.'

Jalaabad, Brydon's hoped-for refuge, was under the command of Sir Robert Sale, who was as yet unaware of the fate of the British Army. Indeed, he had only just written to the Commander-in-Chief in India: 'I have to mention with much regret and in confidence to your Excellency, that our troops at Cabool are entirely dispirited. I conclude therefore that the force is wholly at the mercy of its enemies.' Little did Sale realise so soon afterwards he would see living proof of the 'remnants of an army', as later depicted in Lady Butler's painting of that name.

Kaye reconstructed the scene as it appeared to those on the ramparts, 'looking out with throbbing hearts, through unsteady telescopes, or with straining eyes tracing the road. A shudder ran through the garrison. That solitary horseman looked like the

Messenger of Death—few doubted that he was the bearer of intelligence that would fill their souls with horror and dismay.' Brydon is remembered in history as the one man left alive to tell the tale of the destruction of the army. In fact, there were reports of a few Indian soldiers reaching Jalalabad a few days later. In addition, several hundred camp followers staggered back to Kabul, frost-bitten but just alive.

The Army of Retribution

The British defeat in Afghanistan resulted in an enormous loss of pride. 'No failure so totally overwhelming as this is recorded in the pages of history', pronounced Kaye. 'No lesson so grand and impressive is to be found in all the annals of the world.' Writing ten years after the event, he took a fairly critical view of British actions: 'The Afghans are an unforgiving race and everywhere from Candahar to Caubul and from Caubul to Peshawar are traces of the injuries we have inflicted upon the tribes.' But at the time all honour was to the British, all hatred for the Afghans, not least because Akbar was unwilling to hand over the hostages. These were a significant feather in the cap of the Afghan chieftain: a general, a brigadier, twenty-two British officers, including Pottinger, Eyre, Warburton, Lawrence, John Connolly (brother of the unfortunate Arthur), and both nephews of Macnaghten, Mien, who had dragged Sturt through the Khurd Kabul pass, as well as thirty-five soldiers, twelve women and twenty-two children. As the Duke of Wellington, who was obviously frustrated at being too old to 'go to the spot and set it all right', chose to point out:

> There is not a Moslem heart from Peking to Constantinople which will not vibrate when reflecting upon the fact that the European ladies and other females attached to the troops at Cabul were made over to the tender mercies of the Moslem chief who had with his own hand murdered Sir William Macnaghten, the representative of the British Government at the Court of the Sovereign of Afghanistan.

As a hostage, Eyre felt the hostility of the local inhabitants:

We were greeted 'en passant' in no measured terms of abuse, in which exercise of speech the fair sex, I am sorry to say, bore a conspicuous part, pronouncing the English ladies not only immoral in character but downright scarecrows in appearance, and the gentlemen dogs, baseborn infidels, devils, with many other unpronounceable titles equally complimentary, the whole being wound up with an assurance of certain death to our whole party 'ere many hours should elapse.

To make matters worse for the British, Sir Robert Sale was besieged by Akbar in Jalalabad and was running seriously short of food; but he managed to stand his ground throughout the winter months and, according to Havelock, who had gone with Sale, the month of April commenced 'auspiciously'. 'For a long time large flocks of sheep had been seen grazing within cannon shot of the place,' and on 1 April Sale decided to make a sortie and capture some of these 'fleecy people'. This forage resulted in the capture of some 500 sheep and saved Sale and his men from certain starvation. Soon afterwards they felt emboldened to attack Akbar, in spite of being greatly outnumbered, and succeeded in raising the siege. The hostages meanwhile, had been taken to a fort in the hills south of Tezin away from Kabul. There, General Elphinstone, ill and disheartened, died. He was sixty years old.

Soon after Sale's fight against Akbar, Major-General George Pollock arrived at Jalalabad. He had been delayed by having to fight his way through the Khyber pass; his eventual success was due to a new strategy: that of putting up pickets on the surrounding hills to protect the column from attack by those in possession of the heights. Well into the next century the tribesmen remembered this feature of the British advance, noting that the *feringhees* had adopted their own tactics.

Further delays, however, prevented the 'Army of Retribution' from moving directly to release the hostages. Lady Sale became frustrated, not so much for her own distress but because of the 'honour' of the British army: 'Now is the time to strike', she wrote. 'What are our lives compared with the honour of our country? Not that I am at all inclined to have my throat cut: on the contrary, I hope that I shall live to see the British flag once more triumphant in Afghanistan; and then I have no objection at the Amir Dost Muhammad being reinstated; only let us first show them that we can conquer them and humble their treacherous chiefs in the dust.'

Vincent Eyre, when not writing his journals, occupied his time sketching the other captives. His pictures were sent home for the amusement of his private friends at their request, 'with no idea on his part that they would meet the public'. He drew his fellow officers in native dress—a costume they had adopted in order to gain greater protection against the hostile Afghans. 'I am sitting cross-legged on the bare ground', wrote Captain Johnson, formerly of Shah Shuja's force, to his family; 'Naked feet— turban on my head; and my dress consists of a pair of loose trowsers, an Afghan shirt and a large "chintz" wrapper, called a "chogha", covering the whole of my body.'

As Pollock advanced from Jalalabad, and Major-General Nott from Kandahar, Akbar withdrew to Bamian with his prisoners, and Eyre proceeded to sketch the enormous statues of Buddha, nearly 200 feet high, which Hsüan-Tsang had seen on his travels. Originally encrusted in gold, they are believed to date from the seventh century; in spite of the ravages of time and the Muslims, they 'seemed really stupendous' to Eyre.

As the British army came nearer, their fate remained uncertain. 'If Akbar procures even one lakh of ready cash he can do much mischief by raising troops even for a few weeks to annoy our force,' mused Lady Sale; and Lieutenant Willis Atty, who was with the Army of Retribution, wrote, 'I am sadly afraid that our advance will cause Akbar to murder them all. Now the only satisfaction we shall get will be the destroying of Cabul and dying like rotten sheep in the snow on our retreat.' The general opinion was that 'We shall lose one third of our men going and two thirds coming back.'

The Army of Retribution did not, however, suffer as the Army of the Indus had done. By the middle of September the British flag was flying over Kabul again. Akbar was defeated and the hostages were released after nine months in captivity. The British had, however, learnt a serious lesson. They did not attempt to occupy Kabul again. Once they had exacted their retribution, burning the bazaar and leaving 'razed houses and blackened walls', they departed. Shah Shuja remained on the throne for only a short time, falling at the hand of an assassin. Conceding total failure in the objective of the expedition to Kabul, the British allowed Dost Muhammad to return to his kingdom once again as Amir. He ruled for twenty more years until his death in 1863. The memory of the foreign invader took a long time to fade, however. The Governor-General of India in the 1850s, Lord Dalhousie, noted that relations between the two countries were of a 'sullen quiescence on either side, without goodwill or intercourse.'

Sind, the Sikhs and the Punjab

The British were never again free from what came to be the North-West Frontier of their dominions. The first step in acquiring political control of the valley of the Indus was to annex Sind. The amirs of Sind, who had already suffered the hardships of having the British Army of the Indus pass through their lands, now saw a humiliated Britain retreat from Afghanistan. It looked as though they might have a chance to escape from treaty obligations imposed upon them; the British, however, decided to annex the province before they were even provoked. Sir Charles Napier described the campaign as 'a good honest piece of rascality'. His despatch announcing his victory—'Peccavi' ('I have sinned', i.e. Sind)—was the shortest in military history.

Ever since the death of Ranjit Singh in June 1839, the Sikhs had become suspicious that the British had been intriguing against them. It was well known that Burnes and Macnaghten had favoured annulling the Tripartite Treaty and returning Peshawar and the other possessions which Shah Shuja had ceded back to the Afghans. The annexation of Sind added to the Sikhs' fears of encirclement, and it was not long before they attacked British territory across the river Sutlej, bringing the British into war against their one-time ally in early 1846.

'The Sikhs are reported to have lots of guns,' wrote Captain George Macandrew of the Bengal Native Infantry to his father in Scotland, 'in which case we must meet with some losses and as the chances of war are uncertain I may come in for my turn; if so, all I can say is I hope I have done my duty and you may be sure my best and last wishes will be for you all at home.' But

Macandrew was lucky—the British defeated the Sikhs in a campaign which lasted sixty days. However, they wavered from annexation, preferring to set up Ranjit Singh's young son, Duleep Singh, on the throne. The territory of the Sikh state was reduced and subordinated to the British government with a Resident in Lahore, Henry Lawrence, one of the three Lawrence brothers who all devoted themselves to service in India. His elder brother, George, had been a hostage in the first Afghan war and had returned to the Frontier as the Political Agent in Peshawar. These were among the 'cream of the men' available, who came to the Frontier first to help prop up the Sikh empire and then to rule as administrators in the new British acquisition—the province of the Punjab. They are still recalled with pride and their achievements have been handed down from one generation to another: James Abbott, who laid down the boundaries of Hazara and whose name is remembered in the town of Abbottabad; John Nicholson—the Lion of the Punjab—is honoured by a monument outside Rawalpindi on the spot where he commanded troops fighting against the Sikhs. One of the first Political Agents was Frederick Mackeson, who was in Peshawar throughout the first Afghan war. His advice caused Pollock to picket the hills of the Khyber which enabled him to force the pass in 1842. When Britain annexed the Punjab he became the first Commissioner in Peshawar.

At the same time Harry Lumsden was asked to set up an irregular corps of troops, both cavalry and infantry, known as the Guides. Based at Mardan, they became part of a larger force of a similar nature later known as the Punjab Frontier Force, the Piffers. At the beginning of the next century they formed part of the regular Indian Army. Dressed in dust-coloured cloth, known as khaki, their uniforms replaced the traditional scarlet of the British Army.

After the war in 1846 Duleep Singh knelt before the Governor-General, Lord Hardinge, and begged his forgiveness, which was granted. But as Lieutenant Herbert Edwardes observed, 'It was easier for Lord Hardinge to reseat Duleep Singh upon the throne of the Punjab than for the poor child to sit there.' And increasingly the Sikhs relied on the British to assist in the administration of their empire.

One of the successes of this administration was that of

Edwardes in Bannu. The Sikhs had never endeared themselves to the local people, and for twenty-five years the region round Bannu had remained completely unsubdued. It was therefore decided in 1847 to send Edwardes at the head of a Sikh force, with the task of trying to collect the revenues due. His progress through the area surprised the Sikhs as much as it did the local people.

> For the first time, a Sikh army under the influence of a single British officer had passed, unmolesting and unmolested, through a country, which before it never entered but to devastate and never left but with heavy loss . . . Long indulged in military licence, the Sikh soldiers could not believe that they were no longer to be allowed to help themselves from every farmer's field, pull their firewood from every hedge and drag a bed from under its slumbering owner, in order that they might take a nap on it themselves.

When news of Edwardes's 'anti-plunder' regulations spread through the country, he found that he was able to collect at least a part of the revenue. Shortly afterwards he obtained permission to return to Bannu with a small force and persuade the warring tribes to destroy their forts, four hundred in number, and erect one for the Crown, which was to be for universal protection.

While Edwardes was in Bannu he received an urgent plea for help from another British officer, Lieutenant Agnew, who was in Multan, a city ruled by a Sikh chieftain, Dewan Moolraj. Both Agnew and his companion, Anderson, had been seriously wounded by the Sikhs. Edwardes replied immediately that he was on his way, but his assurance of help never reached them. The two men were cut to pieces; and Moolraj declared himself independent. Edwardes managed to raise a force of men from amongst the tribes he had so recently subdued and marched on Multan. Having dedicated himself to the task of establishing peace in Bannu, he considered it natural that the men would follow him. 'No man assisted me without being rewarded, and no man opposed me without being punished. This was well known; and when I held up my hand for soldiers, the soldiers came.' Although he was criticised for rushing in 'where generals feared to tread', his action was later hailed as one of the gallant episodes in the war.

At the same time the British sent some of their own troops to attack the city. 'It is determined we are to conquer and get lots for our trouble,' Lieutenant Thomas Cubitt wrote to his mother at the end of August. He described the splendid mangoes, 'but they are scarce. The dates are also very fine; our supplies are not very large or good just now but directly we have walked into the city, all will be different.' Unluckily for Cubitt, he was one of the young soldiers who did not walk triumphant into the city; he was killed less than two weeks after his hopeful letter. Multan held out for several months.

Meanwhile, rebellion broke out in Hazara where James Abbott was the Political Agent and Chattar Singh the Governor; the latter was determined to restore Sikh sovereignty, which had been eroded since the arrival of the British. Abbott was obliged to take refuge with the Mashwani tribe in their stronghold of Srikot. A century later Olaf Caroe was travelling in Hazara and met an old man, a centenarian, who said he remembered James Abbott well. 'I was in the *jirga* when he was asking us if we would stand and fight the Sikhs if he stood by us. We swore we would stand and fight and there were tears in our eyes, and a tear in Abbott Sahib's eye too. And we did! He was our father and we were his children. There are no Angrez like Abbott Sahib now.'

Matters were made even worse for the British by the activities of Dost Muhammad who was reported to be moving troops in the direction of Jalalabad. Initially the British saw no cause for alarm. George Lawrence noted that the Amir 'has too much sense to come again into collision with us', but such confidence was misplaced. Dost Muhammad had indeed decided to throw in his lot with his old enemies the Sikhs and Chattar Singh. According to information reaching Abbott, 'the bribe offered to Dost Muhammad Khan is, so far as I can learn, all the territory west of the Jhelum [river in the Punjab], a tempting bribe certainly. We shall see whether it can be realised.' Abbott also learnt that there was 'an absurd story' circulating which boosted the morale of Sikhs and Afghans about 'the death of Her Majesty without issue and of England being in confusion in consequence'.

By December 1848 Dost Muhammad had reached the former winter capital of the Durrani empire and had taken the fort, laying claim to Peshawar, Derajat and Hazara. Abbott, however, felt confident that he could withstand Dost Muhammad. 'I hope to defeat his army if he really attacks me and so long as the Mishwanis continue faithful, have no apprehensions.' Meanwhile, in January, Multan at last fell. 'The last acount is that the town has been taken but not the fort, and Moolraj having had two wives and all his jewels blown up in his chief powder magazine (by one of our shells) is talking of surrendering,' Captain Thompson wrote to his father in January 1849.

Finally in March the remnants of the Sikh army and a force of Dost Muhammad's cavalry, which he had sent to fight on the side of the Sikhs, were defeated by the British at the battle of Gujrat. With the rebels defeated, the young Duleep Singh was dethroned and the British took the decision to annex the Punjab. The Koh-i-Noor diamond was swiftly retrieved and presented to Queen Victoria, in the possession of whose successors it remains. Dost Muhammad, hotly pursued, had no alternative but to retreat back down the Khyber pass, withdrawing from the Frontier for the last time. Never again did he and his Afghans come as conquerors to Peshawar.

By 1849 the British had advanced as far as the foothills of the mountains bordering Afghanistan. The question as to where the border stood was still undetermined. What was clear was that the British were back in close proximity with the Afghans once more. However, they made no attempt to advance into the mountains nor take control of the Khyber pass. Of the 'frontier districts' of the Punjab, Hazara, Peshawar and Kohat came under the Commissioner of Peshawar; while Bannu, Dera Ismail Khan and Dera Ghazi Khan came under the Commissioner of the Derajat. What contact there was with tribal territory was carried out through local chiefs who would liaise with the political officer in the area adjacent to the tribal territory. To all appearances British rule was welcomed. 'My old friends, the chiefs of the Eusofzye country,' said George Lawrence, who had been detained as an 'honoured guest' by the Sikhs during the war, 'came in to tender their allegiance, expressing their great joy at the annexation of the Punjab to the British territory.'

The evangelists

Along with military control and political administration came the spirit of evangelism. The political officers who became administrators in the new province of the Punjab, like Herbert Edwardes and John Nicholson, were intensely religious and were anxious to spread the word of God as much as the rule of the British. Soon after Edwardes became Commissioner of Peshawar, succeeding Frederick Mackeson, who had been assassinated by a tribesman, he opened a mission there. 'That man must have a very narrow mind who thinks that this immense India has been given to our little England for no purpose than that of our aggrandisement, for the sake of remitting money to our homes and providing writerships and cadetships for our poor relations,' he said in his opening speech.

Edwardes firmly believed that the duty of bringing Christianity to India lay 'at the door of every private Christian'. And part of that evangelism lay in education. Edwardes was personally responsible for the foundation of a mission school in Peshawar. And as other missions were founded, more schools were set up to educate the local people in the English tradition.

Some missionaries were former Army officers; the first of these was Major W. Martin, who was so strict in his observances that he prevented Edwardes and Nicholson, Deputy Commissioner at the time, from going for a drive to Nowshera on a Sunday. 'That God should be dishonoured amongst the heathen, he could not endure.'

Throughout the years to come, the religious battle was waged unabated. Each mission sent back detailed reports to the Church Missionary Society in England, outlining its activities, successes, setbacks and social events, such as the first visit of Royalty to the Frontier, when the Duke and Duchess of Connaught came for a two-day visit in 1884. A high point was reached in 1883 when the Reverend Worthington Jukes, who headed the Peshawar mission at the time, was able to report on the opening of a new church: 'We cannot thank God sufficiently for the house of prayer he has enabled us to build to His honour and glory in the midst of this bigoted Afghan city filled with mosques and temples.' Rather to his own surprise, he was able to note that it had been up for a whole year without 'anything of an unseemly nature ever having happened to it'. All the same he noted that many mosques had been restored and others built, 'as if in protest at its [the church's] erection.'

The missionaries also took pride in their converts: few in number, but 'men of mark'. One was a policeman, afterwards a soldier; another, 'formerly a robber and a plunderer, a killer of "infidels"', who ended up as a soldier fighting with the British; another became converted by a dream: he saw first Muhammad teaching, and then a door opened and an even more venerable-looking man appeared, and carried on teaching. This man he believed was Christ; and so he interpreted his dream to mean that Christ was a greater teacher than Muhammad. Theodore Pennell, who spent much of his time in Bannu, wrote enthusiastically about Jehan Khan, a convert from the valley of Laghman in Afghanistan, who went as a missionary to the Persian gulf and then started a mission hospital in Kohat district. 'The Afghan makes an excellent pioneer. His pride of race and self-reliance enable him to work in an isolated and difficult field, where a convert from the plains of India would quickly lose heart.'

There were of course setbacks. It was quite possible for converts to return to the Muslim faith, especially with a degree of pressure from their families. The Reverend Mayer lost his only convert amidst the people of Bannu in the 1880s and could not help writing in his report about his bitter disappointment. 'Truly, in this country, it is casting bread upon the waters, and much of our preaching seems carried away by a strong and merciless stream.' Even so he continued his work translating the Bible for the Afghans.

Very early on in its existence, the Peshawar mission turned its attention towards Kafiristan, the area of Afghanistan where the people had resisted Islam (until they were converted in 1895). 'Native' missionaries ventured to go there and were received with apparent friendliness by the local people. And it was with great delight that the Peshawar mission accepted an extra £100 'for the maintenance of the communications which had been already made with that country and with the intervening tribes'.

The duty of the missionary was seen as healing both the mind and the body; and there was great emphasis not just on education, but also on medicine. 'There is a door everywhere that can be opened by love and sympathy and practical service,' wrote

Pennell, 'and no one is more in a position to have a key for every door than the doctor.' There was also the considerable advantage of having a medical missionary from amongst the people themselves. 'He is probably now the only Christian man in India who can travel unarmed without any escort, yet uninjured,' the Reverend Thwaites wrote in 1885 of a local convert, who took the name John Williams, who was in charge of the mission at Tank. 'His work is among a people whose hearts seem to be as hard as their own hills, yet some have not been altogether able to resist the loving gentleness of their *faqir* [holy] doctor.' Thwaites noted that in one year alone Williams performed over 11,000 minor operations and ninety-nine major ones.

As Pennell saw, whether they were missionaries or administrators, the strength of the British lay in the men themselves.

> For it has always been the man, and not the system that governs the country; and there are names of officers now dead and gone which are still a living power along that frontier, because they were men who thoroughly knew the people with whom they had to deal, and whose dauntless and strong characters moulded the tribes to their will, and exerted such a mesmeric influence over those wild Afghans that they were ready to follow their 'feringi' masters through fire and sword with the most unswerving loyalty, even though they were of an alien faith.

Hold on to Peshawar!

The men to whom Pennell was referring were those like Edwardes and Nicholson, whose achievements earned them the title of the great Frontiersmen of their times. Less than ten years after the British annexation of the Punjab, British power in India suffered one of its most testing times: the Indian mutiny in 1857. The fact that the Frontier tribes remained quiet was attributed to the sheer force of personality of Herbert Edwardes in Peshawar. What little trouble occurred was quelled swiftly.

It was, after all, only fifteen years since the British had retreated in humiliation from Afghanistan, and although Dost Muhammad had himself failed to regain Peshawar during the second Sikh War, he might easily have tried again. However, earlier in the year he had come to Peshawar as a guest to sign a treaty of friendship with the British in the face of growing Persian power to the west. Herat had been attacked again by the Persians, and the Amir felt better disposed to treating with the British than he had in previous years. Exhibiting those character-istics which Burnes had discerned in him twenty years pre-viously, he kept his word: 'I have now made an alliance with the British government, and come what may I will keep it till death.' Harry Lumsden, who was on a mission to Kandahar, recorded in his diary:

> We ought indeed to be grateful to Providence for having permitted our relations with Afghanistan to be so success-fully arranged before the arrival of this crisis, for I am convinced that, had it not been that the minds of the Afghans were in a measure prepared for the Amir's non-interference, he could not have prevented a general rush down the passes, which must have added greatly to our embarrassment at Peshawar and along the Frontier.

So troubled were the British by the mutiny in India that the chief administrator of the Punjab, Sir John Lawrence, brother of George and Henry, even suggested that Peshawar should be given to Dost Muhammad in return for his co-operation. Once again the ancient valley of Gandhara was within reach of becoming the eastern frontier of the Afghan kingdom. But the proposal was rejected out of hand by the Governor-General, Lord Canning: 'Hold on to Peshawar to the last,' Lawrence was told.

Peace in 1857 did not beguile the British into thinking that they could expect tranquillity all the time. In the aftermath of the mutiny, there was trouble from the Yusufzais, and the British soon found themselves undertaking punitive action against the tribes, who consistently raided into what was now British administered territory. Even so, since any attempt to enter tribal territory involve fierce fighting and casualties, the British deter-mined not to involve themselves with the tribes any more than was necessary, and they made no attempt to build garrisons in tribal territory. This policy effectively closed the border for the first thirty years of their administration. As the raids did not cease, however, there came to be those who had doubts about the 'closed border policy', especially since it was extended to the British government's dealings with Afghanistan. It was, the critics said, 'masterly inactivity'.

At the same time, there was the belief, at least on the part of the British soldier, that they were a match for the tribesmen: 'I am quite well and in capital spirits,' Lieutenant Hewett of the Bengal Cavalry wrote to his wife in 1863, when the British were engaged in fighting against the Mohmand tribe north of Khyber.

> The enemy only consists of four petty tribes, and when they fired, their attempts were so futile and they were not joined by the other tribes. I think you will find they will disperse. The other tribes hold aloof and hold back to see what we intend doing and when they see we are so well prepared for war, they will, I am sure, think twice before they attack the British lion in his own Lair.

Although the British retained superiority in their weapons, they nevertheless saw that they could not afford to embroil themselves in mountain warfare, as Hewett explained.

> They are armed only with matchlocks and swords, and they can do but very little against our artillery and rifles, so as soon as we advance, they retire and try to entice us into the hills which is their ground, as they know every inch of it and we know nothing; so it usually ends in our watching them and then returning into the fort at sundown. Really the enemy is most despicable and our only hope is to try and entice him into the plains and then get at him with our cavalry.

The second Kabul tragedy

In view of Britain's new presence in the Punjab and the frontier districts, the question of who ruled in Afghanistan could be even more important than it had been in the 1830s. There was still no fixed 'frontier' and the tribes straggled from one side to the other with no apparent concern as to whether they owed allegiance to the Amir of Afghanistan or to the British government in India. Since the mutiny in 1857, control of Britain's affairs was now in the hands of the Queen's representative, the Viceroy, and his government in Calcutta.

Upon Dost Muhammad's death in 1863 the throne was contested by twelve of his sixteen sons, of whom three emerged as the main protagonists: Sher Ali, who had been named as the heir to the throne, and his two brothers Muhammad Afzul and Muhammad Azim, who held the principal cities of Kabul and Kandahar. British experience in the past made them consider that any active interference in Afghanistan 'would engender irritation, defiance, and hatred in the minds of the Afghans, without in the least strengthening our power either for attack or defence.' So Sher Ali was left to secure his throne without British assistance.

In the meantime, Russia, to the north, was exerting its influence. In 1860 the Tsar's armies had defeated the Khan of Khokand; in 1865 Tashkent fell; in Bokhara, just as the Amir had incarcerated Stoddart and Connolly, so had he decided to imprison a Russian mission—the Russian Army, however, was close enough to be able to help its officers. In 1866 the Bokharans were routed and obliged to accept Russian suzerainty. Samarkand fell in 1868; finally, in 1873, Khiva was absorbed within Russia's dominions. Januarius Aloysius MacGahan, an American correspondent for the New York *Herald* married to a Russian, witnessed the Russian advance on Khiva under General Verevkin. 'The troops started forward at a run. In a moment they found themselves in an open field before the walls of the city, in front of one of the gates.' As the infantry moved forward the Russian artillery got to work, 'and the storming party, placed between two fires, heard the solid shot of the Khivans and the shells of the Russians pass shrieking over their heads so low as to almost touch them.' The Russians continued to shell the city for several hours. 'Then a messenger arrived from the Khan, asking for a suspension of hostilities and begging that the bombardment might cease, in order to negotiate terms of capitulation.'

All this increased Russian activity had alarmed the British and they had called for negotiations to determine 'some territory as neutral' between them in Central Asia. Eventually the discussion centred on what would constitute the northern limit of Afghan territory. Although loosely defined, the British and Russians agreed in 1873 that this would be at the river Oxus.

When the Conservatives under Benjamin Disraeli came to power in 1874, a change in government marked a change in policy. The new Viceroy, Lord Lytton, attributed Sher Ali's by now obvious estrangement from Britain to Britain's own neglect of him. 'Afghanistan is a state far too weak and barbarous to remain isolated, and wholly uninfluenced, between two great military empires such as England and Russia,' he said, comparing Sher Ali's position with that of an earthen pipkin between two iron pots. Once again, the constant preoccupation of the British was that Sher Ali would go over to Russia. 'A tool in the hands of Russia, I will never allow him to become. Such a tool, it would be my duty to break before it could be used.'

Sher Ali was, however, distrustful of British advances of friendship. He had been angered by Britain's comparative indifference to his earlier request for help when he was trying to secure his throne, and he was not pleased that the independent state of Kalat, formerly a part of Afghanistan, had become a British sphere of influence. Britain's advance to Kalat and Quetta was one of the first signs that the 'forward' policy was beginning to take root: Quetta, close to the Bolan pass, at least secured one point of entry into Afghanistan.

The British for their part were annoyed that Sher Ali was not willing to accept a British agent in Kabul, whereas his attitude to the Russians was much more cordial. Sher Ali's excuse was the 'bigotry' of his subjects: if any agent were assassinated, the English would charge him with being the instigator. 'In this country of Afghans, I am myself surrounded with enemies who desire nothing better than my ruin, and would designedly be guilty of acts of violence for which I would be held responsible. Let them relinquish Quetta and I am as ever their friend.'

As the vision of Russia establishing herself at Kabul loomed larger, British concern increased: 'We cannot rely on her [Russia's] friendship,' said Lytton in September 1878, 'and the rich plains of India might prove a too alluring bait to the occupiers of the barren and profitless mountains of Afghanistan.'

In the summer of 1878 a Russian agent arrived in Afghanistan. Lytton reacted swiftly and ordered a British envoy—Major

Louis Cavagnari, a descendant of one of Napoleon's generals—to proceed there as well, accompanied by a small escort of Guides; but Cavagnari was refused entry at Ali Masjid in the Khyber pass. Smarting under the apparent insult, Lytton requested an apology from the Amir. When this was not forthcoming, he gave the go-ahead for an invasion. '*Jacta est alea* [the die is cast],' he wrote. British forces invaded Afghanistan along the three main routes from the east—Khyber, Kurram and Quetta—and by early 1879 they were in possession of Jalalabad, Peiwar Kotal near Kurram, and Kandahar.

Sher Ali, the earthen pipkin, was swiftly crushed between the iron pots: with the British occupying his country, the Russians, rather surprisingly, refused him their help. They excused themselves on account of the difficulty for Russian troops in crossing the mountains of the Hindu Kush in winter. Sher Ali left Kabul, planning to plead his case before the Tsar in St Petersburg, but the Russians dissuaded him from doing so and in February he died at Mazar-i-Sharif. He was succeeded by his son Yaqub Khan, whilst the British remained in occupation of Afghanistan.

This second Afghan war was a talking point in India for the next fifty years and more. Mollie Kaye, whose ancestor was the historian of the first Afghan war, Sir John William Kaye, remembers being told, as a girl of seven living with her parents in Delhi, the story of the heroism of the Guides by her father. 'It was talked about in much the same way as we talk about the Second World War.' Her interest in the Afghan war was strengthened by her marriage to an officer from the Guides, whose grandfather's first cousin, Lieutenant Walter Hamilton, played a leading role in the early stages of the war.

Being a keen historian herself she realised that it would be much easier for readers to become interested in the history of the second Afghan war if it were woven into a romantic love story set in the North-West Frontier. So it was that a hundred years after the event she wrote the best-selling book, *The Far Pavilions*, in which Walter Hamilton featured alongside her fictitious hero.

With foreign troops once more in occupation of their country, resistance from the Afghans was not long in coming. At Fattehebad near Kabul, they had assembled in large numbers to confront the British troops. The night before the battle, an advance party of Hussars and Lancers were sent to cross the ford at Kabul river. Lieutenant Walter Hamilton of the Guides was safe in camp; so too was Captain B. A. Combe. But soon news came of disaster: 'A most awful thing has happened,' Combe wrote in a letter home. 'As I was writing, I heard a great clattering of horses galloping, and, on running out, found some twenty horses riderless, with the saddles wet through. Guessing what had happened some of us galloped down to the river.'

The river had been too strong and 'in a moment horses and men were all down.' Over forty men died. The next day their luck turned and they defeated the tribesmen in what Combe described as 'a very smart little affair'. But the Commanding Officer of the Guides Cavalry, Major Wigram Battye, was killed, leaving the twenty-three-year-old Hamilton to lead the men on to victory. Mollie Kaye captured the sensation of elation mingled with sorrow that her husband's victorious ancestor must have felt on hearing that he was to be awarded the Victoria Cross for a battle in which so many of his comrades had died: 'But even as he listened to the unbelievable words . . . the blood that rushed to his face drained away again, and he realised that he would gladly exchange that coveted Cross for Wigram's life . . . or any of those other men of his squadron who would never ride back to Mardan again.'

Within months of Yaqub Khan's accession, the British managed to conclude the Treaty at Gandamak with him, allowing not only a British envoy, but also giving Britain full control over Afghanistan's foreign affairs along with control of the Khyber, Kurram, Pishin and Chaman near Kandahar. There were those, including Combe, who felt that the treaty had been reached too easily. He had heard that one of the chiefs had a letter from Yaqub which, Combe said, incited all the people 'to attack, kill and burn the Kafirs [i.e. the British], wherever they met them; not to be afraid, as we only had a small force, and adding that if we pushed on, he himself had horse, foot and guns, and a large arsenal and we should all be sent to some hot place below.' Combe added that the letter had been written only a few days after a very submissive one to Cavagnari inviting him to have a small embassy in Kabul and professing Yaqub's inability to fight any more. 'It was a great find and will, we hope, open the eyes of the Home Government to what they may expect,' Combe concluded with an unwarranted degree of optimism.

Some of those in high places were also apprehensive. Sir Frederick (later Field-Marshal Lord) Roberts escorted Cavagnari on his way to Kabul via Kurram. He had to give a toast to the envoy and his escort of Guides; now led by Lieutenant Walter Hamilton; but he noted later, 'Somehow I did not feel equal to the task; I was so thoroughly depressed, and my mind was filled with such gloomy forebodings as to the fate of these fine fellows, that I could not utter a word.'

During what turned out to be but a brief stay in Kabul, Hamilton visited Beymaru, the scene of one of the first battles of the 1841 disaster. He put his thoughts to verse in a poem which was full of all the patriotism of the time, evincing the belief that God was very much on their side:

> Though all is changed, yet remnants of the past
> Point to the scenes of bloodshed, and alas!
> Of Murder foul; and ruined houses cast
> Their mournful shadow o'er the graves of grass;
> England's soldiery, who faced a lot
> That few, thank heaven! before or since have shared.

Within a week of posting the poem to his family in England, Hamilton himself was dead; so were Cavagnari, two other British officers and the whole escort of the Guides: seventy-five Indian soldiers in all. Resentment against the British in Kabul had already been building up when a riot broke out in early September, caused by unpaid soldiers who directed their anger towards the British Residency. Cavagnari, like Burnes before him, confronted the hostile crowd and was amongst the first to die. For several hours the Residency held out against the barrage of attack; even when all the British officers were known to have died, the Indian soldiers refused to surrender—they were killed to the last man.

The slaughter of British officers led inevitably to another army of retribution; this time it was called the Avenging Army. Yet again the British occupied Jalalabad and Kandahar, which they had so recently vacated. Roberts himself marched directly on Kabul. Lord Lytton gave him full freedom of action to exact what retribution he deemed necessary: 'There will be more clamour at home over the fall of a single head six months hence than over a hundred heads that fall at once.'

Soon after Roberts arrived in Kabul, he paid a visit to the Embassy.

> The walls of the Residency, closely pitted with bullet holes, gave proof of the determined nature of the attack and the length of the resistance. The floors were covered with blood stains and amidst the embers of a fire were found a heap of human bones. It may be imagined how British soldiers' hearts burned within them at such a sight and how difficult it was to suppress feelings of hatred and animosity towards the perpetrators of such a dastardly crime.

Roberts's own position in Kabul was altered by Yaqub Khan's sudden abdication, leaving him as the only authority. 'His life,' he said, 'had been most miserable and he would rather be a grass cutter in the English camp than Ruler of Afghanistan.' It also meant that temporarily Roberts became 'King of Kabul'. 'It is not a kingdom I covet and I shall be right glad to get out of it,' he confided to his wife. Since much of the fortress of Bala Hissar had been destroyed by explosions, Roberts set up his force in the cantonment of Sherpur constructed by Sher Ali on the site of the old British cantonment in the days of their first occupation of Afghanistan. For a short time there was a period of calm, making Combe bemoan the lack of interest in the Kabul campaign back in Britain. 'I wish,' he wrote, 'we *could* get up a real good fight—the news would astonish you at home who evidently think it all over—but it is, as you say, no use unless we can show a good butcher's bill.' Neither the fight nor the butcher's bill were long in coming.

The Afghans were certainly not inclined to let the British remain in their country unchallenged. Thousands rallied to the cause of the holy war against the infidel; once more the British come under attack, and were forced to withdraw into Sherpur. Conditions for a siege were, however, far more favourable than in 1841: there were supplies and provisions to blunt cold and hunger, and Sherpur was more easily defensible than the old cantonment. Even so, it was quite a turn of events which caused Combe to write:

By Jove: and really that is all one has breath to say. A change has indeed come over the vision of our dream—last night we were all cock-a-hoop, thinking ourselves fine fellows and all that we had to do was to walk around and burn some villages; and within 24 hours we were locked up, closely besieged after a jolly good licking and all communication with the outer world completely cut off!

But the Afghans did not have the necessary ammunition to attack Sherpur; nor was Roberts prepared to negotiate and consign himself and the army to an evacuation which could have the same outcome as the one in 1842. Reinforcements soon arrived, enabling the British to return victorious once more into Kabul and Combe to write home in triumph.

The grand attack was made the day before yesterday and ended in a general skedaddle. Yesterday morning the whole country was quite clear, city—re-occupied . . . Heavy snow yesterday and we are enjoying a real 'old-fashioned Xmas' all well and jolly, but shall be glad of a little peace and quiet and think we have had enough fighting if we are only to get a clasp to the old medal. Love to all.

The 'butcher's bill' Combe had so fervently wanted in his earlier letter was reported to be over 2,500 Afghans killed.

A thought however passed through Combe's mind: 'My own idea is that they have not had nearly licking enough and that we shall have them all back before very long.' The Afghans, he said, had written letters saying 'that they would never cease their efforts till they had kicked us out of the country'—a warning for the Russians when they in their turn occupied Kabul at Christmas time exactly one hundred years later. The British were snowed up in Kabul all winter.

The elections in Britain the following year meant that those in Afghanistan would have to bide their time before they knew what direction their own fortunes would take. Ever since the telegraph could be used for communication between the Viceroy and the British government in London, the direction of Asian policy followed much more closely the tide of political sentiment in England. So when the election brought William Gladstone and the Liberals to power, they were all, as Combe wrote, 'taken aback . . . We expect a change of government will entail a great change in Afghan policy; we shall most likely retire from Cabul in a month or so and then all this will have to be done over again within a very few years.'

But as it was, even Lytton had changed his tune; before he had handed over to the new Viceroy, Lord Ripon, he was already arguing in favour of withdrawing British troops and setting up a ruler who would be subservient to British power, though nominally independent. The sort of man the British had in mind was Abdur Rehman, the nephew of Sher Ali and son of Muhammad Afzul. He had spent several years in exile in Russia while Sher Ali was on the throne, but, provided he could be detached from any allegiance to the Russians, he seemed as suitable a ruler as any. With a band of followers, he had managed to consolidate his hold on northern Afghanistan in the lands across the Hindu Kush. It remained only for the British to agree to let him take over Kabul and establish himself as Amir of Afghanistan. However, the British were quite emphatic in their terms to him: Kabul was to have no diplomatic relations with any other power than the government of India. In return for accepting British control over his foreign policy, Abdur Rehman could rely on British aid against unprovoked foreign aggression. Abdur Rehman demurred before he replied; when he did so, he agreed to accept the terms as being in accordance with those 'settled of old by Treaty with my noble grandfather, the Amir Dost Muhammad Khan'.

There remained, however, the problem of Kandahar. This was still regarded by the 'forward thinkers' as being essential to defend British India's north-west frontier. They proposed to set it up as an independent principality very much within the British sphere of influence. This plan backfired when the brother of the abdicated Yaqub and second son of Sher Ali, Ayub, who was in possession of Herat, decided to try and wrest the throne from Abdur Rehman by first taking Kandahar. Ayub had inherited his father's old army, which was well trained and surprisingly well armed, and he also had the support of several thousand tribesmen. With these forces he was able to inflict a severe defeat on the British at Maiwand, one of the worst ever suffered by British arms in a pitched battle. He then advanced and laid siege to

Kandahar. In order to relieve the city Lord Roberts marched from Kabul, with a force of ten thousand men. He took less than three weeks to cover the distance of nearly three hundred miles: a record speed for that time. As he advanced past Ghazni green valleys turned into dry and dusty ravines. 'But the worst torment which pursued us was unquenchable thirst. Lips and throat were parched beyond the power of beakers of water to cool and dreams of impossible draughts used to haunt my imagination till I thought I must drink something or perish,' recalled Roberts.

Yet again the British succeeded in turning defeat into victory. But by the time Ayub and his forces were routed, the policy-makers back in London had begun to rethink their Afghan strategy. The feeling was in favour of withdrawal from Kandahar, with the possibility of relinquishing even Quetta and Pishin. Finally, after a long debate in Parliament, it was decided to withdraw to Quetta, while retaining nominal control of the Khyber and Kurram to the north.

For the officers and soldiers, withdrawal from Afghanistan meant a long journey back to India. Combe was at pains to tell his family about some of the discomforts.

> We have to sit for hours in the sun waiting for our baggage, and when at last it straggles in, our servants are too dead beat to do much for us. No trees grow in this lovely country, so there is 'never no firewood' only brambles and thorns, the gathering of which may be awful fun at a picnic, but is apt to be considered in the light of an ill-timed joke when you are dying for a cup of tea.

To make matters worse:

> . . . it blows a regular dust storm almost every afternoon, and it is difficult to write till after dark when somehow the dust subsides, and then one is so deadly sleepy that writing is sheer physical pain. Then the sun blisters one's face, nose, ears and lips, the wind and dust get into cracks and make huge chasms across the back of one's hands, and at all the finger joints.

Forward!

They [the Frontier wars] are but the surf which marks the edge and the
advance of the wave of civilisation.

Lord Salisbury, 1892

In spite of their withdrawal from Afghanistan, the war gave
considerable impetus to an active forward policy for the next
twenty years on the North-West Frontier. The British had
already secured Quetta and Kalat, as well as the Khyber,
Kurram, Pishin and Chaman. Sir Robert Sandeman managed to
bring the whole of Baluchistan within British control, carefully
negotiating with the local chiefs, and pushed forward from
Pishin into the Zhob valley, making his headquarters at Apozai,
renamed Fort Sandeman.

Following this, the British decided to pursue a new scheme to
open up the Gomal pass, which was used by the caravans of the
tribesman and would provide them with entry into Afghanistan
to the north of the Bolan pass. They found, however, that the
peoples north of the Gomal river were very different from those
to the south, and fiercely resisted incursion into their lands.

At the same time as advancing in Baluchistan, the British were
also securing their position in the Khyber and the Kurram. In
1879 Robert Warburton, whose father had been a hostage in the
first Afghan War, was appointed to deal directly with the tribes
in the Khyber as opposed to relying on the local chiefs as
mediators. He succeeded in opening up the pass to its western
end, and formed the force of 'Khyber Rifles'. Originally they
were known as the 'Jezailchis', and as Warburton himself admitted 'they were an untidy unkempt band of excellent men, very
good material for warfare in any country, but without discipline
or "esprit de corps".' Nevertheless, he persevered in his
endeavours, contrary to the advice of 'certain people who
objected to seeing the Khyber levies either properly dressed or
fairly drilled'. He knew from his own experience that 'the Afridi
recruit was just as proud of a good, well-disciplined corps as
either Goorkha, Pathan or Sikh;' all that the Afridi objected to
was interference with his ancestral tribal customs. However,
Warburton and his assistants never succeeded in bringing under
control the tribal territory of Tirah.

The advance into the Kurram valley took place in the 1890s. The British had first to secure the entry through the Miranzai valley which meant taking possession of the Samana ridge, overlooking the valley. Without having control of the heights, they could not guarantee a safe route to Kurram. As was to be expected, they were strongly opposed by the tribesmen.

Dr Hugh Luard of the Indian Medical Service, who had joined the Bengal Lancers at Rawalpindi and spent much time treating sword wounds from the Afghan War, was sent to help the wounded from the Miranzai expedition. 'Some were slashed up by sword cuts, but most were bullet wounds, fractures of arms and legs, three shot through the lungs.' Using the only drug available—opium—he tried to make them more comfortable.

Eventually they advanced on the Samana range: 'The hillside was steep and rocky and offered great obstacles to my medical pannier mule, so that I was soon left behind, entangled in the baggage train.' Luard managed to catch the regiment up, and the cavalry proceeded up the river-bed: 'a piece of bluff as they could do no good, but the hillmen have a great dread of cavalry and were duly dismayed at seeing cavalry in their innermost recesses.' Penetrating further up the river, Luard and his companions came under severe fire from snipers. The men were ordered to lie down while the Commanding Officer walked up and down, directing their volleys, and, wrote Luard, 'the rest of us did the same. (I must confess I should have much liked to lie down too!) There were a few casualties: one sepoy was knocked down by a bullet hitting him on the head, but after a short time got up and picked the round bullet out of his enormous puggarree, quite unhurt.'

Once the British had succeeded in taking the ridge, most of the force withdrew to India. Three forts were built along the range: at Mastan (named Fort Lockhart after Sir William, who commanded the whole operation), Sarighar and Gulistan. Luard was amongst those who remained in the fort at Gulistan; 'We made a set of chessmen out of Martini and Snider cartridge cases and bullets, and had chess tournaments to while away the time; or played quoits. The Sikhs devoted themselves to great tug-of-war contests in teams every evening with tremendous zeal, the whole regiment wildly excited, shouting and cheering them on.' It had the effect of wearing the skin of their hands down, 'which

RUSSIA

Caspian Sea

Aral Sea

TURKESTAN

Oxus

Jaxartes

(1873)

(1873)
Khiva

(1873)

(1881)

Gok Tepe

Bokhara

(1868)
Samarkand

Tashkent

Khokand

1895

Pamirs

Merv
(1885)
Panjdeh

Balkh

(1979)

Herat

Kabul

NORTH WEST FRONTIER

PERSIA

Kandahar

Quetta

BALUCHISTAN

INDIA

0   500 km

- - - Boundary of Russia, 1855
- · - · - Boundary of USSR before 1979
——— Afghanistan's borders

Russian advances towards the Oxus up to 1979

wounds they concealed in fear they should have to leave the teams, till I had some in hospital with chronic ulcers.'

The tribesmen who were obliged to give their submission were not pleased by the intrusion of the British into their territory, as Luard discovered: 'They said many armies had marched through the Miranzai valley since the days of Alexander [as had the British in the second Afghan war] but had never tried to establish themselves on the Samana range, and that they would kick us out of it now if they could, but that we were too strong for them.'

Abdur Rehman, the Durrani chief

His mercy fills the Khyber hills—his grace is manifold;
He has taken toll of the North and South—his glory reacheth far,
And they tell the tale of his charity, from Balkh to Kandahar.

Rudyard Kipling, 'The Ballad of the King's Mercy'

In the intervening years, Abdur Rehman had managed to assert his authority throughout Afghanistan and had unified the country to a greater degree than the British had ever anticipated. He had also been anxious to maintain a pragmatic balance between his neighbours, the Russian Bear and the British Lion. While watching, with a certain amount of alarm, Britain's movements in the east, he also kept an eye on those of Russia to the north. In 1885 the Russians invaded Panjdeh, a small tract of land close to Herat. It was the first time during their advance south that they had actually entered land claimed by Afghanistan. Had Abdur Rehman chosen to uphold his claim, the British, who had guaranteed the 'integrity and independence' of Afghanistan after the second Afghan war, might have had to support the Amir and declare war on Russia. But Abdur Rehman, who happened to be on a State visit to India as a guest of the Viceroy, defused the issue by renouncing any claim he had on the Panjdeh.

Soon afterwards, by agreement between Russia and Britain, Afghanistan's northern boundary was fixed along the river Oxus, as established in 1873. The fertile Oxus valley north of the Hindu Kush was left in Afghanistan. In spite of all Britain's efforts and Afghanistan's wars throughout the nineteenth century, however, Russia had still managed to come within striking distance both of Afghanistan and India, in what had been a slow and measured advance. Abdur Rehman chose to compare the Russians' habit of forward movement to that of an elephant, 'who examines a spot thoroughly before he places his foot upon it and when once he puts his weight there is no going back, and no taking another step in a hurry until he has put his full weight on the first foot and has smashed everything that lies under it.'

What was equally significant for Britain was the drawing of a border line in 1893 between British India and Afghanistan. The Amir was careful to record the discussions of his meetings with Britain's negotiator, Sir Mortimer Durand. He described in his autobiography how he had arranged for one of his men 'to sit behind a curtain without being seen or heard, or his presence known of by anyone else except myself, to write down every word they spoke to me, or among themselves, either in English or Persian'. Durand found the Amir at times 'very touching'. 'There was something which went to one's heart about the man, standing there between England and Russia, playing his lone hand. Like all men who have got accustomed to unlimited power, he was impatient of opposition, and his temper was quick; but it was easy to bring him round, and he was soon laughing.'

After weeks of negotiations, the Durand line was fixed and the agreement signed by both parties. At the time Abdur Rehman seemed pleased with the outcome. 'The misunderstandings and disputes which were arising about these Frontier matters were put to an end, and after the boundary had been marked out according to the above-mentioned agreements by the Commissioners of both governments a general peace and harmony reigned which I pray God may continue for ever.'

One of the few European men to converse with Abdur Rehman informally was the Honourable George Curzon, soon to become Lord Curzon of Kedleston, Viceroy of India. As well as being a politician, Curzon was also an enthusiastic traveller, and while things were relatively peaceful in 1894 he decided to try and visit the Amir. In a letter to Abdur Rehman he proposed his journey on the grounds that, although he had visited Bokhara, Samarkand, Chaman and Peshawar, he had never visited the territories situated in the middle, 'like unto a rich

stone in the middle of a ring'. No Englishman had been extended
a private invitation—Durand's visit the previous year had been
on official business; the British government was not anxious for
Curzon to go, and notified him that if he did, it would be as a
private individual, without an official escort.

So on 13 November 1894, having received his invitation,
Curzon rode alone into Afghanistan, crossing the newly drawn
Durand line at Torkham to be the guest of Abdur Rehman for
two weeks. He noted that the Afghan ruler had not learned to
read and write until he was twenty: 'at a time when most
European lads had their knees under a desk, he was engaged in
manufacturing rifled gun-barrels and in casting guns.' Abdur
Rehman was pleased to recount that, during his exile in Russia,
whilst Sher Ali was precariously holding the throne, he had
secretly learnt the Russian language and had never enjoyed
himself so much as when he heard Russians discussing affairs of
state 'in the presence of the seemingly simple-minded and
unsophisticated Afghan'.

The Amir suffered severely from gout. When the Indian press
wished to criticise him, it would say, instead of 'gout', that the
Afghan ruler was suffering from a bad attack of 'govt'. Curzon
found that it was 'inveterate in his nature' to be cruel, and it came
as no surprise to him to learn of the severe punishments meted
out: for theft, a hand would be amputated and the stump plunged
into burning oil; men were flayed alive, blown out of guns,
beaten to death or thrown down wells. Yet, in spite of this, 'this
man of blood loved scents and colours and gardens and singing
birds and flowers'. This terribly cruel man, he said, could be
'affable, gracious and considerate to a degree'.

Curzon believed that the Amir's friendship with Britain came
from expediency. 'As an independent sovereign he was compel-
led for the sake of appearances with his own people, to exhibit a
truculence that was often inoffensive and at times unsupportable.
But at a crisis it was to British advice and British arms that he
invariably turned.' Curzon also discovered, during the course of
his conversations with the Amir (through an interpreter), that he
was fascinated by the customs of marriage in other countries.
Calling monogamy 'a most pernicious system', the Amir
claimed that since there were more women than men, it was
unnatural for some women to remain unmarried. But he excused

the system in Britain, saying that it was due to the damp climate: the British were raised in water and mud, and were like rice; whereas eastern people who lived in dry soil were like wheat and could manage four wives.

One favourite topic of conversation was the Amir's impending visit to England; to Curzon's dismay, the Amir outlined the manner in which he would behave. He would not, he announced, say a word, 'and the Queen will then ask me why I refuse to say anything; and I shall answer: "Send for Roberts!" And there will be a pause until Roberts comes, and when Roberts has come and is standing before the Queen and the two Mejilises [the House of Lords and the House of Commons—the Amir assumed he would be able to address both Houses at the same time], then I will speak.' Abdur Rehman had determined on this course of action because he held Lord Roberts personally responsible for the executions carried out when he was in charge of Kabul during the second Afghan war, and felt that he should be punished.

'It was in vain,' Curzon later wrote, 'that I indicated to the Amir that things were not done exactly in that way and that the ceremonial of his reception would hardly be of the nature described.' In fact, rather to Curzon's relief, so insecure did the Amir feel on his throne towards the end of his reign that he did not leave the country and the visit never took place. As it happened he was one of the few Afghan rulers who both retained his throne and died in his bed: at the age of fifty-seven in 1901.

Chitral and the route through Malakand

The British were no less concerned by Russian movements in the Pamirs and had seen to it that they had established cordial relations with the ruler of Chitral, the Mehtar, Aman-ul-Mulk. When he died in 1892 the throne passed first to one son, then another, Nizam-ul-Mulk. But in January 1895 he was murdered by a third son, his half-brother Amir-ul-Mulk who seized the throne. The British, however, judged him to be 'unfit to rule', and were worried that he was in the hands of men opposed to British influence in the area. They therefore decided to support Amir's younger brother, the fourteen-year-old Shuja-ul-Mulk.

Soon afterwards, Sir George Robertson, the assistant to the British Agent in Gilgit, arrived with a small force to ensure the succession for Shuja, only to find himself besieged by one of the local chiefs who supported Amir in the fort at Chitral.

In order to relieve the fort, the British decided to take a hitherto unexplored route through the lands of Dir and Swat and the Malakand pass. Ever since 1863, when fierce fighting against the Yusufzais had shown them how much the tribesmen resented intruders into their lands, the British had approached Chitral from Gilgit. But as a matter of urgency it seemed necessary to send a strong force under General Sir Robert Low through the Malakand, whilst a smaller one under Colonel Kelly would come from Gilgit.

Meanwhile, Robertson recorded that in the fort, 'food was scantier than we expected . . . all unnecessary mouths—that is to say, useless prisoners and so forth—were sent away, but there remained inside the walls no less than five hundred and fifty persons to be fed. We had just over 340 riflemen . . . but, excluding those in hospital, only 83 of them were Sikhs—good shots and trustworthy soldiers.'

The relieving force was strongly opposed by the tribesmen in the Malakand pass. The Guides, who made up part of the force, emulated the strategy of the tribesmen and managed to climb the heights—to this day called Guides Hill—and gain a position of advantage. For the first time since Akbar, an army had entered the Swat valley from the south, but only after fierce opposition did the ruler of Dir submit and allow the British to cross the Lowarai pass and reach Chitral, pulling their heavy guns through the snow.

The besieged spent most of the time strengthening their defences, although prolonged rainfall made conditions very unpleasant. 'The men could hardly get dry in the daytime before being drenched again in the evening, when they had to stay near their alarm posts,' wrote Robertson. Their greatest sufferings, however, were, he said, the anxiety, confinement, bad sanitation, overcrowding and foetid smells: 'Imagine what it must be for 550 persons to be cooped up in a space 80 yards square for 47 days!' When, after six weeks, the two British relief forces converged on Chitral and rescued them, they were greeted with great applause. Kelly's officers were wonderfully nice fellows,

Robertson enthused, noting that they had sent over their supplies of tobacco. 'All seemed to think, from Kelly downwards, that their march was a mere trifle, their hardships undeserving of reference.'

From Malakand to Tirah

The gradual penetration of the British into tribal strongholds over the past twenty years had engendered increasing alarm among the tribesmen, and for a short time in 1897 the tribes united to oppose the British in the severest rebellion on the Frontier so far. From Malakand to Tirah a call for a holy war against the infidel brought the tribesmen out to fight the *feringhee*. Saidullah, a mullah in Swat, known as the Mad Mullah or Faqir, did a great deal to inflame the tribes against the British. In his report to the *Daily Telegraph* Winston Churchill, who was with the Malakand Field Force sent to deal with the unrest, compared Saidullah to the eleventh-century Franciscan monk who preached the First Crusade: 'Civilisation is face to face with militant Mohammedanism. What Peter the Hermit was to the regular bishops and cardinals of the Church, the Mad Mullah has been to the ordinary priesthood of the Afghan border.'

There were also those amongst the British officers who were convinced that the Amir of Afghanistan, in spite of his protestations of friendship, and the Durand line, had his part to play. 'Three months ago the Amir sent agents all over Afghanistan telling all to be ready for a "jihad". This was all in the papers but of course it never occurred to anyone that it could be directed against us, though there is absolutely no one else against whom he could possible proclaim a "jihad",' wrote Lieutenant T. P. Dowdall. 'He then sold 80,000 rifles (made in Cabul under English supervision) to the frontier tribes at 2/6 each . . . he could afford this as we give him a large subsidy yearly to insure his friendship.'

Tirah too fell victim to the cry for a holy war, and the tribesmen did not hesitate to show the British their resentment at the three apparently 'impregnable' forts built on the Samana range earlier in the decade. Dr Theodore Pennell was in camp on the range and read the service on the Sunday before the fighting at the fort at Sarighar began. 'The Sikhs knew that the Pathans would give them no quarter, so they prepared to sell their lives dearly. The Afridis worked nearer and nearer, and many of the brave defenders fell . . . finally there was only one Sikh left. The Afridis swarmed over the walls and cut his throat. So the noble garrison fell at their posts to a man.' The tribesmen nearly succeeded in capturing the Gulistan fort as well.

Warburton had just retired from his eighteen years on the Khyber, but when he heard of trouble he offered to return at once. 'My mind is very heavy over this hideous disaster, which I feel could have been staved off even up to the day of mischief. It makes me quite sad to think how easily the labour of years—of a lifetime—can be ruined and destroyed in a few days.'

Sir William Lockhart, who arrived to take command of the British Army, determined to advance into the unknown territory of Tirah, promising that he would announce his final terms to the tribesmen from the heart of their lands at Maidan. Captain Shadwell of the Suffolk Regiment was with the expedition and subsequently wrote about its early stages. The British troops were at a disadvantage from the start, knowing little about the country into which they were venturing: 'From native information it was supposed that a large portion of Tirah was covered with forests of pine trees; and one had pictured the blazing camp fires which could be made at night by the help of resinous wood.' When they got to Tirah they found that there was nothing like a forest in the whole area. Private Walter Ware with the Devonshire Regiment wrote to his parents complaining about the maps. 'Far from being accurate, they are only got on native information, as no white man has ever been in the country so there is nothing definitely known.' The maps were almost blank apart from a few main streams dotted in. The British forces sustained severe casualties whilst taking the surrounding ridges from which the enemy could open fire; on the Dargai heights there were nearly 200 casualties, including thirty-six killed. Finally, in November, they reached Maidan, having forced the intervening passes.

'We are being fired on every night now but they can't hurt us much as we have built fortifications all round the camp and they won't come too near us so we don't take any notice of them,' wrote Ware. Before that, they had had a 'rough' time. 'Afridis used to come down on the low hills in the night. Thousands of them, and fire in our camps, in fact we had to sleep in our trenches all night long. I say sleep, but it was very little of that.' The soldiers were also obliged to fight against men they themselves had trained. 'They are ex-sepoys', wrote Surgeon-Captain Pollock, 'armed with Martinis and Lee-Mitfords and drop their men at 1,000 yards. They never show and don't stand up to be killed. Hope to get back safe.'

But to eager young officers like Lieutenant Thomas Percy Dowdall, action meant glory. 'Service and medals are everything,' he wrote to his mother from Rawalpindi, itching to be in the front line. At the time he felt they would not get any fighting in spite of the need to prepare for battle, which cost between £50 and £100. 'It is hard luck getting no show for all this worry and expense, but there is still a little hope . . . I fancy they must want more men pretty soon, for sixty or seventy British soldiers are sent back daily, some wounded, but most of them with dysentery and pneumonia. You needn't be nervous about me though. I have lungs like a horse and insides like an ostrich.' Soon afterwards, in immense delight, he wrote, '*We are off at last* . . . every single man in the regiment is as keen as blazes and we are all in tearing spirits.' This time he felt certain of a medal, 'though we are sorry to say we mayn't see much fighting . . . Isn't it champion good luck so far!' He suggested that his mother go to a shop in Trafalgar Square and buy a map 'for about 6d or 1/-' so that she could see where he was.

As January passed, Dowdall seemed to think that, with Lockhart firmly in possession of Maidan, the chances of fighting were diminishing. Even so, he wrote, 'If by any luck we do get some fighting later on, and if by any chance I get wounded, I'll send you a wire as I hear Government has a habit of frightening the lives out of one's Mamma by wiring that one is wounded, and I hear that one's Mamma invariably imagines that it must be a dangerous wound when as a matter of fact, it very rarely is.' Dowdall never had a chance to wire his mother. At the end of January he was killed in action at Shinkamar ('The Green Meadow') near the Bara valley leading to Khyber. The next letter his mother received was one informing her that, 'owing to some mistaken order a high and rocky hill was vacated too soon by a portion of the force . . . it happened that your son's company was nearest to this position, and was one of the companies ordered to retake the hill.' Dowdall succeeded in doing so, but 'in the moment of triumph' hidden tribesmen opened fire, killing him outright, and several others. There was, his fellow officer wrote, 'nothing of the drawing room or carpet soldier about him, only a plucky desire to be in the thick of the fight and share the danger with his men by whom his loss will be deeply regretted.'

By spring the fighting against the tribesmen was over. Dr Hugh Luard went to treat the sick at Landi Kotal, and he talked with some of the local *maliks*.

Why did you become our enemies? One man said, 'It was the Mullahs;' the others nodded; another old man made a long oration the drift of which was that they had two strong reasons for being discontented; the first was the increase of the salt tax from four annas to two rupees, and the second, that their women who ran away to the Punjab were not given up by the Sirkar.

Luard could not help admiring 'these fine fellows; one man had lost a son in the war. They were grim, earnest serious men, in dirty clothes, but with piercing blue eyes, firm strong mouths, strength of character strongly marked on their weather-beaten faces. It is absurd to call them savages.'

'If we give you the Khyber,' he asked them, 'you will again burn out the forts as you did before?'—'No,' came the reply, 'we are the friends of the Sirkar and of the Amir: leave us alone. We will fight the Russians or any other European armies that come against India.'

Closed!

I have no wish to join the bands who ride out to do battle with the windmills of the forward or backward policy . . . For the man on the Frontier sees but his own square on the chessboard and can know but little of the whole game in which he is a pawn.

Colonel Algernon Durand

The widespread fighting on the Frontier in the 1890s made the British government wonder whether they would not do better to leave the tribes to themselves rather than try and pacify them. 'If we can conciliate and attach to us these tribes,' Lord Hamilton, the Secretary of State, wrote to Lord Elgin, the Viceroy, in 1897, 'then from a military point of view we are greatly the gainers. If we only make them more hostile, whatever benefit we gain theoretically in strategy, by occupying their country, we lose tactically by the forces locked up in maintaining our communications.'

In addition, any operation in tribal territory generally resulted in a loss of British and Indian lives, and in the Tirah campaign they had been particularly high. 'To send our gallant officers and men in mere handfuls into those gorges to risk entanglement among death traps, with cunning and daring hillmen hidden on every side, really seems demanding too much,' was just one newspaper comment. Those like Winston Churchill, who advocated firm action before it was too late, were of a diminishing school of thought. 'Every year the tribesmen will have better weapons, and the difficulties of dealing with them will be increased; therefore we must go on as quickly as possible.' In his opinion, British policy amounted to 'an interference more galling than complete control, a timidity more rash than recklessness, a clemency more cruel than the utmost severity'.

Even Churchill, however, conceded the difficulty of moving an army about in mountainous territory.

> People talk of moving columns hither and thither as if they were mobile groups of men who had only to march about the country and fight the enemy wherever found; and a very few understand that an army is a ponderous mass which drags painfully after it a long chain of advanced depots, stages, rest camps and communications, by which it is securely fastened to a stationary base. In these valleys, where wheeled traffic is impossible, the difficulties and cost of moving supplies are enormous.

Once the fighting was over in 1898, the men in power put into action their plan to withdraw from tribal territory. With the dawn of a new century came a new policy, personified in the new Viceroy Lord Curzon, who took power in 1899. It was to be enacted in a new province: that of the North-West Frontier. No longer were the Frontier districts to be an annexe to the Punjab.

CHAPTER FOUR

Amongst the Tribesmen

The land was made for the men in it, not men for the land . . . The truth
is that the history of the Pathans has never been unrolled. There are tribal
annals, there is legend, there is myth.

Olaf Caroe, *The Pathans*

Before the Europeans began to excavate the land and search the
archives it was easy enough to explain away the origins of the
local people by saying they were 'lost in the mists of time'. But
modern researchers would not rest until they found out who
were the ancestors of the people called 'Pathans', or alternatively
'Afghans', who seemed to predominate in the area over which
the British armies fought in the nineteenth century.

Herodotus referred to a people called Paktyes who formed part
of the thirteenth division of the Persian empire subject to Darius
the Great. They were men who wore 'cloaks of skin and carried
the bow of their country and the dagger'. These Paktyes are now
generally considered to be the first traceable mention of the
modern-day Pathan. But the connection is tenuous and they
disappear from the records until many centuries later. In the
meantime a great deal of immigrant blood was diffused widely
among the local people from the time of Alexander onwards.

'Afghans' are mentioned by Al Otbi, the secretary of Mahmud
of Ghazni, as making up part of the Ghaznavid armies in the
eleventh century; and in the fourteenth century Ibn Batuta, the
Arab traveller from Tangier, found that a tribe called Afghans
lived east of Kabul. 'They hold mountains and defiles and possess
considerable strength and are mostly highwaymen.' In addition
there are a number of tribes living in the area who are not
considered to be 'Pathan': they speak their own dialects and have
their own customs.

A popular theory in the nineteenth century was that the various tribes to be found in the area were in fact the descendants of the ten lost tribes of Israel, and the Amir Abdur Rehman even prided himself on this heritage. But Olaf Caroe, who made a lifetime study tracing the origins of the Pathans, points out that as the issue has been debated, so have the weaknesses of the argument emerged. In the end it seems to rest on not much more than the similarity of names. 'David, Solomon, Abraham, Job, Jacob', remarked Theodore Pennell, 'are constant inmates of our hospital wards.'

The British came to call the tribesmen who lived in British India 'Pathans', those in Afghanistan 'Afghans'. But the two names indicate a difference which does not necessarily exist. When referring to race, the Pathan will still say that Pathan and Afghan are synonymous. Nowadays, the name Afghan has been used to embrace in national terms all those tribes living within Afghanistan, whether they are Durranis, Ghilzais, Tajiks, Uzbegs, Hazaras, Turkmen, Kirghiz or Nuristanis. And across the border in what was the North-West Frontier of British India (and what is now Pakistan) there live in the north tribes like the Swatis and Chitralis who are not Pathans.

Strictly speaking, the Pathans are only those who speak Pashtu, a language of eastern Iranian origin, which is quite distinct from Persian and Urdu (spoken in the areas to the west and east) and which forms an important part of their culture. The Pathans prefer to call themselves Pakhtuns as the word Pathan is an Indian name. In the south, where they speak with a softer variant as opposed to the more guttural 'kh' accent in the north, they are called Pashtuns. Roughly speaking, the Pashtu-speaking people live in an area from just north of Peshawar, south to Baluchistan and across the mountains into eastern Afghanistan. Of the estimated sixteen million Pathans, about half live in the settled areas in Pakistan, over two million in tribal territory, and the remainder in Afghanistan.

In the days of the Afghan wars the British cared little whether they were dealing with Pathans or non-Pathans. They had Elphinstone's account to guide them, which described a people, 'whose vices are revenge, envy, avarice, rapacity and obstinacy; on the other hand they are fond of liberty, faithful to their friends, kind to their dependants, hospitable, brave, hardy, frugal, laborious and prudent.' And it had not taken the British soldiers long to realise that the tribesmen were indeed very fond of their liberty and could be expected to resist foreign domination at all costs. When the Professor of History at Kabul University, Muhammad Ali, described the Afghans in 1965, he was writing as much for the future as for the past.

> One of the most dominant characteristics of the Afghan is his intense love of independence. The Afghan patiently bears his misfortune or poverty but he cannot be made to reconcile himself to foreign rule . . . Foreigners who have failed to understand this point and who have tried to deprive him of his national independence or personal freedom have had to pay heavily for the price of folly.

Also notable is how, at all times, the tribesmen have been able to assemble an army in double quick time. 'The celerity with which troops are raised is quite astonishing to us, who are accustomed to see recruits drilled for a length of time,' wrote Lady Sale in 1842. 'Here every man is born a soldier, every child has his knife . . . every Afghan is armed complete with some three or four of these knives of different sizes—from that as long as a sword, to a small dagger—pistols and a jezail.' The jezail was the long flintlock rifle which used brass cartridges filled with gunpowder, and which, according to Lady Sale, predominated over the muskets of the British, 'so that when our men are beyond range to hit them, they pour a destructing fire on us'. As the British weapons improved so did those of the tribesmen, and they infuriated their opponents by either stealing their weapons or copying their models to perfection. Whereas they used Martini-Henrys and Lee-Enfields against the British in the nineteenth and twentieth centuries, today they have automatic Kalashnikovs to use against the Russians, for they continue to steal and reproduce the rifles of their enemies with dexterity.

Apart from individual friendships such as that between Warburton and the Afridis, there was little love lost between the British and the tribesmen. They are 'amongst the most miserable and brutal creatures of the earth', Winston Churchill wrote for the consumption of readers at home in 1897. 'Their intelligence only enables them to be more cruel, more dangerous, more destructive than wild beasts.'

The fact that the British were infidels in the sight of all the tribesmen hampered good relations between them. The call to raise a holy war—a *jihad*—had been a powerful weapon against the British in the nineteenth century and it was to be again in the twentieth; and in spite of the Durand line, the Muslim tribes in British India still looked to the Amir of Afghanistan for political and religious inspiration.

The way of the Pashtun—Pashtunwali

Who today is disgraced, tomorrow will be lost.

Pashtu proverb

The Pathan has found that his varied past has presented him with a series of contradictions: once a Buddhist, he was then converted to Islam; in the North-West Frontier Province he lived under the rule of the British for one hundred years. In the present day, insofar as nationality is concerned, he is either a Pakistani or an Afghan, depending on which side of the Durand line he lives. But the dominant loyalty is to his Pathan heritage, which centres on his tribal lore, Pashtunwali. This strict code of behaviour operates alongside the observance of the teachings of Islam and the Koran.

The code is maintained by observing many tenets, of which *melmastia* (hospitality), *badal* (revenge), and *nang* (honour) play an important role. The *jirga* (tribal assembly) of elders decides together on all main issues: whether to wage war or make peace. In a society where public business is decided without the aid of letters, 'the tribesman learns to speak lucidly, persuasively and often wittily,' said Gerald Curtis, who had much experience of the jirga whilst a political officer in Waziristan. The decision of the jirga could be implemented through the *lashkar* (tribal army). When a visitor enters the land of a particular tribe, a *badragga* (tribal escort) will be sent to meet him in order to give him a safe passage. Most important of all, quarrels have to be settled honourably. In the time of the British they arose frequently over issues such as *zar, zan* and *zamin* (gold, women and land), and so the tribes often feuded with each other in what Curtis called the 'Tweedledums and Tweedledees of tribal life'.

'Each tribe or clan maintains an account, as it were of profit and loss, not only in matters economic, but also in matters of *ghairat* (self respect); and that account must be kept in balance. Nowadays money is often the solvent of a debt; but it is a kind of paper currency the validity of which may always be questioned. The gold in tribal transactions is life.' This is the basis of the blood feud, which obliges a man to avenge the death of his closest relation. To the British it appeared to be both blood-thirsty and a waste of life. 'However,' added Curtis, 'it can be argued that in a country where there is no Government to enforce sanctions on those whose conduct is injurious to others, the blood feud spares as much life as it destroys. The fear of provoking a feud to be the curse of generations of his descendants must give a man pause.'

The blood feud also meant that the tribesman devoted a great deal of time defending himself against his enemies: his defence was not only a good supply of rifles but a strong tower from where he could view his enemies and keep his family safe. Charles Masson once came across a plain with twenty-four such towers, and in South Waziristan Herbert Emerson, the Assistant Political Agent in the 1940s, came across two watch-towers, each a hundred feet high: '"Wouldn't it be very awkward," I asked my host, "if that other tower was held by an enemy?" "It *was* very awkward," he said. "For nearly a year my cousin and I were fighting each other and I was shut up here like a prisoner. It was only when the family made peace between us that I could come down."'

The blood feud was alien to the Christian beliefs of the British, which taught that a man should forgive his enemies. Inevitably the two beliefs came face to face when a man wounded in a blood feud ended up in a mission hospital. Theodore Pennell tried to teach the tribesmen what he called the 'Christian's revenge'. At one time a tribesman was brought into the hospital at Bannu with his eyes slashed and blinded. His main concern, as Pennell relates, was for his sight to be restored: 'Oh, Sahib,' the man begged him, 'if you can give me some sight only just long enough to go and shoot my enemy, then I shall be satisfied to be blind all the rest of my life.'

It so happened that the tribesman was lying in the bed which had above it a plaque: 'The Connolly bed'. While the patient was recovering, Pennell told the story of Arthur Connolly who, together with Charles Stoddart, was executed at Bokhara in 1842. Having refused to convert to Islam, he had gained great solace during his imprisonment from the Book of Common Prayer, and wrote a diary of their sufferings on the flyleaf. The prayer book was not found until over twenty years later when a Russian, who had obtained it from a Polish prisoner of the Amir, returned it to Connolly's sister. In spite of reading about the terrible time he had in captivity at the mercy of Muslims, who taunted him for his faith, she wrote to the hospital in Bannu when it was opened, and requested that she might support a bed in memory of her brother. So, said Pennell, we tell the tribesmen that this is 'the Christian's revenge'—Connolly's sister was paying for the recovery of men who were of the same faith as those who had killed her brother.

Another patient, Theodore Pennell recalled, asked him for cartridges in order that when he left the hospital he might kill his uncle. Pennell refused and pointed out that they had spent a lot of time nursing him back to good health. 'I suppose in a few days we shall be having your uncle brought here on a bed likewise and having to take the same trouble over him'. 'Don't fear that, Sahib,' was the prompt reply. 'I am a better shot than he is'. Pennell noted that he never had to deal with the uncle, 'though I never gave him the cartridges; probably he got them elsewhere'.

In the next century, in the Mission Hospital in Peshawar, Dr Jonathan Shaw would receive similar requests. 'Listen, doctor, I want good sight. I have enemies at home and I've got to be able to shoot them.' He also found that it was quite possible to have two feuding men in beds alongside each other living in perfect harmony until they recovered; as soon as they left the hospital, the feud would be resumed.

When the British caught a man who had killed in a feud in the administered areas of the North-West Frontier, he would be treated according to British law as a murderer. Sir Courtenay Latimer, who served in the Indian Civil Service in the early twentieth century, saw the dilemma for the tribesmen. 'One can't help feeling a good deal of sympathy with a man who murders to carry on a blood feud,' he wrote to his wife.

'Probably the last murder was that of a member of his family by one of the opposite faction, and public opinion insists that retaliation must be made—certainly the public opinion of the murderer's own family was insistent about it—and the murderer was probably chosen out by the head of the family and told what he must do.' In the case Latimer witnessed, the murderer was a man of forty or fifty with grown-up sons, 'and was probably chosen for that reason; a young man I am told is seldom chosen, as the man to commit the murder is virtually sacrificed.' The convicted murderer turned to Latimer and asked him if he was angry. 'And then before I could answer he said, "Don't be angry, it's not God's will that men should be angry with each other." (Not perhaps, very convincing for the committer of a cold-blooded murder.) Then I smiled and said, "No, I am not angry with you." Then they led him off to the scaffold.'

Even as progress has come to the Frontier, the blood feud has remained. Mike Edwards, writing for the *National Geographic* in 1977, was amazed by an incident in a classroom of students who were studying to become teachers, doctors, engineers. 'When I had to leave, they asked if I would take their picture. "But wait," said a slender lad, who hoped to study medicine. He returned a minute later, with a pistol strapped on his shoulder. "I have a feud," he said when I asked why. "Years ago my family killed a man. It has never been avenged."' He could not be photographed without his weapon of defence.

If revenge is the way of the Pathans, so too is hospitality, both to each other and to the foreigner. A man is disgraced if he does not offer hospitality to a visitor. 'May you never be tired!' he will say, to which the traveller will respond, 'May you never be poor!' When Dr Pennell went to visit a chief rather late at night he found that the chief was away. None the less, his son welcomed him and killed a fowl for his dinner, 'after which, wearied with the labours of the day, we were soon fast asleep'. But later on, the chief arrived and, on hearing that his son had only killed a fowl for his guests, insisted that a lamb be prepared. 'This will be a lasting shame for me, if it is known that, when the Bannu Daktar Sahib came to my village, I cooked for him nothing more than a fowl. Go at once to the flock and take a *dumba* [lamb] and slay and dress it, and when all is ready, call me.' Dr Pennell and his companions were accordingly woken at about one in the morning to be told that dinner was ready. 'It would not only have been useless to protest that we were more in the mood for sleep than for dinner, but it would also have been an insult to his hospitality.' So they got up and ate another dinner.

Hospitality must also be given to those who seek help, even if they are considered to be outlaws by another authority, such as that of the British. This is *Nanawatai*, from the verb meaning 'to go in', when the vanquished party was prepared to go into the house of the victor to beg forgiveness. In the days of the British, it affected their dealings with the tribes, since outlaws fleeing from the settled districts and British law could expect to be given refuge in tribal territory according to the way of the Pathans. The Pathan will tell the story from amongst his folklore of how Sultan Mahmud was out hunting and wounded a deer. The injured creature made its way to a shepherd's home; when Mahmud requested the shepherd to give him the deer, offering in exchange a good sheep, he was refused. The deer had come to him in distress, the shepherd said, and he boldly advised the great sultan to learn the customs of the country.

Afghans

The Afghan wars enabled the British to gain a fair knowledge of the various tribes of Afghanistan. As early as 1809, Mountstuart Elphinstone had realised that the Durranis—some of whom spoke Persian, others Pashtu—were rather different from the other tribes because of their connections with the royal family. 'The Douranees,' he wrote, 'are distinguished from the other Afghans by their consciousness of superiority, combined with a sense of national dignity which gives them more spirit, courage and elevation of character than the other tribes; at the same time it renders their behaviour more liberal and humanised.' He also recognised in them a characteristic prevalent in all the tribes. 'The Douranees are all religious; there is not a village or a camp, however small, without a Moollah, and there probably is not a man who omits his prayers.' In general, he concluded, no people could be more regular in the hours they worshipped.

The most numerous tribal grouping, the Ghilzais—also referred to as Ghaljis—are of Turkish origin and speak a soft variation of Pashtu, as a result of which they are sometimes claimed not to be true Pathans. There is a legend which says that the name 'Ghil-zai', meaning 'son of a thief', arose because the founder of the tribe was the product of an illicit love affair. It was the Ghilzais, living in the land east of Kabul towards Jalalabad, who inflicted on the British the first of a series of disasters at the time of the first Afghan war. They border other small tribes of Pashtu-speakers living in the Khost valley. In the twentieth century the British found that these tribes would reappear across the Durand line and join in whatever fighting might be going on in British India 'just for the fun of it'.

Non-Pashtu-speaking Uzbegs, Turkmen and Tajiks all live to the north as well as in Kabul. The advance of Tsarist Russia in the nineteenth century, like that of Britain, also left their lands divided. Elphinstone said that, according to his information, the Uzbegs were not as ferocious as people made out. They were said to be 'comparatively sincere and honest. They have few quarrels among individuals and scarcely any murders.' The Hazaras, of Mongol origin, living in a large tract of land in central Afghanistan, he found 'very passionate, and exceedingly fickle and capricious'. But, they are 'a good people, merry, conversable, good-natured and hospitable'. When Babur had tried to enforce a levy on the Hazaras, the result was open rebellion, leading him to comment in his memoirs: 'This country is of the sword, not the pen.' Their name is believed to come from the Persian for a thousand, after the force of a thousand men left behind by Genghis Khan when he passed through Afghanistan on his voyage of conquest. Throughout the time of the British it was common to see Hazaras, Uzbegs and the fair-skinned Tajiks in the market of Peshawar. It was only a day's journey for them and the Durand line meant little to them.

To the north, bordering Chitral, the Kafirs remained in virtual isolation until Abdur Rehman forcibly converted them to Islam in 1895, as part of his programme of consolidation for the country. They accordingly turned from being 'unbelievers' to 'enlightened' people and adopted the name of Nuristanis. Of all the various tribes who were supposed to have a drop of the blood of Alexander's armies, the Nuristanis were supposed to have the most, though in fact modern research has revealed that the

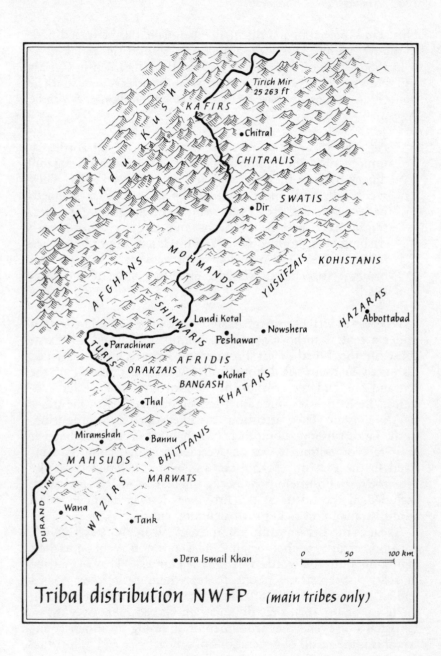

Tirich Mir
25 263 ft

HINDU KUSH

KAFIRS

• Chitral

CHITRALIS

SWATIS

• Dir

MOHMANDS

AFGHANS

YUSUFZAIS   KOHISTANIS

SHINWARIS

HAZARAS
• Abbottabad

• Landi Kotal

• Nowshera

TURIS

• Parachinar

• Peshawar

AFRIDIS

ORAKZAIS

• Kohat

BANGASH

KHATAKS

• Thal

• Miramshah

• Bannu

MAHSUDS   BHITTANIS

WAZIRS

MARWATS

DURAND LINE

• Wana

• Tank

• Dera Ismail Khan

0   50   100 km

Tribal distribution NWFP (main tribes only)

Nuristanis' pale skin and distinctive language can be traced back
to the Aryan invasions some 1,500 years before Alexander.

In 1956, while on their 'short walk' in the Hindu Kush, Carless
and Newby felt their encounter with the Nuristanis in their
homespun clothes and bare feet was like being back in the Middle
Ages.

> As they came bounding up they gave an extraordinary
> impression of being out of the past. They were all extraor-
> dinary because they were all different, no two alike. They
> were tall and short, light-skinned and dark-skinned,
> brown-eyed and grey-eyed; some, with long straight noses,
> might have passed for Serbs and Croats; others, with
> flashing eyes, hooked noses and black hair might have been
> Jews. There were men like gypsies with a lock of hair
> brought forward in ringlets on either side of the fore-
> head.

Whereas the tribes in Afghanistan came to be brought together
under a central authority, belying a unity which did not exist,
those in the North-West Frontier of British India remained
disunited in their tribal homelands. With the drawing of the
Durand line and the creation of the North-West Frontier Province, the British became rather less preoccupied with the tribes
in Afghanistan. Their attention was fixed squarely on the tribes
in the lands running along their North-West Frontier, whatever
their race or origin. It was an accepted fact that some Pathans
lived in the east of Afghanistan and were excluded from the
North-West Frontier Province, whereas non-Pathans were
included in the north of the Province. It was designed as an
administrative unit rather than a cultural entity.

As far as the British could see, the tribes were united only by 'a
common error as to their origins and a common aversion to their
neighbours'. In the words of Ambrose Dundas, 'They are a tribe
in order to keep strangers out, to keep them out of their houses
and off their lands and off their grazing grounds; they resent
intrusion of any sort, they do not want Government of Sikhs or
Christians or even other tribesmen or anything into their country; this is the result of generations of self-defence and of justified
fear, suspicion and resentment.'

Amongst the non-Pathans of the North

When two lords meet, who shall hold their horses?

Chitrali proverb

There was one distinct difference for foreigners living amongst the tribes in the north who were not Pathans and did not observe Pashtunwali. They could be sure that whatever troubles they might have, personal vendetta and revenge would not be one of them. 'No Deputy Commissioner of Hazara,' said Gerald Curtis, who held that post in 1939, 'need expect to be rung up in the middle of the night and be told that one of his villages or towns was being raided, the noise of shots being heard as a background to the agitated voice of the reporter. Nor had he to take blood feuds into account. They were not a feature of existence in Hazara.'

Hazara was the northernmost of the administered districts. The tribes are of mixed origin with strains from the Punjab and Kashmir, although some speak Pashtu, chiefly in Mansehra. One tribe, the Dilazaks, were driven from Afghanistan by Babur and from Swat by the Yusufzais. In the northern part of Hazara, and across the Indus in Swat, live the Kohistanis ('the People of the Mountain'). They have Mongol, Aryan and Chinese ancestors; some also claim to be descended from Alexander.

Herbert Emerson discovered a people living a pastoral and pleasant life in the unknown valleys of Indus Kohistan in Hazara and was reminded of Kipling's poem, 'The Explorer': 'Anybody might have found it, but—His Whisper came to Me.' 'The landowners and their families,' Emerson noted, 'move up with their animals and spread out over a series of magnificent grazing grounds. The upward move is complete by the beginning of July and the move down begins in October.' Government officials, he said, had been under the impression that the Kohistanis were illiterate beggars, but in some cases 'they are well off and do not lack any of the usual necessities of life.'

When, on his way to find Aornos in 1926, Sir Aurel Stein went to Swat Kohistan, on the other side of the Indus in Swat, he sensed the past all around him: 'I enjoyed perhaps more than anywhere else on this expedition, what seemed like a bodily translation into an earlier phase of human society and life. It is

difficult to express clearly in a few words the effect, for one
endowed with historical instincts, of close and constant contact
with men whose ways of thought and actions reflect conditions
that the West has left centuries behind.'

Also living in Hazara are the dark-skinned Gujars, a nomadic
race of herdsmen who spend their lives grazing their buffaloes on
the high mountain pastures in summer, and in the valley during
the winter. In one large settled village in the plains of Haripur,
Gerald Curtis found that many old soldiers and Viceroy's
Commissioned Officers were living there. 'The senior of them
had been one of the King's Indian orderly officers. When I visited
the village he put on his full dress uniform, resplendent with
medals.' Among them was the campaign medal awarded to all
those who had served in the assault on Ghazni in 1839.

Working amongst the tribes in Hazara was an ideal appointment for a British officer, and Curtis recognised his luck.

> The Deputy Commissioner of Hazara was greatly to be
> envied on more than one account. He had a pleasant house
> on the fringes of Abbottabad which was at an elevation of
> more than 4,000 feet and consequently was never exces-
> sively hot judged by the standard of the plains. He also had
> a summer residence under the deodars at Nathia Gali. . . .
> Climatically, it was an enviable job.

In some respects the political officer in Chitral could feel the
same. 'Whereas elsewhere you were an administrator, in Chitral
you were just a presence,' said John Dent who came to Chitral in
1945. Ever since the troubles in 1895 the lands of Dir, Swat and
Chitral had been formed into the Malakand Agency. But since
they did not fall into the administered territory of the North-
West Frontier, their rulers were allowed to carry on as before,
paying lip-service to the orders and wishes of the British
government. 'Likewise, if you did anything likely to undermine
the ruler, you could lead almost unintentionally to his downfall.'

One of the first British officers to visit the Chitralis was
Colonel Algernon Durand in 1889. Before the establishment of
the Malakand Agency, Chitral was observed from neighbouring
Gilgit, of which he was the Political Agent. Quite apart from the
Chitralis, he found of great fascination the fairies of Tirich Mir,

who still exist in Chitrali folklore. 'They are exactly like men and women, but very beautiful and dressed mostly in white. Their only peculiarity seems to be that they have no knee or ankle joints and that the toes of their feet point to the rear, the heel being to the front.' Durand regretted not having more time to pursue his interest in the fairies; he did however ascertain how they managed to feed themselves: if a man declared he had produced ten sacks of grain when in fact he had twenty, the fairies, with an eye to justice, would take the balance.

After the dynastic wars of the early nineties, the British aimed at keeping friendly relations with the ruler, the Mehtar; in return the British political officer could expect a hearty welcome. Colonel McMahon described a visit to Chitral at the close of the nineteenth century.

> About three miles out we are met by a band of ragged musicians playing drums and reed instruments accompanied by dancers and matchlock men. The band precedes us and a crowd of men dance and sing all the way along in front of it, while the matchlock men periodically blaze off their pieces, generally when your horse has arrived at a more than usually giddy piece of road. This goes on till we get near the polo ground. Here we find more groups of men dancing and sometimes as yesterday a group of kafirs, men and women, solemnly dancing what is exactly like our 'pas de quatre' to a whistling accompaniment in a dusty ploughed field. Everyone who has one, gives off his gun and all the wild weird horsemen who have been riding after us all day proceed to gallop wildly up the polo ground.

If the British did not have to worry about the blood feud amongst the non-Pathans, there were other practices they attempted to discourage. In Yasin country, which borders Chitral, McMahon said the population was scanty 'as the chiefs had a pleasing habit, until we stopped it, of selling off a few hundred of the younger population every now and then, when they wanted ready cash, as slaves in Turkestan in Central Asia.'

Slaves were not the only merchandise which flowed between Chitral and Afghanistan. One of the most popular pastimes of the Chitralis was polo, for which they needed the sturdy Central

Asian ponies which came from Badakhshan in north-eastern
Afghanistan. 'At frequent intervals, when the Durah pass leading
from Badakhshan was open,' recalled John Dent, 'trains of
ponies, ten or twelve at a time, would make the journey. But
before they were sold to the Chitralis for their sport, a valuable
cargo would be unloaded: opium.' The opium would then make
its journey down to Nowshera in marked bags containing a rare
metal mined in Chitral, antimony, used for making type-metal
for printing presses and certain grades of steel. The mining of it
was generally very uneconomical because of the low percentage
yield from the rock, but if it was transported along with the
opium it proved to be more cost effective. Once at Nowshera the
opium was transferred into bags which contained a very
pungent-smelling type of pear grown in Nowshera to disguise it
on its way to the ports of India. 'It was a trade,' said Dent,
'which seemed harmless to the Chitralis whose need for ponies
for polo far outweighed all other considerations.'

There also remain pockets of unconverted Kafirs in Chitral,
and whilst mountaineering Fosco Maraini and his group were
pleased to be welcomed by the Kafirs of Bumboret.

> People came and went or sat down and chatted to us in the
> most charmingly unselfconscious way. When holding a
> conversation with the Kafirs, we were instantly aware of
> that characteristic lessening of tension in human relation-
> ships which is almost always found on passing from an
> Islamic to a non-Islamic society. Here men and women
> mingled in the circle around us, without the crushing
> weight of taboo to keep them apart; and it was pleasant to
> feel, for once, that the concept 'foreigner' was not exclu-
> sively and passionately identified with 'infidel'.

Pathans of the Malakand and Peshawar

No need to worry about 'slave mentality' here.

Yvonne Gertrude Fitzroy

In the early part of the fifteenth century the Yusufzais drove the
Swatis out of the Swat valley to the upper banks of the Indus.

These 'sons of Joseph' had fled from Afghanistan and the armies of the Moguls. Later on they used the help of another tribe which came from near Jalalabad, the Muhammadzais, to force the Dilazaks to the east. For their services the Muhammadzais were allowed to settle in the area near the ancient city of Charsadda; they wished to be able to grow rice as they had in Afghanistan and the land here was considered to be fertile and promising. Numerous and powerful, the various *khels* (clans) of the Yusufzais have remained in the Swat valley and the mountains of Dir in the Malakand Agency. They also inhabit the plains of Mardan in the administered district of Peshawar which later came to form the separate district of Mardan. Of Turco-Iranian stock, whose forebears lived by the Caspian sea, they speak Pashtu with a hard 'kh' as opposed to the less guttural accent of the southern tribes.

As the hated enemies of Khushhal Khan, the Khatak, they have been immortalised in his poems:

> Swat is meant to give kings gladness;
> Every place in it befits a prince.
> But the Yusufzais have no such feelings
> And have made of it a desolate hostel.

Before the Yusufzais were favoured with the patronage of Aurangzeb, they had fiercely resisted the earlier Mogul emperors and their victory against Akbar in the sixteenth century was part of their folklore. Olaf Caroe asked one ruler, Miangul Gulshah-zada Abdul Wadud, if he could tell him anything about the battle three centuries previously.

> I saw his eyes gleam. He knew the whole story, the very spurs down which the tribal ghazis charged, and the names of the leaders and sections engaged. He could reconstruct the tactics and explain the reasons for victory and defeat. But more than all this, one sentence sticks in the mind: 'Never in all history,' he said, 'not even in the time of Akbar or Aurangzeb, much less under the Durranis, were the Yusufzais of this country the subjects of any empire.'

But the Yusufzais were just as liable to war with each other as with other tribes. 'They are a turbulent lot,' said McMahon in

1899, 'They are always fighting and intriguing and so on, and give me plenty of mental exercise in frustrating their wishes . . . at present they seem friendly disposed towards us but you never know with these devils when they won't be up to mischief. The only way is to keep a very tight hand on them.'

Until the Mohmand Agency was created by independent Pakistan in 1951, the Mohmands, along with the tribes of Bajaur to the north, came under the jurisdiction of Peshawar. The Mohmands live in the land between the Swat and Kabul rivers, skirted by the Kunar, with the 'hill Mohmands' also living to the south of the Kabul river. Of all the tribes, they had the most cause for grievance against the Durand line, which sliced through their territory. This frontier line was not without its advantages for the locals, however. Winston Churchill, when fighting with the Malakand Field Force in 1897, noticed that a small village at the western end of the Mohmand valley near the Durand line had managed to defend itself rather well: 'I cannot refrain from suggesting that the proximity of the Afghan frontier and of this Afghan army [camped nearby] may perhaps explain how it was that the defenders of an obscure village were numbered by thousands and that the weapons of a poverty-stricken tribe were excellent Martini-Henry rifles.'

The Mohmands—along with the Swatis and Bunerwals (a sub-tribe of the Yusufzais)—were, said Churchill, 'brave and warlike—nothing but a bullet stops their career.'

In the heartland of Tirah

Living independently one from the other in Tirah are the khels of the Afridis, a people with whom the British became familiar on their expeditions into Afghanistan. A hostile race, in the early days the toll to pass through the Khyber would be left unpaid at peril: five rupees for a laden camel, three rupees if the load was food, half a rupee for an unladen camel or a man on foot. All Afridis consider Tirah to be exclusively their homeland, where no European may venture.

In spite of the troubles in 1897, Warburton for one retained his respect for the Afridis.

The Afridi lad from his earliest childhood is taught by the circumstances of his existence and life to distrust all mankind; and very often his near relations, heirs to his small plot of land by right of inheritance, are his deadliest enemies. Distrust of all mankind and readiness to strike the first blow for the safety of his own life have therefore become the maxims of the Afridi. If you can overcome this mistrust, be kind in words to him, he will put up with any punishment you like to give him except abuse.

His opinion of the Afridis compared very favourably with that of Elphinstone who said that they were 'the greatest robbers among the Afghans', and of Mackeson: 'The Afridis are a most avaricious race, desperately fond of money. Their fidelity is measured by the length of the purse of the seducer, and they transfer their obedience and support from one party to another of their own clansmen, according to the comparative liberality of the donation.'

At the turn of the century the Afridis were carrying on a handsome trade in rifles which were coming from the Mekran coast into tribal territory. Most of them were surplus guns which dated from the Boer War. Within a short time the British became alarmed at the arming of the tribesmen, and determined that the trade should be stifled; which they effectively did by blockading the Mekran coast. However, while this upset a valuable system of obtaining weapons, it also took away part of the Afridis' livelihood, and in order to supplement the rifles which they manufactured locally at Darrah, they set about raiding government supplies.

One khel of the Afridis, the Bosti Khel, carried out a raid which resulted in an episode which is remembered to this day: the kidnap of an English girl, Molly Ellis, and her abduction into the heartland of Tirah.

In February 1923 over forty rifles were stolen from the police station in Kohat. The leader of the gang was Ajab Khan, a known rifle-thief and the suspected murderer of a British couple three years previously. After careful negotiations and secret meetings on the part of the Superintendent of Police, Rana Talia Muhammad, some of the rifles were returned. But those remaining with Ajab and his brother Shahzada were not surrendered, so

Rana arranged for a raid on Ajab's house. The two brothers were away, but in order to escape the wrath of the British the other men disguised themselves as women; they might have avoided detection but for their large feet which gave them away. The rifles were discovered and to make matters worse, their women jeered at them for having tried to escape the danger by posing as women. When Ajab heard about the raid, he swore revenge.

First he attempted to capture a British officer who was cycling back to his quarters from the Club, but he succeeded only in absconding with the bicycle. Next, Ajab and Shahzada secretly entered Major Ellis's house, a divided bungalow on the outskirts of Kohat. He was away in Bannu, and his wife and seventeen-year-old daughter Molly were sleeping in the same room. 'It was about 1.45 in the morning on 14th April that I was woken by something unusual,' wrote Molly Ellis, trying to describe her adventure to her school friends when she returned to England. 'When I became fully awake I realised that there were two men in the room stopping my mother from giving an alarm and trying to take her away. My first impulse was to struggle, which I did and successfully put out the light they had; but they must have had another as they produced a light very quickly and I could see that one of them had drawn a dagger.'

Suddenly she saw that her mother was not struggling any more, and the next thing she knew was that she was 'half dragged, half carried across the road and onto the football ground opposite the bungalow' by two strong men—Ajab and Shahzada—who kept a firm hold on either side of her. They were accompanied by two others who had been plundering items from the house during the kidnap. The gang was making for the hills north of Kohat into tribal territory, but in order to disguise their route they set off to the east and then doubled back. 'I was determined to make sure whether we were going north or south so that I should know where I was if I had a chance to escape.' Molly recognised a hill called the Old Woman's Nose which she knew was due north of Kohat. But there was little chance of escape in the unknown land of Tirah. After covering eighty miles on foot in five days, they arrived at their destination—a small village in the hills above Khanki Bazar which was a group of forts at the head of the Khanki valley. Molly—who was footsore but had been reasonably well looked after—was taken to a room

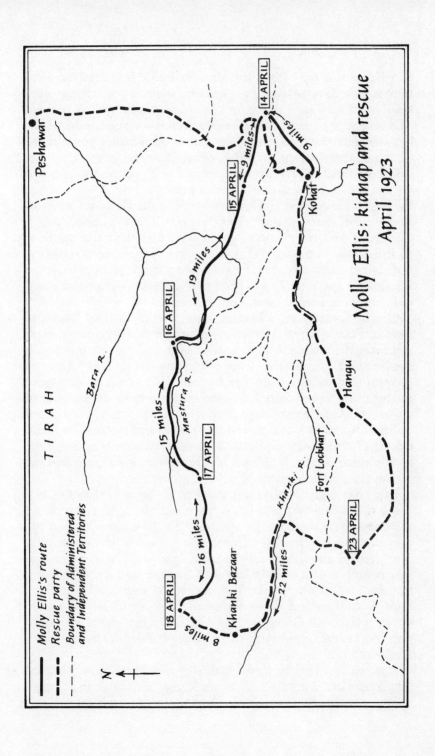

Molly Ellis: kidnap and rescue
April 1923

Molly Ellis's route
Rescue party
Boundary of Administered
and Independent Territories

N

T I R A H

Peshawar

14 APRIL

15 APRIL

9 miles
9 miles

6 miles

Kohat

19 miles

16 APRIL

Bara R.

Mastura R.

15 miles

17 APRIL

Khanki R.

Fort Lockhart

Hangu

23 APRIL

16 miles

22 miles

18 APRIL

8 miles

Khanki Bazaar

in a house where, 'although I did not know it, I was to spend
four weary days of waiting . . . The women treated me very
kindly and massaged me from head to foot when I first arrived.
The rest of the time I was there they used to spend most of the
day staring at me through the open door of a smaller, inner room
on which there was an armed guard all the time.'

On the third day, Shahzada appeared with pen and paper, and
his dagger, indicating that if she did not use one, he would use
the other. He requested Molly to write to the Deputy Commissioner at Kohat, stating their terms for her release, which
amounted to a large sum of money and the release of some of
their gang from prison. 'This was rather disheartening as it was
with great difficulty that I could understand at all what they
wanted. At any rate, I had a pretty good guess and, as they could
not read what I wrote, it did not matter.'

On the fourth day, a hamper arrived with clothes, food and
letters. 'I could hardly believe my eyes, but there were the letters
and I tore them open. One was just a note with the hamper that it
might reach me safely. The other was from Kuli Khan, a
government official from the Kurram, who said he was only
twelve miles from where I was and that he would stay there until
I was released.' Khan Bahadhur Kuli Khan was the Assistant
Political Agent at Kurram, and as a Pathan had managed to walk
over the hills into Tirah; he had met with Ajab at the house of the
local mullah and secured from him the admission that he had the
girl and her whereabouts.

Late that night Molly was awoken to be told that she was
being taken to a 'white lady', but she did not believe this, since
she knew there were no Europeans in Tirah. It did not of course
occur to her that the Chief Commissioner in Peshawar, Sir John
Maffey, had asked Mrs Lillian Starr, who worked as a nurse in
the mission hospital in Peshawar to venture into Tirah to bring
her back. In spite of the unprecedented event of sending a
woman to Tirah, it was considered far safer to send a nurse,
rather than a battalion of troops which the British feared might
only make the gang take their hostage over the border into
Afghanistan.

Accompanied by Sir John Maffey's political assistant, Moghul
Baz Khan and a mullah, without whose assistance the British
recognised that they would not be able to enter tribal territory,

Lillian Starr managed to pass through the lands of five different khels, with permission given at each boundary. She reached Khanki Bazar, but still they could not be sure of obtaining Molly's release. 'The whole scheme was based on rumour and nothing more, and it was on rumour and conjecture alone we set out to find her.' The press in England stated that Mrs Starr was armed; but, she said, 'nothing would have induced me to carry a pistol, considering the errand on which I was going, had I even known how to shoot!'

Eventually Molly was brought down from her hiding place eight miles away. Still guarded by Ajab and his gang, they proceeded to negotiate terms for her release. But they soon lost their bargaining power: angry at reports that their village was being burned, they burst into the house of the mullah where Molly Ellis and Lillian Starr had been offered refuge on what was considered to be neutral territory. This intrusion so angered the mullah that he cursed them, and, having incurred his wrath, they could not now hold out for fantastic terms for the release of Molly. In the end they had to settle for exchanging the English girl for two petty thieves, locked up in Kohat jail. No ransom was paid.

Molly's meeting with Lillian Starr confirmed to her the news she had feared: that her mother was dead. Unable to restrain the two struggling women and escape from the bungalow before they were apprehended, Shahzada was believed to have been the one who had cut Mrs Ellis's throat.

Lillian Starr returned after her mission of rescue to continue her work in Peshawar. When the patients found out that she had been to Tirah, they seemed pleased. 'Now you are one of us,' an old woman said. 'None but Afridis walk abroad in Tirah.' However, the whole episode had made the name of the Afridis a terror on the Frontier. The British public were appalled that a white English girl had been kidnapped by Pathan tribesmen. 'Outrage at Kohat,' reported *The Times*, calling the murder of Mrs Ellis 'an act of callous brutality'. Lillian Starr admitted her feelings before she was called upon to go to Tirah:

> It was not easy to go round the wards; for as we looked first at one patient, then another, into faces, some strong and manly, some coarse and even brutal, we would say to one

another: Think of her in the hands of that one—or that. And there we were, spending time and trouble mending up these very people, and being at times criticised for doing so by our fellow countrymen in India too.

She also recognised, however, 'If it was Afridis who had committed the crime, it was Afridis who had gone back to her rescue.'

Molly Ellis and her father left the Frontier for good. It was not until sixty years later, in March 1983, that Mrs Molly Wade, as she is now, returned to the scene of the crime for the first time, to be warmly welcomed by the sons, daughters and grandchildren of her rescuers, Kuli Khan and Moghul Baz. For the first time she saw the grave of her mother, decked with freshly picked flowers and she saw again the familiar hill looking like and called the Old Woman's Nose. Whilst pointing out the hills which she recalled crossing to her companions, a Pathan claiming to be Ajab's nephew actually emerged to confirm the story. Tribal chiefs travelled from Tirah to greet her in Peshawar and invite her to a reception. In Kohat she planted a lemon tree in the grounds of her parents' old bungalow, now a smart two-storeyed house. She also observed for the first time her own contribution to the map of the area: Ellis Post, which lies at a point near where she had been taken into tribal territory. For a long time to come, the Afridis will sing about the story of 'Ajab and Ellis'.

In days of old, the Afridis were compared to their neighbours, the Shinwaris, for their fierceness. The latter live in the west end of the Khyber and in part of Afghanistan towards Jalalabad. In the 1820s Charles Masson was attacked by them on his trip through the Khyber to Afghanistan. Among the various possessions of his that they took was his 'memorandum book', but when he asked for it back saying that it was a religious book (*keetab-e-moolah*), they returned it to him. The loss he suffered from the attack was 'trifling', but he was somewhat surprised by it. 'From all previous accounts I had heard Afredees were the most to be dreaded, it being asserted that the Sheenwarrees from their commercial pursuits were not so savage as their neighbours.'

Close to the Afridis of Tirah are the Orakzais, who live on

both sides of the Khanki valley as well as in the hills that look down on the Kurram. Their name *Orak zai* (meaning 'lost son') is believed to derive from a romantic legend about their ancestor Sikander Shah, a prince of Iran, who was exiled, or 'lost', for many years and, after several adventures, married and ruled in Tirah. In 1879 the Orakzais were drawn into the fighting against the British when, together with the Afridis, they attacked the British forts on the Samana range.

The Zaimusht—a tribe living in a small pocket of Tirah to the south—could not, however, be persuaded to join in the fighting; their chief, Chikki, 'resisted all the allurements of the Mullahs to take part in the campaign against the Kafirs, the English, and restrained the men of his own tribe from any participation in the warfare.' This, Dr Theodore Pennell said, made a great difference to the troops in the Kurram and Miranzai valleys. Chikki, 'the Lifter', had at one time been a cattle thief, but had turned to contract murders and built up a large following. Eventually he had succeeded in being accepted as chief of the Zaimusht and had under his command 8,000 riflemen, 'all armed with weapons of precision'. 'Yet, withal he maintained his simple mode of life and plain hillman's costume,' Pennell remarked. 'He wore simply shirt and trousers of plain homespun and a black turban, ornamented only by a fringe with a few beads on, and had on his feet a pair of palm leaf sandals, such as could be bought in any bazaar for the sum of one anna. But his rifle was the best there.'

Pennell had visited Chikki's household in order to tend the sick; he also preached to his followers. 'There they were with a devil-may-care look in their truculent faces, which made you feel that they would take half a dozen lives to rob a cottage, with as little compunction as if they were cutting sugar cane.' Before he went, Pennell left some Pashtu bibles and other literature with Chikki, 'and I have reason to believe that he studied them with interest'. It was to this that Pennell attributed the fact that the Zaimusht did not join in the Tirah uprising.

Kurram Shias

Part of the reason why the British managed to establish themselves in the Kurram valley in 1892 was because the main tribe, the Turis, requested British protection. The Turis were Shias, as opposed to the tribes which surrounded them, who were Sunnis. They differed principally in their belief as to who was the rightful successor of the Prophet, and this division caused great enmity between them. Added to this the Turis were in possession of the beautiful land of Kurram, which they had managed to take from the Orakzais some centuries previously.

The Turis' request to the British contained all the eloquence of a court petition.

> O English gentlemen! We appeal to you in God's name. By the Durranis we have been ruined and reduced to the last extremes of distress. They plunder us without restrain. With sighs and tears we appeal to you to free us from these oppressors . . . Durrani rule we loathe. For British rule we yearn . . . Kurram is a well-favoured and fertile country. Move but a step forward and you will free us from the burden . . . If ye refuse aid to us, rest assured that at the last great day of judgement we will seize the skirts of your garments and accurse you of this injustice before God himself! A tall man with a silk turban will deliver this our petition. Treat him kindly.

The lands of the Turis merged directly with those of other Pashtu tribes in the plains of Afghanistan, and the British were not anxious to see them reintegrated into the Amir's possession after Kurram had been ceded to them in 1879 by the Treaty of Gandamak. They therefore took on the charge and the Kurram Agency formed one of their 'forward' positions, leading towards Afghanistan.

Guardians of Attock

In a large stretch of land centred on the administered district of Kohat, running along the edge of the Indus from Attock, are the Khataks. They are both warriors and farmers and have what Olaf Caroe calls 'a collective character' partly due to their tradition of service under the Mogul emperors as custodians of Attock and the road to Peshawar.

An old story gives meaning to their name. There were four brothers—Lukman, Usman, Utman, Hadran—who, while out hunting one day, encountered four veiled girls. The three younger brothers wanted to cast lots, but Lukman said that, since he was the oldest, he should be given the first choice. He picked the girl in the finest clothes, but when all was revealed she turned out to be the ugliest. The others teased him, saying 'Lukman has got into the *khata* [mud]', and so it was that his descendants were known as the Khataks. Usman was said to be very ugly and when people saw him, they would say, 'Who or what is that?' to which the servants would reply: 'That too is *afridah* [a creature of God—i.e. human]; and so his descendants are the Afridis. Utman's descendants were the Utman Khel, one of the lesser tribes living near the Khataks and Afridis.

Buster Goodwin, an Armenian by birth who served in the British army and civil service for over twenty years, found the Khataks the most fascinating of all the tribesmen. 'They are a loyal, industrious, and happy folk, strict in the observance of the doctrines of Islam, and keep strictly to the Pathan code of Pushtoonwali.'

The Khataks are fortunate in having in their well-known ancestor, Khushhal Khan, one whose poems have added so much character to their history. They also have the Khatak dance, described by Goodwin.

> [It] is seen at its best when performed on a dark night with a large bonfire of logs and brushwood flaming in the centre of the dancers. Swords which flash in the firelight when whirled are necessary. Brushwood is thrown on the fire, which, bursting into flame, sends sparks high into the air, the sparks looking like a swarm of fire-flies. An important item is the orchestra—two flageolets and two drums. The flageolets when played sound something like the pipes of Scotland. Unless all these conditions are fulfilled, the dance is a tame affair.

Close to the Khataks and centred on the towns of Hangu and Kohat are the Bangash. On his travels, Babur was never able to control the area where they lived mainly because he was 'occupied by many affairs of superior importance, such as the conquest of Kandahar, Balkh, Badakhshan and Hindustan'. He determined, however, that 'if Almighty God prosper my wishes, my first moments of leisure shall be devoted to the settlement of that district, and of its plundering neighbours'. In the time of the British, the Bangash were widely recruited in the Scouts.

South of the Khataks and Bangash tribes, the Marwats live in the Bannu district towards the tribes of Dera Ismail Khan. Their lands adjoin those Pathans living in Baluchistan in the Zhob valley. Close by in Mianwali are the Niazis, whose lands border the Indus. 'Our tribe,' said Dr Zafar Niazi, 'was noted for its good physique so they were preferred for the police force', which under the British was considered to be a more prestigious job than working as a clerk or a postman.

The wolf and the panther

Living in enmity with each other are the Mahsuds and the Wazirs, who occupy the inhospitable country of Waziristan. Any attempt to explain to a Mahsud, said James Spain, who made a detailed study of the tribes of the Pathan borderland, that his tribe is no more than a division of the Wazirs is 'to invite a sudden and violent end to scholarship'. Olaf Caroe likened the Mahsud to a wolf, the Wazir to a panther: 'Both are splendid creatures; the panther is slyer, sleeker and has more grace, the wolf pack is more purposeful, more united and more dangerous.' At the time the British were fighting them, their strength was put at 30,000 Wazirs, 18,000 Mahsuds.

The Mahsuds are divided into three main tribes and are frequently referred to as Dre Mahsud, 'all Mahsuds'. These three divisions were subdivided into numerous other tribes of which the Shabi Khel 'were probably the most savage of all the Mahsud clans', said Gerald Curtis. 'They had few contacts with civilisation. They had never served in the army and their attitude can be summed up in a remark one of their Maliks made to me: "We want neither your honey nor your sting."'

In the early twentieth century the leader of the Mahsuds was the Mullah Powindah who, the British believed, had the backing of Afghanistan. He led a prolonged rebellion against British rule, but in spite of all the trouble he caused, Evelyn Howell, who was in Waziristan at the time, felt that his character could not be judged by the standards current amongst Englishmen. 'By these he must be set down quite simply as a "first-class scoundrel". But by those who have made allowances for the environment in which he lived, he cannot be denied some tribute and admiration as a determined and astute, though not altogether single-minded patriot and champion of his tribe's independence.'

Nevertheless, the Mahsuds exhibited some of the characteristics which British officers found most trying: 'It is quite impossible to issue a flat order to any tribe, or even to any single tribesman over anything,' wrote Jack Lowis, a political officer at the time of the Waziristan troubles in 1937. 'You have to argue them into agreement. If you don't, in the case of a man he just walks out on you and leaves you flat; in the case of a tribe it does the same and if a tribe walks out on you at a time like the present you probably start a Mahsud war.'

They also had their endearing qualities. Herbert Emerson was told by one of the three lady missionaries at Tank how a Mahsud tribesman came to see her one day with an offer of help. He was a tough-looking fellow, but he said that he wanted to show gratitude for the help she and her colleagues had given to his wife and little girl when they were ill. He turned his hand to many useful jobs about the hospital, as Emerson recounted.

> One very dark night he was carrying a basin of water along the verandah and she was amazed at his sureness of foot. 'How is it that you can see like a cat in the dark?' she asked. He hesitated a moment, and then a broad grin spread slowly over his face. 'It's like this, Miss,' he said. 'If you had been on as many night-raiding parties as I have, you would be able to see in the dark too!'

Even other tribesmen thought the Mahsuds were treacherous. When Ian Stephens was travelling with his Yusufzai servant, Rahim, they came across some Mahsuds, quite by chance. As Stephens had fallen ill they were obliged to make for the Mahsud camp in spite of the protestations of Rahim: 'You could never spend a night with such people, they're not to be trusted. No doubt they'd rob you, then slit your throat'. But Stephens, who had little choice in the matter since he was badly in need of rest, was welcomed by them, fed on breast of chicken with spiced rice and curd, wrapped in blankets and brought out to watch a display of Mahsud dancing in his honour. 'It was,' he said, 'the most unorganised, aboundingly vital, blood-stirring of all the Pathan dance styles, scores of strong, handsome young men rhythmically circling, stamping and twirling their black bobbed hair round a seemingly crazed drummer, against a background of notched snowpeaks and apple-green sunset.' He was struck by the variety of faces amongst the Mahsuds: 'Interesting faces, all hard and lean; some so handsome that you could hardly believe it, catching your breath; others amusingly ugly, others again diabolical, apparently incarnations of scheming, pitiless evil.'

Close to the Mahsuds, who live in the centre of Waziristan, is the smaller tribe of the Bhittanis. Their lands in Waziristan extend from the Marwat plain south to Gomal. To the east of them are the Wazirs, also known as the Darwesh Khel, with whom the Mahsuds were constantly feuding. They are divided into two main groups, the Ahmedzai or Wana Wazirs and the Utmanzai or Tochi Wazirs. They subdivide into almost three hundred separate clans. When the British first came into contact with the Wazirs, they found them to be peaceful tribes. Both Elphinstone and Herbert Edwardes wrote favourably of them. Babur, however, had noted that they had been very irregular in paying their taxes, and seemed rather surprised that they brought him 300 sheep as a tribute.

Like the Mahsuds, the Wazirs had their turbulent priest who troubled the British throughout the 1930s. He was Mirza Ali Khan, a Tori Khel Wazir, better known as the Faqir of Ipi. He steadfastly opposed the British, and as a mark of respect was known by his followers as Haji Sahib. 'But,' said Robin Latimer, a political officer, like his father, Sir Courtenay, 'we tried not to refer to him as such because it was too respectful a title. He had a tremendous amount of influence but we regarded him as a nuisance.'

For administrative purposes Waziristan was divided into two Agencies: North Waziristan and South Waziristan. Unintentionally it came to be the only tribal territory which the British actually garrisoned, and hence they aroused more hostility from the tribes there than those elsewhere. Places like Miramshah in the Tochi valley in North Waziristan, and Razmak and Wana to the south, all featured on the maps of the British as forward positions in their defensive strategy.

Townsmen and Hindus

On the plains in the district of Bannu live the Bannuchis, people who are not true Pathans. 'They are not of pure descent from any common stock but represent the ebb and flow of might, right, possession, and spoilation in a corner of the Cabul empire whose remoteness and fertility offered to outlaws and vagabonds a secure asylum against both laws and labour.' Herbert Edwardes saw in them the clear proof of centuries of interbreeding: 'Every stature, from that of the weak Indian to that of the tall Durrani, every complexion, from the ebony of Bengal to the rosy cheek of Kabul, every dress from the linen garments of the south to the heavy goat skins of the eternal snows is to be seen promiscuously among them, reduced only to a harmonious whole by the neutral tint of universal dirt.' They were, he said, a ferocious people. 'Blood was just a red fluid, and to remove a neighbour's head at the shoulder as easy as cutting cucumbers.'

Charles Masson, in Bannu just twenty years before Edwardes, found great hospitality amongst the people of Bannu, which led him to observe that 'their manners had been unjustly censured and decried'. But he was wise enough to realise that they might not always be so friendly to others as they were to him, and that they were as likely to rob a rich visitor as they were to be generous to a poor one.

In Peshawar live the Peshawaris, again a people of mixed descent. In 1809 Mountstuart Elphinstone saw 'men of all nations and languages, in every variety of dress and appearance . . . mixed people of the town in white turbans, some in large white or blue frocks and others in sheepskin coats . . . Persians and Afghans in brown woollen tunics or flowing mantles and capes of black sheepskin or coloured silk—Khyberees with the straw sandals and the wild dress and air of their mountain.' In this large, busy, thriving population 'of wild and warlike people', observed Herbert Edwardes, all were 'armed with knives and daggers, and naturally inclined to think little of pointing their arguments with the sword.'

Peshawar's first census in 1868 revealed an interesting combination of people: 2,767 government employees, 1,452 police, 2,151 priests, four printers, one jeweller, five drug sellers, 2,411 blacksmiths, 1,701 goldsmiths, 4,806 beggars, 1,202 female musicians, 147 dancing girls, 307 prostitutes and seventeen Americans.

Also to be found chiefly in the towns of the North-West Frontier were the Hindus who constituted only six per cent of the population. Herbert Edwardes found that they were rather superior to the Muslims in Bannu because they could read and write. He also noticed how all trade was in the hands of the Hindus, 'with the exception (characteristic of the two races) of gunpowder, firearms and swords, which were exclusively manufactured and sold by Muhammadans'. But they were often despised by the tribesmen themselves. 'Quite a number of Mahsud villages had a Hindu shopkeeper who would be escorted to Tank in cold weather to stock up,' said Gerald Curtis. ' "I have brought my little Hindu down to fill up," a Malik would say— he spoke very much as a farmer might of putting the cow to the bull.'

Communal riots, especially at times of religious festivals, were always a cause for concern. 'The Hindus were in an awful funk they were going to be massacred,' Sir Courtenay Latimer wrote to his wife in 1926, before the festival of Id, which ends Ramzan. 'We are so much at the mercy of events elsewhere.' There had been serious riots in Calcutta and Rawalpindi, which were seen as retaliation for earlier riots in Kohat in 1924, and the British always feared that disturbances in the rest of India would spill over into the Frontier. 'In the event,' Latimer was pleased to conclude, 'the Id passed off quietly.' However, as time passed the British saw the riots as 'a manifestation of the anxieties and ambitions aroused in both the communities by the prospect of India's political future'. The conclusion which the British government in India drew from this was that 'so long as authority was firmly establishing in British hands and self-government was not thought of, Hindu-Muslim rivalry was confined within a narrow field.'

Powindahs

The Powindahs are the nomads who live around Kandahar and the plains. They travel in long kafilahs, or caravans. In a typical caravan there would be several hundred to a thousand camels, cows and donkeys. During his travels in 1960 Arnold Toynbee saw a group of Powindahs on the road to Kandahar, who, to his surprise, treated the animals more tenderly than they treated themselves.

> Even when it is snowing, and the ground is sodden, many of the human tribesmen go barefoot, and all of them sleep in tents that let in the wind and the sleet. When the caravan is on the march, few of the human travellers are mounted. In the particular party, my eye was caught by one little boy riding with a grave countenance on a donkey. Baby camels riding in panniers slung on either side of a grown-up camel's back are a more frequent sight. A young camel of walking age wears a quilted coat, with a hole cut in to let his tufted hump poke through. Even grown-up camels have coats of sackcloth issued to them when they reach the higher altitudes.

Toynbee was amazed to see lambs carried like babes in arms.

The Powindahs have been frequent inmates of the mission hospitals. Often, hearing of a good doctor in British India, they would make the long journey, leaving the sick members of the family at the hospital to be collected when they came back again in spring. On her way to Tirah, Lillian Starr observed a group of nomads making for the cool of Kurram.

> The camels are tied loosely together, the tail of the foremost looped to the nose of the next, forming a long string; and if one camel, fancy-free, starts to wander almost aimlessly across the road, woe to the motor or pony-cart behind; for whether he has patience or not, the driver must wait till all the ungainly beasts thus strung together have resorted themselves into a tidy line. To the nomad time is not; it is we of the West who rush and worry and fret over such details.

As all those who have come into contact with the tribesmen have come to learn, they are a world and a law unto themselves. Those who have lacked the patience to try and understand tribal ways have become frustrated with what they consider to be backwardness and ignorance. Whilst there was and still is a timeless attraction about their lives, the clash of cultures between peoples of such different backgrounds has meant that it has been hard to reconcile the one with the other. The British, with their 'railways, roads, aeroplanes, motors and modern thought', felt that whereas they were living in the present, beyond the Frontier the people were living 'in the customs and habits of some six hundred years back. Perhaps, did we but know it,' Lillian Starr commented, 'this strange collision of the centuries accounts far more than we realise for the constant friction on the Border.'

CHAPTER FIVE

Frontier Forces

Honour ate up the mountains, and taxes ate up the plains.

Pashtu proverb

Provincial status

The creation of the North-West Frontier Province in 1901 by Lord Curzon, the Viceroy, was designed to separate it from the administration of the Punjab and focus attention on the area as an entity in itself. The new province was to have its own Chief Commissioner, with Deputy Commissioners reporting to him. The first Chief Commissioner was Sir Harold Deane, who had been the first Political Agent of the Malakand in 1895. Later travellers, however, who are unaware of his contribution to the North-West Frontier, bring to mind his name only when they think of the popular Deane's Hotel in Peshawar. Deane was followed by Sir George Roos-Keppel in 1908. He spoke Pashtu fluently and many future political officers learnt from his Pashtu grammar. He was greatly respected by the officers who served under him and was admired for his ability in dealing with the tribes. 'We must accept that all Muslims feel themselves to be members of one great family—however widely scattered,' he wrote to the Viceroy in 1912.

Curzon, who remained in office until 1905, evolved the strategy of closing the line dividing tribal territory from the settled districts, much as Lawrence had tried to do fifty years before. The tribes were to be left in their mountain strongholds to govern themselves; British forces were to be withdrawn from their advanced positions, and tribal militias, commanded by British officers, would, it was hoped, keep the peace. 'This was indeed setting the poacher to act as gamekeeper,' wrote Evelyn Howell in his report, *Mizh* ('We'), on relations with the Mahsud tribe. It was also open recognition that there was still no immediate prospect of bringing the tribal territory within the confines of civilised empire.

However, leaving the tribes to manage their own affairs did not bring the hoped-for harmony. Within no time there was rebellion amongst the Mahsuds. The murder of the Political Agent in South Waziristan, Captain Bowring, in 1904, and soon¹ afterwards that of Lieutenant-Colonel Richard Harman, the Commandant of the South Waziristan Militia, meant trouble. Evelyn Howell, who was present at Harman's murder, discovered that the Mahsuds had planned to seize the garrison at Wana and proclaim the Mullah Powindah as independent King of Waziristan.

'Life in the little frontier cantonments was anything but secure in the days before barbed wire, when the firebrand of the Mahsud tribe, the notorious Mullah Powindah, was sending down his fanatical emissaries from across the border to murder a white man if they could get one, and so secure certain entry into Paradise,' wrote a young subaltern in the Frontier cavalry, W. K. Fraser-Tytler (later Sir Kerr), who was to become well known as a diplomat and historian. 'And always there were the raids, the sudden alarm, the long dust-choked ride through the stifling heat of a July night, clattering out onto the stony glacis of the frontier hills, and away forty miles before dawn only to find as often as not that the birds have flown, leaving a trail of death and destruction behind them.'

Mullah Powindah's death in 1913 deprived the Mahsuds of their most effective leader, but it did not really solve the problem. 'To keep the Mahsud from raiding in British India is a considerable achievement, but cannot be a final end of policy. What is the final end? The old welter may continue, or Mahsud country may become part of Afghanistan and the Mahsud throw in his lot with the inhabitants of that country, or he must be trained to take his place in the federation of India.' In Howell's opinion, this last option was the only one 'to which our officers can worthily address themselves'.

Meanwhile, in 1907, much to the annoyance of the Afghans who were not consulted, the British and Russians signed the St

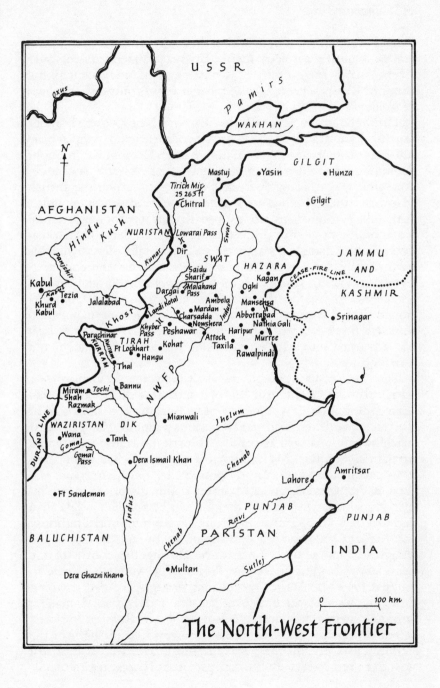

The North-West Frontier

Petersburg Convention, in which they agreed to keep Afghanistan as a buffer between them. Britain retained control over Afghanistan's foreign affairs, whilst agreeing not to annex the country; Russia accepted that Afghanistan was outside her sphere of influence.

Throughout the First World War the North-West Frontier remained calm and Afghanistan stayed neutral. However, the murder in February 1919 of the Amir, Habibullah, brought about a change. It was immediately clear that his successor, Amanullah, was going to be less co-operative with the British than his father. Taking advantage of political unrest in India, Amanullah ordered his troops into British territory near Landi Kotal on the pretext of protecting his own borders. The British interpreted Amanullah's actions as a bid to rally support for his own rule by drawing together young nationalist and conservative Islamic sentiment in a holy war against the 'infidel'. Roos-Keppel, who was on the verge of retiring as Chief Commissioner, learnt from an informer that the Afghans planned to mount a three-pronged attack in the same way that the British had advanced into Afghanistan using the Khyber, Kurram and Quetta routes.

The war, such as it was, came at a time when the British were weary from the fighting in Europe and most of the troops had been demobilised. It would have been much more serious but for the fact that they had far superior weapons, in particular machine-guns, as well as the use of lorries to transport supplies up the Khyber pass. Most important of all, they had aeroplanes, which while they were already obsolete by European standards, were nevertheless capable of bombing strategic places in Afghanistan, including by mistake the tomb of Habibullah in Jalalabad and that of Abdur Rehman in Kabul. Within a month of fighting, the Afghans sued for peace, bringing to an end the last of the 'Afghan Wars' against the British. During the course of the negotiations leading up to the Treaty of Rawalpindi, signed in August 1919, the Afghan representative suggested that it would be in the interests of both Afghanistan and Britain to make a common struggle against the Bolsheviks in Russia, who had seized power in 1917. The British, however, made light of the Communists, maintaining that the old threat from Russia had now been removed with the collapse of the Tsarist regime.

Somewhat reluctantly the British government agreed to restore to Afghanistan control over its foreign affairs, ceded forty years previously. With the Treaty of Versailles proclaiming self-determination for all in Europe, the British realised that they could not hold onto the strings of a policy which dated from the 1840s. Amanullah was therefore free to conduct his own foreign policy; in an effort to maintain the balance between the two powers between whom his country was still a buffer, he concluded formal treaties with both the new Soviet power and the old British Empire in 1921.

Once the British had settled their Afghan affairs, they turned on Waziristan. Unsettled by the fighting on the Frontier, large numbers of Mahsuds and Wazirs had deserted from the militias, taking with them their rifles. Likewise the Afridis of the Khyber Rifles had left in such large numbers that the force was disbanded. Roos-Keppel felt it was better for them to leave without their rifles than desert with them. In 1919 and 1920 it was reported that over 600 raids were launched on Peshawar, Kohat, Bannu and Dera Ismail Khan, resulting in the death of nearly 300 British subjects, as well as nearly 400 wounded and 463 kidnaps. It was a toll which, in the eyes of the British, called for action. At the same time they had to cope with the effects of the Khilafat Movement, of which the *Hijrat* (pilgrimage) was the offshoot. The Muslims of India, including those of the Frontier, were angered by Greece's attack on Turkey in 1920 and held the British responsible for dismantling the Ottoman Empire by the terms of the Treaty of Versailles. In their opinion, not only was Turkey a Muslim state, but the Sultan was proclaimed as the Caliph, the twentieth-century successor to the Prophet. In an attempt to express solidarity with the Turks, thousands of these Muslims left India to go on a pilgrimage—*haj*—to a 'peaceful' land, namely Afghanistan, where they stayed for a few months, to the discomfort of Amanullah and, eventually, their own.

In view of the unsettled situation in Waziristan, the British decided to advance into tribal territory and occupy the plateau of Razmak. The events of the recent past showed that the 'closed border' policy could not work, especially insofar as the Mahsuds and Wazirs were concerned. However, the move forward only succeeded after some of the fiercest fighting yet seen on the Frontier, and the use of the fledgling airforce.

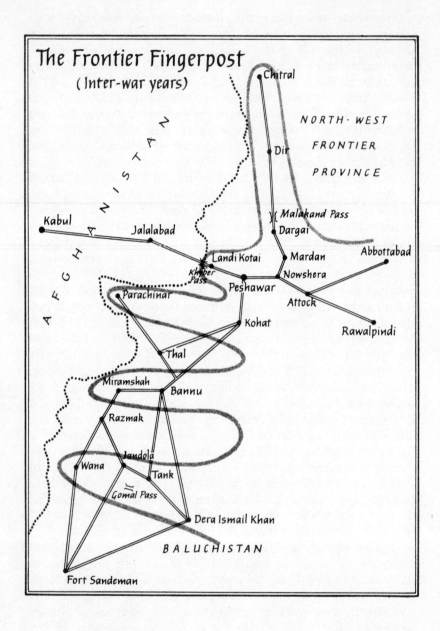

The Frontier Fingerpost
(Inter-war years)

NORTH-WEST FRONTIER PROVINCE

AFGHANISTAN

Chitral

Dir

Malakand Pass

Kabul

Jalalabad

Dargai

Mardan

Abbottabad

Landi Kotai

Khyber Pass

Nowshera

Peshawar

Parachinar

Attock

Rawalpindi

Kohat

Thal

Miramshah

Bannu

Razmak

Jandola

Wana

Tank

Gomal Pass

Dera Ismail Khan

BALUCHISTAN

Fort Sandeman

In order to safeguard their interests, the British decided to maintain fingers of entry by the construction of garrisons and forts at strategic places along the whole borderline. This was to have the double objective of guarding the routes of entry into the sub-continent as well as enabling them to keep an eye on the tribesmen. The Province of the Frontier, said Evelyn Howell—who became Foreign Secretary to the government of India in 1930—was comparable to an outstretched hand: the five settled districts lying in the palm, 'while the thumb and four fingers stretched out to occupy and close against aggression the five gateways of the Malakand (with Chitral), the Khyber, Kurram, Tochi and Gomal. Incidentally, the clenching of the hand exercises pressure upon the turbulent tribal areas lying between the fingers.' The garrisons were all linked by a network of roads upon which the writ of British law ran, manned by Scouts and tribal police, the Khassadars. This was the modified 'forward' policy which was in operation throughout the time the British remained on the Frontier. There were also the railways, of which the construction of the Khyber railway in 1925 was considered to be a feat in itself. Even experts had said it would be impossible: 26½ miles long, it needed 34 tunnels (three miles in all) and 94 bridges and culverts. Major-General G. J. (Goff) Hamilton, who served in the Guides Infantry during the inter-war years, found that the system was comparable to the policy of the Romans towards the barbarous tribes on the borders of their domain.

> The Romans used their auxiliary forces in the first place and only brought up their own legions in time of dire need. In much the same way the area dividing the tribal territory from the administered areas was manned first by the Scouts; if they could not deal with a particular situation, the Indian Army regiments would be committed; the British regiments were usually kept in reserve.

After the First World War, the Royal Air Force also had its part to play.

In spite of fervent efforts to keep the peace, both the Army in India and the Air Force were never very far from action, whether it was preventing full-scale rebellion or serious inter-tribal warfare. 'Not that we would have shed salt tears over any small reduction in the fighting strength of the tribes,' confessed one political officer, Jack Lowis, 'but we certainly did not want the general disturbance which would inevitably have been caused.'

Of continuing importance was the work of teaching and healing carried out by the medical missionaries of the Church Missionary Society and other denominations. It was not for nothing that Lord Roberts had said that Theodore Pennell, as one single missionary, was worth a battalion of troops in keeping the peace.

It was still, as always, a hazardous life, and most Englishmen who ventured to spend a lifetime on the Frontier could call to mind at least some of Kipling's lines, inspired by events of the previous century: 'The "captives of our bow and spear"/Are cheap, alas! as we are dear.'

In the footsteps of their forefathers

Many of those young Englishmen who went to serve in India did so because of family connections. The list of those who joined either the military or the civil service is studded with the names of fathers and grandfathers who had served there before them, as well as uncles and cousins. Some wished to be political officers, starting off in the Indian Civil Service (ICS), with the possibility of later transferring to the Foreign and Political (F & P, which was later changed to the Indian Political Service—IPS). In the F & P, postings stretched from the Indian states, Baluchistan and the NWFP to Aden and the Persian Gulf. Those at Oxford and Cambridge who felt they would like to make a career in India had to sit the ICS exam, spending another year at university, where they learnt Indian law, history and a basic language— Urdu for the north, Tamil for the south—and phonetics to enable them to pick up other languages, such as Pashtu on the Frontier.

Others felt themselves cut out for a career of excitement and danger in the Army in India, as the British and Indian armies were collectively called. The Indian Army was more attractive than the British Army, partly because of its higher pay, which enabled those who did not have a private income to enjoy a reasonable existence. There was also the chance of earlier promotion and responsibility, as well as active service. 'Aldershot must have been pretty deadly between the wars,' remarked Goff Hamilton. Finally, there was the glamour of the East and the attraction of serving in a family regiment. Those who joined the Indian Army had first, however, to serve one year's apprenticeship with a British regiment. It was also possible for Army officers to transfer to a career in the political service, which looked to the Army as a source of recruits.

As time wore on, there were those who felt they might not be able to finish their careers in India. Herbert Emerson, whose father was in the ICS for over thirty years, had spent his youth in India and for several years had wanted to follow in his father's footsteps. Accordingly he sat the ICS exam in 1927 at Cambridge. But he was apprehensive about the future. 'Before going out to India, I discussed with my father whether he thought I would be able to complete a career in India and he thought it would be possible.' But a family friend, Sir Everard Upton, solicitor to the government of India, was more doubtful. He advised the young Emerson to get a professional qualification, so he joined the Inner Temple and was called to the Bar before going to India. 'This eventually proved to have been a very wise step to take.'

With the dawn of the new century, however, such doubts were far from men's minds. 'I don't think we shall lose India in a hundred years,' Sir Courtenay Latimer wrote to his wife in 1910, following some anti-British comment in the Indian press. 'I am a very firm believer in the value of one Englishman against a hundred nations and we are not going to be turned out of India in a hurry even if all the Indians did what they never can do, until they change their character entirely, and really combined against us.'

This feeling lasted throughout the twenties and thirties. 'Only if you were a thinker,' said Colonel Henry Lowe, who was with the Gurkhas in Waziristan, 'did you know what would happen.' And, especially for a soldier, 'Yours not to reason why.'

The tradition for sons whose fathers and grandfathers had served in the Army to follow in their footsteps was perhaps even stronger than in the political service, the preference being to join the regiment of one's father. For Major Robin Hodson, the choice was clear. His family had served with the popular regiment of the Guides, including his great-uncle whose father was first cousin to W. S. R. Hodson, the founder of the cavalry regiment which bore his name, Hodson's Horse; he was later killed in the Indian Mutiny in Lucknow in 1857. 'My one and only ambition was to go into the Guides and become a Frontier officer,' Hodson said. 'I loved the language and I was attracted to the personality and problems and country of the Pathan.' Goff Hamilton also joined the Guides for family reasons. His father had been in the Guides; so too had his grandfather's first cousin, Lieutenant Walter Hamilton, who was killed in the massacre at Kabul in 1879. Many were attracted by the life of the Scouts who patrolled the tribal territory. 'It was the ambition of all of us to go to the Scouts,' said Brigadier Bill Boulter, who served with the Tochi Scouts in North Waziristan, 'because you were more likely to see active service.'

Unfortunately for Robin Hodson, early on in his career in the Army he had a serious accident when travelling from Razmak to Bannu and was advised to transfer to the Political Service. Another Guide, Lieutenant-Colonel Sir John Dring also left to become 'a political'. He had thoroughly enjoyed his time in the Army, but had become friendly with the Assistant Commissioner in Mardan, Olaf Caroe—'I didn't even know that the Foreign & Political existed before then.' Caroe asked him to accompany him on trips around the country away from Mardan. 'To me it was an absolute eye-opener: watching him deal with the people. So I decided to transfer to the F & P because I thought it would be more interesting to get to know the people and their problems.'

Once accepted, Dring was posted back to the Frontier, which pleased him. 'I think there was something very special about the Frontier. People had funny ideas about life in India: that it was life on a pedestal; but it was very far from that, especially on the Frontier. The Pathan was not servile or submissive and it was much easier to make real friends among the locals than to try and get a good friendship with, say, an African.' As Lieutenant-Colonel Michael Wilcox, who served with Coke's Rifles, said: 'You always considered it to be a feather in your cap to be on the Frontier rather than in the sloth belt of the rest of India.' But, as they all realised, 'It was rather an arrogant attitude to think that the rest of India was soft compared with the Frontier. Now we know that's not true,' was Robin Hodson's conclusion.

Numerous Indians filled the lower ranks of the Civil Service, and Indians also formed the backbone of the Indian Army, their numbers increasing with the process of Indianisation. In accordance with the old strategy of divide and rule, there were mixed regiments, composed of Sikhs, Punjabi Mussulmans, Dogras (who were Hindus) and Pathans. It seemed to work very well. 'We were a happy band,' Goff Hamilton said of the men with whom he served, 'and I was intensely proud to be their leader; and they knew it. We fought and played together undeterred by race, rank, class or creed, or age for that matter.' In his early twenties, Hamilton was in command of men who were considerably senior to him in age.

When it came to recruitment, the British went to the same areas: 'Sons followed fathers and grandfathers in the same regiment, so how could the Indian sepoy be a coward? His whole village would hear of it if he were, and his name would be mud,' John Prendergast pointed out. 'The fact that he was a servant of the Sirkar [government] made him a figure of substance.' There was also the possibility of receiving an award for gallantry.

As in the rest of India, Pathans could work their way up from being sepoys to jemadars and subadars; and subadar-majors. As commissions were granted by the Viceroy, they became VCOs—Viceroy's Commissioned Officers.

Although Pathans might find themselves fighting Pathans, they proved loyal to their regiment. 'It was very rare,' said Bill Boulter, 'for a Pathan to break his oath of allegiance to his regiment, in spite of the fact they were fighting against their co-religionists. We always respected each other's religion, and were very polite about one another's beliefs.' Even so the experience of the past meant that certain tribes were not enlisted for service in the Army: Orakzais, Khataks and Yusufzais were considered to be the most trustworthy; Wazirs, Mashuds, Mohmands and Afridis were confined to being Scouts and Khassadars. As such, they would have to provide their own weapons.

Watch and ward

The trouble with British rule was that although the basic aim—
to get the tribes to control themselves through a mixture of
inducement and fear—ran unchanged from north to south, it
worked differently in different places, generally in descending
order of merit according to Ambrose Dundas. 'In the north, they
have monarchy, next a feudal aristocracy, next a fairly well-
working democracy and finally, in Waziristan, anarchy.'
Whereas in Swat and Chitral the British only needed to get the
agreement of the ruler to carry out a particular order, in
Waziristan the Political Agent had 'to convince a jirga numbering
1,500 or more, uneducated and fanatical, any one of the 1,500
prepared to heckle the Political Agent and none of them intending to obey the jirga's decision unless he personally agrees with
it.' Gerald Curtis found that here, 'if anywhere in the world, was
to be found the dictatorship of the proletariat expressed, not in
the tyranny of the few, but in the licence of the many.'

For the greater part of their time on the Frontier, the British in
the twentieth century were watching and warding the tribes:
some three million inhabitants. The aim remained to prevent
those in the barren mountains from sweeping down and attacking those living in the fertile plains; they would watch the one,
and ward the other. If there was nothing to do but remain in their
barracks, the military could find life rather dull. For the politicals
it was a chance to get on with the day-to-day administration of
the province. But it was a slow process. 'Constructive work on
the Frontier resembles the erection of a lighthouse,' said Evelyn
Howell. 'The builders know that storms will come and that from
time to time their operations will be interrupted. Meanwhile,
they have to get on with the job. "The work is with them," as
Kipling said long ago, "The event with Allah."'

Men of War: Army

The garrison which was built at Razmak, after the troubles in
Waziristan in 1919, was high up in the Mahsud highlands. It
housed a strong brigade of six battalions from the Indian Army
and one from the British Army. 'Here on a plateau 6,500 feet

above sea level, secluded behind a triple circle of barbed wire and arc lights, had sprung up an unnatural town with a population of 10,000 men and 3,000 mules. It bristled with guns, armoured cars, and all the panoply of war; but its inhabitants spent their time waiting for something to happen,' wrote John Masters of his year there with the Duke of Cornwall's Light Infantry in 1935.

When there was peace, life followed its set pattern: parades, training, mess, siesta, tea and games. After dinner in the mess, there was the possibility of night operations; if not, some would have sing-songs, others played bridge.

Confined though they might have felt in their barracks, there was the obvious reason of safety which prevented the soldiers exposing themselves unnecessarily to attack from the tribesmen. John Masters saw it all as a diplomatic battle between the political officers and the Army chiefs as to whether or not they should be allowed out.

> The political officers would have liked us to stay behind our barbed wire for ever: all Pathans are at all times in need of rifles and ammunition to carry on their private wars and blood feuds. The temptation to steal them from us was great, and the easiest way to get a soldier's rifle was to shoot the soldier when he was on training manoeuvres. On the other hand, the Generals knew that the soldiers would go mad if they were cooped up for two years on end in this monastic wilderness [Razmak]. They therefore insisted that we be allowed to take periodic walks through the country-side to admire the views, smell the rare flowers and keep fit.

And so they did. 'We would think nothing of having to march twenty miles a day,' said Michael Wilcox. Since they never quite knew when there would be trouble, they had to be prepared. 'One day a week we put the mules into lorries, about ten per lorry, so they would be used to being moved and would not be afraid when the day of action came.' In general, the mules carried the ammunition and light artillery; they were followed by the camels with the tents and luggage. If it was a light column the tents would be left behind and they would have to bivouac— sleep under the stars as they were, on what was available. Gone were the days when they would travel laden down with luggage and camp followers: the lesson of the Afghan wars had been painfully learnt. A subaltern—the rank at which most young Englishmen started their army career—was limited to ten pounds of baggage. Henry Lowe's mother gave him a camel-hair sleeping bag, for which he was envied by others who were less fortunate. It weighed just seven pounds and could be incorporated into his kit for protection against the cold winters. He was also imaginative enough to provide himself with a rubber ring which he could use when bivouacking to soften the hard ground. Later he got a lilo, a novelty on the Frontier, which gave much comfort until it was punctured by a thorn bush. Such 'luxury' items could greatly enhance the life of the soldier.

The column would go out either on training manoeuvres or to make a display of force if a tribal chief was suspected of 'intriguing or harbouring outlaws or hatching embarrassments to the Afghan government', said Masters. They used to spend 'a week or ten days stamping noisily around in the suspected headman's section of country'. The outing was called a column because that was what it was: 'a double string of men and animals defiling down the narrow valleys and stony passes'. It moved at the rate of about two miles an hour, and because of this was a ready target for the tribesmen, especially since, with the camels, it had to keep to the valleys. Exactly as the army had been picked off in the Khurd Kabul pass in 1842, so could a column be an easy prey to tribesmen if they had command of the heights above the valley. To guard against this and any intermittent sniping, the advance guard would put up Khassadars as pickets to secure the passage of the troops, in the same way that Pollock had managed to pass through the Khyber in 1842. If the column was going through a valley, the rear guard would take the pickets down. Along with scanning the horizon for tribesmen on the hill tops, they also had to watch out for a sudden cloudburst which could flood a narrow valley within minutes.

Since life in camp was rather routine, there was great enthusiasm when the soldiers knew they were going out to confront the tribesmen. Three wars against the Afghans and the fierce fighting of the previous century had not dulled the desire for battle. 'If you were sitting in Mardan and heard that there was trouble brewing,' enthused Hamilton, 'there was this sense of great excitement. Your life was entirely taken up with your profession and when you went to battle you knew that your men would follow you.'

In a sense part of the glamour inherited from the previous century of fighting to protect Britain's North-West Frontier in a Great Game remained; only now the game was between the tribesmen and the British, whereas before the game of diplomacy had been played between the British and Tsarist Russia. To an army officer, medals and experience were still uppermost in importance. But every so often, there was, as Masters felt, the 'sense-sharpening chance of a sudden storm of bullets, a rush of knifemen, a bloody hand-to-hand struggle,' which would inevitably leave some of their comrades dead.

Goff Hamilton had experience of bitter fighting against the Mohmands which, like so many times before, turned out to be 'another military disaster which never should have happened.' He recalled a day's events.

> There were no bugles that morning on 29 September 1935. My Pathan bearer and friend, Kashmir Khan, leant down into my dugout and shook my shoulder. '*Ek baj gia*, Sahib,'—one o'clock—he muttered, as he thrust a tin mug of steaming tea into my hand, and departed as silently as he had come. No lights in the camp, of course, and no moon yet. No noise either except for the shuffle of sandals on loose stones, the muttered curses, and the snorts of shackled mules sniffing the cold night air: all the age-old sounds of infantry girding themselves for battle in the dark. Except for the muffled roar of a dozen or more oil cookers heating the early morning meal of chupattees and sweet tea, it might have been early dawn at a Roman staging-post on the way to Hadrian's wall.

For the past few weeks Mohmand tribesmen had been attacking cavalry patrols and firing into the British camps; and so the object of the mission on which Hamilton and the Guides infantry were engaged was to capture a strategic ridge with the object of dominating the surrounding country: 'It all boiled down to the Nowshera Brigade, of which we were part, having to capture a 1500-foot-high ridge of rocky peaks ending at the cross of a T with the hill top—Point 4080—at the junction of the two ridges.'

Major Syd Good was the acting Commanding Officer of the Guides, Captain Godfrey Meynell, the Adjutant; Lieutenant Tony Rendall in charge of one company of platoons, Lieutenant Goff Hamilton in command of another; as they were missing one British officer, who had been wounded in an earlier battle, the Subadar-Major, a Khatak Pathan, was in charge of the third. There was also just one doctor from the Indian Medical Service. On the Guides' left side were the other regiments of the Nowshera Brigade. The Peshawar Brigade, commanded by Brigadier Claude Auchinleck was to cover their right flank. The two nearer peaks on the ridge which they had to capture before the assault on Point 4080 were code named 'Teeth' and 'Bare Nipple'.

As they 'wolfed' their porridge at 1.30 am Hamilton chatted with Tony Rendall.

> 'Don't forget! If anything happens I want you to go through my things,' said Tony quietly. 'You can have my silver cigarette case.'
> 'Same here!' I replied as was our custom. We always said it. It blunted the thought of disaster somehow. Good joss, too! Like taking out an umbrella to ensure against rain.

Soon afterwards they set off.

> We plodded along in such silence as we could muster, but it was chilly at that time in the morning and our teeth were chattering. As I shuffled along in the dust and gravel, I pondered on death and women. Queer how the two tend to jostle in one's mind for priority in times of crisis! I had thankfully discarded the former trend of thought and was getting well into the latter when Godfrey jerked me out of my reverie. He whispered that we had reached the spur that led up to the vast cathedral-like outcrops that were Teeth.

In spite of the steep climb in the dark, taking the first two peaks went unopposed according to plan. Hamilton and his company were to hold Teeth, while the second company with two machine-guns made for Bare Nipple. But when the third company, under Tony Rendall, advanced on Point 4080, it was clear that the element of surprise had long since been lost. In the fighting which ensued on Point 4080, Rendall was killed at the head of his men; a few minutes later Godfrey Meynell, who went forward to take over command of the company, also died in fierce hand-to-hand fighting. Syd Good and the gunner officers were all wounded. Hamilton then decided to go forward; he took the Khatak and Dogra platoons with him, leaving the other two platoons to hold Teeth. 'We went like hunted chamois over the rocks, sliding down into the dips on our backsides and scrambling up vertical cliffs with an ease that was the gift of youth and much practice.'

Once they had reached Bare Nipple, they went on to try and get to the lower slopes of Point 4080. 'I had only gone about a hundred yards when I was hit by what felt like the kick of a horse and which spun me round in my tracks. I paused, and I suppose stood gazing with fatuous amazement at Point 4080 from whence the bullet must have come, for I heard my Pathan orderly shout at me, saying, "You can't stand there, we must go forward."' He had received his wound in the stomach, but decided that he could carry on and make for the relative safety of a small outcrop further forward named Pimple. 'I found I could still move on all fours and covered the next 200 yards or so to Pimple like a chimpanzee.' Several of Hamilton's men had also been wounded: one of them, a Khatak, was hit near the edge of the ridge and fell, rolling a thousand feet to the bottom, beyond help. 'He was captured by the tribesmen later that day but was returned during the night on a donkey given to him by an ex-Guide who was now in retirement fighting with his friends.' One of his Dogras was not so fortunate. He was hit in the chest and rolled down the lower foothills of the ridge. 'He did not survive and his body, being Hindu, was found later badly mutilated.'

'For the next two or three hours we did our best to be aggressive and fired at anything that moved on the hill and spurs to our front, but the tribesmen were some hundred feet above us and well concealed. We saw little.' Hamilton was expecting a counter-attack to be launched, if only to recover the wounded. 'We all knew what happened to them if captured. Was there not an age-old unwritten law of the Frontier never to leave wounded in enemy hands if humanly possible?' At about midday, the artillery far down the valley began to shell Point 4080. The counter-attack was never launched. Even so, the Mohmand tribes 'had had enough for the time being and sued for peace the following day. The bodies of Tony and Godfrey and of twenty other Guides were collected and either buried or burnt.' In addition to Good, Hamilton and the two gunner officers, eighty-two others were either captured, wounded or badly injured falling down the mountainside. The tribesmen returned to their villages and the Guides went back to their home in Mardan in the Yusufzai plain. Meynell was awarded the VC posthumously; Hamilton received the DSO.

Even when the Army did not venture out of the safety of its camp, their pickets on the hillsides were always vulnerable to a sudden attack. 'Bloody show this morning,' Jack Lowis noted whilst in Waziristan:

> Just as we were beginning to hope things were settling down. A camp picquet was completely scuppered at 3.30 am. There were seventeen men (thirteen Gurkhas) in the picquet with four sentries and the first thing they knew was a bomb in the middle of them, which laid out about half of them. The *dushman* [enemy] then rushed the picquet, getting away with nine rifles, one VB gun [a light automatic which replaced the old Lewis gun], eight bombs and about 1,500 rounds of ammunition. All the casualties were from bomb fragments—six Gurks killed, ten wounded, only one unhurt. No bullet or knife wounds at all.

Sniping in the camp was less of a problem. The chance of being hit was normally one in seven thousand, John Prendergast estimated. 'More often the mules who stood shackled in serried ranks with no cover sustained the casualties.'

Once the Army had pacified a certain area where there had been trouble, they set about building roads. Many an officer could testify to the amount of time he had spent on the art of road construction. The road was considered to be like 'a needle which pricked the balloon of tribal superstition' by bringing the tribesmen into contact with 'civilised' India. 'These roads in the long run did more than the troops to integrate Waziristan into the Indus Valley,' said Gerald Curtis. 'They put the economy of the country onto wheels. Such exports as it afforded—timber, hides, wool, potatoes, or fruit—made their way down to markets in India and not into Afghanistan to which there were no roads; and tribal consumer needs were supplied from Indian sources.'

Men of War: Scouts

The Army was only called upon if a full-scale operation was to be mounted. With a simple punitive raid, the Scouts in tribal territory, and the Frontier Constabulary in the settled areas, could normally do the job. The Scouts were commanded by officers like Bill Boulter or John Prendergast, seconded from the Indian Army. In their case, they joined the Tochi Scouts which operated in North Waziristan. The South Waziristan Scouts had their headquarters in Jandola, and with the Tochi, they comprised the Frontier Corps. All along the Frontier, the Scouts were relied upon to maintain order. In addition to those in Waziristan, there were the Chitrali Scouts, the Gilgit Scouts, the Kurram Militia and the Zhob Militia, and after 1945 the Khyber Rifles.

Patrolling their respective areas, they were constantly on the move, 'so that they were superbly fit, knew the ground intimately and they were on good terms with the tribesmen in their areas,' said Jack Lowis. The officers wore the same outfit as their men in order not to stand out as a target for the tribesmen—a useless attempt at disguise, as John Prendergast learnt. 'Pathans have always assured me that they could pick out a British officer with no difficulty simply from the way he moved.' In the Scouts it was obligatory for the British officers to learn Pashtu, for which skill they received extra pay. It also meant they could get to know the Pathans better than their counterparts in the Indian Army.

In case they got into difficulties, the Scouts always carried pigeons which they could release to return to headquarters as a signal for help. 'We always sent two birds as, in this hilly country, falcons were common and our messenger could be struck down,' Prendergast recalled. On one occasion, however, once released, both birds settled on a rock and started cooing at each other. 'In desperation we raised ourselves from the ditch and threw pebbles at them hoping no one would shoot us. At last, both messengers took off, circled high and set a course west for Miramshah.' Within half an hour an RAF plane arrived to shoot the Scouts out of their difficulty.

The Scouts were expected to act as the military arm of the political officers in cases not serious enough to call in the Army. On one occasion in Waziristan, the Political Agent, Major Barnes, as Jack Lowis recorded, decided to use the Scouts to 'bring to order' an important tribe of Wazirs, the Zilli Khel, by restricting the autumn movement of their flocks. The Scouts succeeded in capturing nearly a thousand sheep, eight shepherds and two rifles. 'The sheep round-up was wholly successful in its purpose,' Lowis noted, although he himself was criticised by an officer from the Brigade at Wana for cruelty to sheep. 'But there had been no shooting, no casualties and no sheep died.' And, in spite of the criticism, he still continued to play squash with the officer in question.

Jack Lowis, for one, preferred travelling with the swift-moving Scouts, rather than the Army, even though for those about to be punished, the end result could be equally unpleasant: 'The jaunt this morning was fun,' he wrote to his sister, describing a typical punitive raid.

> Just Scouts. Much better than the cumbrous Army. We went to arrest a man starting at 3.45 am but he wasn't there so set about burning his kot [home]. Only we had no explosives so didn't know what to do about the tower till somebody found a 120 lb bomb in the back room. There was some difference of opinion as to whether it would go off, as it must have been there for years, but eventually when the fire was going well in all the roofs, we dashed in and heaved the bomb onto the fire in the bottom room of the tower and ran for it. Surprisingly, the bomb exploded causing the required damage. A first rate show. All modern appliances to hand.

The Scouts also acted as a screen for a military column. As they had no supporting weapons, their own casualties could be high, and fear could come to the best of them. 'Bullets were cracking an inch or two above our heads. Being normal, I had horrid visions of having my brains scattered by the next shot. The crack of the bullets was so unnervingly sharp and so close as to turn my ear-drums into singing deafness. I found myself frightened indeed. I had not known fear could be so intense and it was a terrible shock to me.' Even so, John Prendergast successfully led his men to do battle against the tribesmen in Waziristan and was awarded the MC for 'conduct beyond the call of duty'.

Men of War: the Royal Air Force

Increasingly, a major part of the battle against the tribesmen was performed by the Royal Air Force. It was first used on a large scale in Waziristan in 1919, as well as in the third Afghan war. The prospect of having Kabul in ruins was believed to have been the main reason why Amanullah had sued for peace.

On the Frontier the Air Force was supposed only to be used in accordance with a special code of conduct. 'We played the game strictly according to the rules of cricket,' said Wing-Commander James, who came to the Frontier as a pilot in 1936. 'In other words, if we had to punish for a raid or a kidnapping, we'd fly over the village two days before, giving forty-eight hours' notice, warning them to take their children, cows, goats and wife, and not to come back until the government said it was safe.' The warnings—in the form of bits of paper (which the tribesmen in general could not read) dropped over the villages—were the evidence which gave the Faqir of Ipi his accredited powers of being able to turn bombs into paper.

In the summer the Air Force operated from its base in Miramshah. As many of the bombs dropped on the villages were liable not to go off, the bravest among the tribesmen would dismantle them, and place the explosive into tin cans. At night they used to approach the airstrip and bury them on the runway, as James described:

They would act as little landmines and, because the planes had radiators like a car engine, when they exploded they put the aeroplane out of action. The whole thing was very amateurish on both sides. In fact the tribesmen resented the use of aeroplanes or 'machines of the air', as they called them, because they felt it was taking an unfair advantage of them and their rifles. They wanted us to get down to their level with rifles like the Army.

All the same, there were dangers for the airmen as well: flying in narrow valleys could literally clip their wings. If a forced landing had to be made in tribal territory, they could expect 'a fate worse than death'. 'So we had our blood chits'—in common parlance, money bags, or a sum of money if the pilot was returned unharmed. Their usefulness in reconnaissance could also be limited because it was hard to see the tribesmen hidden away in the hillsides, and sometimes to distinguish friend from foe. 'I recall watching an RAF plane discharging a bomb as it flew over my company position,' said Goff Hamilton. 'It killed two mules.'

In the days of no radios, those on the ground used to communicate with the pilots by a system called the Popham Panel, named after the gentleman who devised it. Large letters were laid out on the ground to indicate to the pilot what kind of distress they were in: whether they were short of ammunition, supplies or had a man wounded.

The aircraft used on the Frontier in the thirties were slow clumsy bi-planes, with the double wings held together by struts and bits of wire and with no nose wheels. The pilot sat in an open cockpit wrapped up in leather right up to his helmet, observing the world below through his huge pair of goggles. The open cockpit could have its bonuses: 'The smell of strawberries, peaches, and seedless grapes,' said Wing-Commander James, 'are missed by the modern aviator.'

At Peshawar airfield, an L-shaped grass strip, the trouble came not so much from bombs in tin cans but from waterlogged land.

The grass on each arm of the L was irrigated in alternate weeks; where it was waterlogged, white canvas warning crosses were displayed to advise pilots not to land. If you were in a hurry and failed to see the crosses, you paid the penalty for your haste by running into the mud, turning completely over and coming to undignified rest, hanging upside down in your open cockpit on your straps.

The British also wanted to make an airfield at Parachinar in Kurram, but they found that land was rather limited and the only place where a good landing strip could be laid down was occupied by the grave of a local saint. The political officer at the time, Khan Bahadur Kuli Khan (the rescuer of Molly Ellis), was requested by the British to do something about the grave, but to be careful not to upset the feelings of the local people. One Friday he went to the local mosque and asked the Mullah to interpret a strange dream he had had: 'I dreamt that the Saint was requesting me, "Please remove me from this place, I don't want to be here any more."' This happened three times; finally the Mullah said that the meaning was clear: 'The Saint must be moved.' Within six months the airfield was laid down to everyone's satisfaction.

There was no doubt that the role of the Air Force in frontier warfare was beginning to compete with that of the Army. Gerald Curtis saw the proof of this in Waziristan. A battalion of Gurkhas had been doing training exercises on the lower slopes of a mountain south of Razmak when they got into a fight with some tribesmen of the Abdullais; by the end of the skirmish fifty rifles and a number of automatic weapons had been lost; among the dead was a British officer. This meant that the tribesmen would have to be punished and the rifles returned; their villages and defensive towers were the objects of the attack. Curtis went along to observe the shoot; it took rather a long time as the mud, goat's hair and timber structures were extraordinarily tough. Eventually one tower was destroyed. 'The other we left standing but in a precarious state. That afternoon the Abdullais brought in a number of the lost weapons.'

But they did not bring in the rest, and so another target was selected.

> And this time it was the Air Force's turn. It was quite a tricky place to hit. The aircraft had to dive over a crest, deliver its missile and pull up to avoid another crest. After a couple of misses an aerial torpedo hit the target, there was a blinding flash and an immense cloud of dust flew up, and when that subsided neither walls nor towers remained. The rest of the weapons, a hundred rifles for security, and the fine were brought in that afternoon . . . The futility of the

occupation of Razmak by the Army and, on the other hand, the efficiency of air power had been made manifest before my eyes.

In general the political officers appreciated the frequent contact they had with both the Army, Scouts and the Air Force, and vice-versa. Even so, there could be disagreements between the Army and the political officers on matters of policy. The politicals were more inclined to try and prevent force being used against the tribesmen unless absolutely necessary; whereas the military preferred at least some action. They felt hampered by the politicals' rule which prevented them from firing on the tribesmen unless they fired first. 'So if you came on a *lashkar* of Wazirs armed to the teeth, obviously bent on trouble, unless they fired on you, you had to let them escape,' said Prendergast. In jest the Army officers attributed the politicals' desire for peace as being as much for themselves as for the tribesmen: 'Peace in our time, O Lord, and God preserve my pension,' was said to be their nightly prayer.

Men of land and law

The twentieth-century political officer was undoubtedly more on his own in terms of responsibility than his counterparts in the armed forces. He could be in a place forty to fifty miles away from the nearest British officer, and anyone who served on the Frontier was only too ready to admit that without the co-operation and respect of the local people, he would not have been either so welcome or so successful. Since the Pathans admired men with powers of leadership such as they had seen in their predecessors, personality still played an important part. The political officer soon found that he would need all his ability to deal with an enormous variety of problems, ranging up and down the Frontier.

Administration of the settled areas was carried out along an established pattern with a Deputy Commissioner for each of the five districts, and political officers who would be expected to assist him. The Resident in the tribal territory of Waziristan co-ordinated the work of the Political Agents in North and South

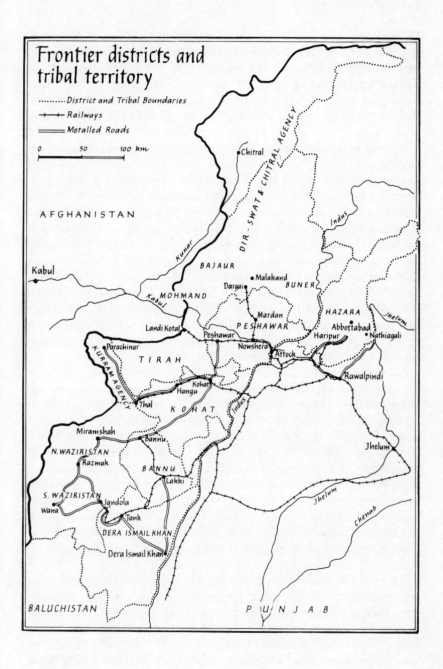

Frontier districts and
tribal territory

.... District and Tribal Boundaries
+—+—+ Railways
════ Metalled Roads

0   50   100 km

AFGHANISTAN

DIR · SWAT & CHITRAL AGENCY

• Chitral

Kunar

Kabul •

Kabul

BAJAUR

• Malakand
Dargai •

BUNER

MOHMAND

HAZARA

Mardan

PESHAWAR

Landi Kotal •

Peshawar •

Abbottabad •

• Nathiagali

Indus

Jhelum

Parachinar •

Nowshera •

Haripur •

TIRAH

Attock •

KURRAM AGENCY

Kohat •

Rawalpindi •

Hangu •

Thal •

KOHAT

Indus

Miramshah •

Bannu •

N. WAZIRISTAN

Razmak •

BANNU

Lakki •

Jhelum

S. WAZIRISTAN

Jandola •

Wana •

Tank •

DERA ISMAIL KHAN

Jhelum

Chenab

Dera Ismail Khan •

BALUCHISTAN

P U N J A B

Waziristan. They in turn were helped by Assistant Political Agents (APAs) as well as Assistant political officers. These men—often Pathans—were invaluable to the Political Agent, as Gerald Curtis recognised: 'It needs a Pathan to unravel the intricacies and lay bare the realities of tribal politics.' They were the 'eyes and ears of the Political Agent'. Part of the APA's duty was to pay the tribal police, the Khassadars, 'who would generally give you a thumbprint in your book in recognition of payment'.

Certainly no political officer could complain about being bored. Upon arrival he was provided with the *Punjab District Administration Manual*, containing a list of his duties. Such were the demands of Frontier life, that Robin Latimer received the advice that 'the first thing to do is to decide which ninety per cent of the work you will leave undone.' It could be a difficult job, thrust upon men whose experience of the world was often confined to the universities of Oxford or Cambridge. 'Somewhere it was written down that an officer's whole time was at the disposal of the government and that leave was a privilege, not a right. There was no such thing as overtime and officers would turn out any time of the day or night, regardless.'

Like the Scouts, it was very important for the men in the political service to learn Pashtu; whereas those in the Army could get by with the lingua franca, Hindustani. When they began their service on the Frontier, an hour's lesson with the *munshi* was an essential part of their daily activity. Some of the political officers took great pleasure in their Pashtu, spending their spare time translating the poems of Khushhal Khan. But a transfer of appointment could present difficulties, as Curtis found when he went from Hazara to Waziristan. 'I had learnt northern Pakhtu and what I had been taught to pronounce as Mong Mahsud ['We Mahsuds'] became on a Mahsud tongue Mizh Mahseet—a drastic change in vowel sounds which took a little getting used to.'

One of the main differences between the British presence in tribal territory and the settled areas was that whereas in the one they would distribute money by way of allowances, in the other they wanted to collect taxes. But in order to do so, a thorough knowledge of the land itself was needed, and each political officer had to be thoroughly trained in land revenue. John Dring was very surprised to find how carefully everything was recorded: 'It astounded me to find that every field was mapped and a record kept of the crops produced.' Before any measurement of the land could be done, a list containing records of ownership and tenancies and rents had to be compiled, which meant studying the family trees. 'You'd sit down with the village people to check the family tree to see what land belonged to whom,' said Robin Latimer. 'And like in biblical times they'd say who was the son of so-and-so, who was the son of someone else. They all knew their family trees by heart and if the village accountant tried to fiddle anything they'd know.'

In tribal territory, the Political Agent would go twice a year to the jirga of all the tribes to distribute their allowances, which were given usually in return for a favour such as keeping the peace on the road through their territory. The jirga presented a bizarre spectacle to the observer, as Curtis found:

> As I looked at the tribesmen I would see a striking display of nose, beard and whisker. But more formidable than these features would be their eyes, which gave at best, a cold, at worst a cruel expression to their faces. The elders of the tribe (in Pashtu *Spin gira*—meaning 'White beard') would be prominently seated. At the back would be the *kasharan*—the young men—noisy and excitable but occasionally reduced to silence by some sour comment from an elder.

Once the allowances had been agreed upon, there was time for a general discussion, which provided an opportunity for the tribesmen to air their grievances. A common complaint was damage by floods to their cultivated land. 'If things went well,' said Jack Lowis, 'it could be disposed of in a light-hearted manner.' But it could also be exhausting. 'Every Malik in the tribe considered himself entitled to a personal and private talk with the PA. It took hours, but it was good to have a personal acquaintance with them and friendly feelings could persist for months.' At the jirga the Political Agent was grateful for the local knowledge of their APAs, who, as Pathans, 'would come up with the one aspect of a case which the tribesmen had found it convenient to forget'.

The political officer's knowledge was not just confined to land revenue and tax; he also had to be well versed in law, which in criminal cases was that of the Indian Penal Code as prepared by Thomas Macaulay in the previous century. Robin Latimer found that the work of the magistrate was the least pleasant. Not only could it be tedious, necessitating long hours in court, but 'you could never tell whether or not a person was telling the truth. It was difficult to feel you had got the right answer.' The task of the magistrate was made harder by the fact that the local police would generally involve all the members of a particular family alleged to have committed a crime. 'Probably only two or three out of seven or eight would be guilty, 'and the difficulty was in knowing which ones were the guilty parties'. Political officers started off as magistrates with third-class powers, whereby they could fine or sentence a person for six months. With time and experience, their powers were increased until as District Magistrates they could sentence a man to up to fourteen years in prison; cases involving the death penalty would go before a Sessions court to be tried by a judge.

Along with the usual cases of murder, theft and rape, and quarrels over women, water rights, and land, occasionally a very unusual one would come before the court, as happened when John Dring was in Tank on the day of Id: 'The holiday spirit was in the air: rich and poor, young and old were dressed in their newest clothes. Mingling in the crowds were men of the Frontier Constabulary.' A local attraction was the Municipal Garden where there were stalls and entertainments, one of which was a snake-charmer. A member of the Frontier Constabulary pushed to the front of the crowd, asking if he might also try. Somewhat startled at this rather unusual request, the snake-charmer, after a certain amount of persuasion, agreed. Within an hour the man was dead.

'The case,' said Dring, 'aroused one of the most amusing cases in the press, although not of course for the dead man.'

In due course, it came before him as District Magistrate, but no one could decide under which section of the law the snake-charmer should be tried. It clearly was not wilful murder, and so eventually they decided that he should be charged with causing death through negligence, under one of the sections governing manslaughter. The snake-charmer was taken into custody and the cobra impounded as the essential prosecution exhibit.

Some time passed before the trial opened in Tank. The police had the snake-charmer locked in one cell, and the cobra in the one next door; they did not take long to appreciate the value of such a deadly reptile in a prison where many outlaws and troublesome characters were unwilling to 'confess' to their alleged crimes. The police therefore adopted the following line of approach: they would ask the accused either to 'confess' or to spend the night in the cell with the cobra; the result was that many such 'confessions' were recorded in the interval before the case came to court.

The actual proceedings were brief. The defence pleaded unwarranted interference in the snake-charmer's performance, attributable to 'youthful exuberance'. The snake-charmer was nevertheless convicted with a penalty of two years' imprisonment for causing death by negligence, under a section more often invoked in fatal motor accidents. He appealed against the decision to the Sessions Court in Dera Ismail Khan, and it was not long before the police in DIK saw the same benefits to be derived from having the cobra in residence. 'The abrupt reduction in the average duration of cases was indeed evident in the monthly statement showing the progress of work in the various courts,' Dring remarked.

> Curiously, the misconduct of the police in resorting to such extreme third-degree methods was not brought to my notice officially as District Magistrate, possibly because the Bar, like the public at large, found the situation so entertaining and the source of endless stories. My conscience was partially soothed by the presumption that the Superintendent of Police would prevent any manifest abuse of the opportunity offered and limit its utilisation to 'selected' cases.

Unluckily for the snake-charmer, the Sessions Judge took a more serious view of the offence and increased his sentence to ten years' imprisonment. The next course of action was to appeal to the High Court in Peshawar. But the cobra's reputation had spread far and wide, and before the snake-charmer and his cobra could be sent to Peshawar, a telegram arrived: 'Prosecution exhibits will not be required'. 'With a sense of some disappointment tinged with reluctance at closing an amusing chapter, I directed that the cobra should be destroyed. It was drowned by the police with unpremeditated ceremony in the turgid waters of the Indus.' In the end the snake-charmer's sentence was once more reduced to two years.

In Peshawar any number of unusual events could take place. At the age of twenty-nine Herbert Thompson became Magistrate with jurisdiction not just over the whole city, but also the cantonment and the tribal suburbs of the city as far as the entrance to the Khyber pass. At one time, he was involved in cracking a drug-smuggling escapade which centred upon a figure who, he said, was the replica of Al Capone. The Assistant Superintendent of Police, with the unlikely name of Twinberrow, tried to trap 'Al Capone'. Having been tipped off as to the gangster's whereabouts, he persuaded Thompson to dress up as a Pathan and venture into a narrow alley of the city for a secret rendezvous. Thompson accordingly put on baggy trousers over his shorts and let his shirt tails hang out, completing his disguise with a ready-wound turban. Alas, the ruse did not work because the member of the gang who had given the tip-off was only using the appearance of the City Magistrate in the street as an indication to the gangleader that trouble was afoot unless he was given his share of the loot.

On another occasion, when Thompson was dealing with civil offences, he had to deal with a case where justice came not so much through a court of law, but by act of God. Two rich brothers had a loose partnership in business matters. A quarrel arose between them, when one brother obtained a valuable contract in timber from the Wali of Swat; the other brother, however, stole the march by marrying his son to the Wali's daughter, with the result that the Wali transferred the contract to the bride's father-in-law, the brother who had originally been excluded from the deal. The other brother therefore took the case to court and prevailed upon one of Thompson's predecessors to pass an order to 'freeze' all the timber, which consequently piled up in the river at Nowshera. The logs were estimated to be worth £3 million. 'I had indeed seen them on my way to Nathia Gali ferrying my family to and from the hill station. It never occurred to me that it would fall to me to deal with that growing mountain,' said Thompson. It piled up for four years until the action freezing the wood was challenged, by which time Thompson was the District Judge. Upon careful consideration, he was obliged to rule that it was not in his jurisdiction; as the ruler of an independent state, the Wali of Swat's action was a sovereign one and could not be challenged in a British court. But for those whose sympathies were with the outmanoeuvred brother, justice was done, said Thompson, because soon afterwards the entire pile of wood was swept down to the Indus in the greatest flood since records were kept.

Clearly the most serious cases the British had to deal with were the murder trials, and the ultimate responsibility lay with those who became judges and had to pass the death sentence. Some British judges felt that their burden was increased because the local Indian judges were not anxious to pass the death sentence themselves. Thompson's Court Inspector of Police once told him how he had lightheartedly asked a co-villager how his blood feud was going, to which the latter had replied, 'I'm waiting until the Sessions Judge goes on leave,' the implication being that the Sessions Judge would be replaced by an Indian one who he knew would be reluctant to pass the death sentence when he committed the murder. In his early thirties Thompson was in the position of having to pass the death sentence. 'A bit young,' he commented, 'to have the authority to decide whether a man should be hanged.' During this time, he had to try 374 people for murder, of which '191 I had to condemn to die'. (Many years later, writing to the author, he apologised for his bad handwriting, which had deteriorated, he said, from having to write so many court orders. 'No wonder I feel old at 84.')

It had, however, been understood that the Penal Code was quite contradictory to the accepted Pathan code of behaviour. And for cases arising out of a blood feud, disputes about women and those which affected the Pathan's sense of 'honour', cases could be tried under the Frontier Crimes Regulations, which had been in force since the previous century. This allowed the magistrate to withdraw the case and submit it to a jirga, which was allowed to sentence a man for a maximum of fourteen years in prison.

'Once an offence had been committed, a group of local

notables who had been accepted by both sides as arbitrators, albeit sometimes reluctantly, could hear the story from both sides. Then they would confer and say, "So and so will be innocent if he and a number of people swear on the Koran that this is so",' said Robin Latimer. If a large number of people, say two hundred, had to swear, this meant, in fact, the man was guilty; his punishment would be having to bribe so many people to swear to his innocence. 'It was the judgement of Solomon in a way. If people would not swear, then he would have to be sentenced. I don't think that a man was ever pronounced guilty outright.' Olaf Caroe felt that it was very unsatisfactory to have the Frontier Crimes Regulations operating as a supplement to British Indian law. 'It satisfied neither the law nor the custom', which required the satisfaction of the aggrieved party rather than the punishment of the aggressor. Thus, said Caroe, 'it fell between two stools'.

Neighbouring tribal territory always meant that if the offender could flee before the British caught him, he could escape punishment altogether. In order to make tribal territory less of a sanctuary, the British adopted a method of *barampta*. This entailed the seizure of all the members of a particular tribe who happened to be in the settled districts, if offenders of their tribe had disappeared into tribal territory. In general, once the offenders had been returned, the innocent hostages would be released. It meant in a way that the tribe had collective responsibility for the good behaviour of all its members. When Molly Ellis was kidnapped, Lillian Starr noticed that the beds in the mission hospital at Peshawar were swiftly emptied of Afridis, who feared they might be the victims of British retaliation. And as a direct result of the kidnap, the British passed a law threatening punishment on those tribes actually in tribal territory who harboured criminals. It meant that henceforward in order to escape British wrath, an offender would only be safe once he had crossed over into neighbouring Afghanistan.

As the writ of British law was deemed also to run on the roads in tribal territory, it meant that if a man killed his enemy on the road, he would be treated as though the murder had taken place in the settled areas. In the same way, it was possible for a man who had a blood feud to tunnel his way from his tower to the road in order to take the air, much to his enemy's annoyance.

The British political officer spent his life performing his duties either at headquarters or on tour, generally conducting business under a tree. There were always countless people who wished to see him about some grievance or other, and it was part of his duties to be available with a sympathetic ear for the *mulaqatis* or molecats, as Jack Lowis used to refer to the visitors in his diary. People would also journey to see the Deputy Commissioner to ask a favour, the DC generally being credited with power and patronage far greater than he had.

Bribery

'Virtually nobody thought it worthwhile to corrupt a British member of the ICS,' said Herbert Thompson, 'such was the success of Victorian morality when it had abolished John Company's method of rewarding its servants by permitting them to shake the Pagoda tree.' Even so: 'I was one of the rare members ever to be offered an open bribe.' Occasionally when Thompson was working as City Magistrate he used to get away from 'that overworked court' to take some exercise before dark on the golf course. On one occasion a young caddy came to him saying: 'My brother is in your court tomorrow. If you let him off I will give you a golf ball.' 'I asked what the offence was: "Murder".' In fact it was one of those cases where the whole family had been accused by the dead man's family. For safety the police had arrested them all, leaving it to the Magistrate to sort out the real culprit. Having ascertained who the murderer was, Thompson was able to discharge the rest, including the caddy's brother: 'But I never got that golf ball.'

Just because the British were deemed not worth trying to bribe, however, it did not mean that a system of patronage did not operate among the locals, although the Army was considered to be immune. 'One felt its presence everywhere,' as Robin Latimer remarked. A particularly difficult task was awarding contracts for cloth, which was especially hard in the war when cloth was rationed and the cotton was highly priced. As Controller of Civil Supplies in Peshawar, Latimer had to allocate the cotton to the Powindahs who came from Afghanistan. 'One would be approached by highly distinguished Maliks who would say that they had the largest family and should have the largest quota.' So the political officer had to make discreet enquiries to find out whether he was telling the truth and whether his family was as large as he said it was, and then give the quota accordingly. Sometimes the Maliks would be disgruntled, at others, they would offer presents in a discreet way.

> One old man offered to bring me a carpet from Afghanistan. I said, 'No, I can't take that, but you can bring some small item typical of your handicrafts,' which he did on his next visit. The idea was that if you had to accept a present of value, you would hand it over to the Toshekhana—the Treasury—which would assess its value and then, if you really wanted to keep it, you could buy it back at their price.
> If people gave you Christmas presents, such as a basket of fruit, usually you would keep an apple or two and then give the rest to the hospital. Sometimes you'd find some rupees tucked inside the basket, in which case you'd have to make sure they knew you were not going to take the money.

A particularly drastic action was taken, Robin Latimer recalled, by a garrison engineer in Miramshah with the Tochi Scouts. He had a certain amount of dealing with the local people for contracts for mending bridges, and other such jobs. On one occasion he found a note with a thousand rupees inside it and an offer to do a particular job. So he waited until the person who had offered his services was nearby and then made sure that he saw his thousand rupees go up in smoke.

Progress

Both in the settled districts and as far as it was possible in tribal territory, the political officers were anxious to do what they could to improve the economic life of the people. Certainly there was plenty of scope, and imaginative schemes could at least be given a try.

In Hazara, as Deputy Commissioner, Gerald Curtis had under his jurisdiction the people of the Kagan valley.

Thinking of means whereby the people might increase their
income, I lighted on the wasteful way in which bees were
kept. Many hill-houses had a hollow in an outside wall with
a small aperture through which bees could enter. Inside
there was a wooden panel which could be removed. When
it was judged the maximum honey had been collected the
inside panel was taken away; with the aid of smoke the bees
were driven out; and the combs removed.

Curtis soon saw that this method destroyed the swarm and
produced poor quality honey in small quantities, mixed with
pollen and grubs. The European method, with hives, queen
excluders and wax sections, was far more efficient, and Curtis
took a lot of trouble getting the equipment from Britain. His
innovation became so popular that an enthusiastic beekeepers'
society used to meet periodically to exchange experiences. The
experiment worked quite well in spite of the problems of heat,
wasps and hornets, and the honey was produced in larger
quantities than before.

In Hazara Curtis was responsible for setting up a small-scale
silk trade. He discovered that in areas below 6,000 feet, the white
mulberry tree was everywhere. In nearby Kashmir, the state
government, the Durbar, produced silk using the white mulberry as fodder. The cocoons were unravelled and the silk carded
at a village on the borders of Hazara. 'I had no difficulty in
persuading a number of Hazara country folk to try their hand at
this enterprise. The Kashmir Durbar had not attempted to breed
the silk moth and we had to buy eggs—seed was the word
used—from Lyons in France. In due course a consignment of
cardboard boxes, flat and round and looking rather like large
pill-boxes, arrived. Each contained two ounces of seed.' For his
own interest, Gerald Curtis and his wife Decima kept one box,
which started off on a mantelpiece, but eventually had to be
accommodated in the loft stretching 'from one side to the other
of our sizeable house, above the living rooms'. Such was the
appetite of the silk worms that providing the mulberry for them
soon became a strenuous business and the crackle of the chewing
was distinctly audible to visitors. Eventually Curtis had the
cocoons processed, and he received back two skeins of bright
orange silk. 'I had thought of keeping a few cocoons back and of

trying to produce the silk moth myself so as to be able to breed
the eggs. But the outbreak of war meant that there was no more
seed from Lyons . . . There was an industry capable of providing
additional income for the peasantry. I do not believe that it has
since been undertaken.'

In Waziristan, Herbert Emerson had ideas of helping the
Mahsuds with their irrigation schemes; but in order to see what
was necessary, he had first to visit the land, which, in view of the
reputation of the Mahsuds, was generally not considered to be
safe. However, he found that he was offered the hospitality
commensurate with his status. 'At first I was inclined to accept a
substantial meal. But I soon realised that I was eating into their
scanty resources, and I did not feel happy about taking more than
a boiled egg and tea, or something equally simple. The main
point was to come openly as friends, unarmed and unescorted
except by our hosts.' When a Mahsud Mullah heard stories of the
political officer 'sitting on a bed by the roadside in some
dangerous defile, calmly eating boiled eggs,' he went to Emerson
and asked him whether he realised why he had not been
murdered. 'I said I thought the Mahsuds knew by now that I was
trying to help them and that I was perfectly safe in their
company.' They were, as Emerson understood very well, only
too grateful for any improvements which would make barren
dry land more yielding.

But there were frustrations for those who wished to break into
the old established way of doing things. Robin Latimer spent a
short amount of time at Hangu near Kohat.

> There was this sort of dwarf palm, out of which the
> villagers would make rope sandals—it was in much
> demand and valuable. Some local tribesmen would say,
> 'You give me the right to cut and market it, and I'll pay
> the village tax.' The villagers would fall for this—but they
> got a pretty bad bargain out of it, because it would often
> be cut without an eye to future growth just to make a
> profit. I tried to tell them not to give away their rights like
> that, but I never got anywhere. I was only at Hangu for
> six months and so was not able to make any progress in
> persuading them, plus the fact I was a foreigner and they
> were local chaps.

Safety, assassination, kidnap

Not all political officers could trust to the goodness of the tribesmen, like Emerson touring around amongst the Mahsuds. Kidnap and assassination were a feature of Frontier life; and the memories of those killed remained fresh in the minds of their fellow officers. There were the assassinations of Bowring and Harman when Mullah Powindah was at the height of his power. In Bowring's case the Mahsud who shot him was reported to have said afterwards, 'The Sahib went to sleep with his feet pointing towards Mecca and so I shot him.' Harman's murder took place just as he was to be relieved of the double duty, which had devolved on him after Bowring's death, of Political Agent and Commandant of the South Waziristan Militia. The man who was to take over as Political Agent, Evelyn Howell, was actually having dinner with Harman when he was murdered. Harman, he said, 'received a bayonet wound right through the heart, and only his wonderful strength and courage enabled him to retain consciousness so long as he did.'

Another officer, Major Dodd, was shot while having a drink on his verandah after a game of tennis. His assassin used the rifle which had been given to him as a present by Dodd: the reason for this apparent lack of gratitude was that Dodd had refused him a favour, and he felt he had lost face with his tribe.

Yet another brutal act of murder happened near Bannu when the District Officer of the Frontier Constabulary, Keith Wagstaffe, decided to lay on an exercise to test their arrangements for closing the routes of escape for fugitives. Geoff Morgan was to assist in the operation by laying a paper trail, and he and his orderly plunged into a sugar cane field to lay a diversion. Unfortunately he met a gang of outlaws who were lying in wait with the intention of raiding the cantonment. They murdered both Morgan and his orderly. In punishment for this unwarranted killing, the British not only chased and killed the gang of outlaws—'of set purpose we took no prisoners,' said Alastair Low, the Deputy Commissioner at the time—but they also had to punish those in whose field the outlaws had been hiding, since they were deemed to have afforded them protection. The village had two or three small towers, Low said; and for a village to be allowed them was a mark of trust by the British on the understanding that the inhabitants of the village would resist outlaws, which they clearly had not done. So the villagers were ordered to destroy the towers themselves or the British would do so. 'In point of fact they got busy with picks and mattocks and the towers were levelled by the villagers themselves within a few hours. We also laid waste the cane field. I could wish to have done this more spectacularly with a bulldozer, but the Brigade did not have one available so the Frontier Constabulary did it by hand. It was the only piece of old-fashioned "laying waste" in which I was personally concerned.'

Patrick Duncan, one of the few British political officers who stayed on the Frontier after independence, was shot by a Mahsud whose pride got the better of him at a jirga. Duncan did not deal with his request at once as he was busy talking to other Maliks, and the tribesman, feeling insulted by this apparent dismissal, shot him. No sooner had Duncan been killed than another Mahsud, Duncan's orderly, avenged his death by killing the murderer. In so doing he incurred a blood feud and therefore had to leave his village. The Mahsuds were so distressed by the murder of Duncan that they collected together a sum of money for his widow, which in their tradition was 'blood money'.

In general such acts of assassination were unpredictable and hard to prevent. But to make sure that there was no sniping at a political officer on tour, he travelled with his bodyguard, his *badragga*. A Pathan, Lieutenant-Colonel Muhammad Yusuf, saw the usefulness of putting the blood feud to work in favour of the British. 'One man from each tribe was chosen to form an escort in a circle with the political officer in the middle. So if a would-be assassin tried to attack the political officer, he might be likely to miss and hit a tribesman of another tribe and thereby incur a blood feud.' But the badragga could fail. Captain Roy Beatty, the APA in North Waziristan, was killed along with his entire escort when he went out to pay the Khassadars.

In times of particular unrest amongst the tribes, the political officer would travel in an armoured lorry. 'It was comforting to have steel plate between the world and oneself when sniping started,' remarked Gerald Curtis, 'and I used to chuckle at the curses of the Mahsuds [his badragga] on the roof who had not this amenity. It was after all their kinsmen who were shooting.'

The badragga was also intended to protect the political officer in the event of an attempted kidnap. In the case of J. O. S. (Jos) Donald, the Political Agent in South Waziristan in 1946, it did not do so. According to Robin Hodson, the Assistant Political Agent at the time, Jos Donald was kidnapped because an influential Shabi Khel Malik was affronted at not being awarded the cloth contract and instigated a sub-section of his tribe, the Bromi Khel, to kidnap the Political Agent. 'The road was blocked and the tyres of his lorry were shot out. His badraggas proved themselves incapable of resistance.' When they discovered where he was being kept, food, blankets and whisky were sent to Donald and as many members of the Shabi Khels as possible were arrested. After ten days he was released on payment of a large ransom.

Such an action could not, however, go unpunished, and the original plan was that Shabi Khel country should be bombed if the ransom was not paid, whilst the Shabi Khel insisted that it was a matter for all the Mahsuds, especially since others had the benefits derived from the contract. In the end, the government of India agreed that the whole tribe should be held responsible. Donald, who had returned from leave after the ordeal of the kidnap, succeeded in securing the agreement of the tribes that the money should be returned. Soon afterwards, towards the end of September, Hodson went to Tank on routine business,

> . . . and found that Donald was in a very depressed and despondent state of mind in spite of his apparent success in settling the fines. Just as I was about to leave for Wana the next day after we had breakfasted together, hearing a pistol shot, I found that poor Donald had shot himself. He left a note saying, 'I have lived a lie. I have failed my duty.' I interpreted that to mean that as head of the Agency he had been paying out allowances to Maliks and pay to Khassadars only to find that they could plot against him and desert their posts at the drop of a hat. The badragga system had failed and all that we had striven for was in vain.

The death of Jos Donald shocked many of his fellow officers. It was a sign that the strains of Frontier life could sometimes take their toll.

Another hazard for the British was illness. In spite of

improved medical facilities from the previous century, malaria and typhoid in particular could plague an officer's career. Thompson suffered severely from typhoid: he had drunk tea which had been stewed but not boiled. 'It would,' he said, 'have been an insult to refuse to drink it.' Whereas the British could normally eat their own food at base, on tour they would eat what was provided for them: generally rice pilau, chicken and goat. 'Often you might accept to eat in the house of a tribesman to the detriment of your health; you'd be offered just a cup of tea and then be confronted with an enormous spread of food, and see someone peeling an egg with his dirty fingers,' Robin Latimer commented.

John Prendergast got chronic malaria in Waziristan which stayed with him for fifteen years. 'Sleeping out in what one wore, being on a light-scale set-a-thief-to-catch-a-thief expedition, one was a ready prey for the mosquito.' If all else failed to bring death or discomfort to the British there were the natural hazards. Gerald Curtis nearly met his end when a buffalo bull came charging towards him. 'Obviously it had not smelt European before and did not like it.' He was saved by a tiny herdsman, who 'could have run under the animal's belly without bending. With a stick and a volley of oaths he put the snorting beast to flight.'

Sport

'Every effort was made to play games.' It was generally reckoned that the harder the soldiers trained and played the more contented they would be, especially in time of peace. If the officers played with the men it would be hockey or football, if not squash or tennis—games also shared and enjoyed by the political officers. John Prendergast found that 'the subject of hockey dominated nearly all conversation *ad nauseam*'. The rivalry was so intense that each side spied upon its opponents in order to work up counter-measures. For some, one of the attractions of life in the Army was the opportunity for sport, which included polo, big game hunting, pig-sticking and shooting.

Whereas the Pathans had an outlet for their energies 'in their vigorous, whirling, Dervish-like sword dances', the Hindus and

Sikhs preferred organised wrestling. It also amused the British officers to introduce the tribesmen to their European sports. On one occasion Lowis was travelling with his bodyguard—a fairly large escort—'which made a gay party—anything from say fifteen to thirty cheerful tribesmen armed to the teeth, and many with flowers behind their ears; with a good proportion sitting and singing songs on the roof of the lorry, they made almost a carnival progress.' Thinking the men needed to take a break and have some exercise, Lowis suggested a game of soccer. They all climbed down from the lorry roof and began to kick the ball around. They didn't know the rules, said Lowis, but it didn't seem to matter.

There was little doubt, however, that shooting was the king of sports; and the duck shoot in Swat was a favourite for everyone from the Wali and the Governor down. Ayub Awan, who served on the Frontier in the police force, enjoyed it as much as anyone. 'We left the Wali's palace very early in the morning when it was still dark and reached the vicinity of the lake within half an hour. It isn't really a lake but an extension of the Swat river, where rice was sprinkled through the year as feed for the birds.' Already the honking and cackle of about ten thousand ducks of all kinds was audible. As it got light, the 'sight which now greets the unaccustomed eye is breathtaking. You stand in the middle of an extensive expanse of water; yonder lies the thin line of the river and, far into the distance, the blue hills. The pale sky, with small patches of cloud here and there, is filled with birds, and as each butt blazes away, the ducks are all over.'

If it was not duck shooting, the British could equally well enjoy the Peshawar Vale hunt, which hunted not the fox but the jackal. In the nineteenth century Sir Robert Warburton found that hunting the wily jackal during the cold season afforded 'excellent sport'. But it also caused a certain amount of amusement to the local people. 'We looked forward eagerly to the hunting season which was for only two or three months of the cold weather and only once a week on Sundays,' said Ayub Awan. The hounds, which were imported from England, were given 'enormous quantities of exotic foods and otherwise pampered' to keep them in good health and humour. On the day of the hunt they were taken in closed motor vans a few miles out of Peshawar. 'Imagine a hundred well-fed sturdy beasts who had been waiting for this picnic for the whole week!'

The huntsmen galloped across fields, flew over hedges, jumped ditches and waded through canals; some even parted company with their mounts. 'Tally ho, they cried, Tally ho! whatever that may mean . . . The local Pathan,' Awan said, 'is a sporting kind of chap at the worst of times, and a hilarious occasion like this was a Godsend for him. So he unhitched his tonga pony; thus suitably mounted he also joined in the fun, using all his Pashtu invective in detriment equally of the hunted and the hunters, the feringhee and all their forefathers put together.'

More upsetting to the Master of the Hounds than the occasional intrusion by Pathans was the behaviour of the Royal Air Force, whose officers, lacking the precision of the cavalrymen, totally lost control of their horses. 'In our case,' confessed Wing-Commander James, 'the order of the field was the jackal first, closely pursued by the Air Force contingent, then came the hounds and the well-ordered rest of the hunt.'

To catch a Faqir

They sought him here, they sought him there
Those columns sought him everywhere!

The main 'opponent' of the British on the Frontier between the two World Wars was the Scarlet Pimpernel of Waziristan—an unknown priest from the small town of Ipi. Like the Mullah Powindah twenty years before him, he declared a holy war against the British and succeeded in eluding capture by hiding out in caves in Waziristan. He tested the endurance of the Politicals, Scouts, Army and Air Force alike; at one time or another, they were all involved in the attempt to catch the Faqir.

He had first started causing trouble in the mid-thirties in what came to be known as the Islam Bibi case: a young Hindu girl was abducted by a Muslim and converted to Islam. The case went to court and the ruling went in favour of the Hindu; but sentiment was on the side of the Muslim. The first hostile demonstration was led by the Faqir of Ipi, at that time an obscure holy man whom the British could not have expected to rise to such notoriety. But after he and his following of no more than a thousand men started making large-scale attacks on troops, destroying bridges and cutting down telephone wires, military action was seen as the only solution.

A major operation of Scouts and Army was mounted 'to sniff him out' with the help of the Air Force. 'There's a ruddy war on but you'll have got it from the BBC before this is posted,' Jack Lowis wrote to his sister in November 1936. 'It looks like a big show and I'm afraid the Mahsuds of the Shaktu valley are sure to join in'. As it happened, the fear of war abated temporarily. In January 1937 Lowis wrote: 'The Faqir is still at large, though he has been completely inactive for some time as he is ill (with pneumonia). Military opinion, of course, is that he should be hounded and hunted, but then they either don't realise or don't believe that the hunting of Faqirs merely prolongs and enlarges the war and never by any chance results in the capture of the Faqir'. John Prendergast recalled how on one occasion the Tochi Scouts synchronised an expedition with the South Waziristan Scouts to catch him. 'We found the ashes of his fire still warm in a cave, but he had flown. Our informer, as usual, had informed both ways'.

As with any operation against the tribes, the British could not expect to escape without casualties, and a political officer travelling with the Army could equally well be a victim. At the same time the operation was a jaunt out which, providing all went well, most men would enjoy. 'This war may go on for some time,' Lowis informed his sister in May 1937, 'and unless I blot my copybook I have every hope and intention of being with the column. I shall always be with the Brigade or Force HQ which is always the safest place, so kindly accept the situation in the same airy way that we always used to and rid your mind of anything but a sense of satisfaction that I'm having fun.' It was, perhaps, only natural that Lowis should write to his sister in such terms. She was, after all, Mrs Godfrey Meynell whose husband had been killed fighting the Mohmands two years previously with Goff Hamilton.

Finally, with three brigades and strong Scout support, the expedition set off, 'to smell out the Faqir who, of course will have left before we get there'. But this time the weather intervened, preventing the attack.

It was the worst hailstorm I've ever seen. Some of the stones were an inch in diameter—as big as walnuts—and it lasted twice as long as the usual spring storm. All the mules, camels and horses with the brigades stampeded, and most of the tents were flooded. In a show like this all tents are dug down about three feet as a protection against sniping so you can imagine the scene and the sort of witches' cauldron that the tents were reduced to. We were lucky in ours, no mainstream came through to us and except for general dampness we are OK but many of the men and a lot of their stuff completely washed away, and all of it soaked. A lot of the supplies have been soaked and become unserviceable and what with one thing and another the war has been postponed for a day.

The objective was to bomb the caves—'difficult and dangerous of access'—in which the Faqir had made his headquarters at Arsal Kot in the Shaktu valley. But, as Lewis pointed out, 'blowing up a cave is apparently a difficult job. Your best efforts are apt merely to enlarge it to the subsequent satisfaction of the owner. However, they made a really good job of it and collapsed the cliff and roofs on top of the lot of them.' In his diary he noted: 'Arsal Kot in ruins as result of aerial bombardment but some houses standing. By the end of day whole place levelled'. Insofar as the caves were concerned, 'We were all full of glamorous stories about the huge lashkars they had housed' during recent months, but they turned out to be 'disappointing little warrens'. Lewis went into the Vicarage—as the Faqir's cave was called—and took a sackful of papers back which 'didn't prove to be of much use'.

As was to be expected, the Faqir himself had already escaped in good time, 'very good time, judging from the hungry condition of the fleas,' Lewis commented. 'That evening it would not have been possible to affix a postage stamp to any part of my body without covering a bite. And they remained with me for the next thirty-six hours, fortunately in decreasing numbers.' Lewis did not take much interest in the rest of the operation as he had caught a chill. 'In fact I was asleep under a bush for most of it.'

The Faqir remained at large for several years. From Arsal Kot he went to Gorwekht, near the Afghan border, where his activities worried the British during the Second World War. He died a natural death in 1960. Whoever wrote his obituary for *The Times* genially overlooked the irritation he had caused his pursuers, describing him as 'a doughty and honourable opponent . . . a man of principle and saintliness . . . a redoubtable orga- niser of tribal warfare'. Later commentators, such as Milan Hauner, have been less sympathetic. 'As a guerrilla leader he was uncompromising, unyielding, obstinate and unscrupulous in the choice of combat methods against his opponents. These included the traditional methods of tribal warfare such as ambush, kidnap- ping and mutilation.' Not surprisingly perhaps, the Faqir's son is now believed to be fighting the Russians.

Men of God

From one year to the next, the work of the missionary was continual and never ending. There was the same vigour and dedication, no matter what might befall the military in battle, or the political in administration. The missionary's aim was still to teach and heal, whatever the cost. And by going to the Frontier, the missionaries knew that they were going to work amongst a people who were as entrenched as always against the 'infidel'. One aspect of their work had however changed since the close of the nineteenth century. With the drawing of the Durand line, their activities in Afghanistan were curtailed. Any Christian who ventured into Afghanistan to make converts did so at the risk of losing his own life.

The names of the missionaries who dedicated their lives to work on the Frontier became almost synonymous with the hospitals where they worked: Vernon Starr in Peshawar; the three ladies at Tank; Pennell in Bannu; Holland in Quetta, which although in Baluchistan would still expect to treat the sick of the North-West Frontier tribes. Sir Henry Holland was rather unusual in that not only did his active influence last for the best part of fifty years, but his work was carried on by his two sons, Harry and Ronald, for another twenty years.

Henry Holland came to Quetta in 1900 as a young man whose ideal had at one time been a private practice somewhere near a trout stream, and when the practice increased, 'a day or two with the local pack of hounds.' But once he had taken the decision to devote his life to God as a doctor rather than going straight into the Church, he had to go where he was told there was a need. 'It was all rather breathtaking. Quetta—I had never even heard of the place! I had hoped that if I should be passed fit to go abroad I might go out to Nigeria.' Nigeria, he thought, was a place with no social distractions. 'I knew how much the world and its pleasures attracted me and thought that there I should be safe.' In general the mission stations were near to a military garrison and Holland found himself part of a large British community made up of army officers and their families. However, 'though the British community as a whole were most friendly and hospitable, few showed any interest in active Christian work'. At twenty-five Holland had had little practical experience of medicine. 'The Latin proverb *experientia docet* [experience teaches] is certainly true of all forms of surgery.' In Quetta he found he was up against the difficulty of giving effective care to patients who had to travel long distances. 'In those days the only means of transport was the horse, camel or donkey. For Afghan patients travelling on foot or by camel it meant a month's journey to reach our hospital.' There was still the battle against time and lack of materials, as well as suspicion of being treated by missionaries who were infidels. But Holland found that as confidence grew in the hospital, more and more patients came to them for help, which they often preferred to the civil and military hospitals.

> But it was obvious that we were touching a mere fraction of the need. Whereas people in contact with the life of the towns would use our hospital freely, it was only occasionally that patients from the far outlying villages would come in for treatment. They had great confidence in their village *hakims*, and in those early days only came to us if their native doctors had failed in their treatment, or if they had been advised to come to us for major surgery.

All over the Frontier, this imbalance was partially altered by treks into the countryside and the setting up of village dispensaries. Holland found that blindness through cataracts was one of the most common ailments. 'Glare and heat, dust and flies, together with vitamin deficiency in diet and calcium excess in water, are all contributory factors.' As this was something that could be combated, Quetta became famous for curing the blind, and Holland as the doctor who did it.

The missionary movement, however, had its setbacks, for the life was a dangerous one. Pennell, who dedicated twenty years of his life 'among the wild tribes of the Afghan Frontier' died in 1912 of septicaemia caught from his assistant, who also died. Whereas the patient they were treating recovered, the hospital at Bannu was left deprived of its guiding force. At the hospital in Peshawar, Vernon Harold Starr was murdered in 1917 by a tribesman. One night, hearing a knock at his door, he assumed that it must be a patient in trouble who had come to see him. But instead Starr was stabbed. The motive was never known, although it was believed that the man had a son who had become interested in Christianity. Having reputedly starved his son to death, the man then supposedly took his revenge upon the doctor in whose hospital his son had come into contact with Christian ideas. Starr's wife, Lillian, did not let this tragic incident upset her own work as a nurse in Peshawar, where she remained for many years.

But the greatest disaster for mission work in Quetta came in 1935. 'There was no more mission hospital, because there was no more Quetta,' said Henry Holland's son Harry, who, hiding under his bed during one of the worst earthquakes on record, managed to escape unscathed amidst the 20,000 dead, 15,000 wounded, 10,000 homeless. Henry Holland himself was saved by the bathroom door and a huge cupboard which prevented the beams of the ceiling from falling on him and crushing him to death. His injuries, however, were sufficient to keep him in hospital for a few days.

> When I was extracted from the ruins of my bungalow and taken to the military hospital, I discovered that I was minus dentures, spectacles and a pipe. It is interesting that quite a considerable item of expenditure under relief work was that of supplying dentures to those who had been buried and rescued! I was more fortunate. I sent my bearer to search in what had been my bathroom in the hope that he might find somewhere under the rubble a tin mug containing what

were extremely valuable to me—my dentures. Within two or three hours, he came back, triumphantly bearing them in his hand.

The work of rebuilding not just the mission hospital, but the whole of Quetta, took five years. In the spring of 1940 the main block of a brand-new mission hospital was opened.

The tradition of the old hospital was carried on into the new. We had become known to thousands on both sides of the Afghan border. It was no longer a question of trying to induce patients to come to us; the difficulty was to find room for them all! Such was the change which had come over the attitude of the tribes of Baluchistan and the Frontier.

The name of Sir Henry Holland—as he came to be in recognition for his work in the Quetta earthquake—was famous throughout the Frontier. On one occasion he was called to treat the Wali of Swat, who was nearly blind from cataracts. 'The first Christian prayer ever heard in the palace preceded the operation,' said Holland. He also went to Kabul to treat the King of Afghanistan.

In general the missionaries could travel with much less fear for their safety than their counterparts in the political and military. A doctor was greatly respected as a healer and would be welcomed in the remotest of villages, in spite of the suspicion which modern medicine aroused. Holland was very disappointed when, following a severe typhoid epidemic in Quetta, hardly anyone was prepared to come forward for the injections which were to be given free of charge.

But insofar as conversion was concerned, the welcome accorded to the missionary was quite different. It had not been easy to make converts in the nineteenth century and it was certainly no easier in the twentieth. If one or two people did show a desire to convert to Christianity, they would generally be ostracised and disowned by their families. It was not uncommon for the convert to be threatened with death at the hands of his own family.

Holland was greatly impressed by a man called Abdul Karim,

the son of a leading Pathan judge in Quetta, who openly professed the Christian faith. But once he had done so, all channels of work were closed to him, and the only job he could get was in the mission hospital as an evangelist. Holland became friends with Karim, and for three years learnt Pashtu with him. But once inspired with 'the word of God', Karim was anxious to spread it further afield—to Afghanistan, in spite of the knowledge that few Christians had journeyed to Afghanistan and returned alive. Holland tried to dissuade his friend from going, but one morning in 1906 Karim was no longer to be found. It was not until thirty years later that Holland found out what had happened to him from a report of a British secret agent who had visited Kabul. 'I saw Abdul Karim with my own eyes. He had a chain round his neck weighing some seventy pounds, fetters round his feet and handcuffs on his wrists; he had a bridle in his mouth.' Karim was released from prison but was apparently seized by the angry crowds; they offered him his life if he would recant; when he refused one arm was struck off, then another, finally his head. 'How often I have thought,' said Holland, 'would I have been prepared to face martyrdom at the hands of the Afghan mob in Kabul, as he did?' And on the Frontier, his son Harry also had to learn that one of the converts he had been close to was similarly hounded by his family to make him recant. They tied a grenade to him threatening to pull the pin out if he did not recant. 'He said he wouldn't, and so they did'.

As the decade of the thirties reached its end, it was clear that a great and sweeping change was in store which would affect the lives of political, military and missionary alike. For the first time in a long while the people of the North-West Frontier were to be ruled by their co-religionists. And perhaps paradoxically, of all the assorted British on the Frontier, only the missionaries stayed on for any length of time, adapting their role as the situation demanded.

CHAPTER SIX

Women with Different Frontiers

I feel that my life has been greatly enriched by my contact with people who are so different and yet still of the same species.

Alison Fookes, Pennell Memorial Hospital 1982

The presence of European women on the Frontier has brought out the stark contrasts between Western and Eastern custom. A sophisticated Western woman, used to the liberties of the times, and an illiterate tribal woman live in different worlds. Whereas men of different race could always meet on the field of battle, there was very little that a Western woman would appear to have in common with her tribal counterparts.

Even so, they are both members of the 'weaker' sex: when the British wives went out to join their husbands in the days of Empire, they, like the tribal women, shared second place in the lives of their menfolk. In the case of the Western women, it was not supposed to have anything to do with status as such; rather it arose because they would inevitably follow their husbands, according to the dictates of his career. Whatever love the man had for his wife, whatever support she provided, the conventional view was that his career came first: what was supposed to fire his enthusiasm was doing his duty for the Empire. Likewise the tribesman's main preoccupation was, and still is, in maintaining his honour. Only when a woman has directly threatened that very reason for his existence does she become the focal point of his attention. Otherwise she is essentially part of his property—an acquisition along with his cattle and other worldly goods.

Memsahib

On account of the dangers of life on the Frontier, men stationed there spent more time away from their wives and families than those elsewhere in India. Female presence was welcomed in those areas like the towns of Peshawar and Kohat which were considered comparatively safe. The introduction of the wives and children to Kabul in 1840 was a sign that the British, for the time being at any rate, were there to stay.

No women before or since could, however, have expected to undergo the ordeal of the retreat and the long months as hostages in the hands of Akbar Khan, the son of Dost Muhammad. Lady Sale's description of her own plight and that of her fellow women indicated the presence of all the sterling qualities which were supposed to be found in the British Memsahib. On the retreat from Kabul the ladies travelled in *kajavas* (camel panniers) and found themselves mixed up with the baggage and the column, with the result that they too became the objects of the Afghans' gunfire. In the Khurd Kabul pass where the army suffered so dreadfully, Lady Sale witnessed what happened to another of the ladies.

> Meeting with a pony laden with treasure, Mrs Mainwaring endeavoured to mount and sit on the boxes but they upset, and in the hurry the pony and treasure were left behind and the unfortunate lady pursued her way on foot until after a time an Afghan asked her if she was wounded and told her to mount behind him. This apparently kind offer she declined, being fearful of treachery, alleging as an excuse that she could not sit behind him on account of the difficulty of holding her child when so mounted. This man shortly after snatched her shawl off her shoulders and left her to her fate. Mrs Mainwaring's sufferings were great and she deserves much credit for having preserved her child through those dreadful scenes. She not only had to walk a considerable distance with her child in her arms through deep snow, but had also to pick her way over the bodies of the dead, dying and wounded, both men and cattle, and constantly to cross streams of water wet up to the knees, pushed and shoved about by men and animals, the enemy keeping up a sharp fire, and several persons being killed

close to her. She, however, got safely to camp with her child but had no opportunity to change her clothes; and I know from experience that it was many days ere my wet habit became thawed and can fully appreciate her discomforts.

Others were less fortunate even than Mrs Mainwaring. Mrs Anderson's four-year-old daughter was carried off in the confusion by Afghans, to be offered for sale in the bazaar back in Kabul. When eventually after several months the little girl was returned, she could still understand English, but could speak only Persian, particularly the phrase: 'My father and mother are infidels, and I am a Mussulman.'

By the time the women and children were surrendered as hostages to Akbar Khan, hardly any of them had a single possession left. During their captivity the women were obliged to make the most of the opportunities afforded them. 'We luxuriated in dressing, although we had no clothes but those on our backs,' wrote Lady Sale, 'but we enjoyed washing our faces very much, having had but one opportunity of doing so before, since we left Kabul. It was a rather painful process, as the cold and the glare of the sun on the snow had three times peeled my face, from which the skin came off in strips.' In spite of being transferred from one place to another, and exposed to heat, cold and rain, Lady Sale was not prepared to complain about the treatment they received from Akbar: 'Honour has been respected. It is true that we have not common comforts, but what we denominate such are unknown to Afghan females; they always sleep on the floor, sit on the floor,' which she said were hardships to Europeans. 'We slept large and small, thirty-four in a room fifteen feet by twelve feet and we lay on the floor, literally packed together, with a wood fire in the centre and using pine torches for candles,' she noted after one day's march to a new hiding place.

Lady Sale, for one, preferred to walk rather than be 'packed into a kajava' or forced to ride 'even without side or any saddles'. Suffering from fever, on one occasion she was obliged to accept the space offered to her by another of the women in the camel pannier; being rather tall she found 'the greatest difficulty in doubling my long legs into the prescribed compass'. She also complained about the lice and fleas, referring to the one as 'infantry' and the other as 'cavalry'.

It was and is very disagreeable but still we are *de facto* prisoners; notwithstanding Akbar still persists in calling us 'honoured guests'; and, as captives, I say we are well treated. He has given us common coarse chintz, and coarse long cloth too, wherewith to clothe ourselves . . . making garments has given us occupation, increased by having to work with raw cotton which we have to twist into thread for ourselves.

Lady Sale was even allowed to celebrate her wedding anniversary 'by dining with the ladies of Muhammad Shah Khan's family'— the father-in-law of Akbar. 'It was an extremely stupid visit. They were, generally speaking, inclined to *embonpoint*, largely formed and coarsely featured; their dress inelegant and of the coarsest of materials,' she wrote, displaying a degree of contempt for the Afghan women. After a time, 'an extremely dirty cloth' was spread over the coarse felt carpet on the floor; dishes of pilau, sweet and sour curds were produced. 'Those who had not taken a spoon with them ate with their fingers, Afghan fashion; an accomplishment in which I am by no means *au fait*. We drank water out of a tea pot.'

One woman, Mrs Wade, the wife of a sergeant, forsook her husband and went to live with an Afghan, earning for herself the title of 'an incorrect personage' from Lady Sale. 'She changed her attire, threw off the European dress and adopted the costume of the Mussulmans', professing to have changed her creed as well. Another—a Persian woman married to Sergeant Deane—was taken by force and married to a younger brother of Muhammad Shah Khan. 'Whenever this man enters her presence, she salutes him with her slipper.'

The imprisonment which the twelve women and twenty-two children were obliged to suffer from January until their release in September was as unique in British experience as had been the annihilation of the Army. When Lady Sale was finally reunited with her husband, who arrived in Kabul at the head of his brigade, she wrote with almost more emotion than she had done throughout their entire period of captivity: 'It is impossible to express our feelings on Sale's approach—to my daughter and myself happiness so long delayed as to be almost unexpected, was actually painful and accompanied by a choking sensation which could not obtain the relief of tears.'

* * *

In time of peace—and generally women were only allowed to be with their husbands when there was peace—the life of the Memsahib was taken up with the day-to-day duties of running the household, wherever the Sahib might be based. And in order to help her, every housewife could make use of the information contained in *Every Memsahib's Daily Account Book*. In the front of the book would appear bits of useful information that every proper Memsahib should know. Since by the twentieth century steady communication with Britain was an accepted and essential part of their lives, there was information about the post, parcels and telegrams. There was also a list of Indian weights and English ones: for instance for dry weights the housewife, who might only ever have heard of pounds and ounces, would now have to learn that five *tolas* was one *chittak*, which equalled two ounces; four *chittaks* was one *powah*, which equalled eight ounces.

She would also need to learn some elementary Urdu and so there was a whole list of household vocabulary with all the vegetables, cooking instructions in roman Urdu (as opposed to the arabic script). Thus they managed to pick up some 'kitchen' Urdu. For the housewife who was not used to hot climates, there was a list of hints on how to keep things clean and fresh: for example, covering cheese with a cloth dipped in vinegar kept it fresh. And so that she would not have to worry herself unduly about arithmetic, there was a ready reckoner on what to pay the servants, depending on the number of days in the month.

On the supposition that women's health was fragile in the hot summer months, it was anticipated that they would retire to the hills with the children, either to Simla or Nathia Gali. They were known as grass widows since their husbands remained in the plains. It was something, however, which Herbert Thompson, in the 1930s, resisted.

> There was no question of my wife going to the hills on her own, for she knew nobody to go to and was not going to live amongst strangers. Incidentally, by braving the hot weather that year she was only anticipating the lesson which fourteen years later the Second Great War was to teach white women: that they were as capable as their husbands of enduring the hot weather of the North, whatever the desirability of giving children the relief of the Hills.

During the War, indeed, many of the women were able to relieve a certain amount of boredom by working in offices and hospitals.

The families of the British were generally of great interest to the local people. Gerald Curtis had four sons, and when he went to Waziristan, he found that the Mahsuds were very impressed by his achievement: '"*Tsaloor Zamin, Tsaloor Toopakoon*"—Four sons, Four rifles. I remember an old Mahsud Malik saying, "You will be a powerful man in your own country."' Herbert Thompson was the only political officer on the Frontier to have twin girls. Apart from causing a great deal of fascination amongst the ayahs—the nannies—it also nearly caused a 'strike' since they insisted that each baby should have its separate ayah. But in general, the birth of a girl was not greeted with much enthusiasm. One woman found that 'the news that our third child was a girl—we have two boys already—was received practically with condolences in the hospital, certainly not congratulations!'

Occasionally an important female visitor would come to the Frontier, accompanying her husband, as did Lady Reading, the Vicereine in 1921. While His Excellency, the Viceroy, would be out on official duties or tiger shooting, she would occupy herself in charitable works, visiting the sick at the hospitals, gaining vicarious pleasure in his activities at the end of the day: 'HE had a wonderful time walking and riding, climbing and motoring and visiting all sorts of strange tribes and peoples.'

At the same time there was the chance to do some shopping. Lady Reading found little of interest—shoes, coloured scarves, china, 'all hideous—the only nice things are the carpets which the caravans bring in from over the Frontier'; but by the time they reached her in Peshawar, she believed they were too expensive. To her delight she found out that the caravans brought the rugs to 'a kind of stable or "caravanserai"', before selling them in Peshawar—'so I sent an aide with a pocket handkerchief to his nose and disinfectant on, to buy me some rugs first hand, and he returned with eleven lovely rugs,' she wrote home, noting with a certain amount of surprise that he had not developed smallpox or typhoid as yet. 'The dirt everywhere is indescribable, and the smells.'

In general the lives of the British women on the Frontier, with their tea parties and tennis matches, were cocooned from those of the tribal women, unless they made a particular effort. They could either visit them in their quarters or do voluntary work in the hospital. At times they found the visits to the homes of the richer women rather tedious since they shared no language in common. Lady Dring remembered having to admire quantities of sarees and bangles on such visits. Since the European ladies could also visit the quarters of the men, they could see how both sides lived. Lady Dring noticed how much shabbier were the quarters of the women than those of the men; she also saw the left-overs of the meal she had just shared with the men being brought in for the women to consume.

The comparative freedom of Western women was often viewed with disfavour by the local people, especially the Mullahs, as Gerald Curtis noted on one occasion.

> Summer seemed to inspire the eloquence of the Mullah of Baffa, a small mud-built market town on the banks of the Swat river in the Mansehra tahsil. He always made it plain in his Friday sermons that he took exception to the country being ruled by unbelieving foreigners. One Friday in June 1939 he made a particular scurrilous attack on European women whose 'unchaste and evil example was a crying scandal and a source of danger to all true believers'.

Gerald Curtis said that he had no idea what occasioned this 'anti-feminist outburst'. The only lady the Mullah might have seen was Drusilla Scott, the wife of Ian Scott, the Assistant Commissioner at Mansehra. 'She was a modest and scholarly lady as became the daughter of a Master of Balliol. Nor could he fairly accuse the wives of the British officers of the Gurkhas at Abbottabad of bad behaviour. They lived quietly, looking after their children and playing tennis at the Club. There was never a breath of scandal about them.' This particular outburst led to a riot and 'sore heads in Baffa': the Mullah lost a handful of his beard. The only inconvenience to Curtis as the Deputy Commissioner was that he was obliged to interrupt his trout fishing in the Kagan valley to deal with the trouble.

The mixed marriage

Love affairs between Pathan women and British officers could be fairly common; marriage was less so, mainly on account of the differences of race and religion. But they did happen, and for those who were smitten with the beauty and oriental attraction of a Pathan woman, there were several examples to go by. Sir Robert Warburton's father—one ot the hostages in 1842—was married to a niece of Dost Muhammad; he himself was born during their captivity in a fort.

There was also the successful and happy union between Lieutenant-Colonel Thomas Maughan, of the Bombay army, and Mermanjan. Early in 1849 Maughan was with his regiment in pursuit of the Sikh and Afghan forces during the second Sikh war. 'The former being hotly pressed, surrendered en masse,' whilst the Afghans escaped to Kabul through the Khyber pass, 'at the foot of which our Brigades assembled.'

> At this time I met one evening when riding, my own dear wife. She was then about sixteen and her national costume, in many respects much resembling the Albanian, set off to advantage as sweet a face and figure as I thought I had ever seen. She was mounted on a spirited black horse which she managed with ease and confidence, and was escorted by men who appeared to be her relatives. Love at first sight, a strong lasting never swerving devotion became our destiny from that moment.

Maughan found out that Mermanjan was of the 'best blood of the Frontier'. But there was no possibility of getting married according to the rites of the Christian Church: to do so would have meant death at the hands of her relations. So they were united 'by a simple but most solemn contract at least as solemn and perhaps as morally binding as a marriage after the set formula of the Protestant Church'. When Maughan had to return to India, Mermanjan followed him on her 'trusty black horse'. Eventually she accompanied him to England where they made their home.

Maughan was pleased to note that he found in Mermanjan 'affectionate attachment uncommon amongst English women'. She was hospitable, generous and had exquisite taste; she was also tolerant of all creeds and 'her mind was quite at ease as to our union, which in fact no Archbishop could have strengthened . . . Such then was my Afghan wife—in accordance with the custom of her race she preferred the seclusion considered by the higher orders indispensable to a woman after marriage.' By this he meant *purdah*. After several years they were married according to the Church of England ceremony—the intention being to give Mermanjan full protection in the event of Maughan's death. This precaution served her in good stead; he died in 1861, she in 1917.

Marriages between Pathan men and British women often arose if the man had been studying abroad in Britain, but in such circumstances when the woman was obliged to go to his home and live according to his customs and traditions, disillusionment could set in. During his time as a judge on the Frontier, Herbert Thompson knew a young Pathan barrister who 'had married a pretty blonde shop-girl when reading for the Bar in London and they had made a success of a marriage which so often resulted in tragedy when the girl came out to the India of her dreams but found that village life had racial problems rather than princely Rolls-Royces.'

The poor, the rich, and the unfaithful

With his Victorian outlook on life, Dr Theodore Pennell described the women of the Frontier as being regarded 'as very distinctly existing for the requirements of the stronger sex.' The wife has to grind the corn, fetch the water, cook the food, tend the children, keep the house clean. But she is not allowed to shop, not even for her own clothes. 'The lady must be content with his selection and make up her dresses at home with what her lord is pleased to bring her. How would their sisters in England approve of that?'

Lady Sale gave one of the first pictures of the Afghan women from a Western woman's viewpoint. Their form of dress, she said, resembled a:

> common night-dress; and has tacked onto it coins, or other pieces of silver or gold, such as crescents, etc. all over the sleeves, the front and the sides, from the shoulders to the feet. They wear their hair in innumerable small plaits hanging down: these are arranged once a week after taking the bath; the tresses are then well stiffened with gum. The Cabul women are much addicted to the use of both white and red paint; and they colour not only the nails, as in

Hindostan but the whole hand up to the wrist which looks as though it has been plunged in blood, and to our ideas is very disgusting.

Pennell took a more sympathetic view of their appearance:

The Powindah women are very fond of blue tattoo marks over their foreheads, while all alike are proud of the row of silver coins which is worn hanging over the forehead. The Hindu women plaster the hair of the forehead and temples with a vermilion paste, not merely for cosmetic reason, but because it is sacred to their god Vishnu. Then, the sturdy sunburnt faces of the Wazir women tell tales of the hard, rough outdoor life they perforce lead, and contrast with the more delicate and gentler faces of the Hindus.

In the present day the description of the tribal women has hardly changed, according to Alison Fookes, who works at the Pennel Memorial Hospital in Bannu.

I love the women in their gaily coloured tribal dresses, moving so gracefully with their skirts swaying almost like a crinoline, their hair intricately woven into hundreds of plaits with beads of silver jewellery worked into them. Many of the tribal and Afghan women are much freer than the local women, most of whom are in strict purdah and who only venture out wearing an all-enveloping burqah.

Whereas the poor women living in tribal territory or rural villages are considered to be far too valuable as labourers to be kept secluded from the stares of strange men, those of the rich would be expected to lead their lives literally behind curtains, which is the meaning of *purdah*. Some believe the custom dates from the time when the men wanted to prevent their beautiful women being carried off by invaders. It is a practice still common throughout all Islamic society, especially where traditional values are strictly maintained, as in the Frontier and Afghanistan. The impact of Western standards and values has altered their behaviour only in areas such as large towns or where the women live in non-Islamic countries.

Nowadays a Pathan who has moved from the village to a large

town will recognise that his daughters are living at a time when their lives must try and combine both the 'traditional' and 'progressive' elements of society. In the village, his daughters would observe purdah, because if the village people—his cousins—came to know that they did not keep purdah, they might resent it. In the towns, they may go about quite freely and will be expected to go to school and receive a Western-type education. At the same time, in the climate of renewed Islamic fervour and the strengthening of standards, women everywhere are expected to cover their heads with a *dupatta* or *chaddar*—a nylon scarf or a thick shawl. In addition, there has been an increased effort to isolate women from what are seen as the worst evils of Western society: materialism, sexual promiscuity and a general godlessness.

When women who keep purdah do go out, they are expected to cover themselves from head to toe in a *burqah*, which to a stranger is not only odd but ugly. Peter Mayne travelled with a group of women in a bus in Hazara and conjectured that probably under all the folds of heavy white cotton, the women might be quite pretty.

> But veiled in this way, against the predatory stares of strangers, they were entirely unattractive. Some twelve to fifteen yards of heavy cotton are draped from a dowdy white cotton cap, and the cap itself is cut into the semblance of a crown with points and decorations . . . My own feeling is that nothing could have been better designed to discourage the interest of strangers.

Even for European women, 'it is somewhat unnerving to watch a burqah slowly rotate as you go by and know that you are being studied by the unseen figure within.' As soon as the woman gets into a private area or the women's quarters of her house, however, 'she will throw it back so that the embroidered edge frames her face, rather becomingly, and billows like a ship in full sail.'

On the Frontier the Pathan woman will accept purdah as much as any other Muslim women. If a family is of high birth, the more strictly the purdah is kept. Such seclusion, however, means that the women, especially in the past, saw little of the world about them and this made the British nurses and Memsahibs feel rather sorry for them. Lillian Starr knew of a girl of nineteen who had married into a rich house, since which time she had not been out in the daylight, except in a closed and darkened carriage. 'No wonder,' she remarked, 'that these women can never become "comrades or helpmeets" to their men.' She felt that it was not surprising that they developed 'stunted minds because of it'.

Thus the European women surmised that the lives of the rich must often be filled with boredom, whereas those of the poor were nothing but hard work. It amazed them how the women accepted their lot as a matter of course. However, Dervla Murphy, an Irishwoman in her early thirties, was one Westerner who, as she travelled through the Frontier area in 1963, could see the logic of their traditions and customs. This was in spite of the fact that she herself was doing something quite unconventional, especially for a woman: going overland from Ireland to India on a bicycle. When she saw the 'contentment' of most of the Pakistani women she encountered on the Frontier, as wives and mothers, she could not help contrasting it 'with the uncertainty as to what *is* fulfilment shown by the young of the West'.

In general, the women, rich and poor alike, have always accepted their role as being in accordance with tradition. On one occasion, Dervla Murphy's host on the Frontier related how he had told his twelve-year-old daughter that she need not observe purdah, but she had insisted on doing so. And when he took his wife to Europe, he could not persuade her to take off her burqah in any of the capital cities of the world. In the present day, Western women have been surprised how, if an attractive offer of marriage is received for an educated girl to marry and lead a sophisticated life in Karachi or Lahore, it may be greeted with cries of dismay: 'I won't be able to keep purdah, wear my burqah and speak Pashtu!' The women also deny that their role is as inferior as Westerners believe. In the household women, especially the older grandmothers, not only command great respect but they also wield considerable power in the hierarchy of the family. On the Frontier they have the important role of acting as the guardians of the standards of Pashtunwali. If a blood feud is to be pursued, it is often the grandmother who will know the entire history of the quarrel. For honour's sake she will also expect her son to avenge a killing, even if she knows that he in turn will be killed.

By the same code the British saw them as admiring certain acts of courage and daring which, according to Christian teaching, should be shunned. Charlotte Vines, who worked with the Church of England Zenana Mission in the 1920s was surprised at the reaction of the tribal women when she told them the story of the Good Samaritan. Whereas normally listeners would groan with pity for the wounded traveller, when she told the story to these women 'there was a stir amongst them, no groans, no sympathy, a laugh of pure joy. "Did the robbers get everything?" "Yes, everything". "Did they escape? Get clear away?" "Yes, they got away". The company broke out into joyful congratulations. No sorrow for the robbed . . . these are the women who after battle go out and maim the wounded.' They were, as Kipling said, the women who 'come out to cut up what remains'.

Even if some women consider that they would like to abandon tradition and discard their veils, the men have stood firm to preserve the custom of purdah and the 'honour' of their women. In Afghanistan, when King Amanullah appeared in public with his wife unveiled, he shocked conservative opinion. When the Communists came to Afghanistan in 1978 they were seen as fulfilling the prophesies of the Mullahs: 'For years, the Mullahs had been saying that the Kafirs would come and take away the women, that they will be made common property'. They felt that in the early days of the revolution that was exactly what happened: 'young women were forced to join the party and discard the veil.'

Lest the same should happen to their own women, many of them determined to shift them across the frontier into neighbouring Pakistan where they could maintain their customs amidst people who shared their culture. Even as refugees they remain in comparative seclusion and so only other women have been able to have any real contact with them. Denyse Giulianotti-Bertoni made a photographic survey of 'women behind their veils' for the UNHCR in 1982. 'They were so happy to see other women showing interest in their problems. Our common feelings as women broke through the barrier of tradition and everything was thrown aside: *chaddar*, taboos and fears.'

While the men will afford protection to the women whatever the danger, as 'chattels of men', though, women can expect to be treated with the utmost severity if they should disgrace their

husbands or their menfolk. If an unmarried woman in the family
becomes pregnant, usually because of the advances of a cousin or
brother since they are secluded from everyone else, she can
expect no mercy.

The murder of close family members because of illicit sex or
infidelity horrified British wives in pre-Independence days. In
1941 the wife of Alastair Low, the Deputy Commissioner in
Bannu, visited the local hospital, where she found the doctor, a
young Hindu woman, about to conduct a post mortem:
'"Perhaps you would care to accompany me?" No, I thought;
but it was rather a shock to realise that I had never seen a dead
body and this was officially wartime. I felt I had better accept.'
To her amazement she saw a beautiful Pathan girl who had been
shot through the back.

> Hurrying home with great indignation about this terrible
> murder, I hoped fervently that the culprit would be caught.
> Later, when I asked my husband, he said, 'No.' He gathered
> that the police were unlikely to prosecute. No witnesses
> would come forward and it was generally rumoured in her
> village that she had been a naughty girl and her brother had
> shot her at close range in order to save the family honour.

According to a nurse at present working on the Frontier, the
custom remains.

> They almost always kill the girl and the man too if they can
> find him. Pushing the girl out of a moving bus is apparently
> a favoured way. One or two girls who have arrived in late
> pregnancy I have offered to admit until the child is born, get
> it adopted (several of the hospital staff would gladly do that)
> and send the girl home to tell what lies she likes about her
> dreadful illness. But none has accepted. We are known not
> to do abortions. Some village *hakims* will, however, do one
> without anaesthetic in the patient's home; we sometimes
> have to sort out the results.

In 1983 a woman who had killed her illegitimate baby was
sentenced to death by the court in Dera Ismail Khan. In addition,
she was, prior to the death sentence being carried out, to receive
twenty lashes, serve seven years in prison and pay a two-

hundred-dollar fine. When she appealed to the High Court she
was acquitted of the murder charge, but found guilty of giving
birth to an illegitimate child. Her punishment was therefore
reduced to two years' hard labour and a fine of one hundred
dollars. It was rumoured at the time that she had been made
pregnant by her cousin who had refused to marry her.

If, in the case of infidelity, the husband did not shoot his wife
outright, in the old days she could expect to have her nose cut off
and sometimes her upper lip as well. In the time of the British
they considered this to be a fearful custom which degraded the
women. Not only would it mar her beauty but it was a lasting
mark of shame that she had been accused of infidelity, true or
false. Inevitably these women ended up in hospital to be patched
up. On one rare occasion Pennell had to deal with the case of a
husband who brought in his wife, regretting the damage done to
his 'property', and requesting the doctor 'to restore to her as far
as possible her pristine beauty'. Generally, a portion of the
forehead would be removed and stitched onto the raw surface
where the nose had been cut off; but in this instance the girl's
forehead was too low for such an operation. Dr Pennell therefore
suggested that he could buy, for thirty rupees, an artificial nose,
made in England. Since a new wife would cost about eighty
rupees, the man agreed to the artificial nose, and, once it was in
place, the couple apparently lived happily ever after.

According to Mountstuart Elphinstone in 1809, the practice of
purchasing wives was recognised by Muslim law. 'The price
varies among the Afghans according to the circumstances of the
bridegroom. The effect of the practice is that women, though
generally well treated, are in some measure considered as property.' And the British of the twentieth century felt that the
purchase of wives was still widespread. Lillian Starr was appalled
by the case of a girl of about fifteen who was brought to the
hospital in an anaemic condition; she had been sold in the bazaar
for six pounds. And while travelling amongst the nomad people
in the Kagan valley in the 1970s, V. S. Naipaul noticed that there
was still a commercial undertone to the young girls he saw as
compared with the wrinkled wives. 'The women or girls in the
tent were beautiful, whereas the older ones were "lined and
brown". These women, wives, were workers . . . and those
girls, pretty as they were with their lovely skins, were really far
away, shut off in their own tribal fantasies, beauties now; well

fed, conscious of their rising price, but soon to be wives and workers.'

Among Pathan families the preference remains for Pathan to marry Pathan, although not necessarily of the same tribe. Whereas those in the villages will still expect to have arranged marriages, those who have been educated and live in the cities may well try and compromise. Although an urban Pathan would not condemn his cousins in the villages for having arranged marriages, he realises that for his daughters it must be a combination of love and background similarity—a principle they themselves accept. 'When my daughter goes to stay in the house of her parents-in-law, she sees the quilts folded in the same way as in her grandmother's house. She is used to having the house full of family members and relations. If she were a town girl from Lahore or Karachi, she might think they were very backward people.' But according to the custom of Pashtunwali, 'she realises they are generous in offering hospitality to the whole family'.

Nurses and doctors

If the wives of British officers on the Frontier found they had little communication with the tribal women, the same is not true for the handful of female medical missionaries—Catholic and Protestant—who have dedicated their lives to helping women less fortunate than themselves. To these have been added doctors and nurses from non-sectarian relief organisations such as the United Nations, the International Red Cross, Aide Medicale Internationale and many others who have come to the Frontier in a time of crisis and desperate need.

One of the first female nurses on the Frontier was Nurse Rose Johnson. The Reverend Thwaites wrote enthusiastically about her work in Dera Ismail Khan in his report to the Church Missionary Society in 1885.

Miss Johnson has now been at work for over a year and has found many and great opportunities for making known the words and also the spirit of the Gospel to the women of the neighbourhood. She is never without patients; women come for medicine, sometimes as many as sixty or seventy in the day; and hardly a day passes without at least one visit to the city, and she is frequently called to the villages. She has had patients from a distance of twenty to thirty miles sometimes on camels, sometimes on bullocks and sometimes on ponies.

He noted that in one year more than four hundred visits were made to her, and of these 'many were Pashtu-speaking women, the wives of Powindah merchants or of Wazirs from the hills'.

For a long time there was no woman doctor in Bannu and Dr Pennell saw between forty and fifty women in the outpatients' department nearly every day. 'If some of our medical ladies and nurses in England saw how their poor Afghan sisters suffered, often in silence and hopelessness, would not some of them come out to do the work of Christ and bear His name amongst them?' he asked. The services of women were particularly valuable because of the suspicion and distrust of the men who objected to having their wives treated by a male doctor. In recent times, many doctors have found it not uncommon to have to diagnose an illness through the folds of a woman's burqah.

Lillian Starr first went to work on the Frontier in 1913. Both her parents had been missionaries and she returned to Peshawar where her father had begun his work in 1863. As was often the case, she met and married a doctor in the hospital, Vernon Harold Starr. The fact that she continued to work in the Peshawar Mission Hospital after his murder in 1917 was a source of amazement to those who felt she might well have preferred to leave the Frontier altogether. The Vicereine, Lady Reading, who went to the Mission Hospital during her visit to the Frontier, remarked on it in her letter to her family. 'Here in hospital is a pretty young Matron whose husband was Doctor there—one night he was called down by a man, shot dead . . . this woman came back to the hospital where her husband was murdered to work amongst his enemies, to devote her life to these people who had taken *his* life!'

Throughout the thirties three ladies managed the Mission Hospital at Tank, receiving the admiration and affection of both the local people and the British political officers based there. Set up for the care of women, especially the Mahsud, the hospital stayed open from September to the end of May, by which time all tribal women had sought refuge from the heat in the hills. For economy's sake, the ladies grew much of the food on a small farm attached to the hospital.

While no attempt was made at conversion, even before Independence—'To do so,' as Gerald Curtis said, 'would have invited assassination'—a chapter of the Gospels in Pashtu was read in the wards daily: 'To this no Muslim could take objection as Jesus is reverenced as a great prophet by Islam.'

The physician and surgeon was Dr Maidie Shearburn. 'Her slight figure, blue eyes and fair hair gave her a totally misleading appearance,' remarked Gerald Curtis, who came into contact with the three ladies when based at Tank. She was a skilful surgeon and was so greatly esteemed that the Mahsuds even asked for a men's ward to be opened. 'To it, desperately wounded men, casualties of tribal conflict, would be borne, to be saved if their arrival had not been unduly delayed.' Dr Shearburn also gained fame for providing women with new noses.

Miss Vera Studd, as hospital Matron, was responsible for running the hospital. She could speak Pashtu well and had been a member of the team who translated the Gospels into Pashtu. The administrator was Miss Ethel Hadow. The daughter of a clergyman, 'with her white hair and rubicund complexion,' said Curtis, 'she looked like an eighteenth-century country parson. I do not suppose that Mahsuds in ill health were any improvement on those with whom I contended; even so, despite the exacting nature of their lives, the ladies were habitually serene and a great refreshment to meet after a day spent with a jirga'.

The ladies were greatly respected and they could drive their mission van along the roads without fear of ambush. 'Even the tribesmen had given instructions that they should not be harmed,' said Herbert Emerson. Likewise, today, Alison Fookes appreciates the safe conduct afforded by the tribesmen: 'I feel much safer with these tall men, with their embroidered waistcoats, huge turbans, guns slung on one shoulder and a small child on the other and often a flower behind the ear to complete the picture, than with the educated young men one may meet in the Punjab or up in Murree.'

Women nurses and doctors are still very much a rarity; the harsh life and conditions, the exposure to danger were all reasons for not going to the Frontier. Dr Ruth Coggan, daughter of the former Archbishop of Canterbury, who now works

at the Pennell Memorial Hospital was given pessimistic assessments from the start.

> You're not tough enough to be a doctor,' my biology
> teacher at St Helen's told me, as I was preparing for 'A'
> levels. 'You'll be stewed in a pot and eaten,' warned the
> medical consultant whose house physician I was when I told
> him of my plans to go abroad as a missionary. 'You'll ruin
> your career. You shouldn't go for more than three years at
> the most,' was the advice from one of the obstetric consul-
> tants.

Alison Fookes was told that Bannu was 'very remote and wild,
with no social life'. Even so, the women find their time is
completely occupied. 'Life is so full that I really don't mind the
lack of social life but make the most of outings or parties we do
have. We get invited to weddings and I enjoy seeing people in
their own environment and wonder how they cope with such
limited resources . . . Occasionally we go out for a walk in the
cantonment or go to the river on bikes.' Pennell's piano also
remains for his successors to play.

In the twentieth century, although there are no longer the
same pressures exerted on Europeans not to become nurses as in
the previous century, this has not, however, been the case with
the local women. Sir Henry Holland found that nursing was still
considered to be a degrading profession for them: 'As in Britain
in the days of Florence Nightingale, it had been looked on by
many people as a work for the lower orders of society and for
those who have no brains for anything else.' He found that it was
virtually impossible to recruit nurses from amongst the Muslims
or Hindus. The local women were also up against their own
traditions: a Muslim man would object to being treated by a
local female nurse since he considered her to be of 'low moral
character'. Thus Holland 'came to the conclusion that male
nurses were best fitted for looking after and nursing the men in
their care'.

Even if the men did not regard European female nurses in the
same light as they might regard their own kind, they still
thought they were a breed apart. Lillian Starr records with some
amusement how, when she went to Tirah, the Mullah who was
accompanying them was in need of treatment. She had some pills

for his complaint but, although he was only too willing to take the treatment, he would not address a word to her. 'Being a Mullah he never spoke to me, a woman, even regarding his ailment, but he sent his servant to describe his symptoms and tell me how he was progressing.'

Alison Fookes, in Bannu, finds that the men 'treat us as a third sex; we don't fit into their ideas of being female'; And French-women, doctors and nurses, who have travelled to Afghanistan during the 1980s, have found that if they dress in men's clothes they are regarded almost as neuters in the traditional areas where they work.

One European nurse at present living in a remote part of the Frontier, where her husband is a doctor in a hospital, felt that she ought to take precautions in order not to offend the traditions of society, and went out in a burqah. 'I don't intend to do so again. They are extremely uncomfortable, hot and one's field of vision is limited to a mesh of net straight ahead.' But even so:

> From the beginning I always kept my eyes lowered and would never catch any man's eye; now my husband prefers me to wrap up in a shawl, non-see-through, and to hold the lower edge across my face. He says that he sees the glances the passers-by give me as an unveiled woman. We have also increased my invisibility when visitors call; if they are men I will let them in, serve tea and then vanish inside leaving my husband to do the entertaining on the verandah. So far we have had very few women dropping in like that; if we did, I would entertain them inside.

At the same time, the nurses and doctors have taken pains to learn the language.

'What struck me was their conviction that if only they spoke loudly enough one would understand, and they obviously thought me very stupid not to. I now speak some Urdu, but my only Pashtu is strictly gynaecological; most of the tribal women seem unable to comprehend that everyone cannot speak Pashtu and are surprised that I need an interpreter.' The varied clientele in the Pennell Memorial Hospital can mean that, as well as Urdu, five or six brands of Pashtu are spoken, plus Punjabi and Hindu. 'You need a sharp ear,' said Alison Fookes. 'We see the local people—Bannuchis—with a very distinctive brand of Pashtu, "settled tribal" people from the surrounding districts, Wazirs, Marwats, Khataks, Mahsuds and those from Afghanistan and Khost, the Powindahs and other nomadic groups.'

The sick

Hard though it may be for the nurses to understand the patients, it could be equally difficult for the tribal women. 'Often when we are trying to explain some directions for treatment in the hospital,' said Pennell, 'they excuse their denseness by saying: "We are only cattle: how can we understand?"'

Charlotte Vines was struck by the trust of one woman brought in a caravan from Turkestan. She had been left at the hospital after a month's journey, amongst complete strangers, while the caravan went on its way.

> Then we found that no one knew her language: no one could be found in the city who knew it. She could not understand any of our languages, but she was led to the operating table; by signs she was made to mount the table, by signs made to inhale the chloroform, and so the operation was performed. It showed the most wonderful faith on her part . . . something she had heard in her far-distant home had made her set out on this long journey to seek healing. How she had heard and who it was had told her, we never found out.

In the present day Alison Fookes finds that the women, particularly the Wazirs, 'are very tough and usually make excellent patients because of this—as long as they are convinced the treatment is right.' Another nurse has found that:

> On the whole the tribal people are less demanding patients and extremely grateful for what is done for them, if one can get them into hospital in the first place. What is really frustrating is to see a patient who needs surgery, often urgently, and to have them say: 'But first I must consult with my husband', and vanish back to their villages . . . One sticks in my mind, bleeding in mid-pregnancy—if she had come in we might have saved both her and the baby.

We certainly could have saved her. But no, her husband was away. There seemed to be no other responsible man with her and so she went home and will be dead by now.

To the nurses neglected childbirth can often be most distressing, as Alison Fookes described.

We so often see the results of ignorance in our midwifery room and have to try and clear up the mess afterwards. Drugs which cause the uterus to contract very strongly are given wrongly in labour by semi-trained or untrained 'doctors' or 'midwives' with horrifying results—stillborn babies, ruptured uterus which often causes the mother to die too, which coupled with unsterile vaginal examinations make for sepsis, sometimes septicaemia and death—to see a week-old baby with tetanus caused by cutting the cord with a dirty knife is horrific.

'Too often the babies are born in cow patches and cow dung would get on the forceps,' said Mrs Shaw, a nurse in the Peshawar hospital where her husband was the doctor. 'They deliver the baby in the dirtiest part of the house so they don't dirty the rest of it.' There is also the problem of serious deformity in women resulting from calcium-deficiency in an illness called osteo-malatia. When the time comes for women to give birth, their pelvises have shrunk to the extent that a caesarian operation is necessary, or else the child will be stillborn.

Infertility is one of the frequent complaints brought to the nurses by the women, who fear that if they cannot conceive, their husbands will divorce them. 'Unless the husband has already fathered a child we always insist that he should be tested too, but for some that is too great a threat to their honour and they remove their wives in a fury. Boy children are, of course, of much more value than girls.' The persistence of the blood feud 'ruins family planning': if a doctor suggests to a woman on her fifth or sixth pregnancy that she might like to be sterilised—'Oh, no, doctor I can't do that, we have enemies'. They reckon on a minimum of four sons to get one into adulthood and producing grandchildren.

Superstitions and old habits die hard; one woman came to Dr Jonathan Shaw with a septic wound in her scalp 'from which I extracted a fragment of the Koran. Of course it was this foreign body which kept her scalp wound open and discharging. It promptly healed when the sacred object was removed.' However, he did find that the practice of cutting off the noses of their allegedly unfaithful wives had died out. 'When we arrived in the fifties we saw the evidence of it having happened, but by the time we left in 1968 we didn't see it any more.'

In general, the nurses and doctors have found that the joy of healing has made up for all the frustrations. In the words of Alison Fookes, 'It is so rewarding to watch a young girl with dreadful pulmonary TB gradually respond to the treatment, to see her fill out and begin to walk about and take an interest in her surroundings.'

In the 1980s the hundreds of thousands of refugees from Afghanistan has meant even more medical help has been necessary, especially for women. For the first time many women from Afghanistan have had the opportunity of receiving medical attention and advice on hygiene and childbirth not available to them before. At the same time the women expect to carry on raising families and with continual fighting in Afghanistan there is an added stigma if the baby born is a girl; they are useless as fighters. UNICEF painted a picture of neglect of a baby girl lying on a 'filthy sodden mattress'.

> There are no sheets or blankets though the tent is chilly, and the cold draughts seep along the floor. Sometimes the baby cries wearily, but more often lies in dull silence. The turmoil of children fighting and playing in front of the tent brings no response from her. She seems deaf and blind to the life around her. She looks ageless, with her shrunken body and her distant stare. Actually she has lived in this less than perfect world for only one year.

In many respects, the need seems as great in the present day as when Pennell called for the more fortunate to help their 'Afghan sisters' at the turn of the century.

CHAPTER SEVEN

War and Independence

The best way to face the Russian danger is to grant us our rights to
become masters of our land. We Pakhtuns are a large community,
stretching from the Amu [Oxus] to the middle of the Punjab, and no one
can dominate us. If one thinks of waging war against us, we are willing
to sacrifice everything for the protection of our country.

Abdul Ghaffar Khan, 1931

Islam expects every Mussulman to do his duty by his people and by his
nation.

Muhammad Ali Jinnah, 1942

In the eyes of the British, the mountains of the north-west
frontier bordering Afghanistan, held and owned by a 'race as
hard and ruthless as its peaks and precipices', constituted the 'one
great imperial land frontier of Britain'. Napoleonic France and
Tsarist Russia were the worry in the nineteenth century, but as
the 1920s turned into the 1930s, it was Hitler's Germany and
even Bolshevik Russia which revived the old nightmare of an
invasion of India through the passes.

In addition, the British found their position threatened not just
by the tribesmen declaring their 'holy war' against the 'infidel',
but also by events in the settled districts. In keeping with the
demand for self-government throughout India, nationalist ideas
had taken root in the Frontier. As early as 1912 Roos-Keppel had
written to the Viceroy: 'It is certain that the last ten years have
seen a gradual breaking down of the isolation and aloofness of
the Frontier, the birth of general interest in politics amongst the
educated, and a steady growth of pan-Islamic feeling among all
classes.' This movement became part of a struggle for independence which swept all over India, making the Frontier in 1947
'temporarily at least, the most explosive spot on the Indian map',

in the words of Ian Stephens. As editor of the *Statesman*, which reported on events in a country equivalent in size to one stretching from Sweden to Greece, he was well placed to see the Frontier in context.

The people of the North-West Frontier resented the fact that when reforms giving a measure of self-government to the rest of India were proposed after the First World War, they were withheld from their own province. The British excuse for this was the Frontier's poor revenue and inability to support itself, and also 'strategic reasons'. Even Roos-Keppel, Chief Commissioner at the time, held back from supporting the reforms. It was unwise, he said, to light matches in a powder magazine. The word went out that the Pathans were not ready for 'responsible government'; thus there was to be no franchise, no elections, not even to local bodies. In terms of friendly relations between the British and the Pathans, this decision cost them dearly.

As it was, events in the rest of India were gaining in momentum. The Indian nationalists were not satisfied with the post-war reforms and a young lawyer, Mohandas K. Gandhi, rose to prominence as the spokesman of the Indian National Congress Party, which had been formed in the previous century to fight for 'home rule' for Indians. In the early days, the predominantly Hindu Congress Party and the Muslim League (established in 1906 to fight for the rights of Muslims) had agreed to act together in opposition to the British. When in 1919 laws were enacted regarding sedition, providing for detention without trial, they were bitterly opposed. 'The bills are unjust,' said Gandhi, 'subversive of the elementary rights of individuals on which the safety of the community as a whole and the state itself is based.' Gandhi's method of opposition to British rule was designed to be one of peaceful non-cooperation, 'with the renunciation of voluntary association with the Government at one end and the refusal to pay taxes at the other'.

For almost thirty years the nationalists of the Frontier made common cause with those in India in order to fight against what they considered to be continuing repression by the British imperialists. Only towards the end did the intense divisions between the Hindus and Muslims make it clear that when the Frontier finally did achieve its independence, it would not be as part of a united India.

The Servants of God

In the forefront of the nationalist movement on the Frontier were the Khan brothers, Abdul Ghaffar Khan and Dr Khan Sahib. They were the sons of a wealthy Muhammadzai landlord living in the village of Utmanzai in the Peshawar district. Whilst Khan Sahib went to England to train as a doctor, returning—with an English wife—after an absence of thirteen years, Ghaffar Khan remained on the Frontier. He had appreciated the value of a good education through his experience at the Edwardes Memorial Mission High School in Peshawar and determined that the Pathans should have their own schools in order to learn about Islam and their Pathan heritage.

In the climate of the nationalist movement in India, however, Ghaffar Khan's activities in promoting Pathan education alarmed the British authorities. They feared that such schools could be used against British interests and objected to Ghaffar Khan touring the various districts of NWFP. In 1921 he was arrested and sentenced to three years' rigorous imprisonment, which time he spent either bound in fetters or grinding corn, according to prison rules. Even so, this period of arrest did not dull his determination to infuse the spirit of Pathan 'consciousness' among the local people. He felt that under the British the proud race of Pathans had become almost soft, and he illustrated his point after his release in 1924.

> Once a pregnant tigress attacked a herd of sheep and gave birth to a cub and died. The cub grew up among the sheep and adopted their ways and manners. Once a tiger attacked them and discovered that there, in the herd of sheep, was a tiger cub bleating while running away with the sheep. The tiger was amazed to hear a tiger cub bleating. The tiger separated the cub from the herd and dragged it to a pool in which it could see its own reflection and realise that it was a tiger and not a sheep. The tiger told the cub, 'You are a tiger and not a sheep, do not bleat but roar like a tiger!' You Pakhtuns are not sheep but tigers. You have been reared in slavery. Don't bleat, roar like a tiger!

Ghaffar Khan gained great inspiration from Gandhi, whom he came to know well. Earning for himself the nickname of the

'Frontier Gandhi', he followed Gandhi's example, and never wore European clothes, unlike his brother who dressed as an English gentleman. He also appreciated the value of Gandhi's teaching of non-violence. 'Among us prevailed family feuds, intrigues, enmities, evil customs, quarrels and riots. Whatever the Pakhtuns earned was squandered on harmful customs and practices and on litigations. Underfed and underclothed Pakhtuns led a miserable life.' To start with, it was with the object of working for the improvement of the people that Ghaffar Khan and his followers founded an organisation in 1929 called the 'Khudai Khidmatgars'—the 'Servants of God'. First and foremost amongst the principles they had to swear to observe was that of non-violence: 'I shall never use violence, I shall not retaliate or take revenge, and I shall forgive anyone who indulges in oppression and excesses against me.'

The Servants of God came to the British attention under the name of 'Red Shirts'. 'Their shirts in fact were not really red,' observed Herbert Thompson, 'but a drab dirty faded crimson because their workaday clothes, shirts and voluminous pyjamas had been dipped in the nearest vegetable dye.' They did this because their white clothes soon became dirty as they travelled through the villages of the Frontier. The 'red' shirts were then adopted as a uniform as a mark of solidarity amongst the followers; but they did not like to be called 'Red Shirts' because it suggested they were linked with Communism and terror.

The Khudai Khidmatgars initially were supposed to be non-political. Ghaffar Khan toured village after village teaching the people about economy and self-reliance. It was a well organised movement with a network of committees in every village, which, when the time came for political action, presented a unified front in the overall struggle for independence. As Ghaffar Khan later admitted, 'the cruel operation the British subjected us to made it impossible for the movement to keep away from politics'.

In spite of the fact that the Red Shirts were supposed to be unarmed 'servants of God', the British did not consider them as such. Rather they saw the organisation as constituting a threat to British rule and stability, and considered that the Red Shirts were like the 'private army' of the Khan brothers. Gerald Curtis for one remembered them doing 'terrible things'. 'I'll never forget that an Assistant Superintendent of Police, Dennis Murphy (with whom I'd been at Westminster School and who was a King's Scholar), had been torn to pieces by the Red Shirts' on the road from Mardan to Malakand.

'The movement was so serious', said John Dring, 'that the High Court invoked an old act dating from the previous century stating that in time of great danger and uprising you could sentence to death anyone who had merely attempted murder.' So, following three attempts on the life of the Assistant Commissioner in Charsadda, close to the Khan brothers' village and the centre of activity, the accused was sentenced to death by the High Court in Peshawar. Dring was on duty and, 'alas, was the Magistrate who had to attend the execution'. It was therefore with some uneasiness—because of his 'participation' in the execution—that he received his orders to be posted to Charsadda.

> Things were very awkward in Charsadda. There was a company of Sikhs camping at the bottom of the garden to guard against trouble, and there were three Deputy Commissioners when there should only have been one. The telegraph lines were all down. It was extremely hot and there was no ice. We were all going about in khaki shorts and shirts. Caroe (one of the three Deputy Commissioners) said to me, 'The only thing you've got to do is to keep the collection of the revenue going; otherwise they think there is no government.'

The suppression of the Khudai Khidmatgars only made them more determined to fight against the British. It came as a surprise to the fourteen-year-old second son of Ghaffar Khan, Wali, to receive the kind attentions of the British teachers in school, and then to witness the devastation of his home in Utmanzai by British soldiers in May 1930. 'I was very nearly killed. A British soldier had taken his bayonet out of his gun and I saw him slit the head open of another man. He was about to attack me.' But an Indian soldier intervened and pushed the boy out of the way. 'And then you go back to school and meet your teachers who love and embrace you.'

At the same time, the Khudai Khidmatgars were regarded with suspicion by some of those amongst their own people, who feared that Ghaffar Khan's efforts at educating and influencing the people would detract from the traditional authority vested in the Muslim clergy. Then, in 1931, came the alliance of the Khudai Khidmatgars with the Indian Congress Party, led by Gandhi, Jawaharlal Nehru and Sardar Patel. Ten years previously, the President of the Muslim League, Muhammad Ali Jinnah, had broken with the Congress Party, over the issue of non-cooperation when it was agreed in 1920 at Nagpur. In fact Gandhi had to call off non-cooperation when there was widespread violence and some policemen were burned. Jinnah also did not want to participate in the boycott of councils in which Indians were represented because it deprived them of a chance 'to fight face to face with the bureaucrats'. There was disagreement between the parties over the proposed constitution, and severe riots served to increase the tensions between the Muslims and Hindus.

Ghaffar Khan's alliance of the Muslim Khudai Khidmatgars with the Congress was therefore seen as siding with Hindus at a time when communal passions were already beginning to run high. However, Ghaffar Khan, from the vantage point of a predominantly Muslim province—where Hindus posed no threat—defended the alliance on account of its support. 'The Congress began to sympathise with our Pathan nation as far as it could, that is, it exposed the oppression on us to the world through newspapers and speeches.' In addition, Congress was prepared to give badly needed financial backing to the Khudai Khidmatgars. On the Frontier, the emotional argument that alliance with the Congress meant Hindu domination had little impact on the growing support for the Khudai Khidmatgars. And on account of their numerical superiority, the Muslims on the Frontier did not have the same reservations about joining the Indian Congress Party as did Muslims in the rest of India, where they were in the minority. What seemed to be most important at the time was the pursuit of every means possible to achieve independence.

When, therefore, Gandhi launched his movement of civil disobedience in 1930, the Khudai Khidmatgars gave it their support. The general strategy was to boycott all things British and picket shops which sold British goods ranging from cloth to alcohol. The British authorities kept a record of Ghaffar Khan's movements and speeches. As a result of one of his 'more objectionable tirades against the "feringhee"', they noted in

November 1931, 'the attitude towards the Government has considerably deteriorated and one of the immediate effects has been that a large number of defaulters [of revenues and taxes] who had previously promised to pay up, have now refused to do so . . . propaganda is being organised in villages against the use of canal water for which water tax is paid.' By the end of 1931 the British Government had decided on tough action throughout India. The Congress Party was banned, as were all organisations affiliated to it, which included the Khudai Khidmatgars. The journal, the *Pakhtun*, which Abdul Ghaffar Khan had started in 1928, was closed down. All the leaders, including the Khan brothers, were arrested and many more besides.

At the same time, the frustration in the North-West Frontier Province did not go unheeded and the decision was taken to raise the province from a Chief Commissionerate to a Governor's Province; the Pathans were to be given political rights and institutions equal to those available in the rest of India. Olaf Caroe admitted that in the previous ten years the British had been 'too slow to recognise all the signs of new-found pride in the Pathan'. The reforms of 1932 were seen at least as a beginning. The first Minister was Sir Abdul Qayyum, who had worked hard to impress upon the British that the Pathans if anything were far in advance of other peoples in terms of their understanding of political and egalitarian concepts. They had their own tribal assemblies by which they chose their spokesmen and ordered their lives. According to Caroe, 'in breadth of vision and determination, Qayyum had few rivals throughout India, and he it was who in the end extracted from the inertia of British governments two instalments of "reforms" within a very few years.' To those who were committed to the cause of complete independence, however, like Ghaffar Khan, the reforms of 1932 were greeted with reservations. 'Reforms? Your reforms?' he had said to Sir Ralph Griffith, the Chief Commissioner in July 1931. 'What is the use of them? The paper reforms will not make any difference. What we want is change of heart.'

After his arrest at the end of 1931, Ghaffar Khan spent his next three years in imprisonment miles away from his own people in Bihar. For a while Dr Khan Sahib was confined with him. On their release, they were banned from the Frontier Province and the Punjab, and so they went to stay with Gandhi at his ashram in Wardha, near Nagpur. 'The Khan brothers are here and I am having a very nice time with them,' Gandhi observed. 'To be with them more is to love them more; they are so nice, so simple and yet so penetrative. They do not beat about the bush.'

The right to political representation in further reforms, granted all over India by the Government of India Act in 1935, paved the way for elections two years later. In the Frontier, the Congress Party, which had managed to gain grass-roots support throughout the Province, won the elections. In a province which could in no way be said to be threatened by Hindu dominance, the Muslim League's manifesto encouraging them to fight for Muslim solidarity fell on deaf ears. The attention of the people was directed to those they had come to regard as their spokesmen for independence. Dr Khan Sahib, who had returned to the Frontier after his period of exile, became Chief Minister and he worked closely with the Governor, Sir George Cunningham; they became great friends, and Cunningham described Khan Sahib as 'being very pleasant and a little self-conscious, having no trace of bitterness'.

After an absence of six years, Ghaffar Khan was also allowed to return to the Frontier. However, he remained outside the political framework as laid down by the British. 'Thank God I am once again with you to share your joys. But the real joy is yet to come, and our happiness is meaningless until we have achieved our goal of independence,' he said to his supporters on his return. When Cunningham met Ghaffar Khan in 1939, he recognised him as being a man whose 'chief object is genuinely the social and economic improvement of the Pathan; he is not bitter against the individual British officer, though he dislikes our system of government.'

With a Congress ministry in power in the Frontier, it was considered appropriate for the Congress President, Jawaharlal Nehru, to visit the Province in the autumn of 1937. He was warmly welcomed, and in his speeches he praised the contribution of Ghaffar Khan to the freedom movement and Hindu-Muslim unity throughout India, calling him 'the one great man in whom all India took pride'. He also expressed the feeling that perhaps the Frontier could teach the rest of India a lesson: 'They are not men of words, and any resolution for them is something which has to be translated into deeds. The most significant example of this has been their adherence to the policy of non-violence during our struggle.'

Gandhi also visited the Frontier twice in 1938, and toured through the villages. Both he and Ghaffar Khan in their conversations dwelt on the importance of the principles of non-violence in the fight against the British as well as in their own lives: 'My conviction is daily growing deeper that more than anything else violence has been the real bane of us Pathans in this province,' Ghaffar Khan told Gandhi during his second visit in the autumn. 'It shattered our solidarity and tore us with wretched internal feuds. The entire strength of the Pathan is today spent in thinking how to cut the throat of his brother. To what fruitful use this energy might not be put if only we could be rid of this curse!' Gandhi assured him that 'times change and systems decay. But it is my faith that in the result it is only non-violence and things that are based on non-violence that will endure.'

The invasion fear

Regardless of the aspirations of the nationalists, India as part of the British Empire was at war in 1939. During the early years of the war, the British were plagued by their fear of an invasion through the passes of the North-West Frontier. They anticipated that Hitler's pact with Stalinist Russia would not last long; and in the event of Hitler turning on the Russians and defeating them, there would be little to prevent a German attack on India from the north-west. They also envisaged German air-raids from the Near East if Hitler managed to capture Iraq and Syria. And when Germany did attack Russia, the British had no option but to accept the Soviets as allies, even though they had earlier once again begun to view the Russians themselves as a potential danger to India.

When calculating how long it would take Germany to reach India, British planners found that the mechanisation of warfare and the use of air power greatly altered their earlier assessments. It was no longer a question of an attacker riding across the plains of Afghanistan; instead, despite the obvious lack of a single railway in Afghanistan to facilitate transport, the widespread use of tanks and armoured vehicles meant that men, supplies and ammunition could be swiftly deployed. The example of Poland in 1939 had shown just how effective were the Germans' methods of *blitzkrieg*.

The British therefore determined in some way to fortify all the strategic points of entry into India and particular attention was paid to the Khyber pass. Major Charles Davidson, who was Assistant Instructor in Gunnery at the Artillery School in Kakul near Abbottabad, was called upon to assist in determining what best could be relied upon to stop German tanks pounding into India. 'Although the main route—which could easily be blocked—was kept open, it was decided to erect huge mountains of concrete—"dragon teeth"—along any areas which could provide an alternative passage for the tanks, and thus prevent them from bypassing the forts guarding the pass.' To this day they remain as monuments to Britain's worst fears, inherited by the new guardians of the Khyber pass and the route to India. One side effect to the invasion fear was that the Guides lost their 'spiritual' home in Mardan; in order to bring them closer to the suspected line of attack, the cavalry went to Quetta, and the infantry to Jamrud and other posts in the Khyber pass.

In anticipation of heavy fighting and casualties, areas were selected where field hospitals could be built, as well as ammunition depots. The idea was that troops would be able to move 'at a moment's notice'. Water was laid on and an appeal was even made to those members of the Indian Army—British and Indian—who had water-divining abilities. They were requested to volunteer to look for supplies of water so that when the time came the British would know where to dig the wells. Plans had also to be made to evacuate those civilians who might wish to leave. 'This entailed the creation of reception centres down country,' said Gerald Curtis. 'Food distribution gave rise to difficulties and the maintenance of security on rail and road.'

In order to bring home the realities of a German invasion into India, the British also carried out military exercises, pretending that Germans had actually arrived in Afghanistan. The *pièce de résistance* of one exercise, Davidson related, was to capture and—in theory—blow up the Attock bridge, which provided an essential link with the rest of India both by rail and road. The Army was aware that a security exercise was taking place and had to prepare itself by mounting a special guard to protect the bridge. The 'Germans' meanwhile set about observing movements on the bridge and soon ascertained that the Royal Indian Army Service Corps was training drivers. Long convoys of up to a hundred lorries would pass over the bridge, drive down to

Rawalpindi, fill up with petrol and return. An obvious ploy was to infiltrate the lorries, anticipating that the Indian student drivers would be none the wiser. The next stage was to cause one lorry to break down on the bridge, and then enlist the assistance of all, including the sentries on duty, to help push the lorry. This ruse provided ample opportunity for the others to slip down the side of the bridge and lay the necessary charges to blow it up. Only when the operation had been completed could the umpires be called in and declare the bridge 'blown'. 'No trains or cars', said Davidson, 'were allowed across the bridge for three days to show just how inconvenient it would be if Germans ever did manage to reach the Frontier.'

But within a year of preparation, the danger passed. Hitler's attack on the Soviet Union had been fiercely resisted by the Russians, and Germany's defeat on the eastern front ensured that there would not be another invasion of India from the north-west. By the time a thorough defence system was fully orga-nised, the danger was coming from the other side, with the entry of Japan into the war and the fall of Singapore. Davidson found himself being trained in jungle warfare and having to reply to questions, when taking his oral exam in Urdu, such as: 'Why do you think we have spent so much money to defend the North-West Frontier when the Japanese are our enemy?'

War and the tribesmen

Coupled with the fear of invasion, was that of rebellion among the tribesmen. A rising in Waziristan in peacetime was bad enough; in wartime it could be far worse. And because there was always potentially the danger, the Frontier could not be denuded of fighting men. In the end Michael Wilcox in Coke's Rifles came to realise what a 'terrible waste of manpower it was having forty to fifty thousand troops on the Frontier when they could have been usefully used in the war effort.'

The Second World War was of course remote from the tribesmen's horizons. 'If you asked them how they felt about the war,' said Robin Latimer, 'they were quite liable to reply, "War? Mmmn. Oh, you mean your war." ' John Dent didn't 'think they felt we were really threatened until the Japanese got into Burma.' Other officers found that the Pathans were both interested and informed. 'Certainly the increased availability of radios meant that the tribesmen knew a little more of what was going on. They might run out of batteries, but at least there was the possibility for them to get news,' Charles Davidson remarked. Even then a little knowledge could have its drawbacks. On one occasion Davidson was stationed near Kohat. With British officers and gunners from Madras, he was engaged in checking the guns to test that they were firing at the same range. The line of fire was marked by wire which they had carefully laid down; but it was not long before the wire disappeared. 'I went to the nearby village and asked the village headman for the wire back, threatening all sorts of punitive action unless it was returned. After a lot of argument the wire eventually reappeared.' Whilst disclaiming all responsibility for the theft, the headman said, almost by way of apology, 'I didn't realise it was an Indian regiment; I thought you were Americans with Negro troops.' He had heard on the radio of the arrival of the Americans in the war, and automatically assumed that the very dark-skinned Madrassis must be American Negroes.

Gerald Curtis found that the Mahsuds were interested in a great deal more than what was going on in India, 'and were convinced that the real enemy was not Nazi Germany but "Rees" [Russia].' This arose from a longstanding hatred of Communism. Initially the British were only too happy to cultivate their feelings against the Russians, and encouraged those Mullahs whom they could influence to preach against them as godless Bolsheviks. However, when the Soviets came into the war on the side of the Allies, it was not so easy, and Cunningham found that some of the Mullahs came to him to ask for guidance as to the line they should take towards Russia. His response was that if a mad dog got loose in Parachinar Bazaar, Shia and Sunni would combine to kill it; in the same way the British and the Russians had united to get rid of Hitler. Likewise the non-aggression pact between Turkey and Germany proved rather embarrassing; up until the pact was made, the British were able to castigate the Axis powers as enemies of Islam. With Islamic Turkey as an ally of Fascist Germany, they had to tread more carefully.

'For the Japanese,' commented Curtis, 'they had a loathing which was based upon accounts of the Burma Front, brought home by members of the Mahsud transport companies serving there.' These companies, along with those which served in the

Western desert, were an exception to the British rule insofar as concerned recruiting Mahsuds. Because of their past history and desertions during the third Afghan war, the Mahsuds were still not recruited into the Indian Army, although as good mechanics they proved useful in the transport companies. The same still applied to the Afridis. In their case, when war broke out, they requested re-enlistment, 'as much for the pay as anything else,' said Robin Hodson, who was sent to help recruit the first Afridi battalion in 1942. Certainly no one was going to blame them for wanting a little extra income 'to make life easier at home'. Their support was, after all, grist to the war effort's mill. The British also saw it as giving useful employment to the young men of the Frontier in order to keep them occupied and out of trouble.

In addition, when it came to fighting in foreign campaigns, the experience which the British and Indian soldiers had gained fighting in the North-West Frontier served the war effort in good stead. 'Independent territory,' remarked Herbert Thompson, 'furnished an area for military manoeuvres more useful than the Salisbury plain. The dramatic advantages of such training came in Ethiopia when, on the advance of the Indian Army, Mussolini's chocolate soldiers melted in territory not unlike the hills of the North-West Frontier.'

Herbert Emerson was greatly heartened when a Mahsud tribesman whom he had not met before—'a man of ordinary status'—asked for an interview.

> He came in clutching two medals in his hand, but the ribbons were too old to identify. 'So you want to sell these?' I asked. 'Oh, no, Sahib, they are mine. I brought them to show you.' I looked more closely. His name was engraved around the rim. They were the Indian Order of Merit and the Indian Distinguished Service Medal. 'Where did you get these?'—'Oh! I won them in France in the 1914-18 War.' I expressed admiration. We discussed the war then being waged during one of the darkest moments. He had not the slightest doubt that the Allies would win. 'The Germans are not supermen,' he said. 'We beat them last time and we will beat them again.' (Note the 'we'.) He had gone to France with the Indian Army, had served in the trenches, won these high awards for bravery, and

returned to live a quiet life in his beloved hills on a minute piece of land. But his heart was with us in the struggle.

On his tours throughout the Frontier during the war, Cunningham observed the reaction of the tribesmen to the war effort. He noted with amusement how the Mohmands, who were in 'friendly form' suggested: 'Why not, instead of giving us allowances, let us go and loot the Japanese and those Hindus who sympathise with the Japs?' On another occasion, when Cunningham was accompanying the Viceroy, Lord Linlithgow, to a jirga of Orakzai tribes in the spring of 1943, he felt it necessary to misrepresent their wishes. 'Some men got up and tried to start asking for doubled allowances, but I told the Viceroy [who did not understand what the men were saying] they were only praying for the success of the British arms.'

The British, however, never felt they could relax their hold on tribal territory. In Waziristan, Gerald Curtis found that although the Mahsuds 'wished us well', it was also a case of 'business as usual. They were determined to extract the maximum profit from their connection with the British.' He also found that 'there were elements in the tribe which were unalterably hostile to the British, and they made sure that if the tribal pot did not actually spill over in Waziristan, it continued to bubble and spit.'

The British political officers considered that their troublemakers came in particular from amongst those Mahsuds who held allowances from the Afghan government. This privilege dated from the political upheaval in Afghanistan in 1928 when, after nearly ten years on the throne, King Amanullah was obliged to leave the country. Once again the British preoccupation with the Russian influence in Afghanistan was believed to have been the reason for his downfall, starting with Amanullah's treaty with the Soviet Union in 1921 and invitation to Russian advisers to help establish the Royal Afghan Air Force in 1924. There was the feeling amongst the Pathans of the Frontier, like Ghaffar Khan, who had appreciated Amanullah's support of his own movement, that the British had encouraged the Mullahs to create disturbances in the country in order to get rid of him. 'They [the Mullahs] declared King Amanullah a Kafir and forced him to leave his beloved land.' However, the British believed that his reforms, particularly regarding the emancipation of women, had alienated large sections of his own society.

Amanullah was succeeded by Habibullah Kalakani, better known as Bacha Saqqao, 'the son of the water-carrier'. As an illiterate Tajik from the north, rather than a Pathan, he was not accepted and was soon overthrown by one of the descendants of the fifty sons of Dost Muhammad's brother. He was Nadir Shah who had fought in the third Afghan war against the British and had been temporarily in exile in Peshawar. In order to assert his claim he relied on the support of the tribes in Waziristan. They were rewarded for their services with allowances from the Afghan government, which privilege they retained after Nadir Shah's assassination in 1933, when he was succeeded by his teenage son, Zahir Shah.

In time of war, this Afghan connection was regarded with even greater suspicion by the British. 'Kabul was full of hostile embassies,' said John Dring, 'who wanted the tribesmen to give us as much trouble as possible to keep our troops tied down there.' So nervous were the British about the harmful influence the Axis powers could have at Kabul and indirectly on the Frontier, that the presence of any foreigners on the Frontier was regarded with the utmost suspicion. Davidson recalled how some of his colleagues had gone to visit a village near the Kabul river. 'Have you seen any foreigners lately?' they asked the local inhabitants. They were rather taken aback when the reply came: 'Yes, two Italians.' Further investigation revealed that they were referring to two Jesuit priests on their way to Peking in the seventeenth century.

In addition, the British had to contend with the influence of the Mullahs, especially that of the Faqir of Ipi who was still at large. He was the most logical person for the Axis powers to approach in order to try and cause trouble for the British amongst the tribesmen. It took a whole year after the outbreak of war for them to establish direct contact with him via their legations in Kabul. According to the testimony of the Italian minister at Kabul, Pietro Quaroni, given to the British after the Italian surrender in 1943, the Faqir had informed his would-be allies, through intermediaries, that he would require the sum of £25,000 every other month to keep the pot boiling; double, if tribal unrest extended to other areas; and for a general uprising three times the amount, as well as supplies of weapons and ammunition. The Germans remained in touch with him throughout the war, although it was clear that he could not bring about the sort of general disturbance which would have tied down British troops all along the Frontier. Even if the Faqir had been given unlimited supplies of weapons, he could only ever have gathered 10,000 followers at the most. He had little influence outside Waziristan and failed in his efforts to embroil the Afridis. Once Germany attacked Russia, it was no longer possible to send through the necessary arms. In any case, the feelings of the Faqir towards his wartime paymasters were ambivalent. In a letter to one of his fellow Mullahs in South Waziristan, written from his hideout in Gorwekht, whilst continuing to show his hatred for the British, he also said that no help should be given to the Germans because they were against Islam. In fact the Faqir was far less trouble to the British during the war than in the years before it.

None the less, the British had to guard against the danger of a tribal uprising inspired either by the Faqir or anyone else. The senior Mahsud Mullah and successor to Mullah Powindah was his son, Shahzadah Fazl Din. His aim, Curtis said, was 'to make the best use of any opportunity which might increase his importance. In my day, wartime scarcity of food and clothing furnished him with a case to exploit.' But his efforts to foment discontent because of the shortages did not meet with much success.

In general, because of Mahsud–Wazir rivalry, Fazl Din could be played off against the Faqir of Ipi. As the Faqir of Ipi was quite irreconciliably hostile to the British, they found that Fazl Din was not without his uses. At one stage, however, it looked as though some agreement might be reached between the two Mullahs. 'It became urgent to warn Fazl Din that if he co-operated with the Faqir life might become very uncomfortable for him.' Like the Mullah Powindah, Fazl Din never visited the Political Agent, but Curtis's Assistant Political Agent managed to persuade his two brothers to visit him at Tank.

> Of course, by pure chance, when the brethren entered my office, they found me looking at photos taken by the Air Force during an aerial survey of Waziristan. I showed them a photo of a hamlet of Makin before kind attentions from the Air Force and afterwards. I then turned up a photo of their own happy home, and genially offered them a copy. They did not seem keen to have one. I did not have to tell

them that it was the policy of Government to bomb any
building in which the Faqir might be sheltering. They
anticipated the point and assured me fervently that it was
unthinkable that the Shahzadah should entertain the Faqir.
He did not do so.

The political officers found that the maliks themselves could
also cause trouble, for their own benefit if for no other reason, as
Curtis found.

It might pay a big malik actually to turn hostile for a while.
While he would lose his allowance and a share in any
lucrative contracts in the Political Agent's hands, he could
reckon on picking something up from Afghan, Italian or
other sources. He would become the focus for malcontents
in the Agency and each Political Agent in turn would try to
get him to 'come in'. Eventually he would be welcomed
back into the fold with the bestowal of contracts and other
delights. We are told that in the Kingdom of Heaven 'there
is more joy over one sinner that repenteth than over nine
and ninety righteous persons'. So it was in Waziristan.

War and the nationalists

As soon as war broke out, the Congress Working Committee
requested the British government to 'declare its war aims'. By
this they meant that they wanted an assurance that independence
would be granted once the war was over. 'India cannot associate
herself in a war said to be for democratic freedom when that very
freedom is denied to her.' The Muslim League, for its part, told
the British government that it could count on its support
provided that the Muslims were given 'justice and fair play' in
those provinces where the Congress Party ruled.

Although the Viceroy, Lord Linlithgow, pledged that 'domin-
ion status' was the objective of British policy in India, and
implicitly accepted the Muslim League's claim to speak for all the
Muslims in India, the Congress Party was not satisfied. Accordingly, while the Muslim League was prepared to back the
British war effort, the Congress Party instructed all its ministries
to resign from office. This called for the compliance of the

Congress ministry led by Dr Khan Sahib on the Frontier and meant that Sir George Cunningham took over the administration of the Province as Governor. When in October 1939 all the Congress ministries resigned, Jinnah declared a 'day of deliverance and thanksgiving, as a mark of relief that the Congress regime has at last ceased to function'. Whilst continuing to press for independence, the Congress Party, inspired by Gandhi, determined to launch a civil disobedience campaign throughout India. In its opinion the British were waging the war 'fundamentally for imperialist ends and for the preservation of her empire'.

The Muslim League's 'Pakistan resolution' in March 1940, however, added a new dimension to the British government's dealings with the Indian nationalists. Jinnah declared that the present unity of India was artificial, dating from the British period, and was only maintained by the British bayonet. 'The Muslims are a nation and they must have their homelands, their territory and their state.' The League resolved that it would not accept any independence plan unless it took into consideration that areas in the north-western and eastern zones of India, where Muslims predominated, should be 'autonomous and sovereign'. From this moment onwards, the discussions no longer related purely to independence for the sub-continent, but independence and partition.

Although Japan's entry into the war threatened India's own security, Gandhi finally launched his 'Quit India' movement in 1942, maintaining that 'arrogant imperialism' was indistinguishable from 'fascist authoritarianism'. On the Frontier, Cunningham did not seem to think the movement would cause too many problems. He recorded in his diary how he had sent Dr Khan Sahib a telegram stating that if he started a movement with the slogan 'English leave India', 'he must come and say it to me first, in which case I would take him at his word and go off to England, taking Mrs Khan Sahib with me'—she was of course English. Dr Khan Sahib did, however, don the red uniform of the Khudai Khidmatgars and deliver the 'Quit India' message on the Frontier, in spite of the fact that Cunningham for one did not seem to take his role very seriously. 'Khan Sahib came to dinner and bridge last evening,' he noted in his diary on 15 September 1942. 'He was wearing a shirt with the faintest suggestion of pink in it, which I suppose satisfied his sense of obligation to the Red

Shirts. He was in very friendly form, but I did not talk politics to him.'

As part of the movement of civil disobedience on the Frontier, the Khudai Khidmatgars directed their attention to marching on government offices and courts in the main towns, as well as picketing shops which sold British goods. Their objective was to break through police lines and occupy the buildings. Eventually Ghaffar Khan was arrested in October 1942 on his way to the District Court at Mardan. He was taken to prison at Abbottabad where, for a while his son, Wali, was imprisoned with him. As a prisoner, Wali Khan had his first taste of British justice. 'The magistrate in Peshawar, who was an Indian, had confiscated my pen and pencil. I requested the Jail Superintendent—an Englishman—to have it back.' In the course of the conversation which followed, he admitted that since the Jail Superintendent was part of the British rule against which he was fighting, then he too was his enemy. 'Yes,' came the reply, 'but the moment you enter this prison, then I shall fight for your rights.' Within a short time he secured for him the use of the pen and pencil. Most of the political prisoners were released after a year, but Ghaffar Khan remained in jail.

By 1943, the Congress Party in the Frontier seemed to have lost a certain amount of its following; this was partly because of its support for civil disobedience, from which the Muslim League had kept aloof; also because at last the Muslim League had begun to gain the backing of influential Muslims on the Frontier. A Peshawar lawyer, Muhammad Aurangzeb Khan, was allowed to form a Muslim League Ministry, under instructions from Cunningham; but it did not manage to consolidate its position and Cunningham found himself reprimanding Aurangzeb for not delegating enough authority on the smaller issues. Aurangzeb, he noted, was 'profuse in his assurance of loyalty and desire to administer wisely, and I think there is a good deal in what he says: that unless he makes a show of taking interest in these small matters, public opinion will go dangerously against the Ministry.' Aurangzeb himself admitted that if the Ministry failed to provide the elementary needs of the population, it had 'no right to subsist' and that 'with the grace of God his administration would not fail in these matters'.

Overall, the Muslim League Ministry was not a success. It was still a middle-class party, and there was too much feeling amongst the local people that the League had profited from the wartime shortages and the rationing of cloth and sugar. Its opponents called it inept and corrupt. Even Cunningham admitted that 'there is no doubt that the name of the Muslim League administration is simply mud nowadays owing to the scandalous way in which they buy votes'. It also became unpopular because political opponents were kept in jail, and Cunningham told Aurangzeb that the 'whole Province was becoming "bad-named" over the thing.' When the Muslim League administration fell in a vote of no confidence in March 1945, Cunningham asked Dr Khan Sahib to form a ministry. One of his first actions was to order the release of his brother, Ghaffar Khan, from prison. This was followed soon afterwards by the end of the war, with the surrender of Germany in May and Japan in August.

Postwar

After the war, the election of a government in Britain determined to hand over power in the sub-continent was an indication that the end of British rule really was in sight. However, even though support for the Muslim League and its demand for separate homelands for the Muslims had increased throughout India, when elections were held on the Frontier in 1946 the Congress Party secured the majority. At the same time, feelings for the Muslim League and the Congress Party were sharply divided. 'It was fairly tense,' reported John Dent, who was Returning Officer. 'People at the polling stations got out rifles.' And in order to explain the result, the leader of the Opposition, Abdul Qayyum Khan, stated that the election officers 'played havoc with the electoral rolls, and names of thousands of bogus voters were entered and those of many who were suspected of League sympathies were removed.' The Muslim Leaguers also believed that during the election campaign Congress issued arms licences to Pathans and made future promises of arms. 'These promises of arms enticed the Pathans and considerably influenced election results in favour of the Congress.'

For their part, the Congress Party on the Frontier felt that the British political officers were beginning to sympathise with the Muslim League. 'At the time of polling,' said Ghaffar Khan, 'the

British authorities and their henchmen put all their weight on the side of the Muslim League and they worked against the Khudai Khidmatgars. But with God's grace, the Muslim League was defeated and our party came out victorious.'

Within a very short time of winning the elections, however, support for the Congress Party began to wane. Abdul Qayyum accused the Congress Ministry of having a tendency to interfere with day-to-day justice in the Province. It was also alleged that instead of looking to the needs of the people, the Congress Party spent its time abusing the League. In addition, the Muslim League complained that supplies were not distributed properly. The Congress Ministry, it claimed, 'withheld supplies of cloth, sugar and kerosene oil from those who had not given their votes to the Congress candidates.'

Within the context of the Independence movement, the realisation that the British really were intending to leave India sharpened Muslim attitudes as to what might happen if India were to remain united. The British political officers observed for themselves that the Muslims on the Frontier, as elsewhere, were at last beginning to worry about the real possibility, as Gerald Curtis noticed, of being 'tied to the chariot wheels of a Hindu-dominated government in India'. Robin Hodson, who had been in Peshawar at the beginning of the war, had originally felt that it was impossible for the division of India as requested by Jinnah and the Muslim League to take place. 'But back there again in 1946, it was not long before riots took place in Bihar and Bengal. I can remember a deputation being sent down and coming back with a burnt Qur'an; and it didn't take very long for feelings to somersault overnight against the Congress in the Frontier, because of its support for a united India under Nehru.' In tribal territory, Curtis realised that the Mahsuds in Waziristan would not be happy with a united India. 'I do not think they believed that we would hand over power in India. But if this came about, they would never have agreed to continue, with a predominantly Hindu government, the relationship which they had had with the British.'

For centuries, especially since Babur and the Mogul dynasty founded by him, the Muslims had regarded themselves as the dominant, albeit minority race. In 1893, long before independence was within sight, Muslim protagonists had asked who was to make them submit 'to the supremacy of the Hindus, whom for seven hundred years they regarded as their slaves?' By 1946, all the arguments which the Muslim League had been advancing about the danger of being dominated by the Hindus sounded more plausible. If they did not accept partition and Pakistan, the Muslims feared they would, as Jinnah had threatened, become 'a mere understudy of the Congress, mere footpages of the Congress leaders, to be used, governed and brought to heel when they had served their purpose.' Not only did the Muslims of the Frontier begin to fear the dawn of the Hindu Raj, but once the other provinces in the north-west and north-east, in which Muslims were in the majority, had thrown their support behind the Muslim League's demand for Pakistan, it seemed no longer possible for the North-West Frontier to go its own way.

Nehru on the Frontier

When Jawaharlal Nehru decided to visit the Frontier in late 1946, in spite of being hailed as one of the great leaders of the Independence movement in India, he met with a very different reception from the welcome accorded to him almost ten years previously. Gerald Curtis, on leave in Peshawar, was able to observe the progress of his tour. 'Nehru hoped to be acclaimed the liberator of the nation and quash the two-nation theory. Khān Sahib hoped that he would be able to persuade Nehru that relations with the tribes should be exercised through him.' The tide, however, had already turned in favour of the Muslim League and Pakistan, and the British feared that the visit would provoke strong reaction. 'The Government of India in Delhi tried to persuade him not to go,' said John Dring, at that time Deputy Commissioner in Peshawar. Sir Olaf Caroe, who had taken over from Cunningham as Governor earlier in the year, also tried to make Nehru abandon the visit, which he considered was 'a brave effort, but ill-conceived and bound to fail'.

The first town in tribal territory on Nehru's itinerary was Miramshah, where he was to address a jirga. But, according to reports reaching the British, the Utmanzai Wazirs were not impressed with his pledge to 'set them free', calling out, 'Why don't you speak Pashtu? Go back to Hindustan.' His reception at Razmak was no better. The tribesmen fired on the plane before it even arrived. Robin Hodson, who was the Political Agent for

South Waziristan, witnessed Nehru's address to the jirga there. 'Instead of remaining seated, to my astonishment Nehru got up and started addressing the tribesmen as though he were at a political rally, waving his arms around and marching up and down. At a jirga it is the custom to sit on the ground and the person addressing the meeting would be seated on a chair. But Nehru's manner did not please them.' Again he said that he would set them free from the slavery of the British; but the reply—in Urdu for Nehru to understand—came: 'We are not the slaves of the British and we are certainly not going to be your slaves.' Using the contemptuous word for an Indian, *kortunai*, they said that if they had to deal with any Indian, it would be Jinnah. The meeting broke up in disorder. When Nehru was advanced upon by a Mahsud with an umbrella, it was Robin Hodson who stood in to protect him. Hodson was therefore somewhat surprised 'to listen to All India Radio saying that the political officers there (us) had arranged a demonstration against Nehru'.

At Wana, the Ahmedzai Wazirs refused to meet him, and debagged the suited and booted Hindus who went to visit him. Abdul Ghaffar Khan, who, together with Dr Khan Sahib, accompanied Nehru throughout the trip, spoke scathingly of the British officers in Waziristan calling them 'suave and cunning'. He attributed the docility of the tribesmen to the allowances given them by the British. Nehru journeyed on to Tank and Jandola, where he met some of the smaller tribes. 'Here the tribesmen received us warmly and brought back sheep to present us,' noted Ghaffar Khan. Back in Peshawar, Nehru's next stop was the Khyber pass. But the Afridis refused to grant the usual tribal protection, and the recently reconstituted Khyber Rifles were called in to protect the party against sniping and stone-throwing. After tea in Torkham, they returned to Peshawar without meeting an Afridi.

In spite of his experiences at Khyber, Nehru wished also to go up the Malakand pass. In view of the dangers, he clearly needed an escort and Gerald Curtis was recalled from leave and put in charge. Like Hodson, he was obliged to listen to the All India Radio making virulent attacks against the British political officers, this time about the Khyber visit. They were accused of having encouraged the tribesmen to insult Nehru, and of having 'intentionally imperilled his life'. 'I looked at Nehru during this tirade and he did not appear to be altogether comfortable,' Curtis wrote to his wife. 'I was the only British officer present.' Afterwards, Curtis went out with Nehru on the verandah and tried to explain the situation from the political officer's point of view. 'I said that on the Frontier we were handpicked and we were most of us English gentlemen. It was unthinkable that we should plan to insult a man of his eminence or to imperil a life the loss of which must embitter Anglo-Indian relations. Nehru thanked me for my frankness and we parted friends.'

But the next day more attacks were made against Nehru and his companions. Dung was thrown: 'What a party! Frantic politicians shouting blue murder behind me,' said Curtis. When they returned from the Malakand, thousands of hostile tribesmen were waiting for them and, according to Ghaffar Khan, began to throw stones. 'I pushed my hand to shield Jawaharlal from a stone aimed at him. Another man lifted an earthen pot filled with night-soil and threw it at us. It missed Jawaharlal and me but hit Dr Khan Sahib and covered him with filth all over his body.' Eventually they returned to Peshawar, and Nehru went safely back to Delhi soon afterwards. 'But the visit,' remarked Curtis, 'had momentous consequences. It revealed that there was no support for the Congress Party amongst the major tribes. Jinnah's hand had been greatly strengthened.'

The Muslim League was of course delighted, and the correspondent of the Muslim League daily paper *Dawn* wrote that Nehru's visit had brought home to the Pathans what it might be like to be under Hindu domination. 'Prior to this it was psychologically difficult for him [the Pathan] in a province where a microscopic Hindu minority is looked upon with amused contempt to realise that Hindus could rule over him.'

The Congress Party believed that the hostile reception had been entirely 'stage-managed' by the British. 'Those very people for whose benefit and progress he [Nehru] undertook this tour, were incited to throw stones at him,' Ghaffar Khan complained. 'It is no good getting excited over them. The Britishers want to ruin us by sowing dissension among the Pakhtun.' So convinced were the Congress supporters that the British were responsible for the hostility towards Nehru, that Gerald Curtis was suspended from his duties by the Congress Ministry; he was later reinstated. For their part, the British officers took the allegations levelled against them as an indication of the rising tension in the

Province. Their position was not made any easier by the fact that they had friends on both sides of the political dispute. After Nehru's visit, the Hindus living on the Frontier had seriously to consider their future; atrocities against them became more frequent, while news came through of Muslim murders in India. At the same time, the support for the Muslim League was voiced in village demonstrations as civil disobedience was used against the Congress Ministry. Ian Stephens, who visited the Frontier in 1947, saw tonga-load after tonga-load of 'hefty Pathan peasants, handcuffed to constables, being borne off stolid but determined' down the Mardan-Peshawar road to prison. In Bannu, Robin Latimer saw that it was futile for the Congress Party to state that the jails were large and could take any number of Muslim League demonstrators. 'When the people came in large numbers begging to be put in jail, it was like a comic opera, because we used to have to say, "We're sorry, the jails have had their quota for today, you'd better come back tomorrow."'

The most testing time for the British political officers came during the arduous negotiations which led to independence. On the Frontier, where the Hindus were in the minority, the British had to pay special attention to their protection. 'Our task was to stop the Hindus being slaughtered,' said Robin Latimer. 'One really did have to apply one's mind quite a lot to signs of disturbances. The Muslims did not of course like the measures taken to protect the Hindus, but we had to do it. It didn't bother us; one couldn't let the side down.'

Independence

In March 1947 Lord Mountbatten, who had been sent to India specifically for the task of handing over power to the Indians, became the new Viceroy in place of Lord Wavell. The following month he went to the Frontier. The trouble and continued riots in Dera Ismail Khan and Tank caused great alarm to the government back in Delhi. There was also the question of what would happen to the semi-autonomous tribesmen in tribal territory. When Wavell had visited the Frontier the previous November, he had found that the Afridis did not seem to be anxious to co-operate. 'Their representation was to the effect that if we were going, we should hand them back the Khyber pass, that they had no intention of being ruled by Hindus and resented Nehru's visit and that anything in the way of a little extra cash would be very acceptable.' Wavell had assured them that no one wanted to interfere with their freedom.

The situation had deteriorated in the intervening months, and when Mountbatten visited the Frontier he also felt it was necessary to address the Afridis.

As I expect you know, I am a sailor and had the honour of fighting in a battle in the North Sea in company with HMS *Afridi*, called after your tribe because of its famous warlike qualities. Although we have had to fight you Afridis in the past on occasions, we respect and like each other. Your jirga has a reputation for wisdom and foresight. For the last sixteen years you have behaved and stuck to your agreements. In this critical time, when power is to be handed over, do not lose that reputation.

Alan Campbell-Johnson, who was Mountbatten's press attaché at the time, found that the scene provided:

. . . an extraordinary contrast with the bleak, austere grandeur of the pass [Khyber] itself. Landi Kotal camp, indeed, was just like a leafy Sussex village in summer time. The jirga itself was a colourful assembly. Many of the tribesmen squatting in the shade of the tree looked very old and benign and it was difficult to imagine that they were some of the toughest warriors in the world.

The best that Mountbatten could offer the people of the Frontier who did not want Pakistan was a referendum. Another referendum was also to be held in the tribal territory to gain the formal agreement of the tribes to join Pakistan. During the run up to the vote in July in the settled areas, 'this traditionally turbulent corner of the sub-continent remained in a highly dangerous state,' wrote Ian Stephens. This was partly because the referendum as offered was rejected out of hand by the Congress Party. Realising that the fight for a united India was over, the Khan brothers requested that the people of the Frontier should at least be given the chance to vote for a semi-autonomous North-West Frontier or Pashtunistan, as they preferred to call it. Just as the Muslims had been frightened of absorption into Hindu India, so were the Pathans anxious not to lose control over their affairs and become part of a Pakistan in which Punjabis predominated. 'If you destroy the Pathan nation, terrible things will happen,' Dr Khan Sahib warned Mountbatten.

The land of the Pashtu-speaking peoples which the Khan brothers envisaged was never very clearly defined. At the time, it appeared as a demand for self-rule whilst maintaining relations with both India and Pakistan. However, the option of Pashtunistan was never presented on the ballot paper and the Congress supporters felt they had no alternative but to boycott the referendum altogether. It therefore came as no surprise that the result of the poll, in which only just over half the registered voters took part, was an overwhelming vote in favour of joining Pakistan. 'Stop the poll,' was the Muslim League's excited cry. 'We've already got a hundred per cent.' In the autumn of 1947, the individual jirgas of the tribes in tribal territory stated that they wished for 'exactly the same relations to subsist between them and Pakistan as had existed between them and the British government'.

Those who had campaigned so long for the departure of the British found that, when the time came, their one-time masters left with exceptional speed. In the case of the Congress Party on the Frontier, which was being obliged to witness a partition it had not wanted, the way in which it was done seemed out of character. 'I told Olaf Caroe,' said Ghaffar Khan's son, Wali, 'that I was amazed that the British, who had given India one government from the Khyber to Cape Comorin should break it up so quickly. It reminded me of when we were children and we used to sit on the river bank and make castles in the sand; and then in one movement we'd kick it all down.' Their disappointment, however, was lost amidst the general excitement over the birth of a new country for the Muslims, Pakistan.

The British officers themselves had to accept the idea of fast-approaching independence with good grace, as much on the Frontier as elsewhere. 'One didn't have much time to brood about independence,' said Robin Latimer. 'People had worked themselves up into a great enthusiasm, with the idea of Pakistan catching on like wildfire.' In many cases the British felt a marked lack of hostility from the people who were about to be released from colonialist rule. 'People said, "Don't go!" Even allowing

for being polite, they seemed really not to want us to leave.'
There was also a certain amount of frustration at having to leave
a job unfinished. This was especially true in the case of tribal
territory. Robin Hodson found that there had been little progress
towards bringing peace to Waziristan, and with independence
coming so quickly British authority seemed to weaken in the
months that remained. Whatever mutual respect there was
between the British and the Pathan, there were still fundamental
differences: 'We'd failed in Waziristan, I suppose,' said Hodson,
'firstly because we were "infidels", secondly because a lot of the
forces of law and order contained Hindus and in Waziristan this
always meant that there was a temptation for the tribesmen to
shoot at them.' In general, the British officers reckoned that,
when ruled by their co-religionists, the Pathans would be far
easier to manage. They also realised that, with independence and
partition taking place at the same time, they were about to
witness one of the most momentous changes in the history of the
sub-continent. The Frontier could not help but be affected.

Pakistan's frontier

Independence was celebrated—at midnight on 14 August
1947—in the North-West Frontier with as much rejoicing as
elsewhere. But it was impossible to ignore the news of atrocities,
'which lost nothing in the telling'. Within a month of independence, the incidents of murders of both Sikhs and Hindus
increased in the North-West Frontier, as did those of Muslims
slaughtered in what was now India. Peshawar became full of
refugees from Kohat, Mardan and Nowshera waiting to be
evacuated to the Indian Punjab. Sir George Cunningham, who
had been invited to return to the Frontier as Governor, replacing
Sir Olaf Caroe, noted in his diary that he had received offers
from almost every tribe to be allowed to go and kill Sikhs in the
Punjab. 'I think I would only have to hold up my little finger to
get a lashkar of 40,000 to 50,000.'

Eventually the minority Hindus and Sikhs were evacuated in
thousands leaving the cities along the Frontier quiet but with
'denuded' populations. The Province differed from western
Punjab, which became part of Pakistan, in that the number of
Hindus and Sikhs who left was far greater than that of Muslim

refugees who came in. On average there was one incoming refugee to every ten who left; the Frontier therefore suffered a considerable loss of trained and educated people. In particular, the civil services of the Frontier were affected. Trade was also severely disrupted since a great deal of it had been in the hands of Hindus. 'We had passed through grim and tragic days,' observed Sir Henry Holland from Quetta, 'so soon after the people's rejoicing over independence.'

At the same time, the political divisions remained between those who supported the Muslim League and Jinnah and those who were loyal to the Khan brothers. In spite of refusing to attend the celebrations of independence, Khan Sahib and the Congress Ministry on the Frontier had not resigned. Jinnah therefore took it upon himself to dismiss the Ministry and form a Muslim League administration under Abdul Qayyum Khan. Muhammad Ali Jinnah himself was a stranger to the North-West Frontier. Born in Karachi, he had lived in Bombay until partition. In April 1948 he decided to visit the province, and when he addressed the people at a rally at Cunningham Park, his most forceful warning was to those who had opposed the Muslim League and 'who had nearly succeeded in handing over the Frontier province to a Hindu Raj.'

Although officially there was supposed to be no repression of the Khudai Khidmatgars, many were imprisoned. Ghaffar Khan and his son Wali spent the next five years in jail in Baluchistan. When they emerged, Pakistan had already embarked on the series of political crises wich were to threaten its stability for the next thirty-five years. Both father and son opposed the merger of all the provinces into 'One Unit' in 1954, in anticipation that it would detract from the degree of autonomy which each province had gained under the 1935 Government of India Act. They considered that by accepting the post of Chief Minister in the One Unit administration, Dr Khan Sahib had deserted the peoples of the North-West Frontier; when he was assassinated in 1958, Ghaffar Khan wrote that he had been killed 'by those people for whom he had forsaken his own people'. In the years to come, both Ghaffar Khan and Wali Khan spent many more years either in jail or under house arrest. What they considered the course of action necessary to promote the cause of the Pashtun people was deemed to be secessionist activity by the successive rulers of Pakistan. The 'Pashtunistan' issue could not be laid to rest, more especially since Pakistan's neighbour, Afghanistan, had seen fit to adopt it.

Relations between the two Islamic countries had been hostile since independence. The Afghans criticised the number of British officers remaining in the Pakistani government. Their presence, according to the Afghans, made Pakistan 'nothing more than a thinly disguised British administration'. Afghanistan also chose to veto Pakistan's application to join the United Nations, in protest at the 'arbitrary' nature of the Durand Line. In spite of Afghanistan's prior recognition of the border, the Afghan government maintained that the validity of the line drawn by the British in 1893 had now lapsed with their departure. Finally, open support was given to Pashtunistan which was referred to in school geography books as 'a mountainous territory between Afghanistan and Pakistan'. For the first thirty years of Pakistan's existence, this issue made two countries, which could so easily have been allies, into potential enemies. A shared history and a common religion could not solve their differences.

Likewise, Pakistan fell out with India. This time the cause for bad relations was the disputed territory of Kashmir. As a predominantly Muslim state, Kashmir would have gone to Pakistan, but for the fact that, as a princely state, its ruler had been given the right to decide which country to join. The Maharajah, Hari Singh, was a Hindu and did not opt for either country; but because of the strategic location of the state, there were many who felt that before they left the British should have forced him into an eventual fusion with one or other country. Not unnaturally, since it was one of the provinces in which Muslims were in the majority, the Pakistanis felt it should have gone to them. While the Maharajah demurred, small parties of tribesmen from the North-West Frontier invaded Kashmir. As their numbers increased, relations between the two countries deteriorated and the Maharajah became nervous that he would be obliged to join Pakistan by force. By October 1947 it was estimated that about 4,000 tribesmen, half of them from tribal territory, mainly Mohmands, Mahsuds and Wazirs, and about the same number from Hazara, had already embarked on a holy war against Kashmir.

Once the Maharajah announced his accession to India, Nehru felt justified in sending Indian troops to the capital, Srinagar. This infuriated the Pakistanis, who felt that they were being deprived of what they considered to be a part of Pakistan. Jinnah did not, however, declare war officially; instead it was hoped that the tribesmen, commanded by those of the Army who were willing to take part, would win the day. The crisis over Kashmir presented difficulties for those British who remained in the administration to help Pakistan through its early existence, like Sir George Cunningham. If he were seen to support the movement, he might encourage thousands more to rush to Kashmir. But if he tried to prevent them from going, the Pakistanis, who he realised desperately wanted Kashmir, would hold him responsible for losing it.

Meanwhile, the number of the tribesmen continued to swell; so did their unpopularity. Since they could in no way be considered comparable to a disciplined army, it was impossible to prevent them from exacting the age-old right of war: loot. Cunningham himself was convinced that the invasion of the tribes had 'thrown Kashmir into the arms of India'. He felt that even the Muslims might prefer to become part of India rather than suffer the looting tribesmen in their midst. But, just as the tribesmen reached the Poonch valley and were on the verge of taking Srinagar, they were obliged to stop. The Pakistani government's acceptance of a three-day ceasefire ultimately resulted in the loss of Kashmir for that nation: without tents in the pouring rain, and fearful of the Indian Air Force and heavy casualties, the tribesmen lost interest in the jihad and returned home, satisfied with the booty they had acquired. To this day, the line dividing Kashmir between India and Pakistan remains along the ceasefire line or 'line of control', guarded by United Nations troops. Divided Kashmir has continually soured relations between the two countries, to the extent that their armies, once part of the same fighting force, have only ever been used in battle against each other. In all the three wars India and Pakistan have fought, Kashmir has been an issue, but its future has never been resolved.

The Frontier tribesmen, who had participated in the first attempt to gain Kashmir, little understood the implications of the jihad. The spoils they brought home decked their houses and provided visible evidence that they had been to war. John Dring remembered seeing numerous items which were clearly of Kashmiri origin in the houses of Waziri maliks. What mattered most to them was which tribe had fought most bravely; in general, without doubt it was their own.

CHAPTER EIGHT

Guests on the Frontier

Everything was the same as it used to be, except for an emptiness and an oldness. My eyes noticed only the recognised things; the unfamiliar things didn't count at all: and it was not until I realised this that I knew I must stop and readjust myself to today. The continuity of my life had been broken.

Peter Mayne, *The Narrow Smile*

The people who remained

The British who did not leave after independence found themselves in what were obviously very changed circumstances. The Frontier was no longer the last line of defence of the British Empire; it was now the border between Pakistan and Afghanistan. For the tribesmen, apart from the occasional hiatus caused by political troubles between the two countries, life went on much as normal: migration from the hills to the plains in winter, back to the hills in summer. Whilst tribal territory adopted the same relationship with Pakistan as it had had with the British Empire, the Pathans of the settled districts had to face the challenge of becoming part of an independent Islamic state, cut off from Hindu India; and those people who were once their masters had technically nothing to do with Pakistan any more. Most of the British went home to try and start a new life after sometimes more than twenty years away. It was clear, however, that for those who wanted to stay, there would be work enough to do. They just had to reconcile themselves to working as employees of a foreign government.

At Muhammad Ali Jinnah's insistence, the former Governor, Sir George Cunningham, who had already retired back to his roots in Scotland in 1946, agreed to return and resume his old office of Governor. His initial reaction, however had been to refuse: 'My desire to help the people of the North-West Frontier Province in any way I can is still as strong as ever it was; and I have so many friends there that it would be a real delight to be with them again. But the reasons against taking up the Governorship again weigh too much.' First there was his age—he was nearly sixty; secondly, 'it was a big break in my life to have to leave the North-West Frontier sixteen months ago, and having made the break once I know how difficult it would be to do it again.' But, once pressed, Cunningham did go back, even though he remained in Pakistan for less than a year; ill health was the reason for his final departure back to Scotland in March 1948.

Cunningham's successor as Governor was Sir Ambrose Dundas, another old Frontiersman. As Secretary was John Dent, who was only too happy to help set up the new country. 'There was tremendous zip and enthusiasm. For the first few years after independence there was the feeling that we must work like mad to show that we could do it.' In a sense, he found that it was more fun than before. In the days before independence, there was no deficit-financing and so there was limited scope for what projects could be undertaken. 'But after independence, aid was flowing in and there was more money available for plans for hospitals and schools and irrigation projects.' The excitement over Pakistan was infectious. 'There was a wonderful feeling,' said Dr Phil Edmonds, who came to Peshawar as Principal of Edwardes College in 1954. 'Everyone was so hopeful. They felt at last they had got what they wanted. They did not think about the problems ahead.'

There were also those who seemed to long for the days gone by: 'Why have you deserted us?' was a question frequently put to Dr Jonathan Shaw and his wife Molly, who came to work at the Peshawar Mission Hospital soon after independence. 'They missed our sense of fairness and at that stage didn't value being part of Pakistan.' Even in the present day, the memory of the British is favourable. 'We have spoken to many, many old Pathans,' said Dr James Newmark who works at Risalpur between Nowshera and Mardan, 'who have sometimes brought out old testimonials from Army officers that have been kept with very great pride. It seems to be mainly the officers' ability to speak Pashtu fluently which commanded respect, as well as their fighting ability.' Once they had got rid of their old rulers, it was possible for a Pathan to admit that it was surprising 'how highly the British were respected in areas where before they were resented as colonisers. When one refers to the British days, one talks about good administration and good justice. To have had a British teacher means quality.'

Foreign help in both the Army and the Air Force was welcomed by Pakistan. The head of the Air Force, along with twenty-five other officers from the RAF, stayed on for several years to help create an air force for Pakistan based in Peshawar. They had to start virtually from scratch, since there were no facilities, very few trained pilots, and poor equipment. The formation of the Army, again assisted by British officers, followed closely the model of the old Indian Army. The mess, if anything, became 'more English than the English'. To this day, as the BBC correspondent Alexander Thompson observed, they still drink tea out of the same china cups. At the same time, there were many British ex-officers who saw the tragedy and misfortune that two peoples—the Indians and the Pakistanis—both of which they had trained, should so swiftly use their knowledge and experience to fight each other. 'To me it's so sad,' Lieutenant-Colonel Michael Wilcox remarked of the pictures, proudly hanging in their messes, showing 'deeds of valour against each other in the three wars.'

In many cases, those who stayed on could not help but identify themselves with Pakistan. Ian Stephens met several junior officers who in their turn had become more Pakistani than the Pakistanis. 'They applied "our" to the government or armed forces of Pakistan as naturally as a Pakistani would. To have said "their", putting a separatist pronoun between themselves and the people they were so fond of, would have outraged their sense of belonging.' It was also a time, on the Frontier as elsewhere, when the Pathans themselves could expect swift promotion, leapfrogging one or two ranks to fill the places of their former masters. In general, the British were happy to admit that they did so with competence and ability. Also, as was to be expected, it was much easier for the Pakistanis—as co-religionists—to deal with the Frontier tribes than it had been for the British. Commander Izzat Awan, who went to North Waziristan in 1949 as Assistant Political Agent, realised that it was important for the young officers like himself who arrived on the Frontier to get to know the 'concept of special treatment that these areas required'. They appreciated the guidance of the old experienced officers, both Pathan and British, whom they could rely on as mentors. But it was clear to the British that in the end they would do themselves out of a job. John Dent rose to become Home Secretary and Revenue Commissioner, which was the top job in the Civil Service. He could rise no higher, and after seven years in the new Pakistan, rather than be posted to the Punjab, he decided it was time to leave.

As a Pathan who had worked closely with the British, Lieutenant-Colonel Yusuf thought of going to live in England after 1947. His experience in the Army and the political service had left him almost too English. In the end, he stayed on to serve Pakistan until his retirement, when he finally went to live in England. 'Strangely, I don't miss the Frontier. There's no music, no opera, no ballet, no books. I would be starving without these things there, not to mention good French wines.' He was, however, exceptional. Most Pathans who had served under the British readily adopted the identity of Pakistan and remained there. Some British officers even retired to Pakistan. Colonel Buster Goodwin, who had admired the Khataks, spent his last years in Rawalpindi.

Even back in England the brotherhood remains, and members of the Punjab Frontier Force still keep in touch with each other through their 'Old Boys' magazine' *Piffer*; the Military Historical Society enables old soldiers to go back and visit the scenes of past battles; and past members of the Indian Political Service still meet at their annual reunion. 'There are only thirty of us left now, and we are dying at the rate of three a year,' said Yusuf in 1982. 'But we have decided that even when there is only one member left, he will sit and drink a toast to the rest of us.'

Missionary work

If the days of the foreign political and military officers were numbered, this was less so in the case of the doctors and nurses. In spite of independence, the expertise of the medical missionary was and still is appreciated by the local people. When they have retired, others have come to take their place. Sir Henry Holland postponed his retirement until after independence, although he was already in his seventies. He saw only too clearly the coming challenge for the missionaries.

> The pattern of things, as I had known it for nearly fifty years under the British Raj, was at an end. A new chapter was opening with fresh possibilities as well as problems of its own. To younger minds and hands than mine would fall the responsibility of discovering how best we could fulfil our Frontier mission in these changing conditions. The world's most powerful Islamic State was in future to be the setting of our work, the environment in which the tiny Frontier Church must continue to give its Christian witness.

In a sense, both the Catholic and Protestant missionaries had long since reconciled themselves to healing those who were not of the same faith, and the idea of offering medical treatment on condition of faith was repugnant to them. Even so, their position did alter after 1947. In Pakistan, the Church Missionary Society now comes under the jurisdiction of the United Church of Pakistan, which has several religious denominations under its wing. They no longer own any property, and although they are free and welcome to carry on their work as doctors and nurses, they feel that their actions have to be even more above reproach than ever before. As Islam has re-asserted itself, all foreigners have become subject to scrutiny and this includes missionaries. The suspicion, attached to Americans in particular, is that they might be working as agents for their own governments. However, the missionaries have taken the changes with good grace: 'There is a certain enrichment in our work, because it has become that much more selfless. We are not a group of people doing things there with instructions from Britain.'

And, in spite of their new status, it is still possible for the missionaries to maintain the Christian element in their work: 'We start the day with prayers in the church which is situated in the hospital compound; have a short time of singing and prayer on the wards, prayers before operations, and give thanks for the birth of babies with the patients; and we always pray in the name of Jesus Christ,' said Alison Fookes, who came to the Frontier in 1976.

> We don't engage in the kind of 'active evangelising' which our predecessors used to do, but we do share our faith with those who are interested. Our main 'spiritual' work is with the Church, that is the local Christians. We sometimes have staff Bible studies and two of us are involved in Sunday-school work. There is more scope for this kind of work and it is more appropriate for us as guests in Pakistan.

The number of missionaries from the Church Missionary Society remains very small; since independence their work has been supplemented by other organisations, particularly from Scandinavia and the United States. In general, it was not a love of the Frontier but a desire to serve God which dictated their future. For Alison Fookes, going to Bannu was in a sense going home.

> I was at Crowther Hall, the CMS training college, when I first heard about Bannu as a mission station. The name rang a bell, however and I guessed it was a place my parents had visited while in the sub-continent during the Second World War. I checked with my mother and discovered that it was the place where they had met in 1943! My father was in the Army and my mother a nursery governess and they met in the tiny garrison church which still stands in the canton-ment in Bannu. When I heard this, it seemed to be a confirmation of the feeling I was getting that Bannu was the place God was calling me to.

In the Pennell Memorial Hospital at Bannu, Dr Ruth Coggan, who arrived there in 1969, found that the wards bore little resemblance to those of Western hospitals, 'appearing dark, dirty and cluttered'. Numbers fluctuate, because 'it is such an easy matter to hire beds from the bazaar, or to walk home with one on one's head.'

> When patients are admitted, their family goods and chattels come with them, so one may often find a chicken tied to the bed leg (alive of course!), a pile of firewood under the bed,

cooking pots and pans to trip over and grease marks on the hospital charts, indicating that they have been used as plates or to keep flies out of the day's milk supply. When I first saw the state of the wards, my heart sank to my boots and I wondered how on earth our operations would heal without dreadful sepsis. Amazingly, they usually do!

Even so, the doctors still find themselves up against local obstacles, particularly in adjusting to ignorance. One patient came to Dr Shaw with a jar of yellow liquid which he had been prescribed by a local hakim which turned out to be urine. 'There is also the tendency for local doctors to prescribe far more tablets and medicine than are required (and sometimes omitting the only one needed) because they have a financial arrangement with a certain chemist's shop.' Or sometimes patients would be given only half the prescription and hence would not recover. 'A common racket,' said Dr Shaw, 'was to give chalk when penicillin was prescribed and then the patient would end up in the mission hospital wondering why he had not recovered.'

Overall, medical facilities advanced steadily in the post-independence period. More money was made available and local hospitals improved in quality and size to the extent that the Mission hospital in Peshawar found that it could turn its attention to other diseases not catered for in the government hospitals. While Dr Shaw became involved in the treatment of leprosy, his successor, Dr John Bavington, found there was a need for treatment in psychiatry. He set up a mental health centre, adapting a section of the hospital, in order to help those suffering from depression and schizophrenia. Prior to this, mental illness had been dealt with in 'mental hospitals' which formed part of the local jails. Bavington found that there was 'a surprising amount of depression about' amongst both the educated and the poor classes. 'The people who came to us were very appreciative of having this facility. Of course the question arises whether you can practise Western psychiatry in an Eastern way because of the intrusion into the cultural feelings of the people.' Along with the use of drugs and anti-depressants, part of the treatment involved group therapy. 'It was strange for them in their culture to talk about their problems. I had a mixed group of men and women and this was considered even more extraordinary.'

Touring the villages, Bavington on occasion found mentally ill people chained up.

> I can't say how common it was. One young man—the son of a Mullah—was chained up on the roof. He was a schizophrenic. I got him to come to the hospital but he would only come with his chain. Eventually I got him to take the chain off, but he ran away and his parents didn't bring him back again. In such a case, the relatives would feel responsible for him, but they also felt a great deal of shame at having produced someone mental. Certainly there were other cases of people being brought to me in chains because they were violent. Sometimes relatives did not understand what I was trying to do. The standard remark would be, 'Well, Doctor Sahib, you are our mother and our father, we trust you to do whatever you feel is best.'

An important offshoot of his work was the provision of facilities for handicapped children, which today is flourishing.

Although the hospitals are increasingly staffed by local medics, there is, in the 1980s, a renewed need for nurses and doctors on the Frontier to help the millions of refugees who have come from Afghanistan. Health workers from various relief organisations have been welcomed to assist with the variety of medical problems arising from the fighting. Those who have ventured across the border to tend the sick have been inspired both by a spirit of adventure and a desire to help the people: 'I think that by instinct I'm more attracted to people who have a hard time in life and a hard time gaining their freedom,' said a French woman doctor working for AMI (Aide Médicale Internationale). 'In Afghanistan, the Mujaheddin are fighting alone for an ideal which attracted me; and the people need doctors, so I came.'

Just as the mission hospitals remained, so did the mission schools, of which Edwardes College holds pride of place on the Frontier. Even today it has an Englishman for its Principal, Tim Woolmer. But the main architect of its future and expansion after independence was Dr Phil Edmonds, who spent twenty-five years as Principal until his retirement in 1979. 'I was very conscious that it was important to be almost more Pathan than the Pathans and to observe their customs as they did.' Unlike so many others who spent a lifetime on the Frontier, however, Edmonds was an exception in that he never learnt either Urdu or Pashtu. 'Unless you're first class at learning languages, it is better not to try and talk them, because you might get something wrong. Rather than risk a gauche or erroneous balance in my speech, I preferred to sit and listen. I would never interrupt the flow of conversation, knowing that in time all would be revealed.'

Edmonds arrived on the Frontier seven years after independence, accompanied by his Australian wife, Belle. They were no strangers to the sub-continent having spent the previous ten years at the mission school in Kashmir. However, he found that partition had left its mark on Edwardes College: most of the staff had been Hindus and had fled; educated Muslims were in short supply. There were no typewriters or files. The students were on strike, complaining in the atmosphere of Islamic independence that they did not want to attend a Christian school. 'For three years it was a real battle to restore the college from absolute bedlam.' He took enormous care with the boys, gaining both their fear and respect. 'I administered the College physically, playing hockey and cricket with them,' putting into practice his belief in the strength of personal leadership. He also worked hard to raise the academic standards, realising that if the boys 'had their noses to the grindstone' and were kept busy at their studies, they could not cause trouble.

Belle Edmonds not only supervised the catering but, as a trained nurse, opened a dispensary. Once a week the doctor from the Peshawar Mission Hospital would come to check the health of the boys. On one occasion, the school was visited by a researcher looking into ethnically 'pure' tribes in three specific areas: the North-West Frontier, Sri Lanka and South America. He asked for some Pathans willing to be tested for their purity of race. Eager to do so, several students came to the surgery, 'with their chests sticking out like turkey cocks'; but when it was clear that the demonstration meant giving a blood sample, 'they all said they'd got Punjabi mothers!' Belle Edmonds found that in spite of the ease with which they could draw a knife in a blood feud, they hated having injections.

Edmonds also worked hard to attract boys from tribal terri-

tory to education. In the old days, while the good athletes had
been the Muslims, the best students were the Hindus and Sikhs.
'The Pathans in a way despised education. They used to be teased
if they went to school; they'd be called girls.' In the same way, if
they did not join in one of the frequent demonstrations they
would be sent bangles and cosmetics. 'But once the Pathan saw
the value of education he would do anything to get it.' As the
years went by, he found himself taking on his former students as
teachers; alternatively, he would often see that they had attained
high office in the Civil Service, armed forces or the government.

One difficulty Edmonds encountered was with the boys who
had not learnt English in primary school. They would arrive at
Edwardes College and be unable to compete with those who had
a fair knowledge of the language. 'The system of education had
fossilised at about 1900,' he commented. 'No grammar was
taught, just English literature.' On the edge of Central Asia the
students would be expected to read selections from the *Spectator*,
the de Coverley Papers and Wordsworth. Edmonds was helped
in the College by several VSO students who came as teachers to
spend their year abroad on the Frontier. One of them devised
some modern exercises based on the English language with the
advice of the British Council, which proved such a success that it
was issued in book form and a second edition came out.

Every so often, there was a clear indication that the students at
Edwardes College were not like English boys learning grammar
and reading Wordsworth. 'You'd be thinking that things were
very much like everywhere else, but then something brought
you back to reality,' remarked a VSO teacher. 'A student would
come up and say, "I've got to abandon my studies; my elder
brother has been killed"—as had his father—"and so I've got to
go back and be with my family."' It was not uncommon in
Edmonds's experience for a truck to arrive and take a boy away
to carry on with a blood feud, never to return.

At the same time Principal and teachers alike noticed how the
feud mentality could pervade even the classroom. 'Once I was
asked to invigilate an exam; one student was cheating. I warned
him once, then again, and finally I said I would report him to the
Principal. He carried on cheating and so I did.' Edmonds sent the
boy down. 'It was very unpleasant; I was amazed that evening
when a Pathan colleague of mine on the staff and the boy came to

my room and said, "He has come to tell you that he doesn't bear any grudge." I hadn't thought about it, but realised what he was saying was that no blood would be shed.'

As a missionary, Edmonds had to take a cautious line over religion in early Pakistan. Although Edwardes College remained a Christian school, it was not a mission school as in the days of old. Both the Bible and Koran were read at public functions. 'The strength of my position as a missionary was that I didn't have to make an apology for what I was. The important thing is that you must be sympathetic with the Muslims.'

Travellers, Pashtunistan and the northerly neighbour

The departure of the British Raj did not suppress the interest of foreigners in the Frontier, whether or not their forebears had served there. James Spain, the American diplomat and historian, met his first Pathan at the age of twelve. He was Kamal the Outlaw who stole the Colonel's horse in Rudyard Kipling's 'Ballad of East and West'.

> It was some time, as a matter of fact, before I was even aware that Kamal was a Pathan. Kipling did not write for boys in the American Mid-West in the thirties and the word 'Pathan' does not appear in 'The Ballad of East and West'. At first, I knew only that Kamal and his fellows were some unusual kind of Indians, rather like our own Indians of the American West, devoted to brave and warlike deeds.

Spain was posted to the American Embassy in Karachi; and a trip to Rawalpindi left him sitting on the station waiting for the Down Mail back to Karachi. But before his train arrived, the Up Mail came in, heading for 'Attock, Nowshera, Peshawar,' in the words of the guard on the station platform. 'The names summoned up others in my mind: the Pathans, the Khyber Pass, Waziristan.' Purely on impulse Spain bought a ticket to take the Up Mail instead.

Thus, in the early fifties, began his fascination with the Frontier. In 1953 he resigned from the Foreign Service and was given a grant from the Ford Foundation to study the Pathans in

New York at Columbia University, in London and on the Frontier. His objective was to write a dissertation on the Pathans; and in so doing, like so many others, he came to love the Frontier and its peoples. 'Even thirty years after I first saw the Frontier and more than a dozen since I last lived there, I still long for the place.'

Those who travelled to the Frontier in the years after independence could not fail, however, to notice that the whole area was embroiled in a dispute which stirred emotions on both sides of the border: 'Afghanistan Unjast! Pashtunistan Unjast!' (This is Afghanistan! this is Pashtunistan!) was the monotonous cry which John Griffiths kept hearing in the lorry from Kabul to Kandahar whilst on his Alexandrine adventure in 1957. 'It was as if a tourist on a motor coast drive down the Wye valley from Monmouth to Chepstow were to find himself the captive audience of a fanatical Welsh Nationalist driver continually crying out "Home Rule for Wales, Monmouthshire is Welsh."'

The issue of autonomy for the Pashtu-speaking people had not died with independence; and it was a talking point in select circles both in Kabul and Peshawar. In Afghanistan, the cause was patronised by the Prime Minister, Daoud Muhammad Khan, who, as a cousin to King Zahir Shah, had come to power in a bloodless coup in 1953. As a Pashtun, Daoud took pains to encourage the idea, without however indicating that there was ever any question of including the Pashtuns in Afghanistan within the new 'Pashtunistan'. In 1954 James Spain discussed the issue of Pashtunistan with Daoud in Kabul: 'He insisted, simply, that the Pathans in Pakistan were entitled to claim independence if they chose to do so and that the Afghans, as the same people, had the right to promote the Pashtun cause.' Spain also detected that 'he obviously was proudly aware that his ancestors had ruled there less than one hundred and fifty years ago—not long as time is reckoned in that part of the world.'

Thus, while the government in Pakistan tried to integrate the North-West Frontier Province and the Pathans into Pakistan, it felt that there was continual pressure and propaganda from across the border, encouraging the Pathans to assert their independence. It was a political tug-of-war which observers found was more of an emotional issue than a feasible proposition. Ian Stephens considered it to be a problem, which, in comparison with that of Kashmir, was 'third rate and largely bogus'. On the maps as made available in Kabul, Pashtunistan appeared very 'strange': it was 'an exceedingly narrow, wriggly object, wedged in between Afghanistan on one flank and the remains of West Pakistan on the other, with the bulk of India behind; and consisted almost entirely of infertile mountainous country whose revenues would be meagre in the extreme. Some railways entered it sideways, but none ran the length of it.'

Peter Mayne found that the Pashtunistan issue isolated him from his Afghan friends in Kabul. As soon as it came up for discussion, 'I would find myself cut off, an agnostic surrounded by fanatical believers.' It became clear to him that in Afghanistan the Pashtunistan issue was real, and that it 'poisoned' relations between the Afghans and the Pakistanis.

The Pakistani government regarded Afghanistan's support for Pashtunistan as a threat to the newly created country's security. As relations deteriorated, Pakistan saw no alternative but to close its own consulates and trade offices in Kabul and request the Afghans to do likewise. In return, the Afghans broke off diplomatic relations, leading to the formal closure of the border in 1961. Apart from cutting off much-needed customs revenue, this move pivoted Afghanistan in the direction of her powerful neighbour to the north. If the Afghans could not use the route east to export their produce, then the Soviet Union was only too happy to help out with their transit problems, even if it meant, as was believed, dumping the fruit which was air-lifted out of the country into the river Oxus.

In fact, the Soviet Union had been increasing its presence in Afghanistan ever since 1947. When Brigadier Prendergast was posted to Kabul as military attaché in 1948, it seemed to him that initially the Russians had not realised that there was such a big vacuum left by the departure of the British. Their presence in Kabul amounted to a Second Secretary who could speak neither English nor Persian and 'was no more than a night watchman'. However, in 1949 they increased their deputation dramatically with the arrival of a well-educated English-speaking retired general as Ambassador, and three military attachés—'in which case,' said Prendergast, 'the Americans sent over two air attachés.'

When John Griffiths met a group of Russians in Herat in 1957, he observed how there was already an element of secrecy about their activities. With his knowledge of Russian, Griffiths was rather surprised to hear the word 'armour plate' being used whilst the Russians were discussing a road-building programme, which, as part of the Soviet Aid Agreement negotiated by Daoud, was supposed to be entirely commercial.

> 'Good day, comrades. And what brings you to Herat?' Confusion, embarrassment, anger. Would I be supposed to know about the vehicle maintenance project? 'We're . . . er . . . ah—on holiday.' 'I'm sorry you're having such a miserable time,' I commiserated. 'But I just love your holiday clothes.' I took in their identical dungarees, pointed hats, and little attaché cases with a patronising sweep.

Later, when he related the incident, and told of how his camera had been seized, he found that most people treated it as a 'typical traveller's tale'.

The border closure had clearly enhanced the Soviet position, and on her way to Bamian in 1963, Dervla Murphy noticed a continual stream of empty trucks heading north across the Hindu Kush to stock up with essential supplies. 'Afghanistan's closing of her border with Pakistan was a classic example of biting off one's nose, etc.; the gesture hurt no one but Afghanistan, and benefited no one but Russia, who now has almost a monopoly of trade with Afghanistan.'

The relationship which developed was exactly the one which Britain had endeavoured to prevent over the past century. Since the Second World War, the United States of America, which had replaced Britain as the opponent of Russian expansion worldwide, had been taking an interest in the area with a view to monitoring the Soviet Union's movements. Both countries were giving aid to Afghanistan in an effort to keep a foothold in the country. Whereas the Soviet Union build the roads in the north, the United States built those in the south, and the all-weather roads provided a welcome change from the usual dirt tracks for the overland traveller. Dervla Murphy with her Rozinante bicycle—called Roz for short—could hardly believe it when five miles out of Herat, the road became perfect. 'I nearly fell off with astonishment and joy and Roz really let herself go and whizzed along at an average of 15 mph. Our unexpected bliss lasted all day—God Bless Russia!' By the time she left Kandahar for Kabul, she was travelling on an American-made road. 'This time it's "God Bless the Americans!" who within four years expect to have completed the 320 miles from Kabul to Kandahar.'

The Russians and Americans even attempted to co-operate on joint projects. Whilst the Soviets built the airport at Kabul, the Americans supplied the electrical and communications equipment. And if the United States would not grant the Afghan requests, particularly if weapons were on their shopping list, then it was likely that the Soviet Union would. The population of Mazar-i-Sharif, close to the Russian border, was already beginning to include Soviet engineers and technicians as a matter of course. As time passed, the Russian connection appeared to be more sinister. Returning to Afghanistan in 1966, John Griffiths noticed the 'absolute strangling grip the Russians were getting on the Afghan economy, and the futility of Western efforts insofar as concerned aid. The Americans would give the grain, the Russians would build the silos to store it in, and they would end up getting all the credit.'

Along with the obvious Russian aid programmes came the ideological influence which clearly penetrated a section of the intellectuals while leaving the rural classes unaffected. 'In classrooms, the students often refuse to listen to anti-Marxist views, and an atmosphere has been created in which few academics can favourably discuss anything relating to the West,' wrote Louis Dupree, the American academic and writer who devoted much of his time to studying Afghanistan and its problems.

> I do not myself believe that the student population is 'pro-Communist', whatever that means today [1968]. Rather I believe that their attitudes, and their strikes and demonstrations are a response to the real inequities in their society as they see them. They attack those ideologies— primarily Islam and Western materialistic philosophies—which they believe have created the inequities and which, as they see it, jointly control the country and ultimately their own destinies.

Whatever their affiliations to the Moscow brand of Communism, a hard core of Communist intellectuals managed to gain an urban following during the period of liberalisation in the early sixties. Daoud had resigned in 1963 over Pashtunistan and King Zahir Shah determined to try an experiment with limited democratic rule. In an attempt to liberalise the press, leftist newspapers, which were named after newly formed political parties, were allowed to circulate. The writers of *Parcham* ('the Banner') which first appeared in March 1968, included Barbrak Karmal. He had first come to the public's attention in a fight in the Wolesi Jirga—the House of the People—two years before. Karmal was taken to hospital and, as Dupree relates, he turned the situation to his advantage. 'He has a great flair for the dramatic, and when his followers demonstrated outside the hospital, he grabbed additional bandages and energetically tied them around his head before appearing, to wave feebly to the spirited crowd.'

Parcham took a more cautious approach to reform than its predecessor *Khalq* ('the People') which had been founded by another committed Communist, Noor Muhammad Taraki. His paper had been banned after calling for a 'class struggle' to promote the interests of the 'oppressed classes'. Both Khalq and Parcham continued to function as rival political parties in the limited circumstances allowed. Khalq drew its recruits mainly from amongst the armed forces, whilst Parcham appealed to the intellectuals.

At the same time King Zahir Shah was trying to listen to the demands of the right-wing religious leaders who wanted to reinforce Islam. The conservatives had been alarmed at some of the more liberal practices which had crept into society, and were anxious for them to be eradicated. Louis Dupree measured the resurgence of Islamic ideas in the late sixties in terms of how difficult it was for a foreigner to purchase alcohol in Afghanistan. There was none available in the bazaar and so his Afghan friends suggested that he apply to the Government Monopolies, 'where, they said, the purchase of booze would be very easy for me, a foreigner. I should have known better for when, three days later, I emerged from the Monopolies with six bottles of twelve-year-old Ballantine Scotch and fourteen bottles of the excellent Pakistani Murree Export Beer, I was almost ready to swear off the sauce.' It took him 102 separate steps to purchase the alcohol, 'and the file, about two inches thick, presumably now lies preserved for posterity in the bowels of the Monopolies. Several of the sheets had been ripped in half by irate officials and then glued together again by lower officials at some stage of their long journey.'

At the same time, foreigners were watching Afghanistan's emergence into the modern world with a kind of bemused amazement. Dupree used to measure progress in general by the length of time it took him and his family to pass through customs. Roland Challis, the BBC's correspondent in Cairo, who spent a week in Afghanistan in 1969, found there was another yardstick. 'When I arrived at my hotel I was asked whether or not I'd booked a room. When I gave the receptionist my name, he said, "Oh, here's a cable for you." Upon opening it, I discovered that it was the one I'd sent requesting a room to be reserved.'

In many respects, for all the ups and downs over Pashtunistan and the increased presence of the Russians, travellers found that Afghanistan was still rather a dream-world where time and reality meant nothing. It was the sort of place where the photographers Roland and Sabrina Michaud could spend months on end observing people whose customs and traditions had hardly altered. A British graduate from Oxford, Keith Best, who travelled through Afghanistan on his way to India and the Far East, believed that 'Afghanistan hadn't changed much since the Afghan wars. People still used old box-cameras and apart from the motor car you could have been there at any stage.' Observing the black tents of the nomads and the long lines of camels making their way across the plains, he felt 'intense sympathy' at the poverty he saw. 'And yet there was almost a longing to be part of such a simple life, where the options are so much fewer. My overall impression was that here is a country that desperately needs to be brought into the twentieth century, but at the same time would resent it.'

Archaeologists and collectors

It had not taken long for foreigners to recognise that the whole of the Frontier area, ranging from Taxila right into Afghanistan, was a vast archaeological preserve. Epoch upon epoch of the area's history could be unravelled by digging into the ground; and since the days of Sir Aurel Stein, scholars and collectors have been anxious to hunt for artefacts—especially coins and bits of pottery—amongst the ruins.

From 1957 onwards the French archaeologists were excavating the only Hellenistic city discovered in Afghanistan on the river Oxus, that of Aï Khanum, which dates from 300-150 BC. The Italians were busy unearthing the palace of one of the later Ghaznavid rulers, Masud III, at Ghazni. With their Buddhist heritage, the Japanese took particular interest in digging up several Buddhist sites near Kandahar. The British became involved in excavating the old city of Kandahar, and the Afghans themselves have successfully uncovered a Buddhist site at Hadda, near Jalalabad. In the eighties, however, the fighting in Afghanistan has meant that this sort of activity has become impossible.

In Pakistan, excavations at Taxila have uncovered towns from three separate epochs, and Charsadda, near Peshawar, remains as an important place for finding Hellenistic art, pottery, jewellery, seal rings and silver. There are also the ruins of the Buddhist stupas in Swat, reminiscent of the travels of Hsüan-Tsang in the seventh century, when he saw them ravaged by Huns. In the sixties, Professor Giuseppe Tucci and his Italian colleagues uncovered the remains of Bukhtara close to the capital of Swat, Saidu Sharif, where piles of rocks revealed what must have been a very tall stupa, surrounded by sixty smaller ones. On one they found a carved Corinthian column, a reminder of the Mediterranean influence which had touched the Frontier.

Initially, the archaeologists found that the Pathans were not much interested in their pre-Islamic heritage in terms of art form. Their interest arose, according to John Suidmak, an art dealer and collector, when they realised its international value. Suidmak acquired a specialist knowledge of the Gandhara period of art from the first to the fourth centuries AD.

The whole art of this period is very much a synthesis of Western and Eastern art; for example, a silver mirror handle could be totally Western in design, but for the peepul tree in the background. This tree is a clear indication of the Indian influence. A frieze is easily recognisable as having Hellenistic influence if it is made in linear form, without depth, but

with each scene divided chronologically. The Indian tendency is not to divide the scenes and the whole thing
becomes much more complex and elaborate.

Suidmak also found that he had to be sure about what was on
offer. On one occasion he was approached by an excited dealer
saying that he had Alexander's ring for sale, quoting as evidence
the legend that Alexander had indeed lost his ring on his travels
to India. He produced a huge seal ring in gold cast with the heads
of a man, a horse and a lion. The dealer's firm conviction that it
was Alexander's ring had made him give it price worthy of such
distinction: 'but I was not convinced'. Nor was he the only one
to be offered *the* ring. Another collector said that he had about
twenty-five rings, all of which had been sold to him as that of
Sikander Sahib.

Unlike tourists who come once or perhaps twice to the
Frontier, an antique collector will come many times and can
therefore establish a good rapport with the people with whom he
has to deal. Once, when Suidmak was expecting to be cheated,
he was assured by one of his Pathan friends that this would not
be so. 'You are one of us.' But he has also found that dealers are
quite likely to produce what has been requested. If he asked for
an object from the fourth century, the next day he would be
contacted with the news that by chance that very object was
obtainable, regardless of the fact that an expert like himself
would be able to tell straightaway whether or not it was
authentic. He discovered in a curious way that he could not do
good business until he had learnt to lie. The lies generally
concerned misinformation about one's destination and one's
other contacts. It was quite common for one dealer to say to
another that he had not seen a mutual friend at all when in fact he
had been in touch only the day before. 'If you don't play the
game, they think you're stupid. In a sense it is the meeting of
Western and Eastern custom.'

Travellers, hippies and the after-effects

In the early days, Westerners were liked and respected. On the
Frontier in Pakistan, they reminded the Pathans of days gone by

and the British heritage, and they were pleased by the interest the foreigners showed in their land. Even in Afghanistan, the residue of hatred left by the Afghan wars was beginning to fade. John Griffiths found that most of the local people assumed that all Europeans must be engineers; either that or doctors, and as such they were welcome.

Some of them were hardened travellers, and at least one a great explorer. He was Wilfred Thesiger, who had walked over the Empty Quarter in Saudi Arabia and had turned his attention to discovering Afghanistan. On his way in 1956, he encountered the novice mountaineers, Carless and Newby, returning from their 'short walk' in the Hindu Kush. With some derision, he watched them blowing up their air beds. 'God, you must be a couple of pansies,' he remarked, as he lay down on ground which according to Newby was 'like iron with sharp rocks sticking up out of it'.

Dervla Murphy, in 1963, provided the startling vision of a lone woman cycling to India, by way of Afghanistan and the North-West Frontier. She left 'a dozen broken hearts' behind her in Kabul: 'Not as romantic as it sounds since they are all in the tourist bureau! . . . they admitted I was one of the few to enter their offices without a list of complaints from here to eternity.' Overwhelmed by the hospitality and generosity of the local people, she for one appreciated the other-worldliness of the places she visited and did not want them modernised for the sake of the tourists. She implored the Afghan tourist officials 'not to pander to outsiders and defile Afghanistan with cafés on every mountain pass and juke boxes in hotels and souvenir shops in Bamian'.

By the mid-sixties, however, another type of tourist, anxious to take advantage of the £37 bus fare from Copenhagen to Katmandu, emerged on the horizon. 'The route from Kabul to Peshawar became a hippie trail with drug addicts, and this tarnished the image of the Westerners.' The people could not necessarily have been expected to appreciate that the hippie movement was the reverse side of the period of questioning and doubt which was gripping the West. 'It destroyed all the fantasies we had about white people. Before the hippies came there was no question of seeing a white person in the street and not inviting him into your home. Nowadays you would think twice.'

The hippies shocked the tough men of the Frontier region, who had been brought up to applaud masculine virtues and physical good looks. To date they had seen in the British only the sort of characteristics they admired: tall, clean-shaven men, who were good horse-riders. 'They wondered if those who had long hair really were English.' It also horrified them to see the offspring of their one-time rulers wandering around in patched blue jeans, with their eyes dilated, begging in the streets. It did not matter whether those who came were Swedes, Danes, Germans or French; in the eyes of the Pathan, they were all English, as, to date, the only foreigners they had known were the *Angrez*. In particular, Western women in their cheesecloth shirts and mini-skirts destroyed the reputation of their kind. 'It was a sad thing to see the white boys using the white girls as prostitutes in order to get drugs.' Even ten, twenty, years later, if a girl wears cheesecloth, she can expect to be asked 'Do you take drugs?'

Keith Best recalled a particular hotel in Kabul, called the Panorama, where Western students used to congregate since it was the only place where they could get fresh orange juice. 'It was full of French and Italians whose governments would not repatriate them when their money ran out, so they were shooting themselves silly with morphine.' Whereas the Pathans were used to opium and hashish, they attributed the introduction of heroin and morphine entirely to the hippies, and although the hippies came and went, the drugs did not. They have created such a serious problem that the Pakistani government has begun to become worried about its own addicts. As the main supplier of heroin to the West in recent years, it has been impossible for the government to prevent the local people becoming interested in refining heroin for financial gain, and large numbers becoming addicted. In this respect, tribal territory, isolated from Pakistani laws and punishments, has proved to be the ideal haven not just for growing poppies, as they have done for centuries, but for making heroin. The town of Darrah in the Kohat pass has graduated from being merely a town where guns are made to one where heroin is refined. So too with Landi Kotal. The problem is made more difficult because, if challenged, the local people have plenty of guns with which to defend their lucrative trade.

The traffic in drugs has rebounded on Western countries

because, with instability in Iran and Afghanistan, the traditional overland markets for export have been disrupted. Consequently the amount of heroin sent out from Karachi to the United States and Europe has increased so dramatically in recent years that the United States' ambassador to Pakistan, Ronald Spires, has listed drugs, together with Pakistan's nuclear programme, human rights and relations with India, as the four 'vulnerabilities' which could damage relations between the two countries.

Since long before the outcry about drugs, the smuggling industry has thrived in an area where the loosely acknowledged border makes crossing from one side to the other relatively simple. Dervla Murphy found that Landi Kotal was like 'an exotic sort of supermarket in the middle of nowhere', where virtually any item could be obtained. Someone with the right contacts could quickly obtain whatever item he might require. As one European living in the Frontier in the 1980s discovered, 'the system is to go to the village, order the item, give your address and wait a couple of days until it appears on your doorstep. Of course, the system is run by the rich for the benefit of the rich and is unlikely to be stopped without great opposition from the rich.' In this way, virtually any luxury item can be acquired without, of course, paying heavy import duties. In the sixties and seventies the main items of interest were television sets, radio equipment and refrigerators. In the eighties, attention is focused on guns—manufactured locally or imported from abroad.

Those who returned

The return journey to the Frontier after a long or short absence could provoke strange reactions amongst those who were now foreigners in what had once been the British Empire. Sir Olaf Caroe expressed the feelings of many: 'For one who has spent a lifetime on the Frontier to cross the bridge at Attock is to come home, and the warmth of a Pathan welcome lifts the heart. The wounds left by the 1947 break begin to heal.'

However, when Peter Mayne went back to the Frontier for a holiday in 1954, he found himself looking at it all with double vision. 'It was a disturbing business this return to what had once seemed home.' Inevitably whilst in Peshawar he went to Deane's Hotel: 'The food was the same to the point where one wondered how they had contrived to keep it warm all these years. The waiters greeted me as if I too had been on the hot-plate ever since we last met.'

He found that the most visible difference was the disappearance of the whites.

> Not that the whites had been other than quite ordinary whites for the most part, but their going had necessarily changed the character of the place . . . The cantonment had been alive with whites—administrators, soldiers, their wives, white children with ayahs in attendance, and yapping bands of the dogs the whites kept, spaniels, fox-terriers, dachshunds, setters and the rest of them.

To add to his depression, he found that most of his old friends were dead through feuds.

> I kept thinking of what was gone, when I ought to have been content with each day as it came . . . What else was it that had died? My love for this country, or I who had loved it? . . . Did it matter so much? I really don't know, but I suppose it did. I only knew that after all reaching back was impossible, and that I should destroy these images once and for all time. I must exorcise the ghosts, amongst them the faded ghost of me so long ago.

Mayne was pleased to encounter one friend from the old days: but even their meeting was too brief for him.

> I said good-bye with a nagging sense of yesterdays uprooted. Perhaps it was wrong to see old friends again; wrong in any case to meet just once for a few hours and then go away, leaving the past shaken out of its ordered and happily remembered frame, and the present fluid, with nothing to hold it in.

Not all those who returned felt quite the same nostalgia as Peter Mayne. When John Dent left the Frontier in 1954, he did not think of going back for twenty-five years, but he was happy to welcome his old Pakistani friends when they came to visit him in England. Finally, after one trip his guests bid farewell to their host 'for the last time', unless he promised to make a return journey and stay with them as their guests. So after a quarter of a century away, he and his wife decided to go back to the Frontier for a holiday. 'It all looked the same; everyone looked very fit and healthy compared with the London Underground crowd. And I'd forgotten really how incredibly friendly everyone is.' They enjoyed themselves so much that they went back again the following year.

At the same time, the Pakistanis who received their former rulers as guests were anxious to show off the Frontier at its best. Izzat Awan hosted John Masters in 1961, by then a celebrated author. He was keen to assure him how safe and peaceful Waziristan was since the British left. When the two set off on a drive from Wana to Tank, however, related Awan, 'my orderly came and placed a shotgun in my hand and a box of twelve-bore cartridges by my side. John remarked, "Well, well, after all we have been talking last night, you need a shotgun when travelling." I remember having replied, "You will find out."' In fact, the drive from Wana to Tank, which before had been so hazardous, was so boring that Awan availed himself of the time 'to bag as many birds on the way as possible: this pursuit broke the monotony of the journey.'

Major-General Goff Hamilton of the Guides was delighted by his trip back to the Frontier when he flew by helicopter over his old battleground where he was wounded in 1935. Sighting all the old landmarks in Mohmand territory, he felt 'I too had come a full circle after forty-five years as we swung around the ridge for the second time. And then we landed and saw it all again from the comfort of leather sofas in a huge tent carried to the top of a mountain by the Mohmand Rifles.' He was greeted by many officers in the Guides mess who had been subalterns in his time. 'One of them said, "I've got a present for you". It was a regimental brooch, which they'd ordered for my wife before the end of the War. It wasn't ready before I left and they'd kept it for thirty-two years.' Returning soldiers often found that they would be greeted with the remark: 'When I heard that you were coming, I said my father has come alive again.'

Even so, the Frontier they saw was in many respects very different from the old North-West Frontier of the British Empire days. The journey which Arthur Reed, writing for *The Times*, made up the Khyber in the late seventies contrasted greatly with that of his father who had been in the Army. Whereas he had accomplished it all in ten and a quarter hours from Piccadilly Circus, London, in what he termed an 'airline-cocooned' trip to Peshawar, his father had been obliged to take 'a month by sea followed by the best part of a week by train and with the final leg up the Khyber on the march, with the Pathans taking pot shots from each hill top.' At the time he was writing he found that it was smiles not bullets along the Khyber. 'All is far from Kiplingesque adventure' on the Frontier: 'a flimsy gate through which an Afghan soldier and his opposite number in the uniform of Pakistan let a constant flow of tribesmen pass without formalities.'

Even Goff Hamilton found that the Frontier had 'lost its sting: no longer do Pathans carry rifles, and by and large the tall towers of the Frontier villages have given way to more practical two-storeyed houses in walled enclosures; for commerce has replaced the blood feud and the transistor radio the Khyber knife.' But he had the percipience to observe that, beneath the surface, 'It's still the Frontier and still reeks with history and suppressed excitement.' So it might: Hamilton made his journey in 1979. By the end of the year Russian tanks had rolled into Afghanistan and the world's attention was back on the North-West Frontier once more.

CHAPTER NINE

The Fight Goes On

Acting otherwise would have meant passively watching the creation on our southern border of a source of serious danger to the security of the Soviet state.

Leonid Brezhnev, 1980

To all appearances, the Frontier in the late seventies was retreating back into its romantic history. Nothing much of international interest was going on there, and it was thought of less for its present-day importance than for the stories of the past. Whatever friction there was seemed to be essentially a local affair between Pakistan and Afghanistan. Whether or not the border dispute had been resolved mattered little to diplomats and politicians, whose attention was fully occupied by the Middle East and oil, economic recession in the industrial countries and poverty in the Third World. However, instability in Iran revealed the first chink in the otherwise satisfactory crescent of comfort established between Western spheres of influence and those of the Soviet Union.

The Banner and the People

Afghanistan, which at one time had been so close to absorption within the British Empire, was about to leave behind its links with the Indian sub-continent, perhaps once and for all. In 1978 the country entered on a new phase of its existence: Communism. Surprisingly, the bloody *coup d'état* in April of that year aroused less concern than might have been expected. It hardly seemed to matter that a Communist regime with close links with Moscow was now in power in Kabul. Muhammad Daoud Khan, the personification of the 'last remnants of monarchy, tyranny and despotism', was dead; and, with a certain amount of symbolism, the clothes and possessions of Daoud and his wife were put on public display. 'It was all in very bad taste,' commented the wife of a diplomat, who refused to go and see them.

The new ruler of Afghanistan was Noor Muhammad Taraki, a committed Communist since the 1950s. When Daoud had staged his comeback in a peaceful coup in 1973 after ten years on the sidelines, he had availed himself of the support of the intellectuals and Communists, especially those of the Parcham (Banner) party led by Barbrak Karmal. Although Daoud's new supporters had trained in the Soviet Union, most of them, thought Louis Dupree, were 'more nationalist than Communist in outlook'. Nonetheless, they were anxious for reform, and initially believed that Daoud, the Red Prince as he was called because of his close ties with the Soviet Union in the fifties, would be the one to open the way to sweeping changes. The monarchy was abolished; Daoud was proclaimed Founder, President and Prime Minister of the Republic of Afghanistan. King Zahir Shah agreed to pass his time in exile for 'medical' reasons.

The rural population of Afghanistan, however, were not prepared to accept either the reforms or the men who proclaimed them. And as Daoud decided to drop the Communists from the administration, disillusion set in amongst them. They began to campaign against the new regime which appeared as nothing more than the old established order with a different name. Daoud, totally devoid of any of their socialist convictions, 'reverted to the behaviour of an old tribal Khan,' said Dupree, 'appointing friends, sons of friends, sycophants' to his cabinet.

At the same time as distancing himself from the Communists, Daoud also turned away from his old supporter, the Soviet Union, and determined to make Afghanistan 'non-aligned'. He looked around for new friends among the other foreign powers. 'When I met him in Kabul in April 1974,' said the Indian journalist, Kudlip Nayar, 'he had said he did not want experts from America or from the Soviet Union; he preferred Indians. In fact, many times the Afghan government sought the advice of Indians on project reports prepared by the Americans, Russians and Japanese.' Daoud also took pains to establish contacts with Iran, Egypt, Saudi Arabia and Kuwait.

Relations with Pakistan had reached an all-time low with Afghanistan's continued support for Pashtunistan. However, both Daoud and the Prime Minister of Pakistan, Zulfikar Ali Bhutto, were anxious for a settlement. Whereas previously each country had torn down the other's flag, it was an indication that relations were on the mend when a dancing and singing troupe from Pakistan came to perform for the Afghan national day celebrations in 1976. 'They were so popular,' said the British Ambassador in Kabul, Roy Crook, 'that they performed again the next night!' However, negotiations for a formal agreement to settle the Pashtunistan issue once and for all could not be finalised by the two men. Bhutto was removed from power in a military coup in July 1977. The Afghan monarch's new negotiating partner was General Zia-ul Haq, before Daoud himself was removed from power in April of the following year.

Many observers believed that, by alienating himself from the Russians, Daoud effectively signed his own death warrant, at least in political terms. So long as Afghanistan came within the orbit of Moscow's control, Daoud could count on the Soviet Union's support. But once he tried to go it alone, the way was open for the Communists in Afghanistan to gain the approval of Moscow to overthrow him.

Exhibiting a unity they had not been able to maintain before, nor since, the factions of Parcham and Khalq began to work together. Muhammad Taraki was considered to be the father figure; his two lieutenants were Hafizullah Amin, a Khalqi and Barbrak Karmal from the Parcham. The actual timing of the coup was forced by events. A huge demonstration against the murder of a leftist sympathiser, followed by mass arrests, was sufficient to give the go-ahead for the coup. Before his arrest, Amin had been able to make contact with the carefully prepared cadres of supporters in the armed forces. Daoud was oblivious of the danger; he was meeting with his cabinet in order to discuss the latest unrest when the army started shelling the palace. It seems that the initial intention was not to kill Daoud, but to take him prisoner. However, astounded at the insult, Daoud resisted, with the result that he and the occupants of the room—cabinet ministers and family members—were all killed.

Although rumours from intelligence sources had been circulating that a coup was imminent, it took foreigners and diplomats by surprise. Even the Russian Ambassador was out of Kabul on a fishing expedition and was almost caught in the swiftly imposed curfew. 'The British occupants in Kabul poured into the embassy,' recalled Roy Crook. 'We slept sixty that night: businessmen, tourists and hippies. We gave them drinks, dinner and showed them a film.' The noise of the shelling was enough to cause some Pakistani tourists to make a tape recording of it all before they actually knew what had happened. Three rockets landed in the British Embassy compound, and the next day the British Ambassador and his wife drove around to the French Embassy to see how they were; they found the Embassy had been badly hit. The entrance to the United States' Embassy was blocked. 'We went round to the back and found them all up on the roof.' One tourist who managed to gain entry into Afghanistan for twenty-four hours after the coup was Stephanie Roberts, an Australian on her way from Australia to England. She was amazed by the relative accuracy of the bombers, whose main targets appeared to have been the rows of government buildings. 'If there was an office in between two non-government buildings, the one in the middle was reduced to rubble, while the other two were left still standing.'

After the Saur revolution, called after the month of April in which it occurred, life for the foreigners changed considerably. What had been a pleasant posting for a diplomat became fraught with anxiety. As Britain's representative in Kabul, the British Ambassador found himself held responsible for the broadcasts of the BBC which the Afghan authorities interpreted as being hostile to the new regime. The Crooks soon discovered that their good Afghan friends were frightened to talk to them. They were also aware that their servants might be obliged to give information on their activities and that their telephones would probably be tapped. 'We knew that one of our servants used to have to report back to the authorities; but his English was so bad, we thought that it was a miracle if he ever did get any information to give them!'

Frequently their staff would come and say that they had to go on marches carrying flags in favour of the new regime. 'Little children who'd learnt to clench their fists would be thrown out of school to go on marches.' They also heard shots and screams of people being arrested. 'I saw one man commit suicide rather than be taken away.' And they became accustomed to the disappearance of Afghans they had known, who were never seen again.

Just after the coup, the curfew was anywhere between 4 and 8 pm; as things calmed down, as a rule it was 11 pm, but if there was trouble it could be put back to 9 or 10. 'They would shoot first and ask questions later,' said Crook. 'There was a common joke about an officer who saw a man at 10.30 and shot him; when asked why he had killed the man when the curfew wasn't until 11 o'clock, the officer replied, "I know where that man lives, he never would have made it."'

In the climate of anti-Western feeling, the British Ambassador realised that he could well be a target of attack. It was not that he suspected the government would be responsible, but that some 'patriot' might think to demonstrate his loyalty to the new regime by shooting the Ambassador to the old imperialist country. Even so, Crook refused to alter his progress through Kabul and continued to travel in his large and conspicuous Daimler. 'We preferred to go around as normal rather than appear frightened.' In February 1979, however, the American Ambassador, Adolph Dubs, was kidnapped by a group of terrorists demanding the release of a political prisoner. The Afghan police blasted their way in, and Dubs was killed in the crossfire. This episode increased the worry about the security of all the Western diplomats.

For the first few weeks after the revolution, the uneasy alliance between Khalq and Parcham remained. Taraki was hailed as 'the great national and revolutionary figure'. He was elected President of the Revolutionary Council and Prime Minister; Amin and Karmal were Deputy Prime Ministers. Now that they had the power, the new leaders were determined to put into practice their socialist revolution. Their programme of reforms amounted to sweeping changes in land tenure—'in the interest of toiling farmers'—and countless other innovations designed to project an old feudal country into a new, modern, socialist one. Everything was supposed to be done 'in the interest of the people and the national interest of the country'. But there was no way in which the rural people of Afghanistan could be transformed overnight from a society rooted in Islam and conservatism to one which accepted Marxist doctrine in a godless world. Once the mullahs started preaching that the revolution amounted to choosing between the Koran and the Communist manifesto, there was little chance that it would ever be greeted with enthusiasm from the majority of the people. Even the new flag, which replaced the old Islamic green with Communist red, offended traditional sentiment.

Amongst the reforms was one 'ensuring the equality of rights of women with men in all social, economic, political, cultural and civil aspects.' The issue of women was one on which many rulers had foundered in Afghanistan: the British had offended the Afghans by the 'traffic' of women during their occupation; Amanullah had outraged the conservative elements of Afghan society by encouraging women to appear in public unveiled in the 1920s. Now the Communists angered the Islamic section of society by prohibiting the price to be paid for a bride.

Most of the reforms were never enacted, but the immediate reaction to them was so strong that the committed Communists were bound to be disappointed with their reception. The dedication of the people to the tenets of Islam, engrained over the last thousand years, was far too strong to give way to revolutionary ideals. In addition, although Taraki expressed a desire to remain within the non-aligned movement, his foreign policy clearly accorded with that of the Soviet Union. Within six months of the Saur revolution the *Kabul Times* proudly announced that thirty agreements had been concluded between Afghanistan and the Soviet Union. On 5 December 1978 Taraki signed the Afghan-Soviet Friendship Treaty.

Large numbers of Russian advisers and technicians were welcomed into Afghanistan. As their numbers increased, however, and the Communists pressed on with enforcing their revolution, unrest spread throughout the country. More and more the people resented the intrusions of the reformers into their traditional society, which seemed to be taking them further away from Islam. Most of the old bureaucrats were purged, leaving inexperienced new administrators to govern the country.

Nuristan was the first province to resist the revolution, when it proclaimed itself a 'free' province—Azad Nuristan; others followed suit. Events in Herat in March 1979 showed anti-Russian sentiment to the full. Some thirty Russian advisers and their families were hacked to pieces and their bodies carried about the town on pikes; in so doing the Afghans exhibited the same degree of hatred they had shown for the dismembered bodies of Burnes and Macnaghten in 1841. The Russians took their revenge and bombarded the city, killing or wounding an estimated ten thousand people. When Kudlip Nayar travelled to

Herat nearly a year later, he remarked how fresh in people's minds was the 'brutal' attack of the Russians. Within a short time, the Afghan authorities found themselves fighting a series of rebellions against disparate sections of the people all united in their opposition to the revolution.

Meanwhile, the alliance between Khalq and Parcham was visibly falling apart. There had already been a divergence of opinion as to whether the revolution should be enacted swiftly or in a more evolutionary manner, and there was intense personal rivalry between Amin and Karmal. In the summer of 1978 the Parchamite members of the party were dropped and their leaders, including Karmal, were 'exiled' abroad as ambassadors; Karmal was sent to Czechoslovakia. In March of the following year Amin secured greater power by assuming the office of Prime Minister devolved on him by Taraki. One of his priorities was to try to discredit the Parchamites by recalling them from their posts under a charge of embezzlement. Needless to say they did not return; instead Karmal went to Moscow.

However, in spite of the uneasy passage of the first year of the revolution, Taraki was proud of its achievements, and liked to compare it with the Russian revolution of 1917—the year in which he was born. 'If the Great October Revolution in 1917 rocked the whole world, the Great Saur Revolution which triumphed with the inspiration of the Great October Revolution also jolted all the toiling people of the world and drew their best wishes,' he said at the anniversary celebrations. Others present at the time felt less secure, and even feared that the celebrations might present an opportunity for Taraki to be assassinated. 'We were sitting very close to him,' said a Western diplomat, 'and I said to my neighbours that I was going down behind a nearby wall if there was any shooting. Suddenly from the vicinity of the Bulgarian representative, who was not supposed to understand English, came the assurance, "Me too!"'

As Amin's power increased and the popularity of the revolution waned, Taraki was requested to stop at Moscow on his way back from the non-aligned summit in Cuba in September 1979. The message he apparently received when he met the Soviet leaders was that Amin had to go, and be replaced by Karmal: it was hoped that he would have a less inflammatory effect on the people. Again, most of the foreigners remaining in Kabul were unaware of the intricacies of the power struggle being waged in

Kabul. When it was announced that Taraki had resigned for reasons of ill health after his return from Cuba (where incidentally he had appeared quite well), and then that he was dead and Amin was now in sole control, it was not clear whether Moscow was behind Taraki's death or not. It is now generally assumed that the attempt to remove Amin failed because of his own suspicions that he was about to be ousted. He therefore took precautions and came to see Taraki with an entourage of armed guards. Taraki was fatally injured in the shoot-out and later died in hospital. The Russians had no alternative but to recognise Amin as his successor, if only for a limited period of time.

Amin himself was lulled into a false sense of security by the Russians' apparent acceptance of him. He continued to rule Afghanistan with great severity and brutality: arrests, murders and purges led to greater opposition from rebel groups, which caused Amin in turn to launch a full-scale offensive, devastating villages and the inhabitants all at the same time. But probably even before Amin took power, the Russians had already been making their own plans for Afghanistan. By mid-December, the Americans were complaining to the Russians about the build-up of forces near the Afghan border. At the same time, they also had other urgent matters to think about: Iran for one, and the seizure in November of personnel in the American Embassy in Teheran.

Amin did not live to see the effects of Russian assistance come to fruition in accordance with the terms of the Afghan–Soviet Friendship Treaty. Supposedly poisoned by his Russian cook, he died soon after their intervention, as did several members of his family. The Russians' new protégé was Barbrak Karmal: he and several thousand Russian troops were going to save the revolution.

The army across the Oxus

When Russian troops occupied Kabul at Christmas 1979, they were following in the footsteps of their old rivals, the British, who had last taken possession of the city one hundred years before. While the Western world digested its turkey, Kabul's residents heard the droning of planes, as the Soviets came in to land with their cargoes of men and machines. Then came the tanks rumbling into the city, firing at anything which moved in order to show that resistance would be a waste of time. At last, the Russians, fulfilling the fears of the British, had come in strength to Kabul. By the time they made the journey, the mountains of the Hindu Kush were less of a barrier than they had been. In the sixties Daoud had negotiated with the Russians to build the Salang tunnel, nearly three kilometres long, to the north of Begram. Although badly ventilated, it provided a far easier passage than the mountain passes, especially in winter, and had already become an essential link in the Soviet Union's line of communications to Afghanistan.

Regardless of the fact that the rest of the world knew very little about the internal political situation in Afghanistan—why Karmal had ousted Amin, who had in turn killed Taraki, all three of whom had had the support of the Soviets at one time or another—the entry of Russian troops into Afghanistan changed the status of the North-West Frontier instantly. The Durand line was no longer the boundary between Pakistan and Afghanistan: it had suddenly become the last line of defence against Soviet Communism.

Pakistan found new favour in Western circles. The military regime of General Zia-ul Haq had been well and truly out in the cold for at least the last nine months, ever since Zia, who overthrew Bhutto in 1977, had ignored the worldwide appeals to spare the former Prime Minister's life. In addition, the military dictator had refused to hold elections and return the country to civilian rule. The United States in particular was also annoyed by Pakistan's nuclear programme; although this was ostensibly for peaceful purposes, the Americans were convinced that Pakistan was intending to explode a nuclear bomb, and had earlier cut off aid because of the nuclear issue. But all these preoccupations were shelved in the light of what was believed to be a greater threat to the stability of world peace. The North-West Frontier became the last foothold of the 'free' world before the Russians could reach India: or, as was considered to be more likely, the warm waters of the Persian Gulf.

Since the industrialised countries had suffered bitterly in the previous decade over oil, they were in no mood to see the Soviet Union take possession of the precious oilfields of the Gulf. To start with, it was automatically assumed that oil must account for the Soviet Union's invasion of Afghanistan and the theory that Russia had always been anxious to secure a warm-water port was once more aired. The severest punishment which President Carter felt he could give to the Russians for their 'act of aggression' was to boycott the Olympic Games due to be held in Moscow later in the year; this diplomatic gesture was supplemented by trade embargoes. To a lesser degree, other governments followed suit. Like the preoccupation with oil, the Olympic debate almost overshadowed events in Afghanistan. At the same time, the occupation was condemned by the vast majority of countries in the United Nations. However much the Soviet Union protested that it had been invited into Afghanistan as a friend to assist a neighbour in time of need, the action was branded as one of aggression.

Both the Afghan authorities and the Soviet Union have been very sensitive about the number of Russian troops in Afghanistan. Barbrak Karmal referred to the Russian force as a 'limited contingent'; however, at the time of the invasion the contingent was estimated at anywhere between 40,000 and 80,000. This number has increased to well over a hundred thousand. Those detachments from the Muslim areas of the Soviet Union which came in first overland were understood to have been sent back quickly, lest the strength of Islam should prove more forceful than the desire to serve the Soviet Socialist Republic.

Alongside the protests of the Western countries, there became apparent a vague hope that just as the British had suffered in Afghanistan in the nineteenth century, so too would the Russians. One old Frontiersman, Brigadier F. Hughes, confided his expectations in a letter to *The Times*: 'As one who has had considerable personal experience of engaging in military operations against the hillmen of those regions, I know exactly what the Russian Army is up against. I firmly believe that the Russians have bitten off a lot more than they can chew. Let them stew in their own juice, and go on wasting a lot of military effort to no purpose.' Like the Americans in Vietnam, it was anticipated that the Russians would get bogged down, harassed by the successors of the Afghans who had fought the British so fearlessly. These were the Mujaheddin—the soldiers of the Holy War—'bandits' in the eyes of the Soviet Union but 'freedom fighters' to everyone else. Ever since the coup of April 1978, they had been carrying on guerrilla warfare hiding out in the hills; with the intervention of Russian troops, they increased their efforts and their following. They also secured the nominal support of the

United States and the Western alliance, as well as a place of refuge in neighbouring Pakistan.

In the weeks which followed the Soviet invasion, foreign journalists flocked to Kabul to report on the new conquerors of the Bala Hissar fort. It appeared that the foreign correspondents were allowed into the country in order that their presence might be seen as giving legitimacy to the Karmal regime. But as their curiosity about the extent of the Russian occupation increased, so did the welcome afforded them diminish. Bruce Loudon of the *Daily Telegraph* was in the first group of foreign journalists to be expelled within days of the invasion: 'A ministry official said members of the new regime were "too busy" to meet correspondents, and warned the visitors, "We cannot guarantee your safety because of bands of armed Amin terrorists."'

With Karmal's ascent to power, Amin was branded as a dictator, tyrant, and a CIA agent. It was announced that he had requested the USA to intervene militarily and that their 'great leader' Taraki had been smothered on Amin's orders. His followers and henchmen fell swiftly from power and all excesses of the past were blamed on Hafizullah Amin. The new regime recognised the damage done to the cause of the revolution by the blatant disregard for Islam, and Karmal was anxious to appear in the guise of a good Muslim attending prayers at the mosque regularly. An attempt was made to win over some of the mullahs in order to show that Communism and Islam were compatible. However, the overall opinion of the Afghan people was that Karmal was a puppet, installed by a foreign power, just as Shah Shuja had been instated by the British in 1839. As such he had no chance of being accepted as a liberator of the people from the unpopular Amin regime.

The early reports of the journalists who were allowed to remain in Kabul gave the impression that Russia had the country well within its control. 'In all but a few isolated towns, the Soviet army seems to have crushed resistance in Afghanistan,' wrote Robert Fisk in *The Times* less than two weeks after the invasion. Richard Beeston, writing for the *Daily Telegraph*, found that there was 'a nightmarish air of normality about Kabul as Russia begins the slow process of digesting her new acquisition. In the bustling streets of the city of turbaned Afghans and veiled women, there is rarely a glimpse of a Russian except an occasional Soviet military vehicle or tank, or the oriental face of a soldier from Central Asia behind a barracks gate.' Robert Fisk believed that Kabul's inhabitants had accepted this latest intrusion of large numbers of foreigners with a certain amount of complacency.

> If anyone believes that Kabul contains a crushed, politically downtrodden community only waiting to rise up against its oppressors, then he or she is way out of tune with this curiously Ruritanian society. Most Afghans are politically uninterested and Kabul has an almost bored air of normality as it sits in its icy basin in the mountains with its wood smoke drifting up into the pale blue sky.

But the journalists also realised that although there was not much evidence of the Russian occupation in Kabul, the army must surely be visible in its tanks and tents outside the capital. When they finally did meet some Russian soldiers their experiences varied. Ian Mather wrote in the *Observer*: 'Soviet troops I have encountered during two weeks in Afghanistan have shown friendly and smiling faces. Attempts to engage them in meaningful conversation about what they are doing here have failed. But their behaviour to me has invariably been polite, disciplined and I would even venture to say sincere.' Even when Mather attempted to go through the Salang tunnel, the Russians were apparently courteous in their refusal; whilst taking an interest in the £20 they found in his wallet, as they searched him, they did not however steal it, although they did confiscate his ordinary tourist map. Peter Niesewand of the *Guardian* was less impressed with the Russians' behaviour. He too was stopped from entering the Salang tunnel, and lost his maps. He also witnessed his Afghan driver have three tape cassettes of Afghan music and about £32 in Afghan money taken. 'The Russian looters had judged their victim well. Whereas we Westerners might complain officially if they were too greedy with our belongings, an Afghan would feel powerless.' An Italian film crew, however, had a camera worth over £22,000 confiscated.

It was also perfectly possible for the Afghans to mistake the Western journalists for Russians. When Philip Jacobson of the *Sunday Times* and his colleagues ventured south out of Kabul, they were apprehended by a group of Afghan guerrilla fighters.

It was not, at first, an entirely amicable encounter. Car doors yanked open, a variety of weapons cocked and aimed in our general direction. 'Russki,' said one rebel with dismaying certainty. 'Britishki,' we replied with some fervour, waving passports, press cards and packets of Marlboro cigarettes. Further explanation from our taxi-driver seemed to do the trick: warm hugs and Marlboros all round.

To the consternation of some Western readers, Robert Fisk actually found himself journeying with a division of Russian soldiers in a transport convoy. Like so many other journalists Fisk had wanted to go north. After passing through three checkpoints, a Soviet army officer recognised him as a European: 'The troops were apologetic that they could not allow me to continue on my bus, but they promised to see me safely back to Kabul.' He was therefore put on the next convoy which passed by. 'The soldier driving the transport lorry offered me oranges from his kit bag as we began to descend the gorge. He asked me in broken English to help him watch the clifftops for tribesmen.' When they caught up with the military convoy, Fisk joined the Commander, Major Yuri. It surprised the British journalist that the Russians seemed to be unsure exactly where they were; even more so, that the convoy had no map. Of the 4,000 maps ordered from Afghanistan's mapmakers before the invasion, there had clearly not been enough to go around, and this possibly accounted for the theft of maps noted by the journalists.

Fisk's experience was rather strange in view of the general outcry against Soviet aggression: 'For more than a hundred miles I had travelled with the Red Army down through the foothills of the Hindu Kush mountains, an extraordinary five-hour journey in the front cab of an army truck, sitting next to Soviet troops who spoke freely to me, shared their rations with me and—for one amazing half-hour—armed me with an automatic rifle so that I could defend myself if the convoy was attacked.' The fact that Fisk had been given a weapon and had 'ridden shotgun' horrified some of those back in the safety of the West, who felt that a journalist had no business being armed, let alone by a Russian.

In their encounters with the Russians the journalists inevitably tried to find out what the soldiers themselves thought they were doing in Afghanistan. When Fisk put the question to Major Yuri, he was referred to Brezhnev's extensive explanation in the Soviet media. 'If you read *Pravda*, you will find that Comrade Leonid Brezhnev has answered this question.' When Liz Thurgood of the *Guardian* visited Soviet troops guarding the Salang tunnel, she found that they were firmly convinced that they were in Afghanistan 'to help a friendly country'. 'The officers believe with what seemed to be a very real sincerity that they are not an occupation army and certainly do not reckon with being the biggest threat to world peace since World War II [as President Carter had said]'. She also found that they were shocked at the poverty in Afghanistan: 'We kave seen men without shoes; houses that you don't see in the Soviet Union.'

In Kabul, the journalists and their probing questions were beginning to exhaust the patience of the Afghan authorities. Barbrak Karmal did not fare particularly well when he gave his first interview to the Western press. 'Although this was supposed to be a conference for Western journalists, who arrived in buses,' wrote Peter Niesewand in the *Guardian*, 'fleets of Mercedes cars had already deposited the large Soviet press contingent, who took the best seats and from time to time broke into appreciative spontaneous clapping.' Karmal challenged 'distinguished correspondents from the friendly countries and distinguished correspondents from the opposition' to put their questions. 'Twenty reporters leapt to their feet.' But the Western journalists could not get the sort of information they wanted from the new president, in particular an answer to the question as to how many Russian troops were in Afghanistan. 'Western groans greeted the intervention of the man from *Pravda*: "Comrade Karmal, would you please express your viewpoint about the prospects for friendly relations between the Soviet Union and Afghanistan?" There was a hoot of laughter and shouts of "good question!"' The whole press conference turned into an uproar of unanswered questions. A week later all the Americans were expelled for 'biased reporting', and there were announcements that the visas of all journalists would be withdrawn unless they wrote 'the truth about the revolution'.

If journalists were considered to be a nuisance, photographers with their cameras were even more so. The last thing the Karmal regime would permit was extensive photography of the Russian army of occupation. In February 1980, when all goodwill towards Western journalists and photographers had long since evaporated, Romano Cagnoni, an Italian professional photographer, decided to enter Afghanistan to photograph the Russian presence throughout the country. He flew from Teheran on a tourist visa for one month. Through personal contacts he was able to stay with some foreign friends still in Kabul; he felt the police would be less likely to keep him under surveillance than if he was in a hotel.

'I prepared my photographic equipment, cutting a hole in a black embroidered scarf. I glued the scarf to the lens of my camera. With the camera and scarf around my neck, I draped an Afghan shawl over the lot.' He was able to operate the camera by pulling aside the shawl with one hand, whilst taking the picture with the other, without of course being able to bring the camera up to his eye to see exactly what he was taking. A timely cough was designed to conceal the click of the camera; he even worked out how to change the film under his shawl.

> I travelled around the city taking pictures from a taxi. The taxi driver saw me, but didn't report me to the police. Then I got a bicycle. Looking like a hippie, I cycled about the city. I shot Russian soldiers, in armoured cars, and in tanks. I shot Russian soldiers shopping, armed with AK47s, Russian soldiers buying American cigarettes, American jeans. They sell their food rations, their mechanical tools, their watches, fuel, anything, to buy Afghan currency. Nobody wants roubles. I followed four Russian soldiers into a bookshop. They all had automatic rifles, but when I tried to talk to them they didn't even smile.

He soon felt the hostility of the Afghans towards the Russians. 'I quickly learnt to speak one brief sentence in Farsi: *Shorawi nistam* (I am not Russian).'

Cagnoni's main aim was to travel out of Kabul to photograph the Russians throughout the country. Like the journalists, he wanted to go north through the Salang tunnel, and he decided to take the local bus which left at 5 am. Since he might well be detected taking photographs, he picked his travelling companion with care. 'I always chose an old man in traditional clothes to sit next to, not a young well-dressed Afghan in European clothes, who might have sympathies with the Communists. And I usually took a seat next to the window. Before the bus set off, I'd go outside to clean the window, pretending that I wanted a good view.' As he approached the Salang tunnel, Cagnoni was able to photograph the intense activity on the main supply route from the Soviet Union. 'I photographed hundreds of tanks, armoured cars, tents, lorries, missile-launching sites. As the bus climbed higher, I looked back. The cannons were pointing towards the city of Kabul.' But unlike so many of the journalists, he was not turned back at the Salang tunnel, even though he had to wait five hours in the bus while a stream of Russian supply convoys passed. 'All were escorted by armoured vehicles. I saw hundreds of fuel tankers, road-building machines, wood for construction, bulldozers, radar equipment, ammunition trucks, generators.'

Cagnoni's destination was the city of Mazar-i-Sharif. After an overnight stop on the way, he finally reached the city and, having told the manager of the hotel he was a tourist eager to buy carpets, he also took time off to visit the mosque. He noticed that it was surrounded by red flags and anti-capitalist posters. 'Hundreds upon hundreds of white doves were swooping about as the Russian helicopters flew overhead.' Cagnoni also managed to go to Balkh and found that the city was deserted, the mosque in ruins. It had never recovered from the ravages of the Huns or the construction in the twelfth century of a shrine at Mazar-i-Sharif for the grandson of the Prophet. The Tomb of the Illustrious attracted pilgrims from far and wide, and it meant that they no longer wished to travel to Balkh, 'the mother of cities'.

On the return journey to Kabul, one of the old men noticed that Cagnoni was taking photographs. 'He made shooting gestures, firing an imaginary bullet at me with his fingers.' In order to gain his friendship, the first thing Cagnoni could think of saying was 'Allah-o-Akbar [God is Great].' The old man smiled.

At the next checkpoint, a Russian officer asked me to step outside. I very quickly unclipped my camera and left it in my carrier bag with oranges and nuts, which I put under my seat in the bus. He wanted my passport and to know whether I was a journalist. I was interrogated for half an hour. I said I was interested in Arabic art. I was terrified the bus might have gone, and I played a bit of the fool, making them feel I was worried about the bus.

Eventually, they let Cagnoni go, and he was embraced by the old man on his return to the bus. When they parted, the Afghan gave the Italian photographer his prayer beads.

In spite of the danger and the long hours in the bus, Cagnoni went to the north twice because there had been bad snow storms which prevented him from photographing as much as he wanted. 'It was a very tough trip to the Hindu Kush.' He also travelled south to Ghazni and Kandahar. At Ghazni, he saw how the old city of the Ghaznavid rulers had been turned into a Soviet Army base. He also noticed signs of fighting. 'The road to Kandahar was littered with hulks of lorries and burnt-out buses.' Five miles out of Kandahar, Cagnoni photographed the airport, built originally by the Americans, now filled with Russian missile-launchers, anti-aircraft positions, armoured cars, tank emplacements tunnelled into the ground: all strategically positioned to defend the airport.

From Kandahar he took a bus west to Herat, where he saw another military base stretching for miles on either side of the road. 'There were tanks, armoured cars, tents, lorries, army engineering equipment, fluttering red flags with hammers and sickles.' Cagnoni then looked forward to the crowded uncomfortable journey back to the capital, in order to return home to develop the twenty rolls of film he had taken during his month's stay. Published worldwide, his photographs gave the first visual proof that the Russians, like the British before them, had occupied the main strategic positions in Afghanistan. But instead of cavalry and artillery, they had come with tanks and rocket-launchers and all the panoply of modern war.

In Kabul

Once the journalists had realised that if they disclosed their professions they would be unlikely to obtain a visa for entry into Afghanistan, they found it prudent to go in 'disguise'. Edith Lederer was one of the first Americans to gain entry into Kabul in the summer of 1980 after the mass expulsion of Americans in January. She was an Associated Press correspondent in Hong

Kong and it was felt that she would be less likely to be recognised than the resident AP correspondent in India. 'I flew from Delhi to Kabul and got a visa at the airport not as a journalist but as a buyer.' She soon found that she was not the only one who had decided to go to Afghanistan in this guise. 'There were also a number of French and Japanese journalists masquerading as rug buyers.' In order to make their occupations appear as authentic as possible, they all ended up buying a number of carpets. 'I even did some legitimate business for a friend who deals in rugs.' Two things surprised her most in Kabul.

> Firstly, the extent of the religious fervour of the Afghans and their hatred of the Russians not just as invaders but as heathens; secondly, the realisation that conceivably I could be a Russian in the eyes of the Afghans. People would hiss or spit and I'd shout to them 'I'm American!' and wave my passport. They were astonished that I was there and then went out of their way to help me and pleaded with me to tell the Americans they needed arms.

The stern reaction of the United States to the invasion, and the boycott of the Moscow Olympics, meant that the Afghan authorities, however, did not particularly welcome Americans to their capital. 'I tried to go out of town with several French "rug-buying" friends in a "safe" car with a good driver. That was the time when Giscard d'Estaing had just been friendly with the Soviet Union [he had not endorsed Carter's boycott of the Olympics, much to the annoyance of the Western alliance] and so there was a lot of warm feeling from the authorities for the French, but none for the Americans.' At one of the checkpoints the Afghan official was not at all pleased to see Lederer's American passport and made them all leave their passports with him whilst they proceeded on their journey. 'He sat there ranting and raving, pointing his gun in the air. Eventually we got our passports back after a certain amount of haggling.'

During her two-week stay in Kabul, Edith Lederer managed to send out a couple of stories; the rest she had to write on her return to Delhi. She found that she had no real problems with her disguise. 'Businessmen took me for a legitimate rug buyer. On Chicken Street—the main shopping street—there was one jeweller who would invite me for tea every day.' The local people admitted that they would try and cheat the Russians when they came to the bazaar. 'There were no cheap prices for them.' She also discovered how some enterprising Afghans had set up a market to sell secondhand American clothes, which they had imported in bulk from the United States, to the Russians. It was still just possible, she learnt, for dealers to go to Kabul; and there remain a few favoured bona-fide buyers who, because of previous shipments and prior contact, can still come and go. At the same time, they realise that their movements are carefully monitored and that the slightest suspicious move or probing question would put an end to their visits.

Kabul has altered greatly since the days when it was full of foreigners, tourists, traders, technicians, all absorbing the culture and climate of Afghanistan. Only a few senior diplomats remain; after the Soviet invasion most of the ambassadors of the Western countries were withdrawn for 'consultation', never to return. The United States keeps a fairly extensive staff in its embassy in order to try to find out what is going on, if for no other reason. In general, no one is anxious to talk politics amongst the local people. 'It is a strange sensation to go into a totally silent political situation, especially if you are used to the talk-ridden city of Peshawar.'

For those diplomats who have remained, life can have its problems. In May 1983 Peter Graham, the Second Secretary in the US Embassy, was expelled for having allegedly tried to sell pornographic literature in exchange for Afghan carpets, a charge which the US State Department described as 'absurd'.

Foreigners who have diplomatic immunity know that at worst they can be deported. The same was not true for Ralph Pinder-Wilson, a British archaeologist in his sixties who, although the Director of the Society of Afghan Studies, had no such immunity. He had been living in Afghanistan for over five years: 'We were excavating the old city of Kandahar, west of the present city, which had been destroyed by Nadir Shah in 1738.' Suddenly, without any warning, he was arrested while visiting Kabul in March 1982, and put on trial for spying and subversion. 'The problem was that I had given money to a student in order to help him leave Afghanistan. He was arrested with the money and a piece of paper with my name and address. It was very foolish, as of course he may have been an informer.'

When the time came for Pinder-Wilson's interrogation, he was faced with the 'evidence' of the student, who claimed that the British archaeologist had told him that there was no future for him in Afghanistan and had promised that he would help him to go via Frankfurt to Britain. Once in England, the student believed that the British government would give him guerrilla training to enable him to return to Pakistan to fight against the Russians. All this, Pinder-Wilson later said, was absolute nonsense.

He was also shown the depositions from two dealers repeating unfavourable remarks he was supposed to have made about the Soviet occupation. Finally, he was charged with smuggling artefacts—about a hundred coins—out of the country. This charge was founded on the fact that Pinder-Wilson had sent some coins to the British Museum in London to be cleaned and studied. However, he was on record as having given clear instructions that they should be returned. 'I can only assume that the officials who gave that permission are no longer in power in Afghanistan following the troubles there,' explained Basil Grey, the President of the Society of Afghan Studies back in London. The Afghan authorities, however, deemed that this alleged crime was serving 'the interests of British imperialism' which for years past 'plundered the riches of our country and transferred them to galleries, banks and museums in the West.'

Initially Pinder-Wilson faced the death penalty, but his sentence was then reduced to ten years in prison. He was confined in a jail in Kabul which he discovered had been built during Amin's time. 'I was the only European; most of the other detainees were very young poor people charged with petty offences.' His companion in the cell was a taxi-driver, who used to sweep out the cell, refusing to allow the archaeologist to do any cleaning. 'You are our guest,' he would say. When the month of Ramzan began in July, Pinder-Wilson found that he too was obliged to fast. 'I said I can't endure this, and so they gave me some yoghurt because the kitchens were all shut.'

As soon as news of Pinder-Wilson's arrest and imprisonment got back to the West, there was considerable pressure for his release, not only from Britain but also from French and Italian archaeologists and the Secretary-General of UNESCO. Finally he was told by the Afghan authorities to make an appeal, 'which I did, but it was sent back after ten days and I was instructed to insert the phrase "knowing as I do that the People's Democratic

Republic has a respect for human rights".' Ten days later he was released after nearly four months in prison and told to leave the country.

To compensate for the foreigners who had left Kabul one way or another, the Afghan authorities had of course welcomed in large numbers of Russians, not just soldiers, but advisers and technicians. In keeping with their efforts to promote the Russian presence as being friendly, an attempt has been made to give publicity to those Russians in Afghanistan whose help appears to be purely unselfish. When David Lomax visited Kabul to make a programme for the BBC, he went to the Chest Clinic in Kabul. Built forty years ago, at one time it received American aid; nowadays it is staffed with Russian doctors. 'The only common language between the Russians and their Afghan colleagues is English.' Lomax also found that the doctors were anxious to make it clear to the British interviewer that they had come to Afghanistan to help the people: 'Only free choice, nothing else' had made them come, they said.

There has also been a dramatic increase in the Afghan population in Kabul. The fighting and devastation in the countryside has meant that those who cannot get work or food come to the capital to try and find either one or the other, preferably both. But once they have been in the centre of Communist power, 'they cannot return to the country as otherwise they will be killed as collaborators with the Karmal regime'. Visitors to Kabul are also convinced that those who profess nominal allegiance to the regime during the day, turn into guerrillas at night. 'Practically everyone in Kabul, or for that matter in Afghanistan, is a Mujahid,' Kudlip Nayar discovered; 'the only difference is that some are with guns and some without.'

Those journalists like David Lomax and his television crew who managed to gain official entry into Afghanistan found that they were greatly restricted in their movements, in spite of the Afghan authorities' assurance that they had got the country well under control. Lomax actually complained to Barbrak Karmal in person: 'If it is true that you do have a strong army and that most of the people in Afghanistan support your revolution, why is it that we are not even allowed to leave the capital?' Much like Sher Ali in the nineteenth century, who said he did not want to have a British resident because he was worried he would not be able to protect him, Karmal excused the restrictions on travel because 'in revolutionary time' there was the problem of security, and they would be unprotected if 'some terrorists come'. It was a precaution, he said, for the time being. At the same time he was anxious to insist that the regime controlled all the main cities. They were in the process of normalising the country. 'You agree or not agree, but it is hard fact.'

Frontier refugees

It was also a hard fact that there was a large number of people who did not like the 'process of normalisation' and were not going to remain in Afghanistan. They had friends in neighbouring Pakistan who shared the same traditions and culture; and the obvious route of exit was along the well-worn caravan trails into the North-West Frontier. Long before the Russian invasion focused attention on the whole area, men, women and children had started journeying across the border, fleeing from the repression of Taraki's and Amin's regime. At first they were hardly distinguishable from the usual flow of nomads and caravans making their way back and forth according to the time of year, and there was some divergence of opinion as to whether they were really refugees or seasonal migrants.

In a Frontier that was otherwise calm, foreign journalists had already become interested in the 'refugee problem', especially since fighters were supposed to be harbouring amongst the refugees, before returning to take up arms against the Afghan government forces in a rapidly escalating civil war. The leaders of various factions would promise to meet the journalists in Peshawar and escort them to their camp, which had sprung up in the tribal territory of Waziristan near Miramshah. One journalist drove all the way from Rawalpindi in November 1978 in order to get his story about the Afghan camp. Having passed Bannu with three bearded Afghans proudly proclaiming the ideals of Islam and their struggle in the back of his jeep, he was stopped before he could reach Miramshah. As in the days of old, no foreigner could enter tribal territory without prior permission.

Until the Russian invasion, the refugee problem was still a small domestic matter to be dealt with by the Pakistani authorities with some assistance from the UN. But as the numbers turned from thousands into millions after the invasion, it attracted enormous attention as 'the largest refugee problem in the world'. In spite of initial scepticism as to who was a refugee, who a seasonal nomad, in 1983 the number was officially presented as over three million—one fifth of the total Afghan population. This figure compared with around 300,000 at the time of the invasion. More than two million are in the North-West Frontier, over half a million in Baluchistan and up to a million in Iran. There are now over three hundred camps dotted along the Frontier.

Right from the start Pakistan gave an assurance of protection. General Zia-ul Haq was anxious to emphasise the brotherhood of Islam and almost welcomed the refugees with open arms. 'We are looking after them ungrudgingly purely for the sake of humanitarian grounds and we will continue to do so even if the population increases,' he proclaimed in September 1982, reinforcing his earlier commitments. At first, aid and housing was at best 'haphazard'—in the words of the UN Refugee Commissioner himself. And as their number increased, a more systematic solution had to be adopted: tents, blankets, food, medical help were all high on the list of priorities.

The decision to leave Afghanistan clearly could not be undertaken lightly, and along with peasants and farmers came intellectuals and city dwellers who were not prepared to live in fear for their lives. Ghulam Zarmalwal, who came from Pakhtia province in eastern Afghanistan, was one of those arrested before the Russian invasion. His immediate fear was for his family; although he found that 'prison was not bad, and there was no torture', he could hear people being killed. For about three weeks he was in solitary confinement. 'Finally, after three months in prison, I was let out. We all knew that if we turned left, then we were going home; if we turned right we would be going to where they killed the prisoners.' As it happened the driver turned right, but then he slammed on the brakes because he had made a mistake and they went left. 'The man next door to me—an airforce colonel—went completely white. In the end he was killed under Amin.'

Zarmalwal said that after his release he received a warning that if he ended up in prison again, he would be killed. In the meantime he wrote a petition asking for his wife, a British subject born in Sri Lanka, to be allowed out. He wrote both to the Ministry of Interior and the Ministry of Foreign Affairs, but was told to write to Hafizullah Amin as well. Finally, after six months he got permission for his wife and two children to leave. In the new socialist Afghanistan, he was sent to work in a construction unit. But by this time he had decided to try and get out himself.

I had to arrange for the marriage of my sister in Pakhtia province, and posed as the driver for her wedding in order to escape detection. Everything was kept very secret; no one knew when the wedding was, and on the day of my departure I gave a colleague at work a few Western records, saying, 'Listen to them and tell me what you think of them', in order to prevent any suspicion that I might not be coming back. Twice I went to Jalalabad to see what was happening, and I could see that it would be impossible to cross there because there were too many people.

Eventually he managed to make the long trek from Pakhtia province to Pakistani Peshawar in June 1979; but before he could be accepted as a genuine refugee, he had to be vetted. 'I was put in prison and kept under investigation for twenty days.' Eventually a member of one of the resistance organisations vouched for him and he was set free. He was able to make his way to England, and he found a job with the BBC World Service in Caversham monitoring the broadcasts from Afghanistan. Even so, the sorrow of a man obliged to leave his country is there: 'I have lost the past, and in a sense I have lost the future. My resentment is that my children will not go back to my country to be brought up in our customs and language.'

For the people in the camps, life is generally hard, especially for the urban people. Whereas the nomads know about ventilation and hygiene, the townspeople have found the transformation from city-dweller to living in a tent more difficult. And as settled refugees, they can no longer move to the hills during the summer to escape the sweltering heat of the plains as they were accustomed to do in their own country.

A large proportion of the refugees are the women and children brought over the border because the men feared that they would be dishonoured in the 'godless' revolution. The women can be seen to work as hard as they did back home, washing, cooking, looking after their children. Only the scenery has changed:

'There were plenty of trees and plants all around my house, vegetables and fruit. Here all we have is the desert, sand everywhere.'

In spite of the upheaval there have also been some acknowledged benefits. The refugees have received both medical care and education which they might not have got in Afghanistan. Health workers from various international agencies have tried to improve medical facilities, and over three hundred primary schools have been established—one or two per camp—for the children of school age, who amount to about half the total population of the refugees. On the assumption that the refugees will eventually go back to their homeland, an effort has been made to direct the curriculum towards Afghan culture and life. Since there is still a conservative fear of educating women, the young boys are the ones who have benefited most from the schools. Attention is also paid to sports: 'No equipment itself is more heartily welcome than a ball and a net!'

Those people who have visited the camps are amazed by the morale of the refugees. 'In visiting camp after camp, spending hours looking around and talking with the refugees,' said Claude Smadja of Television Suisse Romande, 'what we saw was a spectacle of poverty, even complete destitution, but never of abject resignation and despair. We were struck by the dignity of these hundreds of thousands of people.' Bertrand Galimard Flavigny, a French journalist, found, however, that contact was hard: pointing to the sun and moving the earth aside with their feet, the men imitated the sound of an explosion. 'I imagined that they were referring to mines which had been sown by Soviet troops. The fact was that they were trying to explain to me that their tent-poles were unable to stand in the loose soil.'

The good reception the refugees have received in the North-West Frontier has been attributed to the fact that many of them are peoples of the same race. The Pakistani authorities have made an effort to settle the tribes on the basis of ethnic and tribal affiliation in order to prevent as much antagonism as possible. Alexander Thompson visited the refugee camps as BBC correspondent in 1982 and 1983 and concluded that 'all things considered, there is remarkably little violence. It is one of the most successful refugee programmes'.

Even so, the influx of such a large number of people has inevitably placed a strain on the local inhabitants. One particular complaint is that they have taken over the jobs in the transport business, putting local Pathans out of work. There is also the possibility of resentment over the allowances given to the newcomers when the local people have none. Much damage has been done by the refugees in need of firewood and fuel for warmth and cooking. They have cut down trees and shrubs oblivious of the harm it would do in a country already short of forests, which greatly annoyed the local people; the UNHCR stepped into the breach to provide funds for planting more trees and giving the refugees oil-cooking stoves to prevent them taking the trees for fuel.

In both the North-West Frontier and Baluchistan the old inhabitants and the new compete for the scarce supplies of water. Again, the UN has made an effort to regulate the water supply so it is shared between the two. However, in Baluchistan the problem of the refugees is altogether different. The majority of the Baluchis do not share the same Pashtu heritage and although there are Pathans in Baluchistan, and the refugees have only been settled in the Pathan area, Thompson found that 'the influx of Pashtu-speaking people is upsetting the whole balance between the Pathan-Baluchi peoples'. In Hazara clashes have meant that an entire camp of 250,000 refugees had to be dispersed.

The estimated cost to Pakistan of keeping the refugees is put at one million dollars a day, quite apart from what it costs the United Nations and other international aid organisations. In spite of making it clear that Pakistan will continue to provide refuge for the homeless, the hope is that they will find 'suitable conditions' to return to their homes in 'safety and honour'. But in the past four years the refugees have managed to settle in with what looks like an air of permanence. 'Camps which UNHCR has caused to spring out of this arid and poor region of Pakistan don't have much that is temporary about them,' commented Heiner Hug of Television Suisse Alemanique. 'The tents have almost disappeared'. Lieutenant-Colonel Michael Wilcox, who went to the Frontier in 1980 and 1983, also noticed that many of the refugees had graduated from tents to mud houses. 'They have apparently integrated very well and Pakistan is said to have acquired two million new citizens, the majority of whom will never return to Afghanistan even if it is ever liberated.' As Heiner Hug said, 'These huts will soon form villages and even towns which will possibly be included on maps'.

Apart from those who have been able to make their way to Europe and the United States, there is little hope of resettlement elsewhere than in Pakistan. The USA has taken about one thousand Afghans, mainly academics and those who have been educated in the US or who have family connections. However, there was one offer of a 'new life, a television and a radio' given by Turkey. In the biggest airlift the sub-continent has ever seen, over 4,000 engineers, priests and drivers were moved in thirteen stages. The offer was extended to minorities like Uzbegs and Turkmen who speak an old form of Turkish and who, it was hoped, would settle in without too much difficulty amongst their Muslim brothers. The only group which seemed to present a problem was the Kirghiz from the Wakhan corridor who were used to living at high altitudes. They were originally destined for Alaska until the United States found that hashish and bigamy were an accepted part of their lives. Eventually, Turkey agreed to take them, and, as a Turkish official remarked, 'If we don't build the village at the right altitude, they will just wander further up the mountain.'

The Pakistani government has had to recognise that, until there is an end to the fighting, there is little prospect that their Afghan guests will move. From the point of view of Pakistan's own security, the presence of refugees on Pakistani territory is more contentious than it would appear. Whereas the women and children have been brought there for their safety, all the able-bodied men aim at returning to the country to fight the Russians. The Afghan regime of Barbrak Karmal and his Moscow supporters believe that the camps do not only give succour to helpless women and children, but also provide refuge to guerrillas. In this respect Pakistan is considered to be aiding the Mujaheddin, a charge which the Pakistani government has been anxious to deny. Although the authorities have complained of numerous violations of their airspace by the Soviets, in no way would they like to provide a pretext or justification for Soviet troops to enter Pakistani territory in hot pursuit of rebel forces.

Freedom fighters

It is, however, no secret that the open border with Afghanistan has not only enabled the constant flow of refugees to come from the west, but it has let fighters creep back from the east. The Frontier, which has let in more invaders than anywhere in the world, could hardly prevent people either fleeing for their lives or returning to fight for their homeland. The Soviet Union used the open border, along with interference from its two habitual enemies, the USA and China, as a suitable justification for its own invasion. As Brezhnev was reported as saying in *Pravda*:

> For a year and a half armed bands of mercenaries were trained for invasion, including persons who refused to accept the revolutionary changes and wished to restore the monarchy and feudalism in Afghanistan. These mercenaries were instructed by CIA officers together with Chinese advisers and they underwent practical training in Pakistani barracks. Pakistan became a base for launching military operations against the country and its people; war was being waged and is still being waged to this day.

Western correspondents who have visited the Frontier area admit to the existence of some guerrilla training camps, although there are not nearly as many as the Soviet Union likes to think; nor would Pakistan accept that there was any question of its own nationals assisting in the training. A great deal of the trans-border guerrilla activity takes place in the once sleepy Frontier town of Peshawar, which soon became the headquarters for rival liberation groups. In a broadcast for the BBC World Service, Alexander Thompson described the newcomers to the city.

> Everywhere there are crowds of displaced men drifting, often aimlessly, looking for something to do. Many from the mountains and valleys across the border have never been to a city before, let alone a city as grand as Peshawar. And nowhere are the groups of Afghans more noticeable than outside the offices of the Afghan resistance organisation who have their headquarters here.

Sometimes literally hundreds gather outside: 'men back from the fighting fronts wanting to see the party leaders they fight for; men waiting to be sent in; men in flat Chitrali caps or massive untidy turbans hiding long hair, some with mascara and flowers behind their ears, surprisingly feminine in a city where anything female is hardly ever seen.' Apart from a few Japanese tourists, almost every foreigner is assumed to be a journalist looking for a resistance leader to interview. An American diplomat found that 'even if you take a taxi and ask to be taken to the airport, the taxi-driver won't believe that is really where you want to go.'

The various liberation groups have never presented a united front and there has always been intense rivalry and difference of opinion over eventual objectives. After the Russian invasion some sixty groups claimed to have a following, although the Pakistani authorities chose to recognise only six. Of these some wish to fight for a purely Islamic state, while others would like to see the return of the former King, Zahir Shah, now in his late sixties. He himself has been active from his place of exile in Italy in trying to assist the resistance movement, although he has said he has no wish to restore the monarchy. Of the moderate groups, the National Islamic Front of Afghanistan, led by Sayed Ahmed Gailani, allied with two other nationalist groups, originally took the limelight. Gailani, Western in outlook and approach, was seen by some Western observers as the man most favoured by the West to win an eventual power struggle. However, attention has now also been focused on the Islamic fundamentalist groups, who have a considerable following in Afghanistan. Of these, the Hezbi Islami Afghanistan is said to be the most powerful, and its leader, Gulbuddin Hekmatyar, the most ruthless of the guerrilla leaders. He is committed to a long-term struggle in order completely to transform Afghanistan in accordance with the principles of the hard-core Muslim brotherhood. He would like to see Afghanistan become the centre from which to launch the jihad against both Soviet Communism and Western capitalism. Alexander Thompson found, however, that whereas the Pakistanis gave most of their respect—and support—to Hekmatyar, rather surprisingly, many Western observers regarded him as irrelevant. Instead, they concentrated on talking to the rather less radical fundamentalist groups like the Jamiat-i Islami led by Professor Burhanuddin Rabbani, or even the Hezbi Islami faction led by Yunis Khalis.

Great rivalry between the Hezbi Islami and the Jamiat has made each convinced that the other has been infiltrated by Russian agents disguised as Afghan defectors. Quite apart from this, it is believed to be an acknowledged part of Soviet policy to try and subvert the Mujaheddin both in Afghanistan and Pakistan. The KGB is also said to have organised groups to pose as Mujaheddin and create havoc in the country, in order to discredit the genuine 'freedom fighters'. At the same time, the Mujaheddin have been trying to infiltrate the Afghan army in order to encourage defections. Of the various groups, Hekmatyar is believed to have the most efficiently organised cadres.

In addition to the fighters who come and go across the border, there are those who remain in their mountain strongholds, whose objective is to make lightning attacks on the towns and strategic places in order to weaken the hold of the regime of Barbark Karmal and disrupt Soviet lines of communication. Of these, Ahmed Shah Masud is now the most well-known in the West. The son of an army colonel, Masud—a Tajik in his late twenties—belongs to the Jamiat. Having trained in guerrilla fighting in Pakistan, he returned to his native valley, the Panjshir, which lies north-east of Kabul, to fight the Russians. Although Western commentators have portrayed him as the most effective guerrilla leader in Afghanistan, however, it is by no means certain that he will gain sufficient following throughout the country to counteract the influence of Hekmatyar and the Hezbi.

One of the problems which the foreign journalists initially encountered with the Mujaheddin in the city of story-tellers, where rumours are rampant, was finding out the truth. Thompson found that often their stories had an element of fact, but were 'embroidered and expanded, as few can resist the temptation of Afghan hyperbole'. But fantastic claims made it hard for the journalists to believe anything: 'such claims are made with convincing sincerity, but if totalled up, even during the course of a couple of days, they amount to the destruction of the Afghan regular army, their Russian spymasters, and Communist sympathisers, and countless thousands besides,' wrote Kenneth Clarke in the *Daily Telegraph* after journeying into Khost soon after the invasion.

Thompson felt that part of the problem arose because the Afghans relied on notes, scribbled by people who had no idea of the Western calendar and little appreciation of the importance the media attached to exact dates and times.

How can an Afghan guerrilla from the mountains understand the finicky, pedantic, precise needs of a Western correspondent? How can a Western correspondent truly understand what a Jihad involves? . . . It is too easy for the Afghan to accuse the Western reporters of being against him, unsympathetic, distrustful, and for the reporters to be exasperated by a war which does not fit in with any preconceptions—a war fought the Afghan way, in which the men eventually do seem to muddle through.

On one occasion the guerrillas told Thompson that during an offensive in the Panjshir valley they had shot down fifteen helicopter gunships.

> Now this was incredible and the sort of information I either could not use, or if I did, I would cast great doubt on it. Months later I spoke to someone who gave me a much more credible story. He said that the Russians had set up a base for supply helicopters; and amongst the supply squad were twelve MIG helicopters—not gunships, but nonetheless big helicopters. Masud's men surrounded the hills, and, whilst the helicopters were on the ground, bombarded them and managed to put several out of action. That story I could buy.

But of course in terms of Western deadlines, it was too late to report it. However, as time passed, Thompson found that the Mujaheddin realised that they were doing themselves more harm than good by exaggerated claims. 'At the same time it makes it harder for the West to assess what is going on. You can easily dismiss claims of having shot down 600 MIGs but you are less sure if they say they have shot down just one.'

In a strange way, Thompson also felt that the vagueness about what is going on inside Afghanistan served its purpose in confusing the Russians. 'It's argued, perhaps making a virtue out of necessity, that if the guerrillas had deadlines, timetables, radio communication and conventional methods and tactics, the Russians might then be able to understand them. But let them remain to all appearances a rabble, and the Russians will remain confused.' Of course the only way to be really sure how the Mujaheddin operate is to travel with them. Nick Downie spent four months with a group of guerrillas in Kunar in late 1979 before the Russian invasion. On the whole he found them to be lacking in discipline and divided amongst themselves. As a former soldier and member of the SAS, Downie had filmed insurgencies in Eritrea, the Western Sahara, Zimbabwe and Kurdistan, and he found that the Afghan guerrillas were the most disorganised he had seen. Peter Niesewand, the *Guardian*'s Delhi correspondent spent nearly two weeks with the rebels near Jalalabad in June 1980. 'Carry, little,' he was advised by one of his companions, 'because we might have to run.' He also saw the strength of the holy war. 'It is in Islam that their morale is anchored, and Soviet attacks, the prospect of death itself seems scarcely to bother them.'

But in spite of Soviet allegations that the Mujaheddin were trained and equipped in Pakistan, Niesewand found that in the early stages of the war their weapons were mostly of Second World War vintage or earlier. 'There is no sign in Nangrahar province of secret aid from any major power. Only a few new Egyptian-manufactured Kalashnikov assault rifles show that at least someone outside is taking a small active interest.' And because of the shortage of weapons journalists would find that invariably the question they would be asked was 'Why don't you give us what we need—guns and bullets?' Even Her Royal Highness, Princess Anne, was asked for guns, when, as President of the Save the Children Fund, she visited refugee camps in Pakistan in May 1983.

The Dutch journalist Arnot Van Lynden visited Mujaheddin strongholds in 1981 and 1982 and he saw definite improvements in the insurgents' conduct of the war during his second trip. He reported, in a BBC World Service broadcast, on his visit to the group of fighters under the command of Abdul Halim, a twenty-five-year-old ex-policeman, of the Hezbi Islami faction led by Khalis.

What Halim and his three hundred men have achieved in the past year forms one of the major examples of how the war in Afghanistan has developed and escalated during the past twelve months. They're successfully attacking most of the government military posts in the villages and furthest outskirts of the capital. The Mujaheddin have forced government control back, while themselves operating more openly in what they term as 'liberated areas'. Although it has meant that the resistance can move about more freely,

Soviet units are still close enough to be able to move in on any one area within fifteen or twenty minutes, and that constant threat makes for a precarious existence.

A few days after Van Lynden's arrival at Halim's headquarters in 1982, the guerrilla leader and his followers set out on an operation at night, which, due to their difficulties in combating Soviet air power, is when the Mujaheddin can operate most successfully. 'The nights,' Halim told the Dutch journalist, 'belong to us. Then they cannot catch us, for we are birds of the night.' A few weeks afterwards, however, while Halim was conducting another operation—this time against an Afghan post at the Bala Hissar fort in Kabul—Van Lynden witnessed his death. Hit in the head by a bullet from a machine gun, 'he died instantly, and his death brought the operation to an immediate and chaotic end.' As Van Lynden observed, one of the problems throughout Afghanistan is that the Mujaheddin do not have a disciplined command structure, and the loss of a leader can seriously jeopardise their operations.

At the same time, it has been hard for them to maintain their successes. 'We can disrupt life in Kabul in no time, but it is no use doing so when we cannot hold the city,' Kudlip Nayar was told during his visit to Afghanistan in 1980. And although the resistance fighters have improved their tactics since then, their position in Kabul remains the same. Erik Durschmeid, a Canadian television journalist who secured permission to film in Kabul in early 1983, concluded that whilst the Russians may have great difficulty in taking Afghanistan, there is no way in which the Mujaheddin can take Kabul. While few Russians are visible in the capital, he said, there is no doubt that the city is strongly fortified by Soviet forces on the outskirts. Even so, the attacks on Kabul have continued. One main achievement has been to blow up pylons with the result that the city has been without electricity for comparatively long periods. A frequent target has also been the Soviet-built grain silo, whose concrete structure has been badly damaged by rockets. According to one diplomat in Kabul, it is because the Russians have built it that the Mujaheddin wish to destroy it. In July 1983 they attacked the airport at Kabul and succeeded in damaging certain installations. Other airports throughout Afghanistan have also been the target of attack.

Nick Downie witnessed a battle in one of Afghanistan's other main cities, Kandahar, when he made a film for the British Thames Television programme, TV Eye, in December 1981. 'After a cup of tea, we set off in a horse-drawn cart, bells a-jingling,' he wrote to his wife: 'I have to confess that I've been to war in a wide variety of conveyances, but nothing quite as bizarre as this.' He saw that the guerrillas had no heavy weapons apart from about eight rocket launchers. 'There were some 200 Mujaheddin defending the bazaar, of whom only one hundred had arrived as an organised group—the word "organised" being used in the loosest sense—and the rest just happened to be in the bazaar when it started, shopping, and so had no choice but to stay and fight.' In no time, the bazaar was surrounded by troops and gunships and artillery. But although the guerrillas were 'caught like rats in a trap', it surprised Downie that no real counter-attack by the combined forces of the Afghan army and the Russians was launched. With his experience as a soldier, Downie saw how easily they could have been eliminated. 'Any self-respecting army would have wiped us out to the last man, but neither the Government troops nor the Russians did a damned thing.' However, the Mujaheddin's continued resistance in the past three years has meant that Kandahar has been subjected to severe bombing which has reduced about a third of the city's buildings to rubble. Likewise, Herat, close to Afghanistan's border with Iran, has been a constant problem for the Russians. In spite of severe reprisals after the guerrilla attacks, the Soviet forces have never managed to gain complete control of the city.

The Mujaheddin recognise that the presence of a journalist, who himself is prepared to risk life and limb in order to report on the war in Afghanistan, is a great asset in publicising their case. Even if the foreigner is not a journalist, however, he may be welcome all the same. Ian Donaldson, an English banker in his early twenties, who was taking time off work in order to travel around India in early 1982, decided to spend a few days with the Mujaheddin after he had met Sayed Gailani's son in London. It was just a brief encounter, but it was enough to ensure a warm welcome when finally he arrived at Gailani's headquarters in Peshawar. 'I think they were probably rather surprised when I said I'd like to go to Afghanistan.' But just the mention of Gailani's son's name, Muhammad, was sufficient for them to agree to take him and he was invited through the barrier of turbaned freedom fighters, armed with Kalashnikovs, without any need of further credentials.

His first priority, he was told, was to secure a disguise. This proved to be more difficult than it should have been since all he wanted to buy was the everyday dress of the Pakistanis—the *shalwar kameez*, baggy trousers and a long overshirt. Not thinking a foreigner would want such an outfit, the shopkeepers in the bazaar kept offering him a safari suit instead. Eventually, he returned empty-handed to his hosts, who themselves procured it for him, and a traditional Afghan hat as well as a blanket to complete his disguise. The agreement was that he would travel with them and witness an attack on a 'fort' held by the Afghan army and Russian soldiers. A servant, an old man in his sixties, and an interpreter were attached to him for the duration. They decided that since Donaldson, with his pale skin and dark hair, was of similar colouring to people living in the north of Afghanistan, he should travel as an Uzbeg, anticipating that they would be unlikely to encounter any other Uzbegs on their way to south-east Afghanistan. 'Wearing native costume and swathed in a blanket against the cold, and with a couple of days' stubble, I looked almost indistinguishable in the street from the locals. I felt just like Rudyard Kipling's Kim, though he was infinitely more skilful than I could ever be, particularly with my ignorance of the vernacular!' His interpreter turned out to be less use than he could have been because 'his English was poor and he had the annoying habit of pretending he understood when he didn't'.

This strange trio—the old man, the interpreter and a London banker—set off the next day by bus, travelling through the Kohat pass. After a few hours' wait in Thal, Donaldson and several others were taken out of the town in a pick-up truck; then they started walking.

> We walked over some fields—dried-up rice paddies—until we came to a wide rocky river, fast flowing, very cold, which we waded, though I was helped across the deepest part. From here we climbed up the bank and were led to the first 'camp': a mud-built walled enclosure . . . I was introduced to several Mujaheddin, some young, some old, all very wiry, none of whom spoke English. The leader, who was referred to as the Commander, was a giant of a man,

perhaps six foot six inches tall, massively built and with a great moustache: a real chieftain.

After a great deal of talking, one of the Mujaheddin produced a tape recorder and they all listened to the recording of what had apparently been a fierce battle. Donaldson found it sounded just like a lot of noisy crackles. Then he was taken to witness a stone-throwing exercise by a river near the camp. The Mujaheddin had set up rocks less than a foot high and standing back thirty yards or so, they threw smaller stones with such accuracy that they shattered the target into splinters. 'If they were this proficient with stones,' Donaldson wrote to his mother, 'then grenades would be deadly.'

Along with the Kalashnikovs which were an essential part of their weaponry, the group of Mujaheddin's pride and joy was a rocket launcher with three rockets. Also Soviet-made, it was their only heavy weapon, usually carried by the commander, but rarely used. But whereas weapons were a problem, food clearly was not. Donaldson confessed to eating much more elaborate meals with the guerrillas than before he joined them. After this stop-over for the night, the journey to the battlesite continued: 'At 4.30 am I was woken and within five minutes was walking with about seven or eight others, all armed save for my guides, up the rocky but wide valley in the moonlight. The wind was very strong and bitterly cold, blowing down from the mountains.'

Having reached another camp site, breakfast was served. As a foreigner Donaldson was honoured with four eggs. The attack was to take place the following night and they continued the journey either on foot or by tractor. As they progressed, their numbers swelled. Like so many others, Donaldson recognised how hard it was to see just where the Durand line lay. 'The border here is very vague, the exact point where Pakistan ends and Afghanistan begins being obscure, always seemingly over the next range of hills.' When they had negotiated a difficult ravine, called 'robbers pass', they considered themselves to have crossed the border. Once in Afghanistan, they had to be on the look-out for mines, and Donaldson was warned to watch his step. He noticed a few withered remains of a sheep which had exploded a mine, lying surrounded by fragments of plastic. The only other signs of military activity he saw were a few furrows made by tank tracks and the ruins of an old Afghan fort. The Mujaheddin were apparently proud of having destroyed this fort since it controlled a small valley leading to Pakistan. Noticeable amongst the slogans painted on the walls was 'Workers of the World Unite!' in Pashtu.

As they proceeded on their journey, they encountered some men with camels who were carrying dismantled parts from a tractor. With the Afghan's customary bravado, Donaldson's interpreter insisted that these parts came from a tank, although Donaldson maintained that they were easily recognisable as belonging to a tractor; even in a short space of time, he had learnt that these people were inclined to boast about their achievements. Somewhat frustrated at the length of time it took to get to their destination, he wrote to his mother: 'The only thing they don't exaggerate is the time to the next camp—always underestimated.'

The 'fort' which they intended to attack that night amounted to a garrison on a hillock, well fortified with tanks and armoured vehicles. It had all-round visibility overlooking the Khost river in Pakhtia province. The Mujaheddin believed that they were facing Russian soldiers, but Donaldson was sure that they were mainly Afghans. Further upstream there was a village once under government control, now abandoned for the greater security of the hilltop, which itself had to be supplied by helicopter since the road was under the control of the guerrillas. They led Donaldson onto a ridge so that he could take some photographs; he appreciated that this was a favour since any light reflected off the camera lens could well have given away their position. Shortly before the attack, while it was still light, he managed to assemble the band of forty to fifty Mujaheddin for a group photograph. Thinking that he must be from the BBC, 'Many were as pleased as surprised to see me. It was pointless to explain that all I had to do with the BBC was a shared nationality.'

Around eight in the evening the firing began. 'I was rather reminded of a firework display by the tracer bullets. The Mujaheddin fired a lot of shots, but I doubt if any did much harm. It was difficult to know what was happening really as it was pitch black and some distance away. However, the army used a lot of heavy machine-guns as well as firing the main guns, with deafening roars and bright flashes.' All the noise and gunfire withal, this battle amounted only to a short skirmish. Even so,

Donaldson was amazed that there appeared to be no casualties. 'Unless the army—very few of whom are openly pro-regime—had deliberately fired in the wrong direction, chance alone would have meant a few minor injuries from shrapnel.' Donaldson believed that the only explanation was that whereas the guerrillas might not have the weapons to inflict heavy casualties, the Afghan army lacked the will-power.

From the start, the Afghan authorities and the Russians behind the scenes have realised that, as Donaldson noticed, they have a serious problem with the Afghan army. In three years of fighting, a force which numbered between 80,000 and 90,000 has dwindled to between 20,000 and 30,000. One Afghan defector put the number at half that amount. This figure compares with the estimated 105,000 Russian troops at present in Afghanistan, whilst the Mujaheddin, who are fighting in their different groups throughout the country, are believed to number anywhere between 90,000 and 200,000. Like the British, who were obliged to see members of the Khyber Rifles or the Waziristan Militia desert with their rifles, so has the Afghan regime of Barbrak Karmal witnessed the disappearance of numerous men with weapons and crates of ammunition. The problem of keeping up numbers has become so serious that stories abound of forced conscription and press gangs roaming the cities and countryside to impound young men to fight against the so-called 'bandits'. 'To bolster its forces, the government in Kabul has used a dual carrot and stick policy,' said Arnot Van Lynden in a BBC World Service broadcast after one of his trips into Afghanistan. On the one hand, high salaries, by Afghan standards, are offered; on the other, the age for conscription has been widened to include anyone aged between fifteen and fifty. At frequent intervals, Barbrak Karmal has appealed for recruits in order to combat 'internal and external aggression'. However, there is no doubt that but for the Russians, the Afghan army would long since have ceased to oppose the Mujaheddin. Often, the fact that the Afghan soldiers fight at all is said to be simply because the Russians are behind them in the field of battle in order to prevent them running away. And the Afghan authorities themselves seem to realise that there is no prospect of the Russians withdrawing their troops until their own forces can be relied upon to defend the Communist revolution.

In general the offensives seem to follow a cyclical pattern. In the summer, when the crops have been harvested, the Mujaheddin can increase their attacks; in winter, conditions favour Soviet air-power. And whilst the Russians have shown themselves content to let the Mujaheddin exhaust themselves in defending the countryside, they have made a concerted effort to control with their own troops those areas which they consider essential to preserve their lines of communication. One such area is the Panjshir valley lying close to the Salang tunnel. It is here that Ahmed Shah Masud's army of some 5,000 men have fought and repelled the Russian troops, who in their turn have been anxious to flush out the guerrillas from the valley and prevent them from attacking their lines of communication to the north. Called the Lion of the Panjshir, Masud has been likened to Tito and his band of partisans. There is also the comparison between Masud the Tajik and Khushhal Khan the Khatak. Both fought against an 'empire' and both called for unity amongst all the tribes in order to repel the foreign invader. Educated at the French Lycée in Kabul, he speaks French rather than English as a foreign language. Gradually, as reports of his powers of leadership leaked out to the Western world, he and his fighters in the Panjshir valley became a symbol of resistance against the Russian occupation. The first film crew to reach him in his mountain stronghold were two French film-makers, Jérôme Bony and Christophe de Ponfilly, who travelled to the Panjshir in August 1981. Masud said, in his interview with the French, 'My troops want to fight against the enemy and they are not afraid of dying because they will reach the Garden of God—Paradise'. He also perceived that they were at an advantage because 'the enemy does not know us, nor the valley'. Whereas the mountains enable the Mujaheddin to withstand a Russian offensive, they provide little succour to Russian armoured vehicles which lie burnt out along the road into the valley.

The following year, Sandy Gall, the British television journalist for Independent Television News (ITN), decided to go with a small party of experienced colleagues to find Masud, who was still an unknown quantity to British viewers. Like the French, he made the journey to the valley from across the Pakistani border with a convoy of Mujaheddin. 'For us the going was extremely tough,' he remarked, 'but the Mujaheddin seemed oblivious of fatigue.' Since they had only budgeted for horses to carry their camera equipment, which weighed 385 kilos, they themselves had to walk. After only two days Gall wrote in his diary: 'The march begins to become one long blur of acute hardship going uphill, bliss at reaching the top of the pass, a moment of delight taking in the fantastic mountain landscape, then the plunge downhill, almost as hard as the uphill.' Without exception, the journalists lost a great deal of weight. By the end of the two-month journey, Gall had lost a stone and a half—'I felt and looked emaciated.'

Before entering the main valley, Gall and his companions were advised to go ahead without their heavy equipment. 'We went in with a big arms convoy, and they all left their weapons behind as well.' Even at the time, Gall realised that they were breaking one of the golden rules of television journalists: allowing themselves to be separated from their camera and other equipment. But there seemed to be no alternative, and the Afghans accompanying them said that it would all be brought into the valley by porters in a few days' time.

Unfortunately for Gall and the others, a Russian offensive—the sixth since the invasion—intervened. 'It meant that for three weeks we were deprived of our equipment. All we could take were stills of the bombardment.' Although they soon discovered that their possessions had been brought into the valley, the problem was to find them, and at one point Gall even contemplated having to leave the Panjshir without being able to make the film at all. While he and his companions went in search of their camera, which eluded them until the last, they witnessed the devastation caused by the Russian bombs. There was none of the gentlemanly warning exercised by the British when they went on their missions of aerial destruction. 'The damage we saw seemed to be clear evidence of terrorising the villagers.' Eventually they were able to assemble all their boxes of belongings, which miraculously seemed to have escaped being destroyed in the bombardment. Even though they had missed the actual offensive and had almost lost the 'story', they were able to film enough material for their documentary before making the hazardous journey back through Nuristan to Chitral.

Like many of the journalists who have travelled with the 'Muj' as they like to call them, Sandy Gall recognised that the problem facing Masud and his men is a lack of sophisticated weapons: 'To make real headway against the Russians, who have masses of helicopters and jet fighters, they would really need ground-to-air missiles.' Masud told Gall that, despite grandiose words of support from Western countries, they had had to buy most of their weapons—Kalashnikovs, rocket launchers and some heavy artillery—from Afghan deserters or even Russian soldiers, paying for them either in emeralds or hashish, both of which are readily available in the valley.

In spite of rivalry with the Hezbi faction, led by Hekmatyar, Masud's reputation has spread far and wide. Others from different groups have travelled to the Panjshir in order to spend some time training with him, before returning to their own areas to carry on the war more effectively. One Afghan made the six-day trip from Kunar in 1981 to ask Masud if he could send groups of his men to be trained by him because he said that, in Kunar, 'we don't know how to wage the war properly.'

In the spring of 1983 Masud surprised onlookers by accepting a six-month truce with his adversaries, involving safe passage out of the valley for the Soviet troops and immunity from attack for those remaining at the head of the valley. Reports, however, indicated that Masud was anxious to use the time to refurbish his supplies of weapons and food, at the same time as extending his influence to the north where Hezbi supporters had been disrupting his supply lines. But the lull in the fighting was short-lived; whilst the Russians are committed to stemming the tide of guerrilla attack on their lines of communication, the Mujaheddin in the Panjshir clearly intend to fight the Russians to the last.

In addition to the journalists, doctors and nurses have run the gauntlet of Russian air attack in order to help the Mujaheddin. Of the various health agencies, the French have had doctors in Afghanistan from three different organisations: Aide Médicale Internationale (AMI), Médecins du Monde and Médecins sans Frontières. Their main objective is to help the civilian population which has been badly affected by the fighting and general upheaval, but they will also treat the resistance fighters who are wounded and brought to them. Like the journalists, the doctors enter Afghanistan clandestinely from Pakistan, travelling with a band of Mujaheddin, who guide them to their destination. AMI, which started its work in Afghanistan in 1981, sends a team of two doctors and a nurse for periods of three to six months. Over the past three years of fighting, some fifty of their doctors have worked in Afghanistan. Aged between twenty-five and thirty, often they have had little experience other than medical school and their assistance is entirely voluntary. They can expect to treat men, women and children, some of whom will not have seen a doctor since the fighting began. AMI works in three specific areas—the Panjshir, Logar and near Kunduz in the north. They have found that their work in the Panjshir has been perhaps the most successful because of the good working relationship with Masud, who has been able to see that they have a house to use as a makeshift hospital. In addition, they believe that their presence has prevented more people fleeing across the border to become refugees in the North-West Frontier Province of Pakistan. 'It is almost more the psychological effect that foreigners have come to help which is important,' said Odile, a doctor who returned from Logar in 1983, 'rather than the fact of giving treatment.'

On average they may see sixty to seventy patients a day, relying on Afghans who have a knowledge of French to interpret for them. They have found that epidemics of measles and whooping cough rage unchecked. With limited supplies they also try to treat tuberculosis, chest, eye and parasitic infections, as well as having to perform countless amputations, generally for the first time in their own medical careers.

But even though the time for which they come is limited, as are the risks, there has always been the possibility that the Afghan authorities, and in particular the Russians, would view their presence with annoyance, especially in view of the boost it gives to the morale of the Afghans. In January 1983 the twenty-nine-year-old Phillippe Augoyard, sent by AMI to Logar, was captured by a Russian patrol group with a band of Mujaheddin and charged as a counter-revolutionary. At his trial in Kabul he was accused of illegal entry, unlawful photography and a breach of public order, crimes for which the prosecutor demanded the death penalty.

Erik Durschmeid, filming in Kabul at the time, was allowed to take photographs during the trial. He said he observed a nervous Frenchman, somewhat startled by the ordeal. At the end of his statement, 'confessing' that he had sought information about the situation in Logar and taken photographs, Augoyard said: 'I think it would be very good to stop this war between brothers inside Afghanistan; to stop the influence of foreign imperialist countries,' which he named as Egypt, Pakistan, the USA and China. 'They are acting by sending weapons and people to train them.' Whilst some believed that his arrest weakened the position of AMI in Afghanistan, members of the organisation maintain that the Afghan Mujaheddin would realise that his statement had obviously been made under pressure, even though he himself was obliged to tell the court that he had not been tortured into making that statement. While the Afghan judges demurred, Augoyard remained ignorant of his fate until an interpreter came to tell him that he was sentenced to eight years in prison. The Soviet news agency Tass branded Augoyard as a mercenary, warning that 'he and his ilk' would not escape retribution. However, after strong diplomatic pressure he was released in June 1983 and AMI continues to send doctors and nurses into Afghanistan.

The Russian front

With all their superior equipment, the Russians have nevertheless not found it easy to subdue the Afghans, who have been able to hide out in their mountain strongholds. But they have one significant advantage which every foreign journalist who has travelled with the Mujaheddin could not help but notice: the helicopter, of which the Russians have between 500 and 650 in Afghanistan; of these, at least a third are believed to be gunships. Used also for transport and surveillance, the helicopter has done more to assert the superiority of the Russians than anything else. In the days of old, the British had to climb the heights in order to gain the position of advantage and picket the hills to let the column go through, but today the Russians have been able to make use of the helicopters to land squads of men who can then give safe protection to the route below. The helicopters then pick up the men and put them down further along the crest of hills.

In a sense Russia's army in Afghanistan in the 1980s is about as remote to the Russians at home as was that of Britain to the British in the previous century. Probably even less news gets back to the Russians about their troops in combat than the British heard about their victories and defeats. And as regards the United States and Vietnam, the exposure could not be more different. Whereas every action of the American soldiers in Vietnam was open to public scrutiny and condemnation in the United States, in the Soviet Union the activities of about one hundred thousand Russian troops go virtually unmentioned.

However, in keeping with the Soviet Union's assertion that the troops are in Afghanistan to help the Afghans out in time of need, the Soviet media is prepared on occasion to present a picture of friendly Soviet soldiers helping to reconstruct ruined villages, farms and factories. There is of course no mention of their own scorched-earth policy, of the devastation of countless towns and villages and the long list of refugees who have fled their homes. Little is said of fierce fighting which, after well over four years of occupation, has certainly affected the Russian troops more than they would like to admit and has led some Western observers to comment that they may indeed be bogged down in a stalemate.

For the most part the Russians have become an anonymous fighting force with only fragments of news about the individual soldiers who make up the vast army of occupation. Western analysts estimate that some 300,000 soldiers in all have served in Afghanistan, for the Russians, like the Americans in Vietnam, tend to rotate as many officers as possible through Afghanistan on short tours of duty. Of these there have been about 15,000 casualties. From what information there is, it is clear that the Russians do not like it in the front line any more than the British did. Sandy Gall and his companions were given a letter found on the body of a Russian in which he had written that he was 'counting the days until demobilisation'. His longing to be home brings to mind Gunner James Black who wrote to his mother from Jalalabad a hundred and forty years before: 'I am saving every Penney I can get to Purchase my disceage [discharge]; by the will of God I will see you in two years time.' Like the Russian, he had died in Afghanistan.

In spite of casualties and increased involvement in the fighting, there appears to be no indication that the Russians are intending to leave Afghanistan. With the death of Leonid Brezhnev in November 1982, it was hoped in Western circles that his successor, Yuri Andropov, would want to find a way out of Moscow's Afghan adventure. Diplomatic negotiations and consistent world-wide demands for the withdrawal of troops yielded nothing during the fifteen months up to his death in February 1984 and that of Konstantin Chernenko a year later, leadership of the Soviet Union passed to Mikhail Gorbachev. Little has altered regarding their Afghan policy at this point. Whilst Western sympathies are clearly with the Mujaheddin, analysts have admitted that time is probably on the side of the Russians. They consider it unlikely that the Soviets would agree to withdraw their troops without having succeeded in securing Afghanistan once and for all within their own sphere of influence, even if it takes ten or fifteen years. Certainly, there is no pressure from within the Soviet Union for a Russian withdrawal.

Very occasionally the Russians have been told that their citizens are being killed in combat. In February 1983, a special correspondent for the newspaper *Komsomolaksaya Pravda*, the daily newspaper of the Communist party's youth organisation, went to visit a Soviet unit in Afghanistan. The correspondent, V. Snegirev, talked with a soldier called Nikolai Semko and described the 'disgusting, inhumane attacks by guerrillas on women and children'. He also said that the Afghan guerrillas 'masqueraded' in Soviet and Afghan uniforms to launch machine-gun attacks on Soviet forces. While out with Semko, Snegirev saw how he 'became quiet and frowned' as they passed near the place where three of his comrades had died in an attack by the 'bandits'. Despite the obvious interest in the Soviet Union in the welfare of their soldiers, such glimpses, heavily biased in favour of the Soviet soldiers, are rare. Letters often appear in the Soviet press asking to know more about the 'daily life' of their troops. In order to celebrate the fifth anniversary of the 1978 coup, in April 1983 Soviet viewers were given the chance to watch an hour-long television programme, in which the results of bombing and violence featured, but which mostly showed Afghanistan returning to normal after three years of 'undeclared warfare'.

One disaster the Russians could not hide, however, was the incident in the Salang tunnel at the end of October 1982. At first, conflicting reports as to what had happened made the Afghan government deny that anything had happened at all, attributing the news reports to the Western media's efforts to destabilise the country. Eye-witness accounts and heavy casualties, however, confirmed that there had indeed been a serious incident along the main communication route to the north. The story, as told by Abdul, a Tajik farmer in his fifties, was that a convoy of troops collided with another one coming in the opposite direction carrying essential supplies of wheat and oil. Abdul—who feared for his life for disclosing the information and had fled to Peshawar—said he was on a bus on the north side of the tunnel, following a Soviet convoy which had not yet entered the tunnel.

He saw thick black smoke billowing out of the tunnel, and it was thought that one of the trucks in the collision was a tanker full of petrol. As the Salang route had been a frequent target of attack by the Mujaheddin, the Soviets initially believed that the convoy had been ambushed, so they swiftly sealed off each end of the tunnel. As a result, a large number of the casualties were caused by suffocation, and the situation was made even worse by the deadly exhaust fumes from the lorries—many of whose drivers kept their engines running to combat the cold. Abdul saw six lorries loaded with the bodies of Soviet soldiers; the death toll was estimated at between 500 and 700 Russian soldiers, and several hundred Afghan civilians who had been trapped on buses. Those who had survived were withdrawn to a nearby town, where Abdul saw bread offered for sale at ten times its normal price, and noticed a Russian soldier looting money from an Afghan trader.

Back in Kabul, the diplomats realised that something disastrous had happened because of the long lists of death notices broadcast on the domestic radio. Although it was assumed that the incident was an accident, a guerrilla group did come forward to take responsibility, claiming that the tunnel had been mined in three places. 'We killed 600 to 700 Russians. Unfortunately there were some civilian casualties,' said the spokesman. Officially, however, sabotage was discounted and it was agreed that it was an accident, 'one of the worst in the modern history of Afghanistan's highways'. For four days afterwards, the road north was closed.

Like the British before them, the Russians know that if they fall into the hands of the guerrillas, they can expect no mercy. Generally they are shot, but in February 1983 four Soviet technicians were found with their ears and noses sliced off and eyes gouged out as well. Although such mutilations provided the Russians with propaganda material against the Afghan fighters, in their defence the Afghans will say that mutilation has long been an accepted practice in warfare. Some have attributed the reason for such multilation, whether it is facial disfigurement or severing of the head, to the belief that it is a sign of Allah's displeasure and will bar entry into Paradise.

Some Russians have been taken prisoner to be paraded as trophies of war. Compared with those Afghans in jail in Afghanistan, their numbers are very few. Even so, the International Committee of the Red Cross (ICRC) has taken pains to locate them and try and secure their release, at the same time as trying to work towards helping those Afghans detained in Afghanistan. Each year since the invasion, representatives have gone to Kabul in the autumn to check the conditions in which the Afghans are kept, and request that they should be improved. In 1982 the Afghan authorities informed them that their work was finished, and so obliged them to depart prematurely. As there is no hope of the guerrillas being able to offer the Afghan captors in Peshawar a quid pro quo—an Afghan for a Russian—the ICRC representatives there have to try to plead with them to spare the Russians on the grounds of mercy. 'Once a man is wounded and has lost his weapons then he is a defenceless victim of war.' When ICRC representatives do manage to secure meetings with Russian prisoners they try to ascertain whether the prisoner would like to be repatriated to the Soviet Union. For soldiers who have been told that they should shoot themselves rather than fall into the hands of the enemy, the answer is invariably the same. 'If I go back to Russia, they will imprison me.' Some therefore have preferred to stay with their Afghan jailers; others have chosen to risk returning to the Soviet Union and have been sent to Switzerland where, according to the rules of the Geneva Convention, they will wait for the end of the fighting or a maximum period of two years.

The Afghans look more kindly on those Russians who convert to Islam. 'Anybody who accepts Islam as a religion, then he is our brother. There is no question of him being a prisoner. He is free.' However, for all their individual kindnesses and declarations about the brotherhood of Islam, the Afghans consider that they have good reason to resist the Russians in the same way as they have fought and resisted earlier invaders. Apart from the loss to their liberty, their casualties far outnumber any that they are able to inflict. In August 1983 the West German Disarmament spokesman said that the total number of Afghans killed since the fighting began amounted to 700,000. Of these, the United States maintains, over a quarter are civilians. In addition, the population has been reduced by about a fifth by the refugees who have fled to the North-West Frontier in Pakistan. Whilst exact numbers are hard to verify, the extensive aerial bombardments, as well as the use of anti-personnel mines, witnessed by doctors and journalists alike, have clearly caused great suffering amongst the Afghans.

The mines in particular have injured countless women and

children, who do not realise what they are when and if they see them lying on the ground. Some children mistake them for toys which they are eager to pick up, only to have their hands or arms blown off by the explosion. When the former British political officer, John Dent, visited Chitral on holiday in 1981, the proximity of the war in Afghanistan was soon brought home to him. As he was sitting on the verandah with his host, 'an old Badakhshi living across the border put down a sack full of three types of these mines: easily a hundred in the sack of different shapes and sizes. He and his friend had learnt to defuse them and, in another bag, he had the fuses. The man said that the helicopters came and sat on a knoll and scattered them in the pathways into the villages.'

It has frequently been asserted that the Soviets have been using chemical weapons, fired from rockets on the helicopters. They have also been accused of poisoning water supplies in Logar. In Peshawar, in September 1982, the tape-recorded statement of a young Soviet defector, Anatoly Sakharov, confirmed the use of chemical weapons. He told the Afghans to whom he surrendered that deadly gases were stored in canisters labelled 'propane gas', painted blue and kept at the Soviet bases at Kabul and Kunduz, near the Soviet border. Another defector, Hazar Gul, an Afghan Air Force pilot, also said the Soviets were using napalm and 'other poisonous bombs'.

In November 1982, the United States' State Department reported that the Soviet Union was definitely using poison chemicals and toxins in Afghanistan, stating that already some three thousand people had died because of the Soviets' use of chemical warfare. As evidence, they produced two gasmasks, bearing traces of toxin, one of which was taken from the head of a dead Soviet soldier in Afghanistan. In March 1983, a French legal expert Dr Ricardo Fraile assured a United Nations panel of investigators in Norway that he was convinced the Soviets were using Afghanistan to test chemical weapons. However, without further substantiation, scepticism remains and the Soviet Union has chosen to deny all allegations. Tass, the official news agency, condemned the United States' report as a 'brazen lie', stating that it was 'based on the testimony of anonymous eye-witness, experts and counter-revolutionary bandits'. Alexander Thompson, the BBC correspondent, even found, when in the North-West Frontier, that some Afghans were annoyed at the apparent obsession which Western countries have as to whether or not the Soviet Union is using chemical weapons: 'a life is a life, however it is lost'.

For the Afghans who are injured, either by anti-personnel mines or Russian bomb attacks, there is still some hope. But for the compassion of their comrades, who are prepared to carry them over the hills, they would undoubtedly die where they fall; and but for the diligence of a handful of doctors, who perform numerous amputations, and even fit them with artificial limbs, they would never walk again. Sandy Gall was so struck by his journey into Afghanistan that he launched an appeal in the United Kingdom for donations in order to pay for some Afghans to be fitted with artificial limbs. Others have had their new limbs fitted by the International Committee of the Red Cross, which has its own workshop in Peshawar.

The Afghans are no strangers to war, and a missing arm or leg is as sure a sign as any that a war is being waged. For those who cast their minds back to all that has gone before, there is no stranger sight than that of a young man, who comes from one of the oldest civilisations in the world, dressed in tribal clothes hobbling along the road with artificial limbs, intent upon waging a holy war. He has come a long way since the conquests of the Greeks, Mongols, Moguls, Persians and the British. But in reality, his horizons remain the same. His world still ranges from Peshawar to Khyber, Kabul and Kandahar. After hundreds of years of fighting on their lands, the Afghans in Afghanistan are still struggling to preserve an independence, lost and regained so many times before. In many respects, the Russians are just more invaders to be resisted. When one of the doctors who treated the wounded Afghans in Peshawar talked of their determination, he was speaking not just for this decade, but for all time: 'They feel very strongly about getting their country free. I've never seen that strength before.'

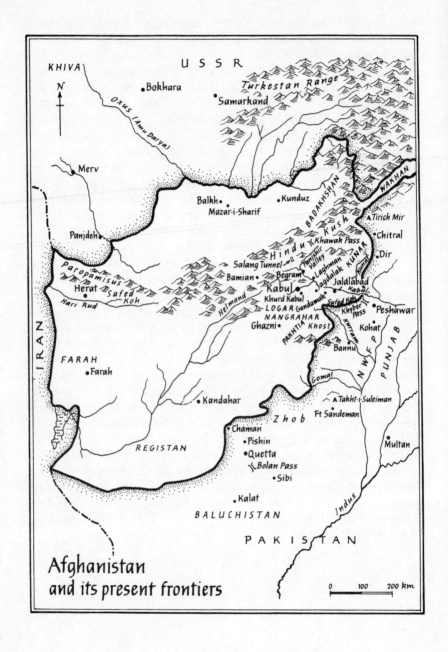

Afghanistan
and its present frontiers

0   100   200 km

A Pathan Warrior's Farewell

Beloved, on a parchment white,
With my heart's blood to thee I write;
My pen a dagger, sharp and clean,
Inlaid with golden damascene,
Which I have used, and not in vain,
To keep my honour free from stain.

Now, when our house its mourning wears,
Do not thyself give way to tears;
Instruct our eldest son that I
Was ever anxious thus to die,
For when Death comes the brave are free—
So in thy dreams remember me.

> (Traditional Pashtu Song: verse
> translation by John Bowen)

Glossary

Badal	revenge
Badragga	tribal escort
Barampta	a round-up; usually of people or members of a tribe whose members have been causing trouble, as an indemnity
Burqah	used by women who keep *purdah* when they go out; a garment which covers them completely
Chaddar	shawl made of cotton or wool, used as a wrap in daytime; worn to cover the head as a sign of modesty
Chappati	flat cakes of coarse bread
Darrah	mountain pass
Daktar	local corruption of 'doctor'
Dumba	fat-tailed Afghan sheep
Dupatta	light shawl or scarf made of nylon worn by women to cover their heads
Durbar	large assembly, court
Dushman	enemy
Faqir	holy man
Feringhi/ee	the name given to Europeans ('the Franks') by the local people
Ghairat	self respect
Ghazi	a fighter for the faith, warrior
Gusht	patrol (for example, of Scouts)
ICS	Indian Civil Service
IMS	Indian Medical Service
IPS	Indian Political Service (replaced the F & P, the Foreign and Political)

Id	Muslim feast day, of which there are two: *Id-el-Fitr* (the day marking the end of the month of fasting, *Ramzan*) and *Id-el-Bakr* (the fast of sacrifice in memory of Abraham's would-be sacrifice of his son)
Izzat	honour
Jemadar	Junior Viceroy's Commissioned Officer
Jihad	holy war
Jirga	tribal assembly
John Company	name given to the Honourable East India Company, which was formed in 1599; from 1833 to 1858 it was recognised as the governing body of British India
Kafilah	camel caravan
Kafir	unbeliever, infidel (applied generally to all non–Muslims)
Khassadar	tribal levy; they wore their own clothes and provided their own weapons
Khel	clan
Khudai Khidmatgars	'Servants of God', called 'Red Shirts' by the British
Koh-i-Noor	'Mountain of Light'; diamond now in the possession of the British Royal Family
Kotal	the crest of a pass, as in Landi Kotal in the Khyber pass
Kujava	camel pannier
Lashkar	a large gang, generally hostile; a tribal army
Malik	tribal chieftain
Mamluk	slave
Masjid	mosque
Melmastia	hospitality
Mizh	dialect of the Pashtu *Mong*, meaning 'We'

Mujaheddin	soldiers of the Holy War
Mulacat(is)	visit(s), corrupted by British to 'molecats'
Mullah	Muslim preacher
Munshi	teacher, interpreter
Nanawati	a deputation (literally 'entrance') from the Pashtu verb 'to enter'
Nang	honour
Nuristan	land of the enlightened (as opposed to Kafiristan, land of the unbeliever)
Pakhtun (also *Pashtun*)	Afghan, Pathan
Pakhtunwali (*Pashtunwali*)	the way of the Pathans, the Pathan code of honour
Piffers	Punjab Frontier Force
Powindah	merchant, trader
Puggaree	turban
Purdah	literally 'curtain': seclusion expected of high class women, generally in Islamic society
Raj	kingdom: used to denote British rule in India 1858-1947
Rajah	ruler (*maharajah:* great ruler)
Rupee	currency of India, Pakistan, Afghanistan. In British India, one rupee was worth about 1s 6d
Ramzan	the month of fasting determined by the lunar calendar
Sardar	chief, Afghan nobleman
Sirkar	the government
Sharm	shame, a disgrace
Subadar (and *Subadar-Major*)	Senior Viceroy's Commissioned Officers
Tahsil	sub-division of an administrative district; centre for the collection of revenue
Tonga	two-wheeled horse-drawn carriage
Zar	gold
Zan	women
Zamin	land

Bibliography and Sources

Published Sources

Abdur Ghaffar Khan, Diaries and statements as quoted in D. G. Tendulkar's biography

Abdur Rehman, Amir of Afghanistan 1882–1901, his autobiography, *Life of Abdurrehman* (1900)

Adler, G. J., *British India's Northern Frontier, 1865–96* (London, 1963)

AFP (Agence France Presse), Selected despatches 1979–83

Ahmed, Akbar S., *Social and economic change in the tribal areas* (Karachi, 1977)

Mansehra: a Journey (1973)

Ali, Muhammad, *The Afghans* (Kabul, 1965)

AMI (Aide Medicale Internationale), work of doctors and nurses in Afghanistan in 1981 as reported by Christophe de Ponfilly and Jérôme Bony (presented by Simon Winchester, 'A Valley against an Empire', BBC Television 3 May 1983)

AP (Associated Press), Selected despatches 1979–83

Awan, A. B., *Across the River and over the Hills* (Islamabad, 1982)

Awan, Cdr Izzat, *Pattern of Administration in the Tribal Areas in Pakistan* (Peshawar, 1972)

Baburnama, *The Memoirs of Babur, first Mogul Emperor*, translated from Turki by A. S. Beveridge, 1921–22; and by John Leyden MD and William Erskine (London, 1826)

Batuta, Ibn, *The Travels of Ibn Batuta* (Hakluyt Society, London, 1958)

Beeston, Richard, 'A nightmarish air of normality in Russian-occupied Kabul' (*Daily Telegraph*, 20 January 1980)

Bhatia, H. S., *Military History of British India* (Delhi, 1977)

Bowen, J. C. E., *The Golden Pomegranate* (London, 1966)

Poems (London, 1968)

Plain Tales of the Afghan Border (1982)

Burnes, Sir Alexander, Note to Sir William Macnaghten, 2 June 1838, as quoted by Fraser-Tytler

Campbell-Johnson, Alan, *Mission with Mountbatten* (London 1951)

Caroe, Olaf, KCIE (1892–1981) Governor of NWFP 1946–7; *The Pathans* (London, 1958, 1962, 1964)

Church Missionary Society, *Proceedings*: selections from reports in nineteenth and twentieth centuries

Churchill, Winston, *Young Winston's Wars: the original despatches of W. S. Churchill, war correspondent,* edited by Frederick Woods (London, 1972)

Clark, Reverend Robert, *History of the CMS 1852–84,* edited by Robert Maconachie (1904)

Clarke, Kenneth, 'Heroic tales told in tall Afghan peaks' (*Daily Telegraph,* January 1980)

de Clavijio, Gonzales, *Embassy to Tamerlane 1403–1406,* trans. from Spanish by Guy le Strange (London, 1928)

Coggan, Dr Ruth, 'Impressions of Ten years on the North-West Frontier' (St Helen's School Magazine)

Combe, Major-General B. A., 10th Hussars, *BAC,* Private publication from diaries and letters (London, 1882)

Cunningham, Sir George, GCIE, CSI, OBE (1888–1964) Governor of the NWFP 1937–46; 1947–8; *Diaries,* as quoted in Norval Mitchel's biography.

Curzon of Kedleston, Lord George, KG, GCSI, GCIE (1859–1925), Viceroy of India 1899–1905; *Tales of Travel* (London, 1923)

Dani, Ahmad Hasan, *Peshawar, Historic City of the Frontier* (Peshawar, 1969)

Dawn Daily newspaper, selected readings 1942–47

Dost Muhammad Khan, Amir of Afghanistan 1826–63, as quoted by Fraser-Tytler

Downie, Nick, Former SAS officer, who filmed in Afghanistan, September-December 1979; and Kandahar, December 1981; 'Shootout at Kandahar Bazaar' (*Observer,* 31 January 1982)

Dundas, Sir Ambrose, KCIE, CSI, (1899–1973); Resident in Waziristan 1941–3; Governor of NWFP 1948–9; 'Watch and Ward on the Frontier'—lecture, 5 August 1944

Dupree, Louis, *Afghanistan* (Princeton, 1973)
Afghanistan (American Univ. Field Staff Report, 1968)

'The tortuous ascent of Barbrak Karmal' (*Guardian* 2 January 1980)

Durand, Colonel Sir Algernon, CB, CIG, *The Making of a Frontier* (London, 1899)

Durand, Sir Mortimer, GCMG, KCSI, KCIE (1850–1924), talk to Central Asian Society 6 November 1907 (as quoted by de Gaury & Winstone)

Economist, The, 'Russia in Afghanistan', 8 January 1983

Edwardes, Major Herbert B., *A Year on the Punjab Frontier* (1851)

Edwardes, Michael, *Playing the Great Game* (London, 1975)

Edwards, Mike, 'An eye for an eye' (*National Geographic,* January 1977)

Elliott, Major-General J. G., *The Frontier 1839–1947* (London, 1968)

Elphinstone, Mountstuart, *Account of the Kingdom of Caubul* (London, 1815)

Eyre, Vincent, *The Military Operations at Kabul with a journal of imprisonment in Afghanistan* (London, 1843)

Flavigny, Bertrand Galimard, French journalist, as quoted in *Refugees* magazine.

Fisk, Robert, 'Russians dig in for winter after crushing most Afghan resistance'; 'Russian troops killed as tribesmen ambush convoy in Hindu Kush'; 'Afghan diary' (*The Times,* January 1980)

Fraser-Tytler, W. K., KBE, CMG, CB, *Afghanistan,* revised by M. C. Gillet (Oxford, 1950, 1953, 1967)

Gall, Sandy, *Behind Russian Lines, an Afghan Journal* (London 1983)

Gandhi, Mohandas, K., (1869–1948) as quoted in *Abdul Ghaffar Khan,* Tendulkar

de Gaury, G. & Winstone, H. V. F., *The Road to Kabul* (London, 1981)

Giulianotti-Bertoni, Denyse, Head of photo library, UNHCR, as quoted in *Refugees* magazine

Goodwin, Buster, *Life Among the Pathans* (Khataks) (1969)

Griffiths, John C., *Afghanistan, Key to a Continent* (London, 1981)

Grousset, René, *In the Footsteps of the Buddha* (London, 1971)

Hamilton, Lord George Francis, (1845–1927) Secretary of

State 1895–1903; Private letter 23 August 1897 as quoted in *Select Documents*

Hamilton, Major-General G. J., 'A Guide Goes Home' (*Piffer*, 1980)

Hamilton, Lt. Walter, (1856–1879) Poem as quoted by Shadbolt

Handbook of India, Burma & Ceylon, A (John Murray, London, 1859; 15th edition, 1938)

Hauner, Milan, 'One Man against the Empire: The Faqir of Ipi and the British in Central Asia on the Eve of and during the Second World War' (pub. in *The Second World War, essays in military and political history*, ed. by Walter Lacquer, 1982)

Heathcote, T. A., *The Afghan Wars 1839–1919* (London, 1980)

Holland, Sir Henry, CIE, MB, ChB, FRSCE (1875–1965): *Frontier Doctor* (London, 1958)

Howell, Sir Evelyn, KCIE, CSI (1877–1971); Resident of Waziristan 1924–6; For. Sec. to Govt of India 1930–2; *Mizh: a monograph on the Government's relations with the Mahsud tribe* (Simla, govt publication, 1931); *Story of the North-West Frontier Province* (Peshawar, 1930)

Hug, Heiner, Television Suisse, Alémanique, Geneva, as quoted in *Refugees* magazine

ICRC (International Committee of the Red Cross) their work in Kabul and Peshawar as reported by David Jessell in *Principles of War* (BBC TV, 19 June 1983)

Isby, David C., *Afghanistan 1982: the war continues (International Defense Review,* November 82)

Jacobson, Philip, 'In search of the war—with cigarettes for protection' (*Sunday Times,* 27 January 1980)

Jehangir, Mogul emperor 1605–27, memoirs as quoted by de Gaury & Winstone.

Journals & Diaries, of the Assistants to the Resident at Lahore 1846–49 (Allahabad, 1911)

Kaye, Sir John William, *The History of the War in Afghanistan* in two volumes (London, 1851)

Khushhal Khan, Poems, as quoted by Caroe

Lahore *Political Diaries 1847–8,* vol III (Allahabad, 1907)

Lane Fox, Robin, *Alexander the Great* (London, 1973)

Lawrence, Sir George, *Forty Years Service in India* (London, 1875)

Lever, Lt. Colonel J. C-G., *AIRO: The Sowar and the Jawan* (1981)

Lomax, David, Reporting for BBC 1 *Panorama* on Afghanistan, 22 March 1982

Loudon, Bruce, 'Russian Ring of Armour' (*Daily Telegraph*, 31 December 1979)

Lumsden, Sir Harry, Diary, 2 July 1857, as quoted by Fraser-Tytler

Lytton, Edward Robert, Earl of (1831–91), Viceroy of India 1876–1880; Private letter dated 27 August 1876; minute on Frontier policy dated 4 September 1878 as quoted in *Select Documents*; and comments on the Second Afghan War as quoted by Heathcote.

MacGahan, J. A., Correspondent of New York *Herald*; *Campaigning on the Oxus and the Fall of Khiva* (London, 1874)

Maraini, Fosco, *Where Four Winds Meet* translated from the Italian by Peter Green (London, 1964)

Marsham, John Clark, *The Memoirs of Major-General Sir Henry Havelock, KCB* (London 1956)

Masters, John, *Bugles and a Tiger* (London, 1956)

Mather, Ian, 'Afghan wall of silence is feared' (*Observer*, 20 January 1979)

Mayne, Peter, *The Narrow Smile* (London, 1955)

Mitchell, Norval, *Sir George Cunningham, a Memoir* (London & Edinburgh, 1968)

Mountbatten of Burma, Lord Louis, KG, PC, GCB, OM, GCSI, GCIE, GCVO DSO, FRS (1900–1979); Viceroy of India 1947, Governor-General of India 1947–8; quoted in *Mission with Mountbatten*, Alan-Campbell Johnson

Murphy, Dervla, *Full Tilt* (London, 1965)

Naipaul, V. S., *Among the Believers* (London, 1981)

Nayer, Kudlip, *Report on Afghanistan* (New Delhi, 1981)

Newby, Eric, *A Short Walk in the Hindu Kush* (London, 1958)

Niesewand, Peter, Correspondent for the *Guardian*—'Western press gives Karmal stormy time', 12 January 1980; 'Russian Troops take to highway looting', 15 January 1980: Series of despatches from inside Afghanistan, June 1980.

NWFP Gazetteers, Peshawar 1934, Hazara 1907, Punjab (Peshawar district) revised edition to 1883–4 edition.

Pakistan *Resolution to Pakistan 1940–7*, edited by L. A. Sherwani (Karachi, 1969)

Pamphlets on National Awami Party, Verdicts in the Supreme Court of Pakistan 1977.

Pennell, Dr Theodore, *Among the Wild Tribes of the Afghan Frontier* (London, 1927)

Prendergast, John, *Prenders' Progress: A Soldier in India 1932–47* (London, 1979)

Refugees Magazine, January 1983 (pub. by Office of UNHCR)

Reed, Arthur, 'Smiles, not bullets on the Frontier' (*The Times*)

Reuters, Selected despatches 1979–83

Roberts, Field-Marshal Lord Frederick, *Forty-one years in India* (London, 1851)

Robertson, Sir George, *Chitral: the story of a Minor Siege* (London, 1898, 1977)

Ronaldshay, Earl of, *India: a Bird's Eye* (London, 1924)

Ryan, Nigel, *A Hitch or Two in Afghanistan: journey behind Russian Lines* (London, 1983)

Sale, Lady Florentia, *Journal of the Disasters in Afghanistan 1841–2* (London, 1843; and edited by Patrick Macrory, London, 1969)

Select Documents on the History of India & Pakistan 1858–1947

Shadbolt, Sydney H., *The Afghan campaigns of 1878–1880* (London, 1882)

Shadwell, Capt. L. J., *Lockhart's Advance through Tirah* (Calcutta, 1898)

Sher Ali, Amir of Afghanistan 1863–78, translation of Persian diary: interview with Turkish mission 1877, as quoted in *Select Documents*

Smadja, Claude, Television Suisse Romande Geneva; as quoted in *Refugees* magazine

Smith, Vincent, *The Early History of India* (Oxford, 1914)

Spain, James W., *The Pathan Borderland* (The Hague, 1963)
The Way of the Pathans (London, 1962)

Starr, Lillian A., *Frontier fold of the Afghan border* (London, 1920)
Tales of Tirah and Lesser Tibet (London, 1924)

Stein, Sir Aurel, KCIE, *On Alexander's Route to the Indus* (London, 1929)

Stephens, Ian, *The Horned Moon* (London, 1953)
Monsoon Morning (London, 1966)
Pakistan (London, 1963, 1964, 1967)

Symonds, Richard, *The Making of Pakistan* (London, 1950)

Tendulkar, D. G., *Abdul Ghaffar Khan, Faith is a Battle* (Pub. for the Gandhi Peace Foundation, Bombay, 1967)

Thompson, Alexander, reporting for BBC World Service ('From Our Own Correspondent', 4 March 1982)

Thurgood, Liz, 'Why Igor was shocked by the Afghan way of life' *Guardian*, 25 January 1980)

Toynbee, Arnold, *Between the Oxus and the Jumna* (Oxford, 1961)

UPI (United Press International), selected despatches 1979–1983

Van Lynden, Arnot, Reporting for BBC World Service ('From Our Own Correspondent', 25 October 1982)

Vines, Charlotte, LRCP & S. Ed. Church of England Zenana Mission work in Peshawar, 1925

Warburton, Colonel Sir Robert, KCIE, *Eighteen Years With The Khyber Rifles* (London, 1900)

de Watteville, H., *Waziristan 1919–20, Campaigns and Their Lessons* (London, 1925)

Wavell, Field-Marshal Lord Archibald (1883–1950), Viceroy of India 1943–7, *The Viceroy's Journal*, edited by Penderel Moon (Oxford, 1973)

Younghusband, Captain Francis, Secret report to the Government of India, 1889, as quoted by de Gaury & Winstone

Yule, Sir Henry, *Marco Polo* (London, 1921) as quoted by de Gaury & Winstone

Unpublished Sources (including private letters and interviews with the author)

AMI (Aide Medicale Internationale) *Interviews in September 1983* with doctors and nurses who have been into Afghanistan (Logar and Panjshir) including Dr Jean-Luc Bremont; others preferred not to give their full names

Atty, Lieutenant William Served with the Army of Retribution; *private letter 27 August 1842 (Gerald Sattin Collection)*

Bavington, Dr John Church Missionary Society; born in Peshawar 1930 (father was a missionary and later chaplain with the British forces in the NWFP); returned to work for CMS in the NWFP 1960–4 and 1970–8 (Peshawar Mission Hospital);

still has links with medical work in NWFP; *telephone interview 17 September 1982*

Best, Keith MP and barrister (b. 1949); travelled through Afghanistan and the North-West Frontier on his way to India 1972; *interview 13 July 1982*

Black, James Gunner in the Army of the East India Company, 1st Brigade, Horse Artillery; served in Afghanistan in first Afghan war; killed on the retreat from Kabul, 1842; *private letter 28 March 1841 (Gerald Sattin Collection)*

Boulter, Brigadier H. E. (b. 1911) Served in 1st Battalion, Prince of Wales's Own Sikhs, 12th Frontier Force Regiment; seconded to Tochi Scouts 1935–8; *interview 24 November 1982*

Bowen, Major John C. E. (b. 1909) Family in India since 1858; served in 6th Duke of Connaught's Own Lancers, Indian Cavalry; transferred to IPS 1934; in NWFP, Assistant Commissioner, Mansehra 1944–5; *interview 5 November 1982*

Cagnoni, Romano Italian photographer who went into Kabul in February–March 1980; *interview 22 August 1982*

Challis, Roland BBC Correspondent in Cairo; visited Afghanistan 1969; *interview 23 November 1982*

Coggan, Ruth (b. 1940) Doctor at Pennell Memorial Hospital, Bannu, 1969 to the present day; *letter 12 July 1982*

Crook, Freda Wife of Roy Crook; *interview 4 November 1982*

Crook, Roy (b. 1921) Deputy High Commissioner, Peshawar, 1962–4; British Ambassador in Kabul, 1976–9; *interview 4 November 1982*

Cubbitt, Lieutenant Thomas Served in 49th Regiment Native Infantry, Bengal Establishment, during second Sikh war; killed at Multan 12 September 1848; *private letter to his mother 29 August 1848 (Gerald Sattin collection)*

Curtis, Gerald, OBE (1904–83) Both father and maternal grandfather served in India; joined F & P 1932; in NWFP: Assistant Commissioner and City Magistrate, Peshawar, 1938; Deputy Commissioner, Mardan, 1938; Hazara, 1938–40; Political Agent S. Waziristan, 1943–6; *private papers (IOL) and correspondence with the author*

Davidson, Major Charles, MBE Assistant Instructor in Gunnery to Artillery School, Kakul, Hazara, 1939; *interview 2 February 1983*

Dent, John (b. 1918) Joined ICS 1940; Assistant Commissioner, Hangu, 1940; Assistant Political Agent, S. Waziristan 1940–2;

Assistant Political Agent, Chitral, 1945–7; NWFP: Secretary to Governor 1947–50; Home Secretary 1950–3; Revenue Commissioner 1953–4; returned to NWFP on holiday 1980 and 1981/2; *interview 15 December 1982*

Donaldson, Ian Banker; travelled in the NWFP and Afghanistan, January 1982; *interview 21 July 1982*

Dowdall, Lieutenant Thomas Percy (1866–98) 2nd King's Own Yorkshire Light Infantry; died in action at Shinkamar in Tirah campaign 29 January 1898; *private papers (IOL)*

Dring, Lieutenant-Colonel Sir Arthur John, KBE, CIE (b. 1902) Father in India as Chief Commissioner East Indian Railways; served Queen Victoria's Own Corps of Guides, Indian Cavalry; 12th Frontier Force Regiment 1923; joined IPS 1927; Assistant Commissioner, Tank; Deputy Commissioner, DIK 1935–6; Secretary to Governor, NWFP 1937–40; Political Agent S. Waziristan 1940–2; Revenue Commissioner; Chief Secretary NWFP 1947; *interview 22 June 1982*

Durschmeid, Erik Canadian film-maker working for NBC; entered Kabul January 1983; his film, *A View from Kabul*, was shown on BBC Television 8 May 1983; *interview 9 September 1983*

Edmonds, Belle Wife of Dr Phil Edmonds; trained nurse; *interview 13 September 1982*

Edmonds, Dr Phil (b. 1908) Principal of Edwardes College, Peshawar 1954–79 (Church Missionary Society); *interview 13 September 1982*

Ellis, Molly (Mrs Eric Wade) (b. 1906) Kidnapped and taken into Tirah by tribesmen in April 1923; rescued by Mrs Lillian Starr; *interview 8 April 1983*

Emerson, Herbert, OBE (b. 1907) Joined ICS 1930; IPS 1935; in NWFP: Assistant Commissioner Nowshera 1937; Assistant Political Agent S. Waziristan 1939; Assistant Commissioner Mansehra 1941; Secretary to Governor NWFP 1941; *private papers (IOL)*

Fitzroy, Yvonne Gertrude (1891–1971) Private secretary to Lady Reading, accompanied her to NWFP April 1922; *private papers (IOL)*

Fookes, Alison (b. 1951) Nurse at the Pennell Memorial Hospital, Bannu 1976 to the present day (Church Missionary Society); *letter 26 July 1982*

Gall, Sandy (b. 1927) Television journalist and reporter; entered

340   *Bibliography and Sources*

Afghanistan from Pakistan in order to make a documentary film in the Panjshir valley for ITV, August 1982; *interview 7 June 1983*

Griffiths, John C. Writer on Afghanistan; travelled to Afghanistan/Pakistan in 1957 (along Alexander's route) and 1966; *interview 22 October 1982*

Hamilton, Major General G. J., CB, CBE, DSO (b. 1912) Descendant of Lieutenant Walter Hamilton; served in Queen Victoria's Own Corps of Guides, Indian Infantry, 12th Frontier Force 1932–47; wounded in action against the Mohmands 1935; *interview 24 November 1982*

Hewett, Lieutenant George 2nd Regiment Bengal Cavalry; arrived in India 1857; *private letter 5 December 1863 (Gerald Sattin Collection)*

Hodson, Major Robin V. E., MBE (b. 1914) Family in India since before the 1857 mutiny; served in Queen Victoria's Own Corps of Guides, Indian Infantry, 12th Frontier Force; transferred IPS 1939; Supervisory Assistant Commissioner, Hazara 1940–1; Assistant Commissioner, Kohat 1941; Assistant Political Agent, Khyber 1941; helped to raise 1st Afridi Battalion of Khyber Rifles 1942; Assistant Political Agent S. Waziristan, 1946–7; Political Agent N. Waziristan 1947; *interview 8 June 1982*

Holland, Dr Harry (b. 1911) Son of Sir Henry Holland; Church Missionary Society: worked for Punjab and NWFP Mission 1935–53; 1964–72 (transferred to Lahore Mission 1966); *interview 4 January 1983*

ICRC (International Committee of the Red Cross) *Telephone interview with information service, Mr Pascale Gondrand, June 1983*

James, Wing-Commander A. G. Trevenen (b. 1915) Served as a pilot in the RAF, no. 20 (Army co-operation) Squadron 1936–9; *interview 24 August 1982*

Kaye, M. M. Descendant of Sir John Wiliam Kaye, historian; Author of *The Far Pavilions*; wife of General G. J. Hamilton; *interview 24 November 1982*

Khan, Abdul Wali Son of Abdul Ghaffar Khan; political leader on the Frontier; still active in politics with his wife, Begum Nasim Wali Khan; *interview 15 June 1983*

Khan, Shameen Grandson of Dr Khan Sahib; *interview 29 November 1982*

Latimer, Sir Courtenay, KCIE, CSI (1880–1944) Joined ICS

1904; political department 1908; in NWFP: Assistant Secretary to Chief Commissioner NWFP 1913–17; Deputy Commissioner DIK 1918–21; Political Agent Malakand 1927; Revenue Commissioner 1929–31; *private letters lent by his son Sir Robert Latimer*

Latimer, Sir (Courtenay) Robert, CBE (Robin) (b. 1911) Joined ICS (Punjab) 1934; IPS 1939; Assistant Commissioner, Bannu 1941; Assistant Political Agent N. Waziristan 1943; Assistant Commissioner Hangu 1943; Political Agent N. Waziristan 1945; Under-Secretary to Govt NWFP; post-war planning 1945; Director Civil Supplies, Peshawar 1945; Secretary to Governor NWFP 1946–7; Deputy Commissioner Bannu 1947; *interviews 18 and 27 June 1982*

Lederer, Edith Correspondent for AP; entered Kabul July 1980; *interview 16 November 1982*

Low, Alastair, OBE (b. 1908) Joined ICS 1929; IPS 1935; Officer on special duty Hazara 1934–5; Assistant Commissioner Charsadda 1938; Additional Assistant Political Agent S. Waziristan 1939; Assistant Commissioner Hangu 1940; Deputy Commissioner Bannu 1941; Financial Secretary to Govt. NWFP 1944–6; *private papers (IOL)*

Low, Mrs Alastair Wife of Alastair Low; 'One May Morning 1941', *private papers (IOL)*

Lowe, Colonel T. M. (Henry) (b. 1910) Served with 3rd Queen Alexandra's Own Gurkha Rifles; in NWFP: 1933–5, 1941, 1946, based at Razmak; *interview 9 March 1982*

Lowis, R. H. D., OBE (Jack) (b. 1905) Served Indian Police; joined IPS 1924; in NWFP: Assistant Political Agent S. Waziristan 1936–7; Assistant Political Agent Chitral 1939; Assistant Commissioner Hangu 1941; Political Agent N. Waziristan 1943–4; Deputy Commissioner Kohat 1945–6; *private letters and diaries (IOL) and correspondence with the author 27 May 1982*

Luard, Dr Hugh Bixby (1862–1944) Indian Medical Service, 11th Bengal Lancers; in NWFP: Miranzai expedition 1891; Gilgit and Chitral 1892–6; Tirah 1897–8; *private papers (IOL)*

Macandrew, Captain George 47th Bengal Native Infantry at the time of the Sikh wars; *private letter to his father 20 January 1846 (Gerald Sattin collection)*

McMahon, Colonel Sir Arthur Henry, GCVO, KCIE, CSI

(1862–1944) In NWFP: Political Agent Gilgit 1897–8; Political Agent Dir, Swat and Chitral 1899–1901; *private letters (IOL)*

Marriott, Lieutenant W. F. Served in Bombay Regiment, Army of the Indus, which marched into Afghanistan 1838–9; *private letter 7 January 1839 (Gerald Sattin collection)*

Masson, Charles (1800–53) Deserter from the Army of the East India Company, whose real name was James Lewis; travelled through the North-West Frontier and Afghanistan in the 1820s; wrote an account of his adventures; pardoned and received a pension up to his death; *unpublished account from memory (IOL)*

Maughan, Lieutenant-Colonel Thomas (1805–61) Served in 12th Regiment, Native Infantry Bombay Army at the time of the Sikh wars; met and later married Mermanjan (1833–1917); *private papers (IOL)*

Moore, John Financial Secretary to the Treasury. As a student he travelled over Alexander's route from Greece through Turkey and Persia to Afghanistan and Pakistan in 1959; *interview 21 June 1982*

Newmark, Dr James (b. 1953) Church Missionary Society, working with his wife Ann, at the Risalpur clinic, NWFP, 1979 to the present day; *letter 21 July 1982*

Niazi, Dr Zafar of Niazi tribe, Mianwali; *interview 27 May 1982*

Pinder-Wilson, Ralph (b. 1919) Archaeologist working with the British Society for Afghan studies in Afghanistan 1977–82; imprisoned in Kabul 1982, later released; left Afghanistan July 1982; *interview 30 March 1983*

Pollock, Surgeon-Captain C. E., RAMC *private letter 26 November 1897 (Gerald Sattin Collection)*

de Ponfilly, Christophe French film-maker, went with his colleague Jérôme Bony to make a film in the Panjshir, August 1981; *interview 9 September 1983*

Prendergast, Brigadier John, DSO, MC and Bar (b. 1910) Served 4th Battalion 15th Punjab Regiment, Indian Infantry 1932–47; seconded to Tochi Scouts 1934–7; Military Attaché in Kabul 1948–50; returned many times to India via NWFP, Pakistan and Afghanistan; *interview 5 September 1983*

Rawlinson, Major-General Sir Henry Political Agent based at Kandahar during the first Afghan war; *private letter 12 August 1941 (Gerald Sattin collection)*

Reading, Alice, Marchioness of, GBE, CI (d. 1930) Vicereine

1921–6; visited NWFP with the Viceroy, Lord Reading, April 1922; *private letters to her family (IOL)*

Roos-Keppel, Sir George, GCIE, KCSI (1866–1921) In NWFP: Indian Army, Kurram Militia 1893–7; Political Agent Khyber 1899; Commandant Khyber Rifles 1903; Chief Commissioner NWFP 1908–19; *private correspondence 1902–15 (IOL)*

Sale, Lady Florentia (1790–1853) Wife of General Sir Robert Sale; imprisoned and kept as a hostage during first Afghan war; *private correspondence 1841–2 (Gerald Sattin collection)*

Sale, Major-General Sir Robert (1782–1845) Called 'Fighting Bob'; successfully defended Jalalabad—the 'illustrious garrison'—during first Afghan war; *private correspondence 11 January 1842 (Gerald Sattin collection)*

Shah, Ghulam Safdar of the Mashwani tribe, Srikot, Hazara; *interview 14 June 1982*

Shaw, Dr Jonathan Church Missionary Society (father also CMS in India): Peshawar Mission Hospital 1951–68, after one year at Quetta; *interview 16 September 1982*

Shaw, Mrs Molly Wife of Dr Jonathan Shaw; nurse at Peshawar Mission Hospital 1951–68; *interview 16 September 1982*

Siudmak, John Art dealer and collector who has travelled frequently to Peshawar and NWFP; *interview 12 November 1982*

Stephens, Ian, CIE (b. 1903) Maternal ancestors in India since 1828; editor of the *Statesman* (Delhi and Calcutta) 1942–51; travelled in Pakistan and Afghanistan 1950s and 1960s; *private papers (Cambridge Centre for South Asian Studies) and interview 26 August 1982*

Thompson, Alexander BBC Correspondent in Pakistan 1981–3, during which time he made frequent visits to Peshawar and NWFP; *interview 17 March 1983*

Thompson, Captain C. W. 2nd European Light Infantry, Bombay establishment during Sikh wars; *private letter 12 January 1849 (Gerald Sattin collection)*

Thompson, Sir Herbert, CIE (b. 1898) Joined ICS 1922; appointed to F & P; in NWFP: Assistant Commissioner DIK 1926; City Magistrate Peshawar 1926; District Judge 1928; District and Sessions Judge Peshawar and Hazara 1931, Derajat 1932; Revenue Commissioner Peshawar 1941; *private papers (IOL) and correspondence with the author 26 May 1982*

Ware, Walter Private in 1st Devonshire Regiment; served in Tirah 1897; *letter to his parents 14 October 1897 (Gerald Sattin Collection)*

Webb, James Private in the army of the East India Company; served in Afghanistan during the first Afghan war; *private letter 12 May 1840 (Gerald Sattin collection)*

Wilcox, Lieutenant-Colonel Michael (b. 1916) Served in 1st Battalion, Coke's Rifles (13th Frontier Force Regiment); in NWFP: Kohat 1937; Thal 1939; Peshawar 1946; returned to NWFP with Military Historical Society 1977, 1980, 1983; *interview 26 November 1982*

Yusuf, Lieutenant-Colonel Muhammad Afghan, born in Peshawar (mother from Bokhara, family from Kandahar); served 6th Battalion Scinde Horse (13th Frontier Force Regiment) 1935–8; S. Waziristan Scouts 1938–43; transferred IPS: Assistant Political Agent N. Waziristan 1944; stayed to work in Pakistan after independence until retirement to England 1969; *interview 27 May 1982*

Zarmalwal, Ghulam Afghan exile; left Afghanistan secretly as refugee, arriving in Peshawar June 1979; at present working in England for BBC monitoring service in Caversham; *interview 17 August 1982*

Index